A Will to Choose

A Will to Choose

The Origins of African American Methodism

J. Gordon Melton

ROWMAN & LITTLEFIELD PUBLISHERS, INC.
Lanham • Boulder • New York • Toronto • Plymouth, UK

ROWMAN & LITTLEFIELD PUBLISHERS, INC.

Published in the United States of America
by Rowman & Littlefield Publishers, Inc.
A wholly owned subsidiary of The Rowman & Littlefield Publishing Group, Inc.
4501 Forbes Boulevard, Suite 200, Lanham, Maryland 20706
www.rowmanlittlefield.com

Estover Road, Plymouth PL6 7PY, United Kingdom

British Library Cataloguing in Publication Information Available

Library of Congress Cataloging-in-Publication Data

Melton, J. Gordon.
   A will to choose : the origins of African American methodism / J. Gordon Melton.
      p. cm.
   Includes bibliographical references and index.
   ISBN-13: 978-0-7425-5264-7 (cloth : alk. paper)
   ISBN-10: 0-7425-5264-0 (cloth : alk. paper)
   ISBN-13: 978-0-7425-5265-4 (pbk. : alk. paper)
   ISBN-10: 0-7425-5265-9 (pbk. : alk. paper)
   1. African American Methodists—History. 2. Methodist Church—United
States—History. 3. United Methodist Church (U.S.)—History. I. Title.
   BX8435.M45 2007
   287'.873—dc22

                                                              2006034686

Printed in the United States of America

Contents

~

Abbreviations

Throughout the text, I have used a standard set of abbreviations for the different churches whose history is traced.

AME	African Methodist Episcopal Church
AMEZ	African Methodist Episcopal Zion Church
AUC	African Union Church
AUFMPC	African Union First Methodist Protestant Church
CME	Colored (now Christian) Methodist Episcopal Church
MEC	Methodist Episcopal Church
MEC,S	Methodist Episcopal Church, South
MPC	Methodist Protestant Church

~

Foreword

Bishop Woodie W. White

A Will to Choose: The Origins of African American Methodism, by J. Gordon Melton, is a story of religion in America, not before told quite as comprehensively as found in these pages. It describes the movement of Methodism across America, as spread through and by its African American followers. It reveals the impact of racism and slavery upon evangelization in the new colonies and emerging nation, and how one church became four denominations defined more by race than theological or doctrinal difference.

This is the story of five streams that emanate from the same source, the Methodist Episcopal Church. It is the unfolding story of the beginning of the African Union First Colored Methodist Protestant Church, African Methodist Episcopal Church, African Methodist Episcopal Zion Church, and the Christian Methodist Episcopal Church. These bodies broke from the Methodist Episcopal Church to form independent Black denominations. The African American members who did not leave the denomination but remained with the denomination they helped found represent the fifth stream.

I am personally formed in some measure by three of these streams: the Methodist Episcopal Church, and the African Methodist Episcopal and Christian Methodist Episcopal Churches. The latter two I attended briefly as a child and in my late teens. The Methodist Episcopal Church is the church of my roots. Both my paternal and maternal families were Methodists from the Eastern Shore of Maryland. Maryland plays a prominent role in the history of Methodism. Interestingly, nearly all the members of my family are buried in two cemeteries related to two little United Methodist Churches,

Macedonia and Asbury, located in Dames Quarter and Nanticoke, Maryland, respectively.

Reading J. Gordon Melton's *A Will to Choose* is in part like looking back at my own beginnings. Here is an effort to capture a period of Methodism that not only shaped the history of a denomination but impacted the history of a nation. More precisely, Melton writes, "*A Will to Choose* attempts to bring together both insights and methodologies from three different disciplines—traditional church history, religious studies, and African American studies" by recapturing the history and telling the story of the beginning of African American Methodism. It concentrates on a limited period of history, namely the antebellum period.

While this is unmistakably a scholarly work, as evidenced by its sixteen pages of primary sources and selected bibliography of antebellum African American Methodism, it is engaging, interesting, informative, and inspiring reading.

One will come from this work with a new appreciation of the importance of the role of African Americans in the expansion of one of the most important denominations in American history: the Methodist Episcopal Church and its successor bodies.

American Methodism has always struggled with its commitment on the one hand to combat and challenge racism and prejudice, and its accommodation to racism on the other. It is not unlike Swedish social scientist Gunner Myrdal's description of *An American Dilemma*, in the book with that title published in 1944—a contradiction of principle and practice, a moral dilemma.

Methodism early took a strong stand against slavery, in keeping with the stance of its founder, John Wesley. In its early formation as a denomination in 1784 it forbade its clergy and members from owning slaves. Yet this position was soon modified and became one of the ongoing debates of the young denomination. It soon found itself in conflict with an economic system upon which an entire region depended as well as a culture of racism in the life of the American colonies, most pronounced in the South.

Melton describes this denominational debates in the General and Annual Conferences as well as in families, among neighbors, within congregations, and among the clergy.

Yet Africans and African Americans have been a part of the Methodist legacy from its earliest beginnings. One meets in these pages slaves with enormous courage and gifts who soon displayed commitment to the faith as well as gifts as preachers, leaders, and organizers.

One of the important contributions made by Melton is the manner in which he connects and maintains a linkage of the African American branches of Methodism and shows their interconnectedness. He describes the formation of the not too familiar African Union Church, the first independent African American Church, later to become known as the African Union First Colored Methodist Protestant Church, "a largely regional body in the Mid-Atlantic states." One is given in detail the founding of the African Methodist Episcopal and African American Episcopal Zion Churches, and their struggles with the Methodist Episcopal Church as well as each other. The formation of the Christian (originally Colored) Methodist Episcopal Church is described with the unique circumstances which brought it into being. Readers will gain a greater appreciation of the complexity of these denominational beginnings.

As a descendent of the stream of African American Methodists who remained in the Methodist Church, I appreciated Melton's depiction of historical detail and information as well as a cast of new leaders about whom not much has been written. Additionally, his treatment of the emergence of congregations and centers of African American Methodism provides a more comprehensive picture of the period of growth and expansion. Indeed many of the historic congregations remain in the United Methodist Church today: Zoar in Philadelphia; Asbury in Washington, D.C.; Zion, in Wilmington, Delaware; Sharp Street in Baltimore; and Mt. Zion, in the Georgetown section of Washington, D.C., to name but a few.

The history of the development and spread of Methodism by African American Methodists is treated here with detail that is rare. In fact, the various divisions among the Black congregations and the moving back and forth by pastors and congregations from one denomination to another will be eye opening to many. Congregations and pastors moved between the AME and the AMEZ Churches as well as the Methodist Episcopal Church with some frequency. Indeed there was a period in the New York area when nearly all the African American members withdrew from the Methodist Episcopal Church to unite with independent African American churches, not returning until after the Civil War.

Melton's careful treatment of the growth of African American Methodism away from the urban areas and the attraction of the church in rural communities as well as the important role of women in the development of the church and its ministries is a new emphasis for consideration. The names, characters, and stories will prove memorable and provide new heroines.

A *Will to Choose* shares the histories of all the strands of Black Methodism in one place, making it easier to follow them and see their relationship to each other. The denominations were far more closely related than many other histories record. Of special interest is the role of White Methodists both as allies and as foes. One will gain some insight into the difference in the growth of Black Methodism in the South and the North and the factors that contributed to those differences. The treatment of the spread of Methodism among African Americans as far north as New England and even Canada may prove to be new material for many.

One area that is often not given a great deal of attention in many histories, but that Melton describes in detail, is the colonization movement and the spread of Methodism in Africa by newly freed slaves and the independent black denominations and churches. Also detailed is the formation of an African Annual Conference by the Methodist Episcopal Church.

The stream of Black Methodists who remained in the Methodist Episcopal Church will find nostalgic reading the formation of the Black Annual Conferences by the Methodist Episcopal Church. Many pastors and laypeople in the United Methodist Church today remember those conferences and those days in the Central Jurisdiction of the Methodist Church with mixed memories—joys and sorrows. A remnant of these annual conferences remained until 1973. When the United Methodist Church was created in 1968 as a result of the merger of the Methodist Church and the Evangelical United Brethren Church, segregated annual conferences and racial structures were discontinued.

What is most telling in A Will to Choose: The Origins of African American Methodism is the ambivalence of White Methodists toward their Black brothers and sisters. They never seemed quite sure how to relate to them or what their position as White Methodists should be—fellow Methodists, objects of mission, or partners in ministry. In fact it was not always clear if White leaders and members wanted Black Methodists to be a part of or to depart from the Methodist Church. They made it both difficult for Black Methodists to remain or leave!

Racism was always a part of Methodism even as it was opposed. In the stream of Methodism that included Black Methodists who remained and continue to this day has been the hope of a united and racially inclusive church. Perhaps it has been achieved beyond any of the forbears' imagining. Yet there is no doubt that those who formed separate and independent Black denominations have made and continue to make a significant impact on the religious life of America. One wonders however, what might have been the impact on America and the world had not racism and prejudice fractured the mission and witness of the people called Methodists.

Atlanta, Georgia
October 2006

~

Introduction

Beginning in the seventeenth century, large numbers of people from Africa made their way to what is now the United States. They came not as explorers, opportunists, refugees of religious repression, but as slaves, destined to be bought and sold and to assume a position at the very bottom of the social ladder. Here they would be expected to do the most back-breaking labor and menial tasks assigned to them in the most arbitrary manner, to work all day without sharing in the fruits of their labor, and to accept their lot in life, if not cheerfully, at least without anger or outward reaction.

In the process of induction into their new life, Africans were stripped of their community and their culture. Members of what were, by most standards, cultures of equal sophistication with their European rivals, they lost their social life, their natural surroundings, and their intellectual environment. While Americans of European extraction tended to see Africans as all the same, they came from a number of different societies that were spread along the west coast of Africa and that spoke dozens of different languages.

Integral to the losses suffered by those taken to the British American colonies was participation in their people's spiritual life, glimpses of which we can see in the modern practitioners of traditional West African religions. Though being squeezed from one direction by Islam and from the other by Christianity, many of the traditional African religions continue into the twenty-first century as vibrant options, and while they show variations from one people to the next (and wide variation over the vast distances from Angola to Senegal), some commonalities have surfaced. The religions were as a rule monotheistic, affirming faith in a single supreme being (while the variant names by which God was called were an indication of the different religions held by each group). The supreme Creator was both transcendent (hence remote for most everyday affairs) and immanent (hence the cause of unpredictable occurrences in the natural realm). God was also believed to have delegated much of the cosmos to oversight by lesser beings—subordinate divinities, different spirits, and ancestors. Humans are often tied to the Supreme Being in His/Her function as the first ancestor. The name for the deity and for one's ancestors are often closely related.

Because the supreme Creator delegated authority in the supernatural realm to the lesser spirits or divinities, much African religious life centers on these lesser beings (which usually also included the ancestors), and in a manner analogous to the saints in Roman Catholicism, their favor is sought by a spectrum of means from prayer to sacrifice to magic. The means chosen are directly related to the dynamic view of the world that permeates traditional African religions. The world is alive and life flows through everything. The life force may be manipulated, most efficiently by specialists, and may be especially focused in different otherwise inanimate objects, from amulets and talismans to medicines.

Religious functionaries, who carry the knowledge of God, the lesser divinities, and the life force, and who understand the manipulation of the life force, were part of an intimate social system into which one would be born. Common to pre-modern societies, sacred and secular would not be separated, and religious functionaries would also commonly assume one or more secular leadership functions. One would turn to different people for different needs, be they priestly, liturgical, pastoral, magical, or protective.

A more complete discussion of African religion would take us far afield from the purposes of this text, but one element in African religions is important—the role of ancestors. Veneration of one's ancestors is a natural extension of the respect one was taught to pay to the older (and hence wiser) people who had built and maintained the community into which one would be born as well as a continuation of the love one had for family members who had passed away. Ancestors continue to exist after death and form a larger community who care for and protect the still visible community and visit it through dreams. Ancestors are to be honored and remembered, and if need be, their displeasure appeased. Access to the ancestors may also occur through another group of religious specialists who operate as entranced mediums.

The all too brief attention to an African past has as its purpose a calling of attention to the social and religious environment inhabited by those Africans who were suddenly captured, forced into slavery, and transported to another land and to note all that was lost, the total way of life—from one's companions who spoke the same language to authority figures who one asked about life questions to the food one consumed day by day to the paths one took as the daily routine unfolded. The new slave in America had to survive in a world in which people might as well have been speaking Martian or Klingon, in which one consumed unfamiliar foodstuffs and not the best of them, and in which surroundings lacked any touch of familiarity, or initially even stability. This totally new environment was also populated by a group of angry and hostile people who ordered you to do things with unknown sounds, beat you at seemingly irrational times, and conducted themselves as if they were completely ignorant of proper behavior. They certainly ignored the rules for proper conduct between the sexes.

Bit by bit, some more quickly than others, individuals gained some appreciation for what had befallen them. The full realization would await the arrival in the New World and their visit to the auctioneer's block and eventual settlement into a new home in some stranger's house, shop, or plantation. Chances are, there would be other Africans close by, though they might or might not speak an intelligible language. Their new masters might or might not be interested in more than the most rudimentary communication, just enough to get the instructions for the day's work across.

If one was lucky, there might be some schooling offered in the new language. If one was motivated, and had the knack, picking up the language could be done over several years, though mastering it was another matter. If one happened to possess some special attributes and had a perceptive master, one's former status as a leader in Africa could, on rare occasions, lift one above the new situation. In the great majority of situations, however, one was stuck with a relatively small number of options, and steps were taken to see that those least alluring to one's master—running away, reactionary violence, or suicide—did not attract the slave.

Slavery became institutionalized in the British American colonies in the seventeenth century, and through the next century, for a variety of reasons, only a minority of the slaves gained their freedom. By the 1760s, communities of free Blacks had arisen in all of the colony's cities. Individual free Africans were scattered across the countryside, many working as skilled artisans—blacksmiths, carpenters, coopers, or shipbuilders. In the cities, though suffering under a variety of laws designed to block direct competition with colonists of European origin, a few free Blacks emerged as relatively prosperous entrepreneurs and professionals.

In the 1760s, Methodism stepped into this world of the slaves and free Blacks. A revitalization movement from the British Isles, Methodism had been designed to spread piety and spirituality among Anglican Christians and had had remarkable success in Great Britain before being brought to America initially by Irish lay immigrants. Though lacking the Christian background of most of the European colonists attracted to Methodism, African Americans were equally attracted to the vibrant spirituality that emerged among the Methodists, and Methodists not only welcomed them into their fellowship but actively recruited them. As it turned out, the first generation of Methodist leadership had been positively affected by the emerging anti-slavery movement. Africans were present when the first American Methodist groups were organized and went on to become an important segment of the membership. Today, one out of three American Methodists are African American.

In spite of the important role that African Americans have played within the larger Methodist movement, their contribution remains among the least documented, a fact all the more noticeable given the high level of interest Methodists have otherwise shown in their own history. A *Will to Choose* is offered as a small contribution to the new effort begun in the 1960s to recover and highlight the role of African Americans in the making of American Methodism. That effort began with attempts to clarify Methodist attitudes toward slavery, an effort punctuated by Donald G. Mathews' groundbreaking *Slavery and Methodism: A Chapter in American Morality, 1780–1845* (1965).

I became interested in African American Methodist history during my years at Garrett Evangelical Theological Seminary, beginning in 1964. I had been born and raised as a Methodist in Birmingham, Alabama, and attended the Methodist-affiliated Birmingham-Southern College during the years of the Civil Rights movement. Having been raised a Methodist, I looked to Methodist history to help me explain my own background as well as the events that were exploding around me. In this endeavor, I was initially disappointed, being informed by my major professor, Frederick Norwood, that he lectured but infrequently on the topic because there was so little material that had survived, and when I got into Garrett's library, which contains one of the finer Methodistica collections in the country, I found he was right—there was not a lot of material with which to work.

Inadvertently, however, Norwood also pointed me in a possible direction. As I moved from my M.Div. program to pursue a Ph.D., he suggested that I should spend my free time in the library reading the journals of the circuit riders, a task I thoroughly enjoyed. And as I indulged myself, I also began to notice all the references to African Americans in those journals and started to copy and assemble them with the hope that while each particular citation carried little information (often saying more about the writer than the subject of his observation), possibly by bringing them all together a story would emerge. Early on, I decided that I wanted to reconstruct the story of African American Methodists, a task that I contrasted with the much more easily documented history of white attitudes toward Black people or the history of slavery relative to Methodism. I was also clear that I wanted to focus on the first century of African American life, the antebellum period. That would prove a more difficult and lengthy endeavor than I imagined.

Though I had gathered a considerable amount of material by the time I finished my graduate work in 1975, it was not yet enough to construct a narrative, and my professional career as the director of the Institute for the Study of American Religion took me far away from this one task. My work otherwise did send me across the United States and allowed some time to continue to gather references, as periodically I was able to spend time in the library of one of the several Methodist seminaries and peruse materials not available at Garrett.

In the meantime, Black Studies emerged as a new discipline, and the first generation of scholars and librarians have done a magnificent job of assembling and making known all of the materials by and about African Americans that did survive—government documents, abolitionist literature, slave narratives, and church records among them. Methodist scholars at the state level also began to assemble the histories of the surviving predominantly African American congregations. Most recently, of course, access has been appreciably heightened by the Internet.

African American historians became a part of the new generation of contemporary historians that demanded that history pay attention to and find means of listening to the voices of the non-elites, the shut-out, and the otherwise inarticulate of the society. They took my search for material on Black Methodists to the slave narratives, where I found a surprising number of African American writers to have been Methodists; to the records of local churches, some of which have survived; and to local church histories, many of which have become available in the years since the destruction of the former Central Jurisdiction of the United Methodist Church. In the end, while nothing like the records of the White church became available, a surprisingly large set of material did surface, far more than I had ever hoped to find when this project was started.

After three decades of gathering materials, by the beginning of the new century, I felt that I had finally assembled enough stuff that an initial narrative of antebellum African American Methodist history could be written. As such, A Will to Choose attempts to bring together both insights and methodologies from three very different disciplines—traditional church history, religious studies, and African American studies—each of which makes its own contribution. Church history, which has traditionally found its life in the exploration of religious institutions, reminds us of the continuing importance of denominations as the primary vehicles of religious life in a free society, an important insight after several generations in which many church leaders claimed that we had entered a post-denominational era and religious historians turned their interests to a variety of other themes in American religion. Religious Studies has pointed out the importance of objectivity in the observation of religious organizations, a significant corrective to the triumphalism that often affects church history, and to the need to call upon more mundane causative factors in explaining the ups and downs of institutions in which supra-mundane forces are regularly invoked.

Meanwhile, African American Studies has done a magnificent job of developing methodologies to tease the maximum amount of information from the surviving materials that document the life of Black America. Far more material on African Americans has surfaced in the last forty years than any of us imagined existed in the 1960s, but African American scholars still have to work in areas in which too much material has been lost and even more never written down in the first place. In the midst of the growth of African American studies one can but stand in awe of the pioneering work on early African American Methodism done by the likes of Will Gravely, Dee Andrews, Gary B. Nash, Sylvia R. Frey, Betty Wood, and the various African Methodist denominational historians, without whom this work would have been a vastly inferior product.

That being said, A Will to Choose attempts to cover the history of African American Methodists through the colonial period and the early national period up to the Civil War, culminating in the organizational discontinuities that occurred following the war. Within a decade, the African Methodist Episcopal Zion Church (AMEZ), a relatively small organization confined to the northeast states, became a national denomination, shot from less than five thousand members to more than a hundred thousand, and reorganized with its new center moved from New York to North Carolina. Simultaneously, the African Methodist Episcopal Church (AME) underwent an equally radical change that would lead to a similar shift from Pennsylvania to Tennessee. As these two churches were transformed, a whole new reality, the Christian Methodist Episcopal Church (CME), came into existence.

While telling the story of the AMEZs and AMEs, and at least of the origin of the CMEs, for two reasons, A Will to Choose concentrates on the story of those African Methodists who were members of the Methodist Episcopal Church (and after 1845 the Methodist Episcopal Church, South). First, at the time this project began at the end of the 1960s, there were multiple book-length histories of the larger African American Methodist churches covering the antebellum period, but material on the antebellum history of those Black Methodists who had chosen to remain in what would become the United Methodist Church was limited to several journal articles and a couple of chapters in books, all of which essentially covered the same material. Only in 1991 did Grant Shockley's *Heritage & Hope: The African American Presence in United Methodism* appear, the chapter on the antebellum period expanding on his earlier article. Second, as this project proceeded, it was obvious that through the antebellum period the overwhelming majority of African American Methodists remained members of the Methodist Episcopal Church, a situation that was reversed only in the last half of the nineteenth century.

In the end, for two additional very good reasons, it became obvious that an inclusive story of all the African Methodists was the most desirable. First, one cannot adequately tell the story of any one branch of the movement without reference to the others, since their histories were so intertwined and constantly interacted. Even when the AMEs, AMEZs, and CMEs became separate organizations, they continued to operate in conjunction with those who remained within the Methodist Episcopal Church, sometimes cooperating and at other times competing. Sometimes they sought a united voice, and at other times issued harsh polemics.

Second, in the present, Black and White Methodists are in a continuing dialogue and mutual exploration of how the Methodist community can find a united voice and even organizational life. What form that might take is still anyone's guess, but it behooves one like myself who would claim the title of Methodist church historian as at least one of his self-identities to see all of Methodist history as his/her history, not just that of the particular branch in which s/he holds primary membership. This particular truth was brought home to me in the 1970s when I pastored a radically multi-cultural congregation, the Emmanuel UMC in Evanston, Illinois, which at the time had equally large contingents of Scandinavian Americans, Black Americans of Jamaican heritage, and a growing number of first-generation immigrants from Gujarat, India. With apologies to the congregation's members for the inadequacies of my youthful pastoral leadership during my five years at Emmanuel, the experience transformed my understanding of what the church was all about.

An Overview

Africans were present in the American Methodist community from its beginning and formed an element in its life everywhere it spread. The African presence had been anticipated by a generation of interaction between African Americans, Moravians, and Methodists that began in the 1730s when a slave from St. Thomas in the Caribbean became the catalyst for the Moravians to launch their world missionary program, which in turn led to their initial contacts with John Wesley and their serving as a catalyst for his personal spiritual awakening and the subsequent birth of Methodism in the 1740s. Initial attitudes of the early Methodists toward the first African American Methodists would be shaped by John Wesley's appropriation of anti-slavery perspectives from the Quakers.

Through the first decades of Methodism's spread in America, growth was concentrated between New York and Baltimore, and Africans were everywhere present. When Irishman Robert Strawbridge came to Baltimore, Maryland, to preach the first Methodist sermon in the New World in June 1765, a young Black man, Caleb Hyland, arranged for the speaking stand from which Strawbridge spoke. When several months later Strawbridge organized the first Methodist class, at least one African American joined. Then early in 1766, when the first class in New York City was formed, another African, as in Maryland, a female, joined.

The pattern set in New York, Philadelphia, and Baltimore would be consistently repeated wherever the Methodist church spread during the next half century. As the church colonized new locations, from Ohio to Texas, Africans were there to participate in the first classes and the first societies. They emerged as exemplars of Methodist piety and faith, and from their midst class leaders and preachers quickly appeared. To tell the story of Methodism without mentioning the ubiquitous presence of Black members and leaders is to miss much of what the church was about and radically distort its history. This truth is nowhere more vividly manifest than in the career of Harry Hosier. Hosier emerged in the 1780s as the single best orator in the church, a fact recognized by Bishop Francis Asbury, who regularly sent him to areas in need of bolstering, where the White preachers had encountered special obstacles to the progress of the church. Without Hosier's contribution, Methodism would have assumed a much different shape at the beginning of the nineteenth century.

Through the early decades of the nineteenth century, the congregations in six urban centers largely carry the African Methodist story. Here a number of free Blacks found Methodism to be a particularly appropriate instrument for orienting their personal and social life, and here they developed new structures that not only provided expression to their faith but also projected their aspirations for full participation in American life. In Baltimore, as early as 1787, they formed an independent Black-led prayer meeting. In Philadelphia, independent Black-led congregations, Bethel and Zoar, emerged, soon to be followed by similar congregations in Baltimore (Sharp Street), New York (Zion), and Wilmington, Delaware (Ezion). Philadelphian Richard Allen would be the first African to be ordained (though only as a deacon), to be followed by seven others serving these independent congregations.

After a decade of waiting for the church to respond to their presence, Wilmington's Ezion church would be the first church to experience a schism when many of the members walked out to found a new African Methodist congregation no longer affiliated with the Methodist Episcopal Church, the African Union Church (1813). Two years later, Daniel Coker led a walkout from the Asbury and Sharp Street churches in Baltimore, and in 1816 Richard Allen founded the African Methodist Episcopal Church, to which Daniel Coker and the Baltimore congregation adhered. In New York, a third independent church, also to grow into a new denomination, the African Methodist Episcopal Zion Church, emerged. While the majority of Africans through the antebellum era remained attached to the Methodist Episcopal Church, these three new branches in the Methodist tree represented a sign of things to come.

Simultaneously with Methodism's development in the northern states, it spread rapidly in the South with early centers in the Tidewater area of Virginia, Wilmington, North Carolina, and further south in Charleston and Savannah. Wilmington proved a singular situation, where the Methodist Church was started and led by an extraordinary Black preacher, Henry Evans. Charleston, a city with an African majority in the general population, also became a unique center of Methodism, with Black membership many times that of the Whites. Charleston, whose only independent Black structures (a quarterly conference within the White-led church and an independent African congregation) were destroyed only a few years after they came into existence, manifested in exaggerated form all of the problems faced by African Methodists trying to struggle with the institution of slavery.

Charleston also became the originating point of the "plantation missions," an effort by White Methodists in the South to both respond to the number of Africans isolated in slavery on plantations and deal with worldwide criticism of their accommodation to and even approval of slavery. Launched in 1829, the plantation missions provided those trapped in the slave states with one outlet, however meager, for an immediate amelioration of their condition and, over the long haul, a means of developing the leadership skills that would be so necessary once emancipation was attained. The slave mission became the major tool for recruiting and organizing African Methodists throughout the American South, especially after the split of Methodism in 1844 into separate northern and southern jurisdictions.

Meanwhile, Methodism was spreading west; it would move into the future Midwestern states all the way to the Mississippi River. Here the same patterns relative to African participation would continue with African members joining the first classes and congregations and Black preachers emerging to lead independent congregations. Louisville, Kentucky, and Dallas, Texas, provide excellent examples of what was occurring in the North and in the South, while the experimental Black Methodist community at Africa, Illinois, symbolized the possibilities.

As the 1810s and 1820s turned into the 1830s and 1840s, African Methodists who had found their freedom did not neglect their sisters and brothers still trapped in the evil institution. The writings of David Walker, a member of the May Street Methodist Episcopal Church in Boston, Massachusetts, would launch a new abolitionist movement that demanded the immediate freeing of the slaves, and caught the great majority of Methodists committed to the gradual elimination of slavery unprepared. Other Methodists such as Harriet Tubman and Samuel Green would help build the Underground Railroad, a massive effort to assist slaves in the South to escape and make the journey to freedom in Canada.

Simultaneously, the very growth of the African American Methodist community necessitated the further development of Black leadership. Beginning in the 1830s, a few Black Methodists within the Methodist Episcopal Church were recruited into the ordained ministry and Black leaders throughout the church began to explore a variety of strategies to gain ministerial and organizational equality for their constituency. Their effort would lead toward the emergence of a parallel synodical structure (the annual conference), full ordination for ministers, and eventually admission into the episcopacy.

The Civil War destroyed the overarching set of social structures governing relations between the African American community and the White community. As the war began, most African American Methodists were slaves, spread across the South as members of the Methodist Episcopal Church, South (MEC,S). Charleston again emerged as the symbolic city, where at the beginning of the war all Black Methodists (numbering in the thousands) were members of one of four White-controlled MEC,S congregations. Following the war, all the African members withdrew from the MEC,S and affiliated with either the African Methodist Episcopal Church or the Methodist Episcopal Church. One former local class leader would head west and emerge as a bishop of the newly formed Colored (now Christian) Methodist Episcopal Church.

For the several independent African Methodist Churches, the end of the war provided the opportunity for advancement previously blocked by slavery and a host of anti-Black laws operating in the North. Both the African Methodist Episcopal Church and the African Methodist Episcopal Zion Church seized the opportunity and experienced significant growth among the freedmen. The more congregationally oriented African Union Methodist Protestant Church fell behind at this point and remained a regional body in the Mid-Atlantic states. A large group of the former members of the MEC,S would reorganize as the new Colored Methodist Episcopal Church, and while having a significant advantage over its African Methodist rivals, it would soon find itself challenged on all sides as the Methodist Episcopal Church, the single church with the most resources, also re-entered the South in an attempt to reconstitute itself as a national church body.

The end of slavery and the reorganization of African American Methodism in the decade after the Civil War set the stage for the next century of African American struggles with America's racial structures. Though slavery had been put behind them, African Americans would quickly discover that the attitudes that had supported their enslavement now supported a host of legal structures that slowed their integration into American life and set obstacles to their attaining their share of the American dream. For those concentrating their attention on this next period, an understanding of the pre–Civil War struggles should broaden insights into the more-recent history.

The story of the antebellum period remains fragmentary, and this volume should not be perceived so much as a finished work as an initial attempt at assembling the available data. I view it far more as an initial attempt to bring some order to a chaos of data and hope that it will stimulate the emergence of more records and prompt the cadre of very able African American scholars to turn their attention to what has previously been a relatively neglected aspect of America's religious history.

Acknowledgments

More than all the several books I have written and edited over the years, this volume calls forth words of thanks to all the people who have assisted me in its preparation. Of these, Larry Murphy, the church historian at Garrett Evangelical Theological Seminary, immediately comes to mind. We have been involved in several projects over the years, especially the editing of the *Encyclopedia of African American Religion*, and I have always appreciated Larry's insights, listened carefully to his words of correction, but most of all been grateful for his friendship. I am also been grateful for the support, assistance, and encouragement of Will Gravely, especially the material he helped me locate once the decision finally to write this book occurred.

No one supplied me with more material and more information, especially on the vitally important story of African Americans in Maryland, than did Ed Schell, one of the leading lights of United Methodist history. Right up to the very end of my research, he located pertinent material, and I offer him and the staff at the Lovely Lane Methodist Museum and Archives in Baltimore my deep thanks for their assistance. In like measure, thanks must go to Brian McClausky at St. George's United Methodist Church in Philadelphia, the staff of the United Methodist Archives at Drew University, the staff of the libraries of the Avery Institute of Afro-American History and Culture and the South Carolina Historical Society in Charleston, and the staff of the Georgia Historical Society in Savannah.

During the later stages of my research, the Religious Studies Department of the College of Charleston hosted me for a week in Charleston, which allowed me the opportunity not only to share some of my findings on African American Methodists with the faculty and students but to get into the files of the archives and other materials at the college and the nearby Avery Institute and the South Carolina Historical Society. My thanks go to Lee Irwin and Elijah Siegler for arranging that visit.

Since my moving to Santa Barbara in 1985, I have been supported by the staff of the Special Collections Department at the Davidson Library of the University of California–Santa Barbara. The library now houses the American Religions Collection, which was initially deposited by the Institute for the Study of American Religion. That collection houses most of the materials that I used in the preparation of this volume. My thanks to David Tambo and his staff for their ongoing assistance.

Last, but by no means least, I want to thank Alyce Harris, who now oversees the Black Studies Collection at the Davidson Library. We have become friends over the years and she graciously agreed to read the final draft of this volume and offer her insights for improving it. I am grateful both for her many kind words over the years that have served to keep me motivated and her specific help on this volume.

Santa Barbara, California
July 2006

CHAPTER ONE

Anthony's Legacy

The Moravian Roots of African American Methodism

While the beginnings of African American Methodism are generally traced to the Black members of the first classes in Maryland and New York, it is illuminating to begin the story somewhat earlier, in 1731, and at some distance from the British American colonies, on the Caribbean island of St. Thomas. Here, on the plantation of a Danish nobleman, Count Larvwig, Anna and her two brothers, Anthony (or Anton) and Abraham—all slaves—resided. It was Anthony's lot to travel to Copenhagen as a member of the Count's personal retinue. While there, Anthony received Christian instructions, was baptized, and received his Christian name, Anthony Ulrich. Once baptized, he was ready to share the story of the plight of his fellow slaves in St. Thomas, especially of his sister Anna and brother Abraham. Anthony pleaded the cause of the slaves in the Indies, and German Count Nicolas Ludwig von Zinzendorf (1700–60), moved by his request, asked permission to take Anthony to Herrnhut, the Moravian center in Germany.[1]

Zinzendorf returned to his estate near Herrnhut on July 23, and Anthony, seizing the opportunity presented by Zinzendorf, accompanied David Nitschmann (1696–1772) to Herrnhut, where he arrived a week later. He immediately spoke of the truly awful state of the Africans trapped on St. Thomas. A heavy work schedule that left little time for religious gatherings probably meant that it would take a slave to reach the slaves. Immediately knowing that they had to respond to Anthony's visit, the Brethren cast lots. Leonhard Dober (1706–66) was thus selected to go to the West Indies for what would become one of the church's most prosperous missionary endeavors. Dober, accompanied by Nitschmann, arrived on St. Thomas on December 13, 1732.

Dober's and Nitschmann's work was made easier by Anna and Abraham, who provided them some initial access to the slaves. However, Nitschmann soon returned to Europe, and Dober's work was hindered by a slave revolt on the nearby island of St. John. During his two years in the Caribbean, Dober's first (and only) convert was Carmel Oly, a young boy whose freedom he purchased and who returned with him to Europe in June 1734. Oly's arrival in Herrnhut brought to the fore another issue. Not having ordained ministers, the Moravians were not authorized to baptize any converts. To receive ordination they needed a bishop. Again, they cast lots, selecting Nitschmann as their new bishop. After suitable arrangements, Nitschmann was consecrated in 1735, and soon afterward Oly was baptized and given the Christian name of Joshua.

Meanwhile, Tobias Leupold continued Dober's work on St. Thomas, assisted by a team of seventeen missionaries, some of whom moved on to St. Croix. The work progressed slowly. The missionaries fell victim to the tropical weather. The most success was had by Friedrich Martin, who had picked up the work with those to whom Dober had introduced the catechism. By 1736, several hundred slaves were regularly gathering to hear him preach. August Spangenberg visited St. Thomas that year and, on September 30, conducted the first baptisms among the converts.

By the end of the decade, the St. Thomas work showed marked progress, as African Christian leaders completed their training and took the lead both on St. Thomas and on the nearby islands of St. John and St. Croix. When Zinzendorf arrived in 1739 he found over eight hundred converts.

As the work on St. Thomas developed, Moravian missionary activity expanded. Zinzendorf arranged for a land grant from James Oglethorpe in Georgia, and in February 1735, August Spangenberg led a small group of Moravians to Savannah to establish a mission to both the Native Americans and the slaves. As chance would have it, the ship that carried the Moravians to Georgia included among its passengers two young clergymen, John Wesley and Charles Wesley, the former having been appointed minister of the Anglican church in Savannah. Midway across the ocean, Spangenberg introduced John Wesley to the Moravians' very personal and pietist faith. Though he was not initially convinced, Wesley's continuing Moravian relationships would become the catalyst for his own religious renewal several years later. Spangenberg stayed in Savannah just long enough to see the church organized, and then moved on to Pennsylvania.

The John Wesley statue located in the historic section of Savannah memorializes his ministry in Georgia and South Carolina.

Zinzendorf was finally consecrated on May 20, 1737, by Daniel Ernst Jablonski (1660–1741), whose orders could be traced back to the Czech Brethren of the sixteenth century. Later that year, on December 15, in his first exercise of the episcopal office, he ordained Peter Böhler to the ministry. Böhler's assignment was to go to South Carolina and initiate a mission to the African slaves. He left Germany soon afterward and joined the small Moravian group in London, where he was to spend some time improving his English. There, on February 7, 1738, Böhler was introduced to John Wesley, the founder of the Methodist movement. The chain of events initiated by Anthony the servant seven years previously would soon have one of its culminating moments. As Böhler worked on his English, he also explained his experiential religious faith to Wesley. Their numerous conversations were crucial to the transformative period leading to his awakening experience on May 24, 1738, at a lay religious gathering on Aldersgate Street.

Wesley's Encounter's with African Americans

While Wesley does not mention the subject in his journal, there is little doubt that an element in his close relationship with Böhler grew out of the connection of his recent experience in Georgia with Böhler's future mission. Wesley's Georgia venture had been supported by the Society for the Propagation of the Gospel (SPG). At its beginning, SPG representative John Burton had instructed Wesley (September 28, 1735), "One end for which we [i.e., the SPG] were associated was the conversion of negro slaves. As yet nothing has been attempted in this way; but a door is opened, and not far from home. The Purryburgers have purchased slaves; they act under our influence; and Mr. Oglethorpe will think it advisable to begin there."[2]

As it turned out, the majority of Wesley's time in Georgia was spent on other concerns, in part because George Oglethorpe, the founder of Georgia, initially kept slaves out of his colony. Wesley's main encounters with Black people would thus come on his several side trips to South Carolina, beginning with his journey to Charleston in the summer of 1736. He included accounts of his encounters in his *Journal* and *Diary*.[3] We know little of the individual Africans Wesley encountered. He recorded only fragments of his conversations, yet from these we can begin to get a hint of the struggle they were having in appropriating Christianity, at least in its Anglican format, and of the general indifference of the Anglicans in trying to communicate with them.

Wesley arrived in Charleston on July 31, and the next day preached in the large Anglican church. Of the service, he later noted:

> I was glad to see several Negroes at church; one of whom told me she was there constantly, and that her mistress (now dead) had many times instructed her in the Christian religion. I asked her what religion she was. She said she could not tell. I asked if she knew what a soul was. She answered, "No." I said, "Don't you know there is something in you different from your body? Something you can't see or feel?" She replied," I never heard so much before." I added, "Do you think, then, a man dies altogether as a horse dies?" She said, "Yes, to be sure."

Somewhat appalled at the level of instruction the woman had received and the level of understanding she evinced, Wesley could only opine, "O God, where are thy tender mercies? Are they not over all thy works? When shall the Sun of Righteousness arise on these outcasts of men, with healing in his wings!"[4]

On his journey back to Georgia, Wesley was disappointed at not being able to visit the plantation of Alexander Skene. Skene, one of the colony's leading citizens, had in 1715 became the first owner who agreed to allow SPG missionaries a free hand to work among his slaves.[5] Wesley's encounters with the few Africans he had been allowed to meet prompted him to obtain and read a copy of the *Negro's Advocate*.

He visited Charleston again in the spring of 1737. High seas prevented his return to Savannah by ship, so a colleague loaned him a horse. On his way home he recorded several conversations with the Africans he encountered. At the home of Rev. Thompson, who had loaned him the horse, for example, he found a young woman who seemed a sensible person. Wesley inquired of her origin. She replied that she had been born in Barbados and had come to South Carolina several years previously. Her tasks included taking the reverend's children to church each Sunday. Eager to find out what she had learned, Wesley was dismayed when she replied, "Nothing: I heard a great deal, but did not understand it." She then added that neither Thompson nor his wife had bothered to explain the faith to her.

Seeing a teaching opportunity, Wesley then offered a basic lesson on the soul to which his audience of one listened attentively. He explained that when she died her soul would go to heaven, where no one would beat her and she would never be in need or hungry. She would be happy. When he saw the young woman the next day, he happily recorded, "She remembered all, readily answered every question, and said she would ask him that made her to show her how to be good."[6]

Wesley used his last journey to South Carolina to reflect upon a more efficient way to evangelize the slaves and reached the same answer adopted a century later by the Methodist missionaries to the plantations. "And perhaps one of the easiest and shortest ways to instruct the American negroes in Christianity would be, first, to inquire after and find out some of the most serious of the planters. Then, having inquired of them which of their slaves *were best inclined*, and understood English, to go to them from plantation to plantation, staying as long as appeared necessary at each. Three or four gentlemen at Carolina I have been with that would be sincerely glad of such an assistant, who might pursue his work with no more hindrances than must everywhere attend the preaching of the gospel."[7]

On this trip, Wesley also first brought up the subject of the brutal treatment of the slaves, of which he had become aware and in a few cases witnessed. While both he and his brother Charles made their protests vocally, Charles recorded his observation in his journal:

> *August 2, 1736.* I had observed much, and heard more, of the cruelty of masters toward their Negroes, but now I received an authentic account of some

horrid instances thereof. The giving a child a slave of its own age to tyrannize over, to beat and abuse out of sport, was, I myself saw, a common practice. Nor is it strange that being thus trained up in cruelty, they should afterwards arrive at so great perfection in it; that Mr. Star, a gentleman I often met at Mr. Laserre's, should, as he himself informed L[aserre], first nail up a Negro by the ear, then order him to be whipped in the severest manner, and then to have scalding water thrown all over him, so that the poor creature could not stir for four months after. Another much applauded punishment is drawing their slaves' teeth. One Col. Lynch is universally known to have cut off a poor Negro's legs, and to kill several of them every year by his barbarities. . . . I shall only mention one more, related to me by a Swiss gentleman, Mr. Zooberbuhler, an eye-witness, of Mr. Hill, a dancing master in Charleston. He whipped a she-slave so long that she fell at his feet for dead. When by the help of a physician she was so far recovered as to show signs of life, he repeated the whippings with equal rigour, and concluded with dropping hot sealing-wax upon her flesh. Her crime was over-filling a teacup.[8]

From December to January 1737–1738, Wesley returned to England. Confined to the small vessel, he developed his first ongoing relationship with several Black people, whom he began to instruct in the faith. The first, a young man, began sitting with Wesley as the minister read the Bible and tried to explain it. They were soon joined in their deliberations by another.[9]

Peter Böhler and George Whitefield in America

In June 1738, Wesley and Böhler parted company when, a few weeks after his "heartwarming" experience at Aldersgate, the former left to visit the Moravian center in Herrnhut. Böhler remained in England through the summer and departed for America in the fall. He landed in Savannah on October 16 and proceeded immediately to the mission station located at the German settlement at Purrysburg, South Carolina. On his first Sunday in the New World, he preached to his German colleagues and then the following week began visiting the African residents in the area.

Böhler arrived in Savannah just after George Whitefield had completed his first visit to America. Whitefield preached at various locations around the colony for some five months (May to September 1738) and began the first of his several charitable enterprises, an orphanage. He also got drawn into the lively debates concerning the reversal of Oglethorpe's banning of African slaves from Georgia. He aligned himself with those who could see no reason that Georgia should be an exception to every other place in the Americas, where slavery was ubiquitous. In fact, Whitefield would prove a factor in the admittance of the practice into the colony.[10]

Whitefield returned to America in October 1739, and after several weeks in the Philadelphia area began to work his way south toward the end of November, preaching as he went. Accompanying him were two supporters, Williams Seward and John Syms.

Whitefield's first real encounters with African Americans occurred on this trip. By the time he reached North Carolina, he had developed a schedule of regular ministry with them. He made it his business to visit with any slaves that resided in the houses in which he stayed. He also saw the brutality with which many Black people lived as a matter of daily routine. Ruminating on these new experiences, Whitefield distanced himself from his earlier stand. First, he developed a belief that Black children, if early brought up in the nurture and admonition of the Lord, would prove to be as devout Christians as any White people. This insight became the foundation of plans for a school for African children, though he set his plans aside to focus energy on stabilizing the orphanage in Savannah.[11]

His new understanding of Black people was quickly put to the test as he neared Charleston. The year 1739 had been a time of slave revolts and rumors of revolts, including accusations against two planters at Purrysburg of inciting a rebellion. Then, in September, a slave named Cato had led an attack on an arsenal at Stono, just south of Charleston. Gathering a following of some seventy-five, he headed for Florida, though he was soon tracked down and his followers either killed outright or captured and later executed.

Now, just a few months later, on January 2 of the new year, Whitefield and his traveling companions were lost and trying to find the house in which they were to spend the night. They ran into some Black people who, when Whitefield and his group inquired about the way to their destination, seemed ignorant of the territory and claimed to be new to the area. Further on, they spied some Black people dancing around a fire. When they finally made it to their destination, they shared their fears that they had encountered remnants of "some of those who lately had made an insurrection in the province, and had run away from their masters." The plantation owners quelled their fears and informed Whitefield whom he had met. This information "afforded us much comfort, after we had ridden nearly three score miles, and as we thought, in great peril of our lives."[12]

Stopping at Charleston, they acquired some Black guides for their journey on to Savannah. Whitefield made it a point of regularly praying with their guides as occasion allowed. By the time they arrived at Savannah, Cato's rebellion aside, Whitefield had now reached a further conclusion: the slave trade was a primary cause of irreligion in the region.[13] He also continued to think about a school for Black children and decided to place it in Pennsylvania, where he was to have a number of notable responses to his preaching from Africans both slave and free. For example, while in Germantown, he found himself "employed for two hours this morning in giving answers to several who came to me under strong convictions; amongst whom was a negro or two, and a young girl of about fourteen years of age, who was turned out of the house where she boarded, because she would hear me, and would not learn to dance."[14] William Seward, now a financial backer of the school project, left an account of "a free Negroe woman [who] came to Mr. Whitefield, who was touched by the free grace of God when he expounded in the prison."[15] Seward shared Whitefield's desire to evangelize the Africans and saw Whitefield's work as a sign that God intended their salvation. Whitefield and his White supporters were encouraged in their work by events such as the one he recorded of the conversion of a Black woman:

> I conversed with a poor negro woman, who has been visited in a very remarkable manner. God was pleased to convert her by my preaching last autumn; but being under dejections on Sunday morning, she prayed that salvation might come to her heart, and that the Lord would be pleased to manifest Himself to her soul that day. Whilst she was at meeting, hearing Mr. M...n, a Baptist preacher, the Word came with such power to her heart, that at last she was obliged to cry out; and a great concern fell upon many in the congregation. The minister stopped, and several persuaded her to hold her peace; but she could not help praising and blessing God. Since this occurrence, many have called her mad, and said she was full of new wine; but the account she gave me was rational and solid, and, I believe in that hour the lord Jesus took a great possession of her soul. Such cases, indeed, have not been very common; but when an extraordinary work is being carried on, God generally manifests himself to some poor negroes who are to be called, God will highly favour them, to wipe off their reproach and shew them that he is no respecter of persons, but that whosoever believeth in Him shall be saved.[16]

Meanwhile, through 1739 the Moravian mission in South Carolina had gone badly. While the missionaries did well through the winter of 1738–1739, they suffered greatly during the hot and humid summer. Böhler sickened first and never fully recovered. Then in July his colleague George Schulius fell ill and died on August 4. They might have persevered, but Georgia was threatened with an attack from the Spanish in Florida, and the locals demanded that Moravians (at the time pacifists) join the defense. Whitefield offered them a way out. Prior to his departure from Savannah in April 1740, he invited Böhler and his colleagues to travel with him to Pennsylvania.

Although the Moravian problem had been handled, the plight of the slaves, and regret at what he had earlier done in Georgia, assumed prominence in Whitefield's thoughts and actions. He hastily penned what he termed "A Letter to the Inhabitants of Maryland, Virginia, and North and South Carolina Concerning their Negroes."[17] Very soon after landing in Philadelphia, he gave the "Letter" to Benjamin Franklin, who printed it as a pamphlet. It was later picked up and reprinted by newspapers throughout the colonies. Having been written by one now so well known throughout the colonies, it constituted a significant attack on slavery.

The letter recounted the miserable treatment the slaves received, worse than the house pets or horses the planters also kept. While not moving to an abolitionist stance, Whitefield weighed in against any cruelty toward those held in bondage and termed those who inflicted it monsters. God's judgment would be upon them. He had not thought about the hostility this widely circulated letter would later provoke among the plantation owners.

The letter done and printed, with the money advanced by Seward, on April 22, 1740, Whitefield brought five thousand acres of land on the forks of the Delaware (north of present-day Easton), and ordered a large house to be built there for the instruction of the Black people. He called his land Nazareth and envisioned many good things from it.[18] In a letter to Dr. Barecroft, the secretary of the SPG in London, he mentioned his hope that he would be able to purchase a number of young slaves at a very low rate so as to benefit from his new project.[19] News quickly spread through the African community, and as Whitefield prepared to return to South Carolina for an extended visit, the local Africans found their way to his lodgings, to express their personal sorrow that they were not to see him for a long time. Near fifty Black people showed up to express their gratitude for what God was doing in their souls. Whitefield was happy that they backed his school project.

> How heartily did those poor creatures throw in their mites for my poor orphans. Some of them have been effectually wrought upon, and in an uncommon manner. Many of them have begun to learn to read. One, who was free, said she would give me her two sons when I settle my school. I believe masters and mistresses will shortly see that Christianity will not make their negroes worse slaves. I intended, had time permitted, to have settled a Society for negro men and negro women; but that must be deferred till it shall please God to bring me to Philadelphia again. I have been much drawn out in prayer for them, and have seen them exceedingly wrought upon under the Word preached.[20]

Whatever his Black supporters thought, Whitefield was no abolitionist. He saw his school as ameliorating the slaves' condition, leading not to freedom and integration into society but to a kinder and more orderly existence as slaves.

The Moravians, however, now found themselves in a predicament, as their brethren, whom they expected to meet upon their arrival in Pennsylvania, were not there. They found some temporary employment and tried to stay together. But again, their needs and Whitefield's plans converged, and Whitefield turned to them (several of whom possessed carpenter's skills) to erect the school on the land he had purchased. He appointed Böhler to superintend the project, and in the last week of May 1740, Böhler and ten others (including two indentured servants) traveled to Nazareth and began work. Word of the work also filtered back to John Wesley, who began to collect money to support the school.[21]

While they worked over the summer and into the late fall, Whitefield continued his evangelistic endeavors in South Carolina, the school never far from his thoughts. He fantasized that if only he had the time and finances, he could also build a like school for the Black people in South Carolina.[22] And as was the case in Pennsylvania, many slaves looked upon Whitefield as a friend and visited him when he became ill during the hot summer months.[23]

In the fall, Whitefield traveled through New England, and on occasion, when Blacks came to hear him, preached out of Acts 8, the story of the conversion of the Ethiopian. And Black people were as moved by his preaching as were White people. He noted the case of one woman in New Jersey who was so filled with the love of God that she wanted to go with Whitefield and join in the work. Her master had even given his consent to the idea. Whitefield declined the offer, however, and bid her return home and serve her present master with a thankful heart.[24]

Back in Pennsylvania in November, Böhler met with Whitefield to report on the progress of the building, but now another matter intruded. It seemed that Whitefield and Wesley were in the process of separating over some theological differences. Instead of receiving Böhler's report, Whitefield turned on his employee and tried to convince him to replace the Moravian belief in free grace with the Calvinist belief in predestination. The theological conflict ended with Whitefield abruptly ordering the Moravians off his land. He relented only in allowing them to remain until spring. As it turned out, not only had their relationship ended, but both the Moravians' and Whitefield's adventure into ministry with African Americans also ceased. Böhler returned to Europe in January 1741. Shortly thereafter, William Seward died, leaving Whitefield financially strapped and unable to continue his project. Work on the school building stopped. In the end, the same Moravians whom he had kicked off his land came to his rescue and in 1743 purchased the land. They finished the school building but put it to other uses that were then high in their consciousness—a new ministry reaching out to Native Americans.

Whitefield's center for Black education never emerged, and though Whitefield would make a number of additional trips to America over the next two decades, he would not revive his attempt to minister to the slaves. In fact, he would himself become a slaveholder. Whatever active interest he retained in the plight of the Africans to whom he preached, he now passed on to Hugh Bryan, a wealthy planter in South Carolina who had developed an interest in educating his own slaves and who to that end had as early as 1734 accepted materials from the Society for the Propagation of the Gospel. Bryan tried to pass on the evangelical faith he had received from Whitefield to his slaves, which was rewarded with rumors that he was attempting to mobilize a slave revolt. He overcame the objections of his neighbors and, having broken with the Church of England, in 1747 formed the Stoney Creek Independent Presbyterian Church to which most (though by no means all) of his slaves would adhere.[25]

As for Whitefield, he would on his many tours of the colonies regularly preach to the Africans in his audiences and occasionally have conversations and encounters that would find their way into his journal. Africans, like Europeans, responded to his oratory, but in neither case did he follow up and attempt to organize them. The Black converts were left to the care of the local ministers. While a few like Samuel Davies in Virginia would welcome Blacks, most were not eager to take them into their churches. It would wait for the coming of the Methodist preachers sent by Wesley in the 1760s before a catalyst for bringing African Americans into a Christian community would operate generally through the colonies.

Wesley's Developing Attitudes toward Slavery

Through the 1740s and 1750s, as Wesley was busy with the initial spread of Methodism across England, Africans all but disappeared from his consciousness. Then suddenly in the mid-1750s, he received a letter from Samuel Davies,[26] the Presbyterian minister in Hanover, Virginia (and later president of Princeton), who expressed a uniquely positive attitude toward the Black residents of his parish. Davies sought Wesley's help, and Wesley was moved by Davies's compassion for the "Poor Africans." He had gathered about three hundred into his church in Hanover, and had instructed and baptized around a hundred. A similar number were attending a nearby church.

Davies happily reported that some had learned to read, and further, since they also loved to sing, Davies had introduced them to the hymns of Isaac Watts, his song books being the major musical tools available to evangelical churches at the time. The slaves were especially responsive.[27] Coincidentally,

Davies' letter had evoked themes voiced in Wesley's *Explanatory Notes on the New Testament* published just at this time (1755). Wesley's comment on I Timothy 1:10 speaks of the "man-stealers" mentioned in a list of sinners: "Man-stealers—the worst of all thieves, in comparison of whom highwaymen and house-breakers are innocent! What then are most traders in negroes, procurers of servants for America, and all who list soldiers by lies, tricks, or enticements?"[28]

Wesley sent Davies a shipment of books to circulate among his African charges. In a letter early in 1756, Davies reported that those who could read sought out the books and read them eagerly during their few leisure hours. "All the books were very acceptable," Davies noted, "but none more so than the *Psalms and Hymns*, which enabled them to gratify their peculiar taste for psalmody. Sundry of them lodged all night in my kitchen, and sometimes, when I have awaked at two or three in the morning, a torrent of sacred psalmody has poured into my chamber. In this exercise some of them spend the whole night." Davies went on to report that "two Sundays ago had the pleasure of seeing forty of their black faces at the Lord's Table, several of whom gave unusual evidence of their sincerity in religion. Last Sunday I baptized seven or eight, who had been catechized for some time. Indeed, many of them appear determined to press into the kingdom, and, I am persuaded, will find an abundant entrance when many of the children of the kingdom are shut out."[29]

Davies continued his correspondence with Wesley, reporting on his success and the continued response from the books Wesley had sent him, "I have baptized near one hundred and fifty adult negroes, of whom about sixty are communicants. Unpolished as they are, I find some of them have the art to dissemble. But, blessed be God, the generality of them, as far as I can learn, are real Christians, and I have no doubt but sundry of them are genuine children of Abraham. Among them in the first place, and then among the poor white people, I have distributed the books you sent me."[30]

The Africans from Antigua

The direct effects of the Wesleyan movement upon the slave population began not in the British American colonies but in Antigua where Nathaniel Gilbert, the brother of Francis Gilbert, one of Wesley's preachers, owned a large plantation. In the mid-1750s he traveled to England to meet Wesley personally, and several slaves accompanied him. Wesley first met the slaves when on January 17, 1757, he " preached at Mr. [Nathaniel] Gilbert's house. Two negro servants of his and a mulatto appear to be much awakened. Shall not his saving health be made known to all the nations?"[31] Then some months later, on December 29, he recorded, "I rode to Wandsworth, and baptized two negroes belonging to Mr. Gilbert, a gentleman lately come from Antigua. One of these is deeply convinced of sin, the other rejoices in God her saviour, and is the first African Christian I have known. But shall not the Lord, in due time, have these heathens also 'for his inheritance'?"[32] Subsequently, Gilbert returned to Antigua and became the fountainhead of the Methodist movement in the West Indies.[33] Gilbert's slaves meeting Wesley would become another step leading to Wesley's later attack on slavery.

Wesley's attitudes toward Black people, especially his seeing them as people ready to receive the gospel in the same manner as any other people, spoke directly to their status as persons. During the last decades of his life, Wesley had little contact with any Africans, there still being few in England, but the few that made their way to the Methodist societies were welcomed. Wesley found one such person in 1780, who was a member of the society in Whitehaven. The demeanor of the members in Whitehaven met with his approval, but one rose above the ordinary: "I was particularly pleased with a poor negro. She seemed to be fuller of love than any of the rest. And not only her voice had an unusual sweetness, but her words were chosen and uttered with a particular propriety. I never heard, either in England or America, such a negro speaker (man or woman) before."[34] Wesley's last recorded encounter with an African would be at Gloucestershire in 1786 when he baptized a young man who, to Wesley, seemed deeply serious and much affected by religion.[35] Of course, by this time, the history in America was beginning to play itself out.

Before we turn from Wesley and the European scene, however, we should visit Wesley's brief 1774 work, written just prior to the American Revolution, titled *Thoughts upon Slavery*. The pamphlet has a direct connection to the two slaves he baptized in 1757, as Francis and Nathaniel Gilbert became the instrument of Wesley's initial contact with the American Quaker abolitionist Anthony Benezet (1713–84). In 1768, Nathaniel Gilbert corresponded with Benezet, the author of four works against slavery written between 1759 and 1771, about which Gilbert concluded, "Your tracts concerning slavery are very just, and it is a matter I have often thought of, even before I became acquainted with the truth. Your arguments are forcible against purchasing slaves, or being anyway concerned with the trade."[36]

Benezet's tracts would subsequently become the major source for Wesley's contribution to the anti-slavery cause. As Wesley was becoming involved in the emerging British and American abolitionist movement, Methodism was extending itself to the North American colonies. The opinions expressed in

Thoughts upon Slavery were shared, more or less, by the early preachers sent from England to superintend the movement and were reflected in the early official position of the Methodist Episcopal Church (MEC) adopted in 1784.

Wesley began his discussion with some historical reflections concerning the revival of the slave trade by the Spanish following the discovery of the Americas. The wrongness of this slave trade came from the innocence of the Africans who had developed their own society in which they lived in an industrious and for the time sophisticated manner. They were rational people who were monotheists. Thus, Europeans procured the future slaves from a people who had done them no wrong, and gained possession of them largely by subterfuge.

Slavers then subjected the people so ingloriously taken into slavery with the barbarities and indignities of the middle passage only to subsequently introduce them into the even worse horrors of the life of American slaves, in which they were beaten, forced to work long hours, and subjected to a range of tortures whenever their strength to perform was exhausted. A particularly horrendous incident that Wesley knew of from his time in South Carolina concerned the roasting of a slave alive. Wesley concluded that the practice of slavery was neither biblical nor in accord with secular notions of justice or mercy. "Where is the justice of inflicting the severest evils on those that have done us no wrong? of depriving those that never injured us in word or deed, of every comfort of life? of tearing them from their native country, and depriving them of liberty itself."[37] The Angolan has the same natural right to the very liberty upon which the Englishman sets so high a value. "Where is the justice of taking away the lives of innocent, inoffensive men; murdering thousands of them in their own land, using their own countrymen; many thousands, year after year, on shipboard, and then casting them like dung into the sea; and tens of thousands in that cruel slavery to which they are so unjustly reduced?"[38]

Wesley then moves to a consideration of the economic arguments for slavery and attacks the assertion that slavery is a necessary evil. Much of the world, he notes, is getting along quite well without it; America could do likewise. But more to the point, he adds, "I deny that villainy is ever necessary. It is impossible that it should ever be necessary for any reasonable creature to violate all the laws of justice, mercy, and truth. No circumstances can make it necessary for a man to burst in sunder all the ties of humanity. It can never be necessary for a rational being to sink himself below a brute. A man can be under no necessity of degrading himself into a wolf. The absurdity of the supposition is so glaring, that one would wonder any one can help seeing it."

Finally Wesley turns to a subsidiary question. Suppose we grant the necessity of slavery: Why the sadistic treatment of the slaves in a manner one would not find even among Turk or Heathen? Agreed, Africans are living a debased life, but it is not because they are inherently inferior to the slave masters. Their condition is a product of the slave system itself, which offers "no means, no opportunity, of improving their understanding; and, indeed, leaves them no motive, either from hope or fear, to attempt any such thing." The negative behavior patterns that appear on the plantation—stubbornness, cunning, pilfering, and diverse other vices—result from the manner of the plantation owners; they cannot be laid at the feet of the slave. And, Wesley adds, "You [the slave owners] must answer for it, before God and man."

Wesley then holds up Hugh Bryan, the plantation owner from South Carolina, as an example of a different path. "He was kind, he shared his faith, and the African residents who worked for him came to love and reverence him as a father, and they cheerfully obeyed him out of love." Bryan contrasts sharply with the average plantation owner who keeps those who he owns ignorant and wicked by severing them from any hope or any opportunities for improvement either in knowledge or virtue. Then their lack of knowledge and goodness becomes the excuse to treat them worse than brute beasts!

Wesley's final words are directed to the man-stealers and the man-buyers—the slave trader who procured the slaves and brought them to America and the planters who purchased the slaves and thus made the traders' business profitable. Harking back to his New Testament commentary, he calls the man-stealer the worst kind of thief, far worse than the highwayman. But he now expands his observation. God's judgment on the man-stealer falls equally on the man-buyer. All slaveholders of whatever rank or degree are exactly on a level with man-stealers. Whatever profits that derive from the labor of slaves amount to ill-gotten gain, derived ultimately from the original dishonest procurement of the slave in Africa.

In what must have been the most infuriating paragraphs to the American readers of his pamphlet, Wesley concludes with a final rhetorical flourish aimed directly at the American slave owners. He places the whole sin of the slave system on their doorstep. The blood of the deceased slaves cries out from wherever they died. Their blood stains the hands, the bed, the furniture, the house, and the lands of the slave owner. He pleads with the man-buyers, "O, whatever it costs, put a stop to its cry before it be too late: . . . Surely it is enough; accumulate no more guilt; spill no more the blood of the innocent!"[39]

Wesley's concluding words would resonate with the words of the American patriots who would take up arms in a few years: "Liberty is the right of every human creature, as soon as he breathes the vital air; and no human law can deprive him of that right which he derives from the law of nature. . . . Let none serve you but by his own act and deed, by his own voluntary choice. Away with all whips, all chains, all compulsions! Be gentle toward all men; and see that you invariably do unto every one as you would he should do unto you."[40]

Methodist Opposition to Slavery

Wesley's anti-slavery stance as expressed in his 1774 pamphlet was reflected in the attitudes of the preachers he sent to America and would lead to the initial statement of the fledgling American Methodist movement concerning slavery. The statement reflects the problem encountered as Methodism spread through a land where slaveholding was a pervasive fact of life. Thus, in 1780, when the preachers gathered, two questions were posed and answered:

> Ques. 16. *Ought this conference to require those Traveling Preachers who hold slaves, to give promises to set them free?*
> Ans. Yes.
> Ques. 17. *Does this conference acknowledge that slave-keeping is contrary to the laws of God, man, and nature, and hurtful to society, contrary to the dictates of conscience and pure religion, and doing that which we would not others do to us and ours.—Do we pass our disapprobation on all our friends who keep slaves and advise their freedom?*
> Ans. Yes.

At the same time, they acknowledged the presence of African members and gave testimony to the common understanding that they were to be treated differently from those of European origin. Question 25 asked, "Ought not the assistant [Mr. Asbury] to meet the colored people himself, and appoint as helpers in his absence proper white persons, and not suffer them to stay late and meet by themselves?," to which the answer was in the affirmative.[41]

It was quite obvious, however, that the slavery question was the issue that was plaguing the growing movement. In 1783 the preachers noted the struggle to get some of the local lay preachers to get rid of their slaves. In 1784 (prior to the Christmas Conference), they voted to turn out the slave-owning local preachers in Maryland, Delaware, Pennsylvania, and New Jersey, but recognize the local nature of the problem in Virginia and give the preachers another year to work things out. At the same time, there is a clear statement than none of the traveling preachers are to be slaveholders.

In 1784, the Methodist movement organized formally as the Methodist Episcopal Church. Discussion of slavery assumed a block of time at the conference, and the preachers adopted a lengthy statement on ridding the new church of its taint (which the preachers saw as contrary to the laws of God and the spirit of the American Revolution). The statement ordered all members to either free or at least make provision for the freeing of all slaves within the next twelve months, and spelled out in some detail how this emancipation was to be accomplished. Those who did not conform were to be excluded from the society and not have access to the sacraments until they complied. No slaveholders would in the future be admitted into membership.

These rules ran into immediate opposition from enough of the members that they were tabled. After appearing in the first edition of the *Discipline* (the church's book of church law), they were deleted from future printings and their implementation postponed to the next General Conference in 1788. The 1784 action did have its effect, however, and ministers such as Philip Gatch moved with all speed to get rid of slaves they had inherited.[42] There were a number of reports of laypeople who also moved to abandon their ownership of slaves. Word spread through the African American community, both free and slave, that the Methodists had joined the Quakers in opposing slavery. Even as the slaves learned of the anti-slavery stance of the Methodists, in 1787 further directions were given to the ministers concerning their approach to African Americans. The ministers were to view them as objects of their evangelical work, and to that end they were to go out of their way to "embrace every opportunity of inquiring into the state of their souls, and to unite in Society those who appear to have a real desire of fleeing from the wrath to come, to meet such in class, and to exercise the whole Methodist Discipline among them."[43] African Americans' knowledge of the church's position against slavery, combined with the systematic recruitment of African Americans by the ministers, largely explains the movement of so many Africans into the Methodist church prior to the Civil War.

Through the early 1790s, the stance of the church on slavery was reconsidered, especially in relation to the spread of Methodism in the slaveholding states of the South. The idealism of ridding the church of slavery pervaded the ministry and the hope of leading the country to forsake the evil institution undergirded their welcoming of African Americans into membership, if not leadership. At the same time the anti-slavery stance was proving ever more difficult to implement. Asbury periodically raised the issue at the different annual conferences and called for commitment to the effort against human bondage.

The dilemma the ministers found themselves in is amply illustrated by the 1795 manifesto produced by a group of the South Carolina ministers several weeks after the discussion of slavery at the 1794 annual conference. They were caught between their own idealism and the fact that even some of their ministerial colleagues had become slave owners. In their declaration, the twenty-two ministers affirmed their agreement that all slave owners who came among them should immediately emancipate them, or, where the law prevents emancipation, pay them a salary for their work, and then free them in their will. They called for all who did not adhere to this action to be removed from the conference and have their ordination rescinded.[44]

The ministers' stance did not prove acceptable to the great body of their peers, and in 1796, the church produced a much watered-down statement on slavery. It advised counseling new members on the problems inherent in slavery. However, rather than excluding slaveholders, it set rules for slaveholding members, rules that would place local churches in the position of regulating the length of servitude of slaves owned by members. The new battle line would be with the ministers. The rule now read, "When any traveling preacher becomes an owner of a slave or slaves, by any means, he shall forfeit his ministerial character in the Methodist Episcopal Church, unless he execute, if it be practicable, a legal instrument of emancipation of such slave or slaves, conformably to the laws of the state in which he lives." The last phrase of this rule, of course, presented an escape clause for ministers in the South.

Relative to the Black membership itself, the next legislation came in 1800 when the General Conference authorized the bishops to ordain some lay preachers among those that had emerged in the Black community as deacons. The rule was meant to accommodate those situations such as had arisen in Baltimore and Philadelphia where separate Black churches served a significant number of free Blacks. According to early Methodist historian Jesse Lee, however, the new rule encountered so much opposition that special legislation was passed to exclude it from the *Discipline* and it was never publicized. Nevertheless, under this rule a modest number of Black preachers were ordained.

Bishop Asbury's own thinking on the slavery issue was deeply affected by several incidents, none so deeply as the attack on two Methodist ministers in Charleston in 1801. Members of a mob had heard a rumor that George Daugherty and John Harper, the two ministers assigned to Charleston that year, were in possession of some materials advocating the abolition of slavery.

The mob initially grabbed Harper as he left the church on a Sunday evening, but he was able to escape their clutches in a moment of confusion. The next evening they grabbed Daugherty as he left the church and this time took him to a water pump under which his head was placed and water pumped into his mouth. He was eventually rescued and left from further attack, though he died a short time later, seemingly from the long-term effects of his ordeal.[45] The incident served as a vivid and traumatic illustration of the temper of the southern states, and helped convince Asbury that he must choose between growing the church in the South and adhering to the hard line against slavery previously articulated by the church's conferences.

The impact of the incident was increased in 1803 when the South Carolina legislature passed a new law forbidding the gathering of Black people between sunset and sunrise and further limiting any daytime meetings to those occasions in which a majority of White people were present.[46] This action kept many Blacks from attending services in the Charleston churches for several years. The 1804 Methodist General Conference would respond to South Carolina by publishing a special edition of the church's *Book of Discipline* with the paragraphs on slavery removed for circulation in the Southern states. In any case, the new statement included a provision that the members of the church in the states of North Carolina, South Carolina, Georgia, and Tennessee were exempted from the overall operation of the remaining anti-slavery rules.

The more substantive accommodation to the state of slavery in the United States occurred in 1808 when the General Conference gutted its opposition to slavery with an authorization for each annual conference to form its own regulations relative to buying and selling slaves. Thus, while the church was on record as opposed to slavery, involvement would no longer be a barrier to participation, even for ministers, in the south. The 1808 legislation moved the Methodists into a position closer to the other Protestant churches as opposed to the Quakers, with whom its earlier anti-slavery stance had originated. Informally, the majority of the church's leadership remained opposed to slavery and they assigned the burden of proof on pro-slavery people to justify their position. By the 1820s, the church adopted a consensus favoring gradual emancipation, a position that tended to remove the sense of urgency from the cause. It also led many White Methodists into alignment with the Colonization movement that advocated the sending of free Black people back to Africa.

The continued formal opposition to slavery, of course, also allowed many individual Methodists and annual conferences to act in ways closer to the original stance. The ineffectual nature of gradualist approaches made abolitionism attractive to many northern Methodists in the 1830s. With gradualists ridiculing abolitionism as a form of extremism, many frustrated abolitionists left the MEC in the early 1840s to form the Wesleyan Methodist Church.

This discussion of the Moravians, Whitefield, Wesley, and the changing attitude of Methodism to slavery serves both to introduce the Methodist movement to anyone less familiar with it and to set the backdrop against which African American Methodism struggled into existence. African Americans, with roots taking them across the Atlantic to Africa, now inherited a second lineage that also takes them across the Atlantic to Europe. The story of Anthony, Peter Böhler, and the slaves of Nathaniel Gilbert also indicates that from the beginning the story of African American Methodists is an interactive history actually initiated by an African and not simply the passive reception of a European reality. As we approach the following account of the African American Methodist community, we should discard former models that pictured the White Methodists as the sole active agents and from the beginning understand the effort demonstrated by the Black pioneers in appropriating Methodism, adapting it to their needs, and in the process contributing to the development of the whole Methodist movement. Had African Americans not been present, there is every reason to believe that Methodism today would look very different. But they were present and to their story we now turn.

Notes

1. On the story of Anthony and Anna, see Sylvia R. Frey and Betty Wood, *Come Shouting to Zion: African American Protestantism in the American South and British Caribbean to 1830* (Chapel Hill, NC: University of North Carolina Press, 1998), and John R. Weinlick, *Count Zinzendorf* (New York: Abingdon Press, 1956), 96–98. On the African American involvement with the Moravians in the eighteenth century see J. Taylor Hamilton and Kenneth G. Hamilton, *History of the Moravian Church* (Winston-Salem, NC: Interprovincial Board of Christian Education, Moravian Church in America, 1983).

2. John Wesley, *The Journal of the Rev. John Wesley* (London: Epworth Press, 1916), 287.

3. It should be noted for the benefit of those unfamiliar with Wesley that during segments of his life he kept a diary of notes that listed what he did hour by hour almost every day. These were written in a private code (deciphered only many years after his death) and not intended for publication. They were one source for his *Journal*, a work written for publication. As not all of the information from the diaries was

passed on to the *Journal*, on many occasions the diaries supply additional insight. Such is the case in relation to Black people Wesley met in Georgia and South Carolina.

The Georgia diaries were published as notes to the 1916 edition of Wesley's *Journal* and are being published along with the *Journal* in the edition of *The Works of John Wesley*, still in the process of being completed. In this book, the new edition of *The Works of John Wesley* is cited where possible. References to those entries in the *Journal* yet to appear are cited from the 1916 edition published by Epworth Press.

4. *The Works of John Wesley. Journal and Diaries, I*, Vol. 18, ed. by W. Reginald Ward and Richard P. Heitzenrater (Nashville, TN: Abingdon Press, 1988), 169.

5. *Works of John Wesley, Journal and Diaries, I*, Vol. 18, 169–70.

6. *Works of John Wesley, Journal and Diaries, I*, Vol. 18, 179–80.

7. *Works of John Wesley, Journal and Diaries, I*, Vol. 18, 181.

8. Charles Wesley, *The Journal of the Rev. Charles Wesley, M.A., sometime student of Christ Church, Oxford: the early journal, 1736–1739* (Taylors, SC: Methodist Reprint Society, 1977): 36. Unlike John's, Charles' journal was not published until after his death (1788).

9. *Works of John Wesley, Journal and Diaries, I*, Vol. 18, 207–8.

10. Helpful sources on Whitefield include Arnold Dallimore, *George Whitefield: The Life and Times of the Great Evangelist of the Eighteenth-Century Revival* (London: Banner of Truth Trust, 1970), and Albert D. Belden, *George Whitefield, the Awakener: a Modern Study of the Evangelical Revival* (New York: Macmillan, 1953).

11. George Whitefield, *George Whitefield's Journals* (Gainesville, FL: Scholars' Facsimiles & Reprints, 1969), 377.

12. Whitefield, *George Whitefield's Journals*, 380.

13. Whitefield, *George Whitefield's Journals*, 386.

14. Whitefield, *George Whitefield's Journals*, 406.

15. From William Seward, *Journal of a Voyage from Savannah to Philadelphia and from Philadelphia to England* (London, 1740); quoted in Dallimore, *George Whitefield*, 499.

16. Whitefield, *George Whitefield's Journals*, 417.

17. George Whitefield, "A Letter to the Inhabitants of Maryland. Virginia, North and South-Carolina," reprinted in *The Works of Rev. George Whitefield* (London: Edward and Charles Dilly/Edinburgh: Kinkaid and Bell, 1771), 35–39.

18. Whitefield, *George Whitefield's Journals*, 406.

19. Quoted in Dallimore, *George Whitefield*, 497.

20. Dallimore, *George Whitefield*, 420.

21. *Works of John Wesley, Journal and Diaries, I*, Vol. 18, (July 29, 1740), 362.

22. Whitefield, *George Whitefield's Journals*, 444.

23. Whitefield, *George Whitefield's Journals*, 446.

24. Whitefield, *George Whitefield's Journals*, 490.

25. Whitefield's preaching would have far-reaching effects. His turning some planters' minds about the desirability of allowing Christianity to grow among the slaves would lead to the conversion of several slaves in Georgia, who would in turn

become the founders of the first African Baptist congregations, the oldest of which survives as the First African Baptist Church of Savannah, Georgia.

26. A brief sketch of Davies is found in William Warren Sweet, *Religion in Colonial America* (New York: Charles Scribner's Sons, 1951), 296–97. For a more detailed treatment see George H. Bost, *Samuel Davies* (Chicago: University of Chicago, M.A. thesis, 1942).

27. *Works of John Wesley, Journal and Diaries*, II, 125–26.

28. John Wesley, *Explanatory Notes on the New Testament* (London: Epworth Press, 1950), 772.

29. *Works of John Wesley, Journal and Diaries*, II, 149–50.

30. *Works of John Wesley, Journal and Diaries*, IV, 194.

31. *Works of John Wesley, Journal and Diaries*, IV, 247–48.

32. *Works of John Wesley, Journal and Diaries*, IV, 292.

33. For more on Gilbert see Frank Baker, "Origins of West Indian Methodism," *London Quarterly Review* (January 1960), 75–86.

34. *Works of John Wesley, Journal and Diaries*, VII, 277.

35. *Works of John Wesley, Journal and Diaries*, VII, 144.

36. From his letter dated October 29, 1786. Quoted by Frank Baker, "The Origins, Character, and Influence of John Wesley's Thoughts upon Slavery," *Methodist History* 22, 2 (January 1984): 77.

37. John Wesley, "Thoughts on Slavery," reprinted in *The Works of John Wesley* (London: Wesleyan Methodist Book-Room, 1872).

38. John Wesley, "Thoughts on Slavery," reprinted in *The Works of John Wesley* (London: Wesleyan Methodist Book-Room, 1872).

39. John Wesley, "Thoughts on Slavery," reprinted in *The Works of John Wesley* (London: Wesleyan Methodist Book-Room, 1872).

40. John Wesley, "Thoughts on Slavery," reprinted in *The Works of John Wesley* (London: Wesleyan Methodist Book-Room, 1872).

41. Question 25 is quoted and commented upon in J. W. Hood, *One Hundred Years of the African Methodist Episcopal Zion Church; or, The Centennial of African Methodism* (New York: A.M.E. Zion Book Concern, 1895), 4.

42. Elizabeth Connor, *Methodist Trail Blazer Philip Gatch. His Life in Maryland, Virginia, and Ohio* (Rutland, VT: Academy Books, 1970), 143–54.

43. For a discussion of the 1787 legislation see Leroy Lee, *The Life and Times of Rev. Jesse Lee* (Richmond, VA: , 1848), 189, and Francis Asbury, *The Journal and Letters of Francis Asbury*. 3 vols. (Nashville, TN: Abingdon Press; London: Epworth Press, 1958). (May 1787): I, 538–41.

44. Will B. Gravely, "Methodism in Black & White," *South Carolina United Methodist Advocate* 135, 11 (March 18, 1971): 8–9, 14.

45. This incident is related in some detail by James O. Andrew, "Letters on Methodist History," *Methodist Magazine* 12 (1830): 21–22.

46. Marina W. Kramanayake, *A World in Shadow: The Free Black in Antebellum South Carolina* (Columbia, SC: University of South Carolina Press, 1973), 122.

CHAPTER TWO

African American
Methodism's Beginnings

The First African Methodists

The story of American Methodism usually begins with an account of the emergence of the first Methodists known to have emigrated to the British American colonies from Europe and their founding of the first classes. But, as we turn our attention to African Americans, from the very beginning the Methodist story changes slightly. It seems that contemporaneous with the appearance of Robert Strawbridge (d. 1781), the Irish lay preacher in Maryland to whom American Methodist beginnings are usually traced, an unnamed Methodist sailor, who happened to be a ship's carpenter, found himself in Philadelphia for a brief visit. While there he met a local carpenter by the name of Peter Dennis and led him to faith in Christ. Dennis' experience suggests that the account of American Methodism's beginning needs to be broadened somewhat to include this account of an African American who would later join St. George's Church in the City of Brotherly Love.[1] Dennis would be remembered as having taken pride that his conversion had been from the preaching of someone who shared his profession.[2]

The recasting of American Methodism continues as we look at the more well-known founders of American Methodism, all three of whom were integrally involved with African Americans. After the account of Peter Dennis, the very first thing we know about American Methodism concerns the career of Robert Strawbridge, the independent-minded Irish preacher from Maryland. In June of 1765, Strawbridge arrived in Baltimore to deliver what appears to be the first Methodist sermon in the New World of which any record has survived. Before he preached, however, a young Black man, Caleb Hyland (spelled differently in various sources), arranged for a speaking stand from which Strawbridge spoke.[3] As James A. Handy (1826–1911) later observed, Strawbridge's "first pulpit was a block in front of a blacksmith shop, at what is now the corner of Front and Bath Street. The next Sunday he preached from a table at the corner of Baltimore and Calvert street, at which time he was mobbed."[4] Hyland, a free Black man, owned the bootblack shop in front of which Strawbridge preached and had supplied him with the table.

Several months after Strawbridge's inaugural sermon, he organized a Methodist class at Sam's Creek, Frederick County, Maryland, some fifty miles from Baltimore. That class included at least one African American, known only as Aunt Annie, a servant in the Switzer family.[5] A short time later, early in 1766, at the instigation of Barbara Heck (1734–1804), with the assistance of Philip Embry (1728–73), both also from Ireland, the first class in New York City was formed. One member of that class was an African American servant woman, remembered only as Betty. Betty would go on to become a charter member of John Street Church, the first Methodist church in the city, and later one of the original members of the first Methodist church in Canada (organized after the American Revolution).[6]

African Americans, both female and male, began their appropriation of Methodism as soon as it became available to them and thus were already an integral part of the Methodist movement when the preachers commissioned by Methodist founder John Wesley for the care of the American members arrived from England. Actually, these preachers, in their journals and letters, created the first records we have of African members. As early as November 4, 1769, the newly arrived Richard Boardman (1738–1782) described his initial perception of the Black attendees in New York and opened comment on what was to be a persistence problem—masters who would not let their servants attend Methodist services.[7]

In New York, the number of people attending Methodist activities grew steadily, and in 1767 the group moved into a rigging loft on Horse and Cart Street (now William Street) and the following year initiated plans to erect a chapel on John Street. About this time a record of the emerging congregation was started, which was kept in a book that came to be called the "Old Book," and which has become a primary source for the early history of New York. Selections from it have been published in various histories of New York Methodism.

As an initial step to erecting the new chapel, following a common practice in the day, the congregation sought subscriptions to underwrite the cost. Amid the subscription accounts, J. B. Wakeley discovered, "We find on 'the

Book' among the subscribers, Rachel, who gave nine shillings, and Margaret, seven shillings. It does not say Rachel who, or Margaret what. Their names are unknown to us, but are written in heaven. From the 'old book' we learn that they were girls hired to take care of the preacher's house, for we read where the trustees paid them their wages. They were colored girls, no doubt, and therefore we have only the first name."[8]

Wesley Chapel, the building erected on John Street, was a stone building sixty by forty-two feet. At some point after the dedication on October 30, 1768, a gallery that was used by the Black members and some of the unmarried young White men was added. According to Wakeley, the chapel was furnished plainly. Seating was on benches with no backs. There were neither stairs nor breastwork to the gallery, access being by way of a ladder. Later stairs would be added to facilitate movement to and from the gallery.

By 1771, there were some one hundred people who identified themselves as Methodists and many times that number who would show up for services when one of the preachers was in town. Notable among the members were a number of Black women. By 1795, the John Street congregation had 155 Black members organized into eight classes, of which two were male and six female.

The presence of African members, a new element in the experience of the British preachers, became the occasion of much consternation and soul searching on their part. In the early 1770s, Joseph Pilmore (1739–1825) recorded the observations of some members in Maryland:

> While we were on our knees wrestling with God, I observed one of the Negroes go out, and thought he was afflicted [in?] his mind and so it happened, for we heard him calling loudly upon God to bless him and save his soul from sin. How many of these poor slaves will rise up in judgment against their Masters, and, perhaps, enter into life, while they are shut out.[9]

In New York in 1773, Thomas Rankin (1738–1810) left his perceptions in his *Journal*:

> May 22, Sunday. I found freedom to declare the word of the Lord this day and I trust the seed sown will produce some fruit to the glory of God. We concluded the evening with a general love-feast, in which meeting the Lord's presence was powerfully felt by many persons. Many declared with great freedom of speech, what God had done for their souls. Some of the poor black people spoke with power and pungency of the loving-kindness of the Lord. If the rich of this society were as much devoted to God as the poor are, we should see wonders done in this city. Holy Jesus, there is nothing impossible with thee.[10]

Again, in November 1774, Thomas Rankin opined over a meeting of the Baltimore Circuit Quarterly Conference:

> Near the close of the meeting, I stood up and called upon all the people to look towards that part of the chapel where the poor blacks were. I then said, "See the number of black Africans, who have stretched out their hands and hearts to God." While I was addressing the people thus, it seemed as if the very house shook with the mighty power and glory of Sinai's God. Many of the people were so overcome, that they were ready to faint, and die under His almighty hand. For about three hours the gale of the spirit thus continued to break upon the dry bones, and they did live, the life of the glorious love. As for myself, I scarce knew whether I was in the body or not; and so it was with all my brethren.[11]

The Methodists erected their first chapel in America at Leesburg, Virginia, on land purchased in 1766. During the later 1770s John Littlejohn settled in Leesburg and roamed through northern Virginia as far away as Richmond. As he traveled the territory he made a resolution to rise early every day and to have morning prayer with the family with whom he stayed so the Black people could be present.[12] At one point, following a colleague's sermon to a Black audience in which he speculated that the Black people will stand in the final judgment over against Whites who only call themselves Christians, Littlejohn exhorted the assemblage to faithfulness and the service of God until "they go where the servant is free from his Master."[13] On May 26 he spoke to a congregation that included many slaves, some of whom he noted were happy and others under conviction of sin. He prayed that the "slaves be made freemen in Jesus Christ."[14]

In January 1790, a revival broke out in Leesburg, accompanied by a variety of extraordinary behavior on the part of those affected by the Christian message. He noted one African woman, a slave, who fell over and was pronounced dead by a local doctor. Littlejohn used the occasion to mock the physicians who did not know God and observed that the woman had "died indeed to sin but was made alive to God." At another time, an African man fell across the arm of a chair, and fearful that the man would break something, Littlejohn eased him to the floor, where he began to turn round like a spinning top. Then another person set him in a position of prayer on his knees. At this point, the man began to pray for mercy and eventually experienced salvation. Throughout the revival, Black and White alike indiscriminately found salvation.[15]

Bethany Veney (b. 1815) grew up in Page County, Virginia, where she became an active Methodist. As a young adult she had to deal with a persistent problem encountered by religious slaves, an unbelieving master hostile to her religion. Deciding to drain the religion from her, her master, David Kibbler, sent her several miles away to work for a Mr. Leaver, where, as she noted, she was

> to stay until I should get over my "religious fever," as he called it. Accordingly, I went as directed; but, when it came night, I asked if I might go down to Mount Asa school-house for meeting. The old man said: "Yes. You can go; and, as it is so far away, you need not come back here till morning. But go home, and stay with the children, as you always do, and have the care of them." I couldn't understand it, but I went; and, when in the morning Kibbler saw me, he scolded, and sent me off to Levers again. Every night, old Mr. Levers would tell me I could go; and I did, till, in the middle of the meeting one night, Master Kibbler came up to me, and, taking me by the arm, carried me out, scolding and fuming, declaring that old Webster (the minister) was a liar, and that for himself he didn't want such a "whoopin' and hollerin' religion," and, if that was the way to heaven, he didn't want to go there. After this, my conscience troubled me very much about going. Mr. Levers would tell me to go; but I knew that Master David had forbidden me to do so. One night, I started out, and, as I came to a persimmon-tree, I felt moved to go down on my knees and ask the Lord to help me, and make Master David willing. In a few minutes, I felt very happy. I wanted to remain on my knees, and wished I could walk on them till I could come before Master David. I tried to do so, and was almost surprised to find I could get along so well. At last, I reached the piazza, and was able to enter the room, where I saw him sitting; and, as I did so, I said, "O Master, *may* I go to meeting?" He saw my position; and, as if "rent by the Spirit," he cried out: "Well, I'll go to the devil if you ain't *my match!* Yes: go to meeting, and stay there."[16]

Especially important to the spread of Methodism in the decade immediately prior to the organization of the Methodist Episcopal Church was the conversion of Harry Dorsey Gough (d. 1808), who owned several plantations near Baltimore. He had initially developed a positive attitude toward the Methodists after hearing Francis Asbury (1745–1816) speak, but the occasion of his actual conversion came later as he overheard one of his slaves praying. A prayer of thanksgiving offered by one so devoid of all material wealth struck home to the very wealthy Gough. His residence became the key Methodist center in the area.[17]

The evidence of the attraction of Methodism to African Americans was everywhere present, and that Black people usually formed the most religiously fervent segment of Methodist congregations would become a problem for Pilmore, Asbury, and their colleagues. African Methodists had not been part of their British experience, and their frequent mention of the Africans points to their initial perplexity. It was a variation of Gough's quandary—the Africans had the least materially—they were the "poor" Africans—but they manifested what the Methodist preachers expected of the entire church. It is of interest, that Acts 10:34 ("God is no respecter of persons") came to mind for these biblically trained ministers, rather than, for example, Galatians 3:28 (In Christ there is neither Jew nor Greek, slave nor free).

The example of the African members certainly reinforced the anti-slavery stance soon to be officially articulated by Wesley in his 1774 *Thoughts on Slavery*, but it was contributing forcefully to the major change of direction that Methodism was undergoing in the New World. Methodism had begun as a revitalization movement in a Christian country, a land where virtually everyone was baptized and raised in some relationship with the church. It viewed itself as bringing new life to Anglicans, bringing personal faith to people who already identified themselves as Christian. The Africans were, however, a radically new phenomenon—they lacked any such Christian background. Most had not been taught to read or write and hence did not have the storehouse of Christian data that the average British youth would learn. They were new converts to the faith in a land where, as the Methodists were also gradually discovering, the great majority of people of European background had little or nothing to do with Christianity. The colonies were being populated by people who had the least to lose by becoming pioneers, those most disconnected—economically, politically, and religiously—from the dominant social structures in England. The Africans now assumed a leading role as a catalyst for changing American Methodism from a revitalization movement to an evangelizing church, and their continued participation would push the movement in some very different directions than those envisioned by its founders.

Restructuring African Methodists

The role that the early Black members played and were to play in the Methodist movement can best be understood in light of the several structures that gave shape to the soon-to-be-organized church. The basic structure, almost always the first to be formed in any new location into which Methodism spread, was the class. Rooted in the German Pietist movement's pious assemblies, classes were small groups within a parish that met for prayer, hymn singing, and general encouragement in the Christian life. Wesley introduced classes from his experience among the Moravians. They could be formed by small groups of five to ten people, who would meet weekly, and add people as they attached themselves to the movement. One person would serve as the class leader. His/her job would include guiding the weekly gathering, collecting the offering, and maintaining knowledge of the religious state and moral behavior of the individual members, about which a report would be made to the preacher on his various visits.[18]

Typically, the Methodist preachers traveled the countryside and stopped wherever they found a friendly welcome and a family who would offer hospitality. Such locations became noted as preaching points, and those who initially responded to the preaching would be organized into the first class. A set of preaching points and classes in relatively close proximity would be organized into circuits. In the beginning, the circuits included a large number of preaching points, not infrequently twenty or more. As members and support grew, circuits would be redrawn around the more stable preaching points, and the preacher's regular visits scheduled well ahead of time. In those cities in which Methodism experienced early growth, one or more preachers would be assigned to a single location (termed a station, as opposed to a circuit).

A station would, as it grew, become the source of multiple congregations. In the older stations, such as Baltimore, several preachers would be assigned to the city and would together have charge of the several congregations in that location. In general, the first congregation would be interracial, though with segregated seating. As the number of classes grew, they would be divided, usually along racial and gender lines. As noted, since 1780, the general policy had been to appoint White class leaders over Black classes, but for a variety of reasons that policy was challenged quite early, especially when there was a shortage of Whites ready to assume leadership and some obviously competent Black leaders.

Beginning in the 1790s, the first predominantly African American congregations were founded. In some cases, African American converts founded a church in a location where there was as yet no White congregation. Others resulted as a growing congregation that had outgrown its building divided along racial lines. At times, a White congregation would construct a new building and leave the original edifice to the Black members. At other times, the African members constructed the new building. On occasion the division came about not from mere growth but from a felt problem within the congregation. White members occasionally found the more exuberant worship style of the Black members disturbing while Black members often found the prerogatives assumed by White members discriminatory, even insulting.

As the preachers traveled the land, they frequently stopped at the manor houses on the various plantations that dotted the rural landscape of the

British American colonies. They sought to preach not only to the plantation owner and his family but as a matter of course to the slaves as well. In the best of situations, the manor house would become a preaching point, the African residents of the plantation (and even neighboring plantations) would be invited to attend services, and those that responded positively would be organized into classes. Frequently, the plantation owner would erect a chapel for the holding of religious meetings. As the membership grew, separate services for Blacks and Whites would often be scheduled.

Through the eighteenth century, a circuit would require two to four weeks to complete. At the annual conference of the preachers, each preacher would be assigned to a circuit. As the new preacher rode the circuit from one location to another for the first time, he would make a schedule of future visits to each location. Preaching services would be held on whatever day the preacher was on site, and thus only a minority of congregational gatherings with the preacher present would be on Sunday. When the preacher was on site, he would often not only preach but meet with one or more of the classes. Meeting with the African classes became the primary means of his getting to know the Black members and discovering emerging leaders.

Of significance in early Methodism was the quarterly conference, a multipurpose meeting in which the presiding elder (who would have oversight of a set of stations and circuits) would be present. These special gatherings would be a time for a general celebration, usually in the form of a love feast. During the conference, all of the congregation, but especially the lay and ministerial leadership, assembled for a time of sharing testimonies concerning their progress and, after 1784, the partaking of the Lord's Supper. Sunday was the big day of the quarterly conference, which would normally include a love feast followed by a sermon, the Lord's Supper, and the baptism of new members. In the evening, there would be a preaching and prayer service that would often last into the wee hours of the morning, as those seeking to flee from the wrath to come struggled to find peace and salvation.[19] Besides the worship meetings, however, the quarterly conference would be a time to conduct business—to collect offerings for the support of the preachers, to discuss the state of the church, and to examine and approve (or disapprove) the conduct of the lay leadership. The quarterly conference would be the meeting at which class leaders were named and exhorters and lay preachers granted their licenses.

Methodist structure is often enigmatic to those who encounter the church from a non-Methodist background, especially those who come from a Baptist milieu in which the sovereignty of the local congregation is emphasized. In contrast, Methodism developed as a connectional movement in which the conferences of ministers were central. The conferences organized the churches in their assigned territory for efficiency in carrying out their tasks of worship and evangelism, and the bishop assigned ministers in a way that maximized their usefulness. Most important, the conference owned all the property, a significant factor often missed by those attempting to understand Methodist history, especially the development of African American Methodism. In Methodism, local trustees hold property in trust for the conference, a crucial factor in the struggle of African American leaders to assert control of their local churches.

The centralized ownership of property in Methodism would become critical, for example, following the building of the new Bethel Church in Philadelphia by Richard Allen in 1805, when the White minister assigned to the city called Allen's attention to the fact that the congregation did not own the new structure. The issue repeatedly emerged through the 1810s and 1820s as the several independent African Methodist denominations struggled to establish themselves. They regularly encountered congregational majorities initially willing to align with them, but then unwilling to give up their church building and start afresh.

The matter of property ownership would again take on a determinative role in shaping denominational life in the years immediately after the Civil War as the several groups vied for the allegiance of the freedmen. As we are now aware, all across the former Confederacy, numerous all-Black Methodist churches worshipping separately in their own buildings with their own ministers that had been established during the days of slavery, especially in the cities,[20] and African American Methodists' choice of their future denominational allegiance became intimately tied up with their ability to maintain control of the church building in which they had been used to worshipping. The annals of the decade from 1865 to 1875 are filled with stories of AME and AMEZ ministers winning the allegiance of a local congregation to their cause only to lose it months or even years later when the property was returned to the Methodist Episcopal Church, South by the courts. While disappointing at the time, of course, such court decisions left the AMEs and AMEZs with little about which to complain, as they too were organizing as connectional churches with central ownership of property.

Developing a Methodist Ministry

Laypeople from the British Isles organized the first Methodist classes in America. Then in 1769, the first preachers recruited by Wesley arrived. These preachers were not ordained; they had authority to preach and lead prayer but were not permitted to serve the sacraments. Wesley's preachers recruited additional lay preachers in America who also traveled (itinerated) among the circuits. The traveling preachers gathered regularly to agree upon the territory they would work for the next year.

It was assumed that Methodists would attend their local Anglican church on Sunday, at which they would partake of Holy Communion. Practically speaking, they might attend if a church happened to be located in their neighborhood.

Methodism spread through the Middle Colonies in the 1770s but experienced a crisis with the American Revolution. Given the withdrawal of most Anglican ministers (as well as all but one of the Methodist preachers) in the wake of the British defeat, Wesley decided to allow the formation of an independent Methodist Church in the former colonies. Since the bishop of London would not cooperate, Wesley assumed the office and authority of a bishop and consecrated Thomas Coke (1747–1814) (already an Anglican minister) as the Methodist "superintendent" to oversee the American organization. During Christmas week of 1784, he met with the preachers and effected the formation of the Methodist Episcopal Church (MEC). Following common practice, the church placed all of the leadership in the hands of males of European descent.

The name of the new church reflected several realities. First, the Church of England had withdrawn from America and in any case had not had a bishop in the former British colonies. The American brethren wanted a church led by a bishop (not a mere superintendent), and they selected Francis Asbury (1745–1816), the only one of Wesley's preachers to remain in America through the war. The choice proved providential. A strong leader, Asbury was totally dedicated to his task, and for the next thirty years, he would grow the movement with his travels through the length and breadth of the land. Immediately after Asbury took charge, those preachers who wished to place themselves at Asbury's disposal and serve where he appointed them, were ordained as deacons and elders. Originally, they met annually with Asbury in conference, at which time Asbury gave them their assignments for the coming year. As the work spread geographically, it was divided into different regional conferences, a process that would continue through the nineteenth century to the present.

Asbury appointed the ministers to their charge, a circuit or station, for the coming year, and each minister would change his appointment annually (originally every six months). Because of the frequent changing of their pastoral charge, and the necessity of itinerating among the various preaching points on their circuit, the ordained ministers became known informally as traveling ministers, as opposed to the unordained local preachers who lived and exercised their ministry in one place.

A set of circuits (and stations) were organized into a district under the leadership of a presiding elder. The presiding elder would generally be present in each one of the circuits under his care once each quarter, his presence being the occasion of the circuit's quarterly conference.

At the congregational level, two kinds of local preachers were distinguished, the preachers and the exhorters. The exhorter, an office also present in the Moravian community, usually spoke immediately after the sermon. He was especially important when the traveling speaker delivered the sermon, usually a general message deemed appropriate for any audience. The exhorter would, with his knowledge of the local situation, drive the message home emphasizing particular ideas aimed at those among whom he worked.[21] While one would be ordained by the conference as a traveling minister, one was licensed by the local church or circuit as an exhorter or local preacher, and the license would have to be periodically reviewed and renewed. Early on, Blacks were appointed to all the offices at the local level—preachers, exhorters, and class leaders—but women, both Black and White, were excluded.

African Americans found a variety of Methodism's attributes appealing, especially the hope and promise that Methodism offered in its early years. Methodism emerged as a new American Christian movement, which, unlike the older Anglican and Puritan churches, had an open future. It also emerged as an anti-slavery church, and Methodists were usually found among the prominent members of the state and local anti-slavery societies that were formed from time to time across the northern states. Through the last quarter of the eighteenth century and into the 1820s, only the Quakers were so identified with the anti-slavery cause as were the Methodists.

Prior to 1784, Methodism existed as a lay-led religious movement. Africans worshipped, testified to their faith, and confessed their struggles in life alongside their European brothers and sisters, and it appeared that in the relatively near future, Africans would be able to assume any role in the movement taken by a European. Initially, the British preachers took charge primarily due to their direct connection with Wesley and the movement in England. Meanwhile, Blacks were integrated into the early classes, worked beside the White members on constructing the early chapels, contributed to building costs, and found themselves accepted in the Sunday worship. As classes were created, they were allowed to form their own classes. While Whites led the classes in some centers, very quickly some Africans were appointed as class leaders.[22]

The first real test of the status of the Black membership would come with the ministry. And within the first decade, Black local preachers and exhorters emerged and were allowed to exercise their talents. As with the White lay preachers, the lack of formal education, even the ability to read and write, ultimately proved no obstacle to their assumption of the role if they manifested a talent for preaching. Some of these early preachers, such as Jacob Toogood, who resided in Maryland, were allowed to preach regularly in spite of being geographically confined due to their slave status.[23]

However, in several cases of free Blacks, even that barrier seemed to be overcome. Richard Allen (1780–1831) began to preach around 1780. He was still a slave at the time, but his obvious talent led his master to allow Allen to purchase his freedom. Over the next years he preached in various locations and was formally licensed in 1784. Following the Christmas Conference, he traveled with a few of the White preachers on their circuits. In 1786, he settled in Philadelphia where there was a large free Black community.

More prominent than Allen at this time was Harry Hosier (d. 1806). He was born a slave in North Carolina; Asbury met him on his travels and immediately recognized his oratorical abilities. Beginning around 1780, he began to travel with Asbury and other Methodist preachers, and he quickly emerged as the most eloquent speaker in the church. An illiterate man, he had a prodigious memory and was able to quote scripture and deliver his sermons without reference to the Bible or any written notes. As the most capable preacher in the fellowship, Asbury frequently sent him to areas (always in the company of a White colleague) that were showing particular resistance to the Methodist message. Once people heard him speak, they always preferred him to any White preacher with whom he traveled.

After the Christmas Conference, both Allen and Hosier had some expectation that they would be ordained and, in spite of the problems created by the social climate, would be able to join the traveling ministry. Such was not to be. Both were passed over. Hosier, in spite of his continuing work, would never be ordained. Within a few years, Allen would form a separate Black congregation in Philadelphia, the Bethel MEC. Later, he became the first of the African Americans whom Asbury ordained as deacons (in Methodism generally a step to full ordination as a elder). Allen waited a decade (1799) to be so recognized, but as additional Black congregations emerged, others were also ordained as deacons: James Varick, Abraham Thompson, and June Scott of New York City (1806); Daniel Coker (New York, 1808); John Charleston (Virginia, 1809); and Jacob Tapsico and James Champion (Philadelphia, 1809).[24] However, after 1809, Asbury refused to countenance further ordinations, and only after his death would additional ordinations be quietly sanctioned.[25]

Harry Hosier, the First Black Preacher

Harry Hosier (d. 1806) was a genuine phenomenon of early American Methodism, and the Methodist Church's development would have been quite different without him. Unfortunately, information about him is by no means as complete as one might wish.[26] It seems, however, that he was born into slavery but later freed, and while a young man he put his oratorical skills to work as a preacher. He compensated for his inability to read with a prodigious memory.[27]

Hosier met Asbury soon after the latter's arrival in the British colonies, and in June 1780 Asbury expressed his wish that Hosier travel with him through Virginia and the Carolinas. Asbury first spoke to the Whites, then Hosier directed words to the slaves. Hosier began traveling with Asbury in 1781, and on May 13 delivered the first sermon by an African Methodist about which some record has survived. We do not know what he said, only that his biblical text was Jesus' parable of the barren fig tree. Hosier's preaching was a novelty to the Whites who nevertheless listened as an attentive audience. Though irritating some who rejected his Methodist theology, Harry was a hit with the White audiences, and initially Asbury feared that his becoming a preacher to the White people might go to his head. That fear proved unfounded, however, and he continued to travel with Asbury for the next few years. At the end of 1784, he was one of only two African preachers to attend the Christmas Conference at which the MEC was founded.[28]

Following the conference, Hosier received one of his more notable assignments: to escort Thomas Coke on a speaking tour. Coke quickly discovered Hosier's unusual skill and on November 29 recorded in his journal, "I sometimes give notice immediately after preaching, that in a little time Harry will preach to the blacks; but the whites always stay to hear him."[29] By this time, Coke had already heard Hosier enough to pronounce him "one of the best preachers in the world." He further noted that "there is such an amazing power attends his preaching, though he cannot read; and he is one of the humblest creatures I ever saw."

After his time with Coke, Hosier rejoined Asbury. In September 1786, we find the pair in New York, where Asbury ordained John Dickins (1747–98) as an elder. At this time, the local newspaper noted Hosier's presence: "Lately came to this city a very singular black man, who, it is said, is quite ignorant of letters, yet he has preached in the Methodist Church several times to the

Harry Hosier attended the consecration of Francis Asbury as a bishop at the 1784 Christmas Conference and is pictured immediately between the pulpit and the window. This picture is an engraving done by A. Gilchrist Campbell based on a painting by Thomas Coke Ruckle and was originally issued by T. C. Ruckle in New York in 1882, in time for the centennial of the ordination (1784).

acceptance of several well-disposed, judicious people. He delivers his discourse with great zeal and pathos, and his language and connection is by no means contemptible. It is the wish of several of our correspondents that this same black man may be, so far successful as to rouse the dormant zeal of our slothful white people, who seem very little affected about the concerns of another world."[30]

In 1790, Hosier traveled with circuit rider Freeborn Garrettson (1752–1827) into Connecticut and Massachusetts. They arrived in Boston on July 1 toward the end of the day and Garrettson first made arrangements for Hosier's lodging at the home of Prince Hall (1735–1807), the famous "master mason for the Africans," and then found a place to stay himself with a lapsed Methodist. Here Hosier would have some of the high points of his preaching career. A week after his arrival, late on a Sunday afternoon, he preached to a congregation of more than a thousand individuals.[31]

Impressed with Hosier's extraordinary oratorical skills, people speculated on their source. Some suggested that he was really a White man, though he showed no manifest evidence of having any European or Native American ancestors. Some Quakers believed that he had to be speaking by inspiration, since no illiterate person could do what he did otherwise.

Raybold described Hosier's speaking thusly, "He also possessed a most musical voice, which he could modulate with the skill of a master, and use with most complete success in the pathetic, terrible, or persuasive parts of a discourse." He further noted that "Harry could remember passages of Scripture and quote them accurately; and hymns, also, which he had heard read, he could repeat or sing. He was never at a loss in preaching, but was very acceptable wherever he went, and few of the white preachers could equal him, in his way. When he was questioned as to his preaching abilities, complete command of voice, aptness in language, and free delivery, as to Scriptural or doctrinal truth, his reply was a description of the Elocution of Faith, 'I sing by faith, pray by faith, preach by faith, and do every thing by faith; without faith in the Lord Jesus I can do nothing.'"[32]

Several years later he traveled with Richard Whatcoat (1736–1806) in New Jersey, and an incident at Hackettstown was added to the church's folklore. A woman who lived in the same residence where the preachers lodged made an issue of not attending the service when Hosier was to speak, as he was a Black man. That very evening the preaching service was held in the residence and after Whatcoat preached, Hosier exhorted. As Whatcoat concluded, Harry arose, stood behind the chair where he had been sitting, and began to speak about sin, the disease with which everyone present had been affected. Hosier's voice slowly rose, "the Lord had sent a remedy by the hands of a physician; but alas! he was black! and some might reject the only means of cure, because of the hands by which it was sent to them that day." As he continued to speak all were moved by his words, and when he concluded with prayer all were caught up in the moment. Even the woman who had earlier slandered Hosier was deeply affected and was among the first to profess conversion.[33]

Hosier's last assignment apart from Asbury appears to have been in 1803, when he returned to New Jersey in the company of John Walker. He then seems to have retired to Philadelphia, where for several years he preached in the Black churches, Bethel and Zoar, and most likely at St. George's, the White church, as well as an occasional camp meeting. In later years, there were rumors that he had for a time forsaken his much-honored status, a victim of alcoholism. John Lednum, writing in the 1850s, suggested that Hosier had become a drunken rag-picker in Philadelphia, though at one point he was able to find his way back to God and have his backsliding healed.[34] There is no contemporaneous evidence of such a period in Hosier's life.

During his last years, William Colbert encountered Hosier, for the first time on June 8, 1803. After hearing Hosier speak, he confirmed the rumors that Hosier was indeed a powerful preacher. He saw him again in 1804 at a camp meeting on the Eastern Shore of Maryland and concluded, "This is not a man made preacher."[35]

Colbert was appointed to Philadelphia in 1805 and was with Harry during his last days. He visited him on April 30, 1806, and believed him to be near death. Harry died a few weeks later. Thus, on May 18, 1806, he was in Kensington (then just north of the Philadelphia city limits) for Hosier's funeral:

I this morning preached at Kensington from I Thes. 5 ch 19th v. and in the afternoon heard Christopher Atkinson, a black man preach the funeral of Harry Hosure another Black man, from Tim. 2d 4 ch 7, 8th. He was very broken but he made out better than I expected. Jeffry Budd spoke after him, and he spoke well—the people were affected.[36]

Raybold said of the same event, "He [Hosier] died in Philadelphia, and was buried in the ground attached to Old Zoar, on which occasion the late Jeffrey Bewley, a coloured preacher, and himself a wonder for capacity and performances, in eulogizing Black Harry, applied a term by which he was well known: 'Here lies the African wonder.'"[37]

Hosier was by no means the only African preacher in the church at the time, but he was by far the best. It was noted by Henry Boehm that Hosier had helped dissipate the early anti-Methodist climate in Wilmington,[38] and he was sent to New Jersey to assist in the building of the work. A better speaker than Asbury, he attracted people to the cause as Asbury traveled the countryside. Even from the scant records we have, it is evident that Hosier had a tremendous positive effect upon the development of American Methodism during its first generation.

One can but wonder, had circumstances been different, how Hosier would have been remembered in American history. Certainly no preacher of his generation received such accolades, of the kind earlier given to Whitefield and later to Charles Finney. Had he not been stereotyped as a African anomaly, he might have been thought of as the Whitefield or Finney or Billy Graham of his age.

Other Early African American Methodist Preachers

Hosier was believed to have been born near Fayetteville, North Carolina, interestingly enough the site of one of the other prominent Black preachers of the church's first generation—Henry Evans (d. 1810). A contemporary of Hosier, Evans was born in the middle of the eighteenth century as a free man in rural Virginia. He earned his living as a shoemaker and had been licensed as a Methodist preacher. As a young man (around 1780), he decided to move to Charleston, but on his way south, he stopped in Fayetteville. Here he observed the slave population living what he considered an unusually depraved existence. There being no church building at the time; the only congregation (Presbyterian) met in what was called the State house. He decided to stay and preach.

The town authorities wanted nothing of Evans, so he moved outside of town and operated in a somewhat clandestine fashion. He preached out of doors, frequently changing the location of his sermons so as to avoid the local constabulary, which sought to arrest him, and the occasional mob that sought to do him bodily harm. One of his preaching sites was the home of Dicey Hammons, the grandmother of Thomas H. Lomax (1832–1908), later a bishop in the African Methodist Episcopal Zion Church.[39] But over several years, some White people noticed a marked improvement in the lives of those slaves known to attend Evans' preaching, and they begin to suggest that their neighbors stop harassing Evans. He continued to preach out of doors through the 1890s, and more and more Whites began to see him as an asset to the community.

In the late 1890s, circuit rider John Jenkins (d. 1847) discovered Evans: "We had no white society there [Fayetteville] at the time; I found however, a small society of coloured people, under the care of a coloured man by the name of Evans, who preached to them regularly, and no ordinary preacher was he. I visited him every round, and encouraged him all I could, and furnished him with a steward's book, in which to register what ever might appertain to his office. About this time [1800] he leased a lot for seven years, and commenced building a church, twenty by thirty feet, out of rough-edged materials. They met the expenses themselves, except five dollars, which were given to them by a white man. This was the first Methodist Church in the place: it was called 'The Negro church.' In a short time it became crowded and an addition of ten feet was made to it."[40]

Arriving in Fayetteville in 1803, Bishop Asbury noted the existence of Evans' meeting house, though he did not preach there; but two years later, he did preach in the "African Church." He found White people were dropping by to listen to Evans and from his work, the first Methodist church of Fayetteville would emerge. Around 1806 an older woman named Maulsby, who had been kicked out of the Presbyterian Church for shouting, inquired of Jenkins if she "might come in among the negroes?" The worship style being exercised at Evans' church had attracted her, and she became the first of many White members who found their way to his services.

Evans' health began to fade around 1806, and circuit riders began to assist with preaching duties.[41] In 1809, William Capers (1790–1855) was assigned to the Pee-Dee Circuit that included Fayetteville. He would leave the most extensive account of Evans. Capers, who did not have the opportunity to hear Hosier, called Evans, even though now in his waning years, "the best preacher of his time in that quarter." He had become the "great curiosity in the town; insomuch that distinguished visitors hardly felt that they might pass a Sunday in Fayetteville without hearing him preach."[42] Evans died in 1810, during Capers' tenure on the circuit. Capers left a moving account of his last days: "On the Sunday before his death . . . the little door between his humble shed and the chancel where I stood was opened, and the dying man entered for a last farewell to his people. He was almost too feeble to stand at all, but supporting himself by the railing of the chancel, he said, 'I have come to say my last word to you. Three times I have broken the ice on the edge of the water and swum across the Cape Fear to preach the gospel to you. And now, if in my last hour I could trust to that, or to anything else but Christ crucified, for my salvation, all should be lost, and my soul perish for ever.'"[43]

Capers preached Evans' funeral sermon, which was attended by what seemed the whole community. They buried his body under the church's chancel. In his will he left the meetinghouse to the Methodists, who would also receive the adjacent home and land after Evans' widow passed on. When Evans died, his congregation included both Black and White members. For a quarter century, the church would be served by both the White circuit riders and the Black preachers that Evans had raised up. Then in 1834, the

White members withdrew and constructed a separate building, the Hay Street Church, and the Black members inherited the original building.[44]

Fayetteville proved a remarkably rich area for the production of Methodist ministers. Besides Hosier and Evans three generations of preachers emerged from the family of Joseph A. Beebe (1832–1905). One of his grandfathers, Adam Counsel, seems to have been an early convert of Evans and like his mentor often preached to the White people, especially in the years immediately after Evans' death. He was said to be amazingly long-lived, having passed away at the age of 115. Beebe's father, Edward Craven, also preached in Fayetteville. Joseph was one of four preachers who emerged among his sixteen children. He had a conversion experience in 1849, and was licensed to preach two years later. After the war he joined the AMEZ Church for several years and was ordained a deacon and then an elder (1866), but he eventually found his way to the CME Church, in which he became a bishop (1873).[45]

In 1822, Hiram Rhodes Revels was born in Fayetteville of free parents. His free status allowed him to leave the state and seek education in the Midwest, topped with attendance at Knox College in Galesburg, Illinois. In 1845 he became an AME minister and served their churches in the Midwest. He served as a chaplain for a regiment of Black troops recruited in Mississippi and after the war organized the AME church in Jackson, Mississippi. Then in 1868 he became an MEC minister in Natchez. He had a brief political career during Reconstruction, including a year as one of the U.S. Senators from the state. He subsequently spent many years as the president of Alcorn State College.[46]

The same year that Beebe was born, Thomas Lomax arrived in Fayetteville. His family had lived in the area since the American Revolution and he joined the MEC,S as a teenager. He helped erect the new brick church (1854–55), renamed for its founder, and remained in Fayetteville through the years of the Civil War. As one of the few local Africans to get an education, he came to the attention of AMEZ minister James W. Hood, who came to Fayetteville in 1866 to reorganize the membership of Evans' church.[47]

John Charleston was born in slavery in Virginia around 1766. He was converted in a Sunday school especially developed for the instruction of slaves and sponsored by Thomas Crenshaw, a Methodist in Hanover County.[48] Charleston began to preach in the 1790s. A few years after the turn of the century, circuit rider Stith Mead purchased Charleston and then raised the money to grant him his freedom. In 1809, Bishop William McKendree ordained the now free Charleston as a deacon.[49]

Once freed, he traveled with Mead on his circuit and then later through central Virginia as conditions suggested. He was a popular preacher among both Black and White members, and was credited with being the instrument of thousands of conversions. After many years as a popular preacher, Charleston, then in his sixties, disappears from the records. Grant Shockley has suggested that Charleston left Virginia, which in 1832, in the wake of the Nat Turner revolt, passed a law to stop African Americans from preaching and prevent the slaves from assembling for worship. After moving to Ohio, Charleston affiliated with the African Methodist Episcopal Church.[50]

Contemporaries of Evans and Charleston could be found throughout the church. In Tennessee, for example, there was Joseph, a resident of Dutch Bottom in Cocke County. He was a slave who had a reputation for deep piety and faith. He gained the confidence of his owner, then of the people of the local Methodist church, who granted him a license to preach in 1818, and then of the people of the county. He so impressed his owner, Francis J. Carter, that Carter supported his effort to attain some formal schooling, at least enough to learn basic reading skills. Afterward he spent a good deal of his time preaching around the county at various locations.

Joseph presented himself as a man of humility and observed the norms of White-Black interaction when out of the pulpit, but when in it aggressively addressed large crowds of both Black and White. He was praised for his gift in public prayer. He was also often compared to an earlier contemporary in the area, Simon Rogers, a free Black. Fellow Methodists judged Rogers the superior in intelligence and culture, and he undoubtedly was a great orator, but was the inferior in piety and thus never gained the popular confidence of the White population enjoyed by Joseph.

Joseph's younger contemporary, Thomas, emerged from a Sunday school class taught by W. Garret, an itinerant in Eastern Tennessee for several years. He learned to read relatively quickly and was noticed by Garret as a capable student who seemed drawn to the Bible. A man recognized by the Methodists for his gifts and graces, he was licensed to preach and delivered sermons regularly for more than forty-five years.[51]

Traveling through another part of Tennessee, circuit rider Jacob Young found a curious situation at a settlement called Fishing Creek. What caught his attention was the local Methodist society. Its sole preacher was a Black man known only as Jacob. He had begun preaching and all the church members had been converted by him. A Mr. Chappel, with whom Young lodged in the neighborhood, had several daughters who assisted Jacob in the organization of the first class, over which he served as the leader. Young observed that Jacob could preach quite well, though unable to read. It appears that Young developed his sermons from listening to his master read the Bible. When he heard a suitable passage, he would request it to be re-read several times, and he would then memorize it and prepare remarks on it for the next Sunday.[52]

James B. Finley (1781–1856) left an account of one local preacher known only as Cuff (a popular name given to slaves), who resided on a plantation somewhere in Western Virginia. On any given Sabbath, if no circuit rider was in the vicinity, the many slaves looked to Cuff to preach and lead the worship. Cuff was a fine orator and at these services, he "would pour out his full heart in exhortations, with an eloquence and power none could resist."[53] On several occasions, local slave owners, some known to be cruel, had come to see Cuff, a great curiosity, and were converted from his preaching.

Cuff's rather tranquil situation changed when the owner of his plantation died. The estate was divided among the several sons, and the one who became Cuff's owner soon squandered his fortune and was forced to sell him. He was purchased by a non-believer, and conflict became inevitable. The new master demanded that Cuff abandon his religious life, even his personal prayer. Cuff refused. The master then tried to beat a promise out of him that he would stop praying. Cuff persisted. Eventually, the master came to some personal crisis, and turned to his wife asking for someone who could come and pray with him. She knew of no one but Cuff.

Cuff was now more than surprised to find the young man asking for prayer. He readily agreed, informing his master that he had been praying for both him and his wife ever since the beating. He prayed all night. The man, having finally experienced forgiveness for his many sins, embraced Cuff and granted his freedom. He subsequently employed the former slave as a "chaplain," and Cuff began to travel through the region as he was able, searching out his brothers and sisters, most of whom remained in slavery. His master also later became a minister.

A. H. Hyde included the story of Punch, a Black preacher in South Carolina, in his popular history of Methodism penned in the 1880s. Bishop Asbury met Punch on one of his early trips to the state. Asked if he ever prayed, Punch replied in the negative. Asbury then introduced him to Christianity, sang a hymn, and prayed with him.

The two would meet again some twenty years later. Punch traveled sixty miles after learning that Asbury was passing through the state just to tell the bishop that he had become a Christian and to thank him for praying with him. Then Punch disappeared and he dropped from most everyone's memory. He would not reappear for several additional decades. In the 1830s, as the plantation missions expanded, the itinerants reached a remote plantation and to their surprise found between two and three hundred slaves already assembled into a worshiping community. The itinerants inquired if there was a preacher who oversaw this flock. They were informed that an excellent preacher, the old "Bishup," resided on the plantation. They were then taken to meet Punch, now an elderly man with white hair and palsied hands. It seems he had been waiting for someone to arrive to replace him, as he felt death approaching.

The itinerants later learned that Punch had begun preaching and praying with his fellow slaves many years previously, but at one point had been forbidden to continue. He did not stop. Then one evening, he was called out by the overseer. Expecting the worst, he was completely surprised when instead of a beating he received a request for prayer. Converted, the overseer went on and became a preacher himself. Punch had no further obstacles placed on his religious work from that time forward.[54]

Solomon grew up in Virginia and after quietly learning to read had secretly assembled a small library that included a Bible and a hymnbook. He was even able to smuggle his treasures with him in the mid-1830s when along with over a hundred other slaves he was taken to Alabama. His preaching was often done in the presence of his White overseer, an unbeliever who went out of his way to mock the religious slaves. Over time, the overseer figured out that some of the slaves could read and discovered that they possessed books. After finding Solomon's library, he burned the Bible and forced Solomon to consume some brandy and some water with ashes of the book, afterward demanding he preach since he now had the word and spirit within him.

Solomon's status among the slaves derived from his stable demeanor and his constantly reminding them that slavery would someday end. One of his fellow slaves stole a Bible and hymnbook to replace the ones previously taken from him. Solomon's demeanor was tested when the same overseer who burnt the Bible had a severe accident. The slaves rejoiced; they wanted him dead. But Solomon reminded them, "God himself willeth not the death of a sinner." The overseer recovered, but was no longer able to swing a whip.[55]

Fanny Kemble, the wife of plantation owner Pierce Butler, spent a period on his plantations on Butler Island in Georgia in 1838–39. There she found London Cooper, a Methodist preacher whom she described as "of no small intelligence and influence," respected by Black and White alike as a person of exemplary conduct and character. He was introduced into her narrative as the leader of a burial service that took place one evening at the end of the slaves' work day. He had picked up the ability to read, and he conducted the funeral service from a prayer book. (He later asked Kemble for a Bible.) He followed the burial liturgy with a sermon on Jesus' raising Lazarus from the dead.

The African residents of the plantation were allowed to leave and attend (a Baptist) church in nearby Darien one Sunday each month. On the other Sundays, London was their worship leader. It was also his task to officiate over wedding services, such as occurred among the slave population.[56]

These early Black preachers exemplified the contributions made by African Americans to the emergence of American Methodism. Their appearance should be expected from a movement whose beginning and vitality were so wrapped up with its African membership. It is also the case that these men led a life of accomplishment, a life that contradicted the common stereotypes about Africans that circulated even within the Methodist leadership and that provided intellectual support for the maintenance of slavery in the South and the anti-Black laws in the North. At the same time, without individuals such as these, Methodism would have fallen far behind in the effort to church America in the post–Revolutionary Period.

Those few mentioned earlier, of course, were not the only preachers to appear among the African American membership, as we shall see as we now turn to the development of the major centers of Methodism during the early decades of the nineteenth century. Through the compilation of the very scattered records of antebellum Black Methodists, the names of and personal information about several hundred of the preachers are now available.

Notes

1. Francis H. Tees, *History of Old St. George's* (Philadelphia: The Author, n.d. [1934]), 13.

2. Dennis competes with Marylander John Evans as the first Methodist convert in America. According to Elliott M. Amos, Evans was converted by Robert Strawbridge in 1763–64. On August 1, 1777, John Littlejohn preached at the Evans' house to a congregation of twenty White and forty Black people. See Edison M. Amos' entry on the John Evans House in Nolan B. Harmon, ed. with Albea Godbold and Louise L. Queen, *Encyclopedia of World Methodism* (Nashville, TN: United Methodist Publishing House, 1974), 816.

3. This story is recounted in James A. Handy, *Scraps of African Methodist Episcopal History* (Philadelphia: A. M. E. Book Concern, 1902). Handy gathered the stories of the founders of the African American Episcopal Church in Baltimore and recorded their memories of the early years. A primary source is Caleb Hyland, who does show up in secular sources and was among the founders of the Bethel congregation in Baltimore, but does not appear in any of the records at the Sharp Street Church. Given the oral sources from which Handy worked, there is some doubt about the exact dating of the events he recorded, though they certainly fit

into what we know otherwise of Strawbridge (much of which is also based on memories collected decades later).

4. J. A. Handy, "On the Introduction of African Methodism in Maryland," In Benjamin W. Arnett, ed., *The Centennial Budget* (N.p.: Benjamin W. Arnett, 1888), 273.

5. Interestingly enough, the primary book on Strawbridge does not mention any of his African American contacts, including the presence of Annie in the original class meeting. Frederick E. Maser, *Robert Strawbridge: First American Methodist Circuit Rider* (Rutland, VT: Academy Books/Strawbridge Shrine Association, 1983).

6. Cf. John Atkinson, *The Beginnings of the Wesleyan Movement in America and the Establishment Therein of Methodism* (New York: Hunt & Eaton, 1896); J. B. Wakeley, *Lost Chapters Recovered from the Early History of American Methodism* (New York: Wilbur B. Ketcham, 1889).

7. Letter from Boardman to John Wesley, November 4, 1769, reproduced in Atkinson, *Beginnings of the Wesleyan Movement,* 248–49.

8. Wakeley, *Lost Chapters Recovered,* 102–3.

9. Joseph Pilmore, *The Journal of Joseph Pilmore: Methodist Itinerant.* Ed. by Frederick E. Maser and Howard T. Maag (Philadelphia, PA: Historical Society of the Philadelphia Annual Conference of the United Methodist Church, 1969), 137.

10. Rankin's unpublished *Journal* is located in the library at Garrett-Evangelical Theological Seminary.

11. Rankin, *Journal.*

12. John Littlejohn, *Journal of John Littlejohn* (Typescript. Nashville, TN: The Upper Room, n.d.), 23.

13. Littlejohn, *Journal,* 39.

14. Littlejohn, *Journal,* 46.

15. Littlejohn, *Journal,* 126–28.

16. Bethany Veney, *The Narrative of Bethany Veney: A Slave Woman.* With Introduction by Rev. Bishop Mallalieu, and Commendatory Notices from Rev. V. A. Cooper, Superintendent of Home for Little Wanderers, Boston, Mass., and Rev. Erastus Spaulding, Millbury, Mass. (Worcester, MA: [The Author], 1889), 16–17.

17. Gough's story is recounted in John Lednum, *A History of the Rise of Methodism in America* (Philadelphia, PA: The Author, 1859), and is discussed more fully in chapter 5.

18. Though often mentioned, class meetings are rarely described in any detail. John Dixon Long attempted to fill this gap in his volume *Pictures of Slavery in Church and State; including Personal Reminiscences, biographical; Sketches, Anecdotes, Etc., Etc., with and Appendix containing the Views of John Wesley and Richard Watson on Slavery* (Philadelphia: The Author, 1857), 288–98.

19. William Warren Sweet, *The Rise of Methodism in the West* (New York: Methodist Book Concern/Nashville: Smith & Lamar, 1920), 43.

20. Much confusion has entered the discussion concerning the development of Black Christianity in the South by an overemphasis on the laws passed by some states

(as for example the laws passed in Virginia and South Carolina following the Vesey and Nat Turner incidents, which were operative only within the states that passed them and which were often ignored as the incident prompting the law faded from immediate consciousness), and/or the ability of Methodists to find loopholes in the laws that allowed them to found separate Black congregations.

21. As a more settled pastorate took over from the circuit rider, the office of exhorter was an office that fell into obsolescence and was eventually dropped altogether. At the same time, as African Americans were welcomed into the ministry, the role of the unordained lay preacher changed considerably.

22. Ed Schell, longtime historian at Lovely Lane, the original Methodist congregation in Baltimore, analyzed the surviving class records and noted that from 1799 all the Black classes had White leaders but that by 1815 Black leaders had been assigned to about half the classes. In Charleston, where Blacks were in the majority almost from the beginning, Black class leaders assumed duties very early.

23. George Roberts remembers, "Old Jacob Toogood was a slave of Mr. Maynard, he had permission to preach to the colored people and often was engaged in this work in his cabin. His master would frequently go to hear him; he would take the precaution to sit where Jacob could not see him for fear of embarrassing him and listen to the word of life, as in great simplicity the old man would give it to his hearers." George C. M. Roberts, *Centenary Pictorial Album: being Contributions of the Early History of Methodism in the State of Maryland* (Baltimore: Printed by J. W. Woods, 1866), 8.

24. We shall meet all of these men who were ordained as deacons in the next chapter as they assume leadership in the larger urban congregations. Eventually all of them would leave the church for one of the independent Black Methodist denominations.

25. In 1810, Coker published a list of Black preachers who had received ordination. Besides those mentioned elsewhere, he also lists one Jeffrey "Buley" as an ordained minister in Philadelphia. Buley (also spelled Budd or Bewley) is best known as one of the speakers at Harry Hosier's funeral in 1806; however, there is no independent mention of his being ordained as a minister in either MEC or AME sources. This is probably the same as Jeffrey Beulah, a member of the Zoar Church who would in 1813 lead a group out to form the Union (later AME) Church and later an active AME preacher. Coker's list appears at the end of his pamphlet *A Dialogue between a Virginian and an African Minister* (Baltimore: Benjamin Edes, 1810).

26. Information on Hosier comes to us primarily from R. A. Raybold, *Methodism in West Jersey* (New York: Lane & Scott, 1847), 165–68; a newspaper account of him from the *New York Packet*, which was reprinted in Samuel Seaman's *A History of Methodism in New York City* (New York: Hunt & Eaton, 1892), 92–93; and a set of references in Francis Asbury's *Journal* (London: Epworth/New York: Abingdon, 1958). There is an unsubstantiated report that he was the slave of Harry Gough and freed after Gough's conversion.

27. Secondary sources on Hosier include Joshua E. Licorish, *Harry Hosier, African Pioneer Preacher, Including [a] Brief History of African Zoar Methodist Church, Founded 1794, Philadelphia, Pennsylvania* (Philadelphia: Afro-American Resources, 1967); Warren Thomas Smith, "Harry Hosier: Black Preacher Extraordinary," *Journal of the Interdenominational Theological Center* 7 (1980), 111–28; and possibly the most important, Warren Thomas Smith, *Harry Hosier: Circuit Rider* (Nashville, TN: The Upper Room, 1981).

28. AME writers regularly assert that Richard Allen attended the Christmas Conference, but as Carol V. R. George and others note, the documentation is extremely sparse, and Allen himself does not claim to have been present. See George's *Segregated Sabbaths: Richard Allen and the Rise of Independent Black Churches, 1760–1840* (New York: Oxford University Press, 1973), 42–43. Allen's biographer, Charles H. Wesley, states only that "it is highly probable that he was present." Charles H. Wesley, *Richard Allen: Apostle of Freedom* (Washington, DC: Associated Publishers, 1935), 32.

29. *The Journals of Dr. Thomas Coke*, ed. by John A. Vickers (Nashville, TN: Kingswood Books, 2005): see journal entry for November 29, 1784.

30. Seaman, *A History of Methodism in New York City*, 92.

31. Nathan Bangs, *Life of Rev. F. Garrettson* (New York: Carlton & Phillips, [1832]), 186–95.

32. Raybold, *Methodism in West Jersey*, 165–68.

33. Raybold, *Methodism in West Jersey*, 165–68.

34. John Lednum, *A History of the Rise of Methodism in America* (Philadelphia, PA: The Author 1859), 281–83.

35. "A Black History Moment: Harry Hosier's Last Days," *Third Century Methodism* 38, 3 (March 1999), 2.

36. From William Colbert's unpublished journal, entry for May 18, 1806.

37. Raybold, *Methodism in West Jersey*, 168.

38. Henry Boehm, *Reminiscences of Rev. Henry Boehm* (New York: Carlton & Porter, 1865), 89

39. William J. Walls, *The African Methodist Episcopal Zion Church: Reality of the Black Church* (Charlotte, NC: A.M.E. Zion Publishing House, 1974), 26.

40. *Experience, Labours and Sufferings of James Jenkins* (N.p.: The Author, 1849), 120–21.

41. Among the preachers who met Evans in these later years was a very young William Capers, who would later concentrate so much of his ministry in dealing with African Americans in South Carolina.

42. William M. Wightman, *Life of William Capers, D.D., One of the Bishops of the Methodist Episcopal Church, South, including an Autobiography* (Nashville, TN: Southern Methodist Publishing House, 1850), 124

43. Wightman, *Life of William Capers, D.D.*, 129.

44. Today, Evans' church is known as the Evans Metropolitan African Methodist Episcopal Zion Church. It appears that the church suffered some discontinuities dur-

ing the Civil War and was revived by James Walker Hood, an AMEZ minister (and later bishop) who reorganized the congregation in 1866 and brought it into the AMEZ Church. Walls, *The African Methodist Episcopal Zion Church*, 189–90.

45. C. H. Phillips, *The History of the Colored Methodist Episcopal Church in America, Comprising Its Organization, Subsequent Development and Present Status*. Third edition. (Jackson, TN: Publishing House C. M. E. Church, 1925), 208–12.

46. Julius Thompson, *Hiram R. Revels, 1827–1901: A Biography* (New York: Arno Press, 1982); Elizabeth Lawson, *The Gentleman from Mississippi: Our First Negro Congressman, Hiram R. Revels* (New York: n.p., 1960); Nolan B. Harmon, ed. With Albea Godbold & Louise L. Queen, *Encyclopedia of World Methodism*. 2 vols. (Nashville, TN: United Methodist Publishing House, 1974), 2005–6.

47. Larry G. Murphy, J. Gordon Melton, and Gary L. Ward., eds., *Encyclopedia of African American Religions* (New York: Garland Publishing, 1993), 458.

48. In the *Centennial History of American Methodism* (New York: Phillips & Hunt, 1884), 175–76, John Atkinson asserts that Crenshaw's Sunday school was the first in America and names Charleston as possibly the first convert of the Sunday school movement.

49. William W. Bennett, *Memorials of Methodism in Virginia* (Richmond: The Author, 1871), 533–34.

50. Grant S. Shockley, "Negro Leaders in American Methodism," *The Garrett Tower* 12, 1 (December 1966): 4.

51. John B. M'Ferrin, *Methodism in Tennessee* (Nashville, TN: Southern Methodist Publishing House, 1873), 3:286–87.

52. Jacob Young, *Autobiography of a Pioneer or, The Nativity, Experience, Travels, and Ministerial Labors of Rev. Jacob Young; with Incidents, Observations, and Reflections* (Cincinnati: Cranston and Curtis, 1857), 90–91.

53. James B. Finley, *Sketches of Western Methodism: Biographical, Historical, and Miscellaneous* (Cincinnati: Methodist Book Concern, 1854), 379ff.

54. A. H. Hyde, *The Story of Methodism Throughout the World, from the Beginning to the Present Time* (Springfield, MA: Willey & Co., 1889). The story of Punch was later picked up and retold by Leroy F. Beaty, *Work of South Carolina Methodism among the Slaves* (Columbia, SC: Historical Society of the South Carolina Conference, Methodist Episcopal Church, South, 1901).

55. [James Williams], *Narrative of James Williams, a American Slave, Who Was for Several years a Driver on a Cotton Plantation in Alabama* (New York: American Anti-Slavery Society/Boston: Isaac Knapp, 1838), 70–77.

56. Fanny Kemble, *Journal of a Residence on a Georgian Plantation in 1838–1839* (New York: Harper & Brothers, 1863). London Cooper became a major building block in Kemble's arguments against slavery. In contrast, her husband and other Whites on the plantation used Cooper's work as the rationale for the slaves' culpability for any wrongdoing, since Cooper supposedly taught them moral correctness.

~

CHAPTER THREE

Emerging Centers of Black Methodism: Baltimore, Washington, D.C., and Wilmington

Methodism has its American beginnings in the British colonies of Maryland, Delaware, Pennsylvania, and New York, and the major city of each of those colonies (Baltimore, Wilmington, Philadelphia, and New York City) would become a prominent early center of Methodism (soon to be joined by Brooklyn, NY, and Washington, D.C.). Relative to both Methodism as a whole and African American Methodism in particular, each of these six cities have been home to different firsts—the first Methodist conversion having occurred in Philadelphia, the first sermon having been preached in Baltimore, the first class formed in New York, and the first independent Black church founded in Wilmington.

The congregations in these six cities assumed a key role as primary carriers of the history of African Methodism in the several generations immediately after the formation of the Methodist Episcopal Church (MEC). As the homes to relatively large free Black communities, these cities also became locations where the struggles of the entire community became visible and where important decisions that would affect the community to the present would be made. Frederick Douglass, who as a young man lived both in Baltimore and on plantations in Maryland's Eastern Shore, discovered the very different life available to urban African Americans: "A city slave is almost a freeman, compared with a slave on the plantation. He is much better fed and clothed, and enjoys privileges altogether unknown to the slave on the plantation. There is a vestige of decency, a sense of shame, that does much to curb and check those outbreaks of atrocious cruelty so commonly enacted upon

the plantation."[1] This very different environment suggests at least one reason the city churches took the lead for the whole of the African American
community.

In any case, within a few years of the foundation of Methodism, we find
Black Methodists in each of these six cities expressing very similar aspirations, encountering much the same obstacles, and considering almost identi-
cal choices. Though leaders in each community took different steps at different times, the somewhat simultaneous encounter with the different issues
and the manner in which decisions in one city interacted with similar decisions elsewhere seem the more important observations. Thus we have somewhat arbitrarily chosen to begin telling the story with the cities further south,
working our way north.

African Methodism in Baltimore

Nine years after Robert Strawbridge preached his initial sermon in Baltimore, the city's Methodists, both Black and White, joined together in the
erection of the first Methodist chapel. It was located on Lovely Lane. This
building would become the scene of one of the more heralded events in
Methodism, the 1784 consecration of Francis Asbury as the first bishop of
the newly formed Methodist Episcopal Church (MEC). In 1776 a second
chapel was opened on Strawberry Alley, at Fell's Point. When statistics of
African members were first reported, in 1787, there were 111 members in
Baltimore, approximately 17 percent of the city's total membership.

The Black members looked on as the movement's leadership passed very
strong policy statements concerning slavery in 1780 and 1784. The newly
founded MEC moved to excommunicate slaveholders who did not free their
slaves. They also watched as these rules were first ignored, then quietly placed
on the table, and then, beginning in 1787, effectively withdrawn.[2] That same
year, 1787, some of the African members at Lovely Lane began to request permission to hold separate worship services. Their actions preceded by a few weeks
(or a few years)[3] the move by some of the Philadelphia members to establish
separate worship services, in effect setting up a separate congregation. Though
the move in Baltimore occurred in a less dramatic fashion than the separation
that followed in Philadelphia, the issue was essentially the same.

In 1787, a few of the Black members in Baltimore, mostly free Blacks, began to gather for an independent prayer service in Caleb Hyland's bootblack
cellar. This meeting was in partial response to the placing of White leaders
over all of the Black classes. Jacob Fortie [also spelled Forty] assumed leadership of the group. The names of a number of the attendees at these prayer

meetings are known—Henry Harden, Thomas Clare, Munday Janey, Jacob Gillard, George Douglas, Daniel Buster, and Caleb Guilly. This prayer group grew and evolved through the 1780s. Not financially able to afford a meetinghouse, for a brief period they rented facilities on Fish Street, but through most of the 1790s they met in members' homes or wherever they could.

In 1797, the Maryland Society for the Abolishment of Slavery, whose leadership included a number of Methodists, purchased a lot on Sharp Street from James Carey, a Quaker. Upon this parcel of land, the Society opened the city's first African American school. The school lasted only two years, and after it became evident that it would not reopen, in 1801 Carey reclaimed his land. In 1802, the African American Methodists purchased Carey's land, which became the meeting site for a Black congregation formed by the Black members of the former Lovely Lane (now Light Street) Church. From its location it took the name Sharp Street. Meanwhile, the Strawberry Alley congregation had built a new chapel on Wilk Street, and in 1801 had turned the Strawberry Alley property over to its African members for their use. Among the first projects of the Sharp Street congregation was the opening of a new school. In 1811, the congregation purchased an additional adjacent lot on Sharp Street.[4]

Also, about 1809–1810, Daniel Coker (c. 1780–1846), soon to be one of the most important figures in the development of Baltimore Black Methodism, arrived in the city.[5] Born into slavery on a Maryland plantation, his mother was White, and he had skin light enough to pass as one of his mother's people. He escaped his home on the plantation, where he had been allowed to receive an education, moved to New York, and there became a Methodist. For some years he lived a clandestine life, awaiting his formal emancipation, which was accomplished by some Quakers raising money to buy his freedom. During this time he dropped his original name (Isaac Wright) and became active in the Zion Church, the African congregation that had grown out of the John Street congregation. He became a local preacher, and in 1808, Bishop Asbury welcomed him into the small circle of Black preachers ordained as deacons. (In the Methodist system, deacon's orders were usually a step to ordination as elder and admission to conference membership.) However, after receiving his deacon's orders, he moved to Maryland, where he became a teacher in the school established on Sharp Street and quickly emerged as the primary leader among Baltimore's African American Methodists.[6] Coker would further solidify his leadership position in 1810 with the publishing of a forty-three-page pamphlet, *A Dialogue between a Virginian and an African Minister*,[7] in which he would make his case for the emancipation of the slaves.

The present Sharp Street United Methodist Church continues the original congregation founded in 1802.

While Coker was the most famous of the Sharp Street ministers, his life is by no means the best documented. That honor belongs to David Smith, who toward the end of his long life published his autobiography.[8] Born in 1784, Smith was raised on a farm owned by a Roman Catholic family. Gaining his freedom by some fortuitous circumstances, he became a Methodist, in 1796. As he later remembered it:

> According to the rules and discipline of the Church, I joined on six month's probation. As nearly as I can recollect, I was about twelve years old. The Rev. Nasey Schin was then pastor of Sharp and Light street Churches, the only colored Churches in Baltimore at that time.[9] When my probation was out (the six months) I was then received into full membership, and very soon after I requested the Rev. Schin to give me a permit to hold prayer-meetings in private houses, which he consented to do.[10]

Though a youth, he enjoyed success in preaching and was soon rewarded with an exhorter's license. He later was able to travel in the region around the city and preach on the plantations.

Another prominent leader at Sharp Street was Edward Waters. Born in West River (south of Annapolis), Maryland, in 1780, as a young man he had moved to Baltimore and in 1798 converted to Christianity. He joined the Methodists and in 1810 was licensed as an exhorter at Sharp Street.[11] Increasingly free Blacks were emerging as the church's leaders.

The several Black groups in the city were formally a part of the city's White-controlled organization, which grew to include four predominantly White congregations—Light Street (the former Lovely Lane church), Green Street (1792), Wilk Street (1801), and Eutaw Street (1808). The MEC saw Baltimore as one charge on its list of ministerial appointments and saw each of the congregations as meeting places of the one Methodist work in the city. There was also originally a single set of trustees over Methodist property in the city, though over time separate trustees were designated for each congregation. While most Black members worshiped at Sharp Street and Dallas Street, some continued to worship at the predominantly White churches. Then in 1810 land was purchased for the building of a third African congregation, which in 1812 first appeared in the records as Asbury Church (now Christ United Methodist Church). By 1815, at least three Black classes were meeting in its building, with others nearby.

Throughout this period (1802–15), the members at Sharp Street were counted as members of the single Baltimore charge and were formally under the authority of the two ministers (both White) annually assigned to the city by the Methodist conference. Baltimore was one of Methodism's strongest centers and Methodism became and remained a force in the city throughout the nineteenth century. Methodism remained the only group really welcoming of Black members, and Sharp Street and its school quickly emerged as the center of the Black Methodist community.

Sharp Street's first decade of existence culminated in one of its first major challenges. In 1812 war opened with Britain. During the hot summer months, White anger became focused on perceived pro-British elements in the city. Scattered riots occurred, and several Whites were killed. Then, at one point, a mob redirected its anger to the free Black community and the homes of several prominent free Blacks. As their homes were put to the torch, someone had a better idea—targeting Sharp Street, a symbol of free Black Baltimorians. The mob headed for Sharp Street and a crowd began to grow in front of the church. The mob's rampage ended only when the church's members, holed up inside the building, made it clear that they would defend their building with force if pressed. The incident prompted the mayor to station troops across the city as a visible sign that no further mob action would be tolerated.[12]

Dividing Methodism

By the second decade of the nineteenth century, it had become obvious to all that the deacon's orders to which a cadre of African American preachers had been admitted were not preparatory to their further ordination as elders and admission into the traveling ministry. The implication was that while the various Black congregations had a significant amount of autonomy, ultimately their affairs remained in the hands of the White ministers and the lay leaders who controlled the White congregations. Blacks served as unordained local preachers, exhorters, and class leaders, but in each case were beholden to the White leadership for the regular annual renewal of their authority. Over time some restlessness with this arrangement became visible.

The first real sign of trouble had emerged in 1813 in Wilmington, Delaware, another center of Methodist strength, where Peter Spencer (1782–1843) led a group out of Ezion, the African Methodist congregation in the Wilmington charge, and organized the African Union Church (AUC) (to be discussed later). This church was not only independent of the local White congregation but autonomous relative to the Methodist Episcopal Church. In the wake of the Wilmington affair, a similar restlessness could be noticed among the Black members in Baltimore. Thus it was that, as James A. Handy notes, in November 1814, a group that included Daniel Coker, Jacob Gilliard,[13] Henry Harden, Stephen Hill, George Douglas, Don C. Hall, and Daniel Brister gathered at Harden's home. They agreed to purchase a plot of ground on Fish Street. That being accomplished, on May 9, 1815, they again assembled and formally organized what they named "The African Methodist Bethel Church Society, of the city of Baltimore."[14]

As of 1815, though tracing its origin to the original independent prayer meetings begun in 1787 and the independent prayer meeting that had met at various locations through the years, a new entity had come into being, a Baltimore congregation whose building was not under the control of the Methodist Episcopal Church. Knowledge of the existence of Baltimore's Bethel Church circulated through African American Methodist circles around the country, and when the group that gathered around Richard Allen in Philadelphia initiated plans early in 1816 to form the African Methodist Episcopal (AME) Church, they included Coker and the Bethel congregation among the invitees.

David Smith sheds much light upon the situation leading to the organization of the Bethel congregation. He claimed that a number of Baltimore's Black exhorters had manifested a significant amount of talent as preachers and that as a result the White exhorters became jealous of them. It was also the case that Daniel Coker, as the only ordained minister among them, was expected to deliver the regular reports to the White elders on the condition of the Black leaders. Based on those reports, the elders often made far-reaching decisions while neglecting what today would be termed due process. Those who felt wronged by such decisions (and their friends) harbored a growing resentment against the church's ministerial leadership.

Coker, the deacon who was not invited into elder's orders, while continuing to preach and teach at Sharp Street, began quietly to talk about schism. As he felt out the exhorters, he found those who were ready to consider leaving the MEC. Smith mentions that the break was somewhat along geographical lines. Namely, the ones who had been longtime residents of Baltimore tended to favor the break (Jacob Fortie,[15] at that time a local preacher, being a prominent exception), and those who had in recent years migrated to Baltimore from the Eastern Shore of Maryland tended to remain attached to the MEC. Many former slaves from the Eastern Shore had moved to Baltimore as there were few jobs for a free Black person at the time in the largely agricultural region.[16]

An analysis of the African American Methodist class membership lists for Baltimore also sheds additional light on the schism. Close to two hundred of the fourteen hundred African members in Baltimore initially left to form Bethel. Interestingly enough, it was the several classes that met at Asbury that were hardest hit by the withdrawal of members. Two of the preachers

who left, Richard Williams and Charles Pierce, were also class leaders at Asbury. Certainly, members left Sharp Street, but it appears that the newer Asbury congregation was the real source of the schism. Sharp Street losses included one preacher, Henry Harden,[17] and the exhorter Edward Waters, the
latter destined to become an AME bishop.[18]

Important to the group if it broke with the MEC would be a meeting
place. Initially, it rented a Presbyterian church not far from Sharp Street, and
then purchased a large building on Fish Street that became the new church's
permanent home. These actions set the Bethel congregation in place to participate in the founding of the AME Church. Coker attended the founding
conference in Philadelphia in April 1816, and was actually elected by the attendees as the church's new bishop. However, Coker refused to accept the
post that subsequently went to Allen.[19]

When the dust settled following the organization of the AMEC, the
Methodist community in Baltimore could be found in four locations. Those
who had left the MEC worshipped at Bethel. The great majority of those who
remained in the MEC could be found at Sharp Street, with smaller groups at
Asbury and Dallas Street. A few still attended the predominately White congregations. In the aftermath of the schism, the Black membership required
some reorganization, especially of the class structure. Several classes that met
at Asbury had been gutted, with a majority of their members leaving. The
encouragement to rebuild Asbury's membership seems the most likely rationale behind the resolution passed by the White leadership on April 9,
1817, that requested the remaining Black members to "retire from the Light
Street, Eutaw, and Old Town churches."[20]

In discussing the establishment of the AME Church, attention has been
almost totally directed to the break of the AMEs from the predominantly
White leadership of the MEC. Meanwhile, no consideration has been given
to the equally important split within the Black Methodist community itself.
The formation of the AME Church forced a choice upon all of Baltimore's
Black Methodists. And it would appear that, at least initially, the majority
chose to remain with the Sharp Street Church. The split was essentially a division among the free Blacks. The majority of members were, however, still
slaves having less choice about their religious allegiance, and of course, many
free Blacks had family who remained in slavery.

There is every reason to believe that almost all the Black members would
have favored the full ordination of their ministers and freedom from the arbitrary control of the church's White leadership. At the same time, there
were strong arguments favoring their staying with the Methodist Episcopal
Church. Most important, breaking with the Methodist Episcopal Church

meant breaking a number of long-term relationships. This issue must have weighed most heavily among those who had close friends and relatives who remained in slavery. Further, leaving Sharp Street would mean reorienting one's access to power, much of which now came through the Methodist hierarchy. White ministers gave individuals an immediate avenue for the amelioration of various practical problems.

It was also the case that even with its backing away from the very strong policies against slavery articulated in the 1780s, the MEC remained one of the stronger loci of anti-slavery sentiment. While accommodating to slavery somewhat, even the southern conferences were calling slavery a moral evil. Hope persisted among many Black people that the church would revert to its earlier position and that the opportunity to call the church to account for its shortcomings relative to its African members would arise. Finally, it was the case that many Black members felt that their participation in the church from its American beginnings gave them a birthright that they refused to abandon.

Possibly the major reason for the African members remaining with Sharp Street (and the MEC congregations in other cities) was their response to a persistent message they had heard from the White ministers and other friendly voices—that it was important that they show the larger White community that Black people did not conform to popular derogatory stereotypes. They were hard working, prosperous, sober, intelligent, and potentially ready to assume any position in the community held by a White person. Sharp Street, along with its school, was to many the primary demonstration of the truth of their life and would be the avenue of their integration into the mainstream of American society. (This argument would actually reappear during debates at the General Conference of the United Methodist Church [UMC] in 1970 when the status of the remaining Black conferences was decided.)

The issues that divided them aside, both groups had a prosperous future ahead of them. They held a high status in what was a growing Black community and both would soon see additional sister congregations form, a sign of their burgeoning membership. A decade after the split, in 1825, Sharp Street, Dallas Street, and Asbury became the seed from which a fourth congregation, the Orchard Street Church (now Metropolitan UMC), would begin to take shape.[21]

The members at Sharp Street were also justly proud of their school. In spite of the split, Coker continued to teach at the school until he readied himself to leave for Africa. He would be succeeded as the primary instructor by William Watkins (c. 1800–58), one of his pupils and a leader in the Sharp Street congregation. Watkins would go on to marry the daughter of Richard

Russell, a Sharp Street trustee, and emerge as a preacher. In 1837, he was ordained as a local deacon in the church. Meanwhile, in 1828, he adopted his three-year-old orphaned niece Frances Ellen Watkins (1825–1911), who attended the church and school and would later become a poet, teacher, and abolitionist in her own right.[22] Watkins remained in Baltimore until after the passage of the Fugitive Slave Act in 1850. He then closed the school and moved to Canada.

Sharp Street and Bethel were tied together somewhat by their common origin and would remain more or less friendly rivals over the succeeding decades and to the present. Once the immediate impact of the schism was put behind them, the two congregations would share the same needs to respond to common issues.

Possibly in response to the formation of the Bethel AME Church in Baltimore and the loyalty of the great majority of Sharp Street's members, which numbered in the multiple thousands, the Baltimore Conference began quietly to admit a few Black preachers into deacon's orders. (These men were retained as local deacons rather than beginning any process leading them to membership in the annual conference as traveling ministers.) The first such person to be ordained appears to have been John Mingo. He was followed by John Fortie three years later. Then over the next three decades fourteen additional deacons were designated: Philip Lee (1822), Lewis Wells (1828), Joseph Wilson (1830), Robert Golder (1830), Isaac Jones (1831), Thomas Watkins (1832), Patrick Hamilton (1834), William Watkins (1837), Benjamin Lynch (1838), John Harden (1847), Welmor Elsey (1858), Jacob Nicolson (1859), Thomas Garretson (1860), and Perry Mathews (1860).[23] The first man admitted to elder's orders (and hence able to serve the sacraments) was Joseph Young in 1843. He would be followed by Mingo, Elsey (1851), and Wesley Brown (1858).

The ordination of deacons obviously assisted Sharp Street in its head-on competition with Bethel AME. In the beginning, the local deacons were, like the unordained local preachers, unpaid. Later on, they would be "hired" to serve Black charges as supply preachers.

Colonization

Even before the Nat Turner incident and the new abolitionist movement, however, Baltimore Methodists were asked to decide about a possible future posed to them by the Colonization movement.[24] Founded at the end of 1816, the American Colonization Society included a number of prominent members, such as former president James Monroe (1758–1831), War of 1812 hero Francis Scott Key (1779–1843), and the notable lawyer Daniel Webster

(1782–1852). Their program was designed to provide passage for free Blacks to Africa. The more altruistic members felt that African Americans would never be able to assimilate into the society, and had concluded that African Americans' repatriation to their ancestors' homeland was the best option. At the same time, slave owners where quite aware of the threat that free Blacks offered, by their very existence, to the institution of slavery.

Free Blacks, including Baltimore's Methodists, aligned themselves along a broad spectrum of opinion concerning colonization. Amid the debate that followed the introduction of the colonization program, Baltimore (and Washington, D.C.) developed centers for its support within the Black community. This support was nowhere more fully illustrated than by Daniel Coker's agreement to become the chaplain for one of the first ships of colonists that sailed for West Africa. In 1820 Coker settled in Sierra Leone, where he lived the rest of his life.[25] David Smith asserted that Coker was initially opposed to the colonization scheme,[26] but was recruited heavily by the Society's leaders and finally consented to go from the inducements he was offered.[27]

While members at Bethel considered Africa, George R. McGill, a prominent lay member at Sharp Street, organized the Maryland Haitian Company that in 1819 chartered a ship, the *Dromo*, which would carry a group of Baltimorians to the Caribbean island. McGill had previously made a trip to meet with the Haitian president and see firsthand the conditions that colonists would encounter. Upon his return he devoted much time to countering rumors as to the poor state of Haiti since its independence. In the meantime, the MEC threw denominational support (though not funding) behind the colonization effort.[28]

The colonization cause, which waxed and waned throughout the nineteenth century, received new support at the end of 1826 when, following meetings at Bethel and Sharp Street, supporters issued "A Memorial of the Free People of Colour." The memorial, actually written by two White men with local political ambitions, did not receive the support of a majority of the conferences' attendees, and it quickly drew the ire of William Watkins, the head of the Sharp Street school, and another lay leader/activist, Jacob Greener, who pointed out the anti-Black statements in the document. In his writings, Watkins emphasized the Americanization of the African community and noted that as a group Black people had no knowledge of Africa and no desire to go there.

A minority in the several Methodist churches did hold some hope for a future in Africa, among them George McGill, who had not joined the Haitian group in 1819 because of an illness that had temporarily taken him out.

Several months prior to the conferences, McGill had begun to organize a group to go to Africa, and he was instrumental in setting up the December conferences. In the end, however, only a small group joined McGill in the move to Liberia. The first would, however, be followed by a second group led by Sharp Street schoolteacher Remus Harvey, which departed for Liberia in October 1827.

Throughout the 1820s, and indeed for the rest of his life, Watkins took the lead in denouncing colonization. This would cause him some discomfort in 1830 when David Walker's *Appeal to the Colored Citizens of the World* appeared, in that the *Appeal* cited Watkins' arguments against colonization with approval.[29] For a brief period, Watkins became unwittingly associated with Walker's approval of violence as a means to end slavery. However, the *Appeal* slowed him only momentarily from his picking up his attacks on colonization, which he published sporadically in William Lloyd Garrison's *Liberator*.[30] At the same time, closer to home, he had to deal with the supporters of colonization and gradual emancipation, that included two preachers, John Fortie at Sharp Street and Nathaniel Peck at Bethel.[31]

To those African Americans who weighed the pros and cons of colonization and abolitionism, one issue often tipped the balance in its favor, namely the fragile nature of the liberty experienced by free Blacks. In places like Baltimore, free Blacks lived with the fear that they could be returned to a state of slavery, and once a slave, the added possibility of being relocated from the relatively permissive atmosphere of the urban North to labor on a plantation in the Deep South.

The First Colored Wesley Methodist Independent Society

The AME Church in Baltimore grew slowly through the 1820s. It was not until 1832 that a second congregation, Ebenezer, was organized and then in 1843 a third, Waters AME Church. In the meantime, in 1842, a small group from Sharp Street left to found the First Colored Wesley Methodist Independent Society of Baltimore. The group was led by Jacob M. Moore, a local preacher, who was soon joined by two other preachers, William Johnson and Severn Johnson. This group then decided to join with the African Methodist Episcopal Zion Church and made application to the Philadelphia Conference in 1844.[32]

It would appear that the Society and the AMEZ Church ran into problems when the denomination asserted some ownership over the Society's property. Initially, the Society prevailed, and in 1847, Moore turned to the Baltimore Conference of the AME Church, asking to be accepted into it. He pointed out that in the five years of its existence the congregation had grown to include 337 members under the leadership of an official board of eleven men, five stewards, nine trustees, seven preachers, and two exhorters. Its Sunday school had 152 students and seven teachers. Having won in court over the AMEZ Church, it now wished to place itself under the authority of the AME Church. A committee appointed by the conference recommended that the conference look with favor on the request.

The Society's relation to the AME Church, however, was short lived. As it turned out, the congregation was heavily in debt, and in 1850 lost its property. The person who took control of it then returned it to the AMEZ Church. At this time, the AME's three churches in Baltimore were not in the best of financial condition, and there was no money to save the Society's chapel. Rev. Moore and his supporters were absorbed into the other AME congregations, while the chapel housed a congregation that survives to this day as the Pennsylvania Avenue AMEZ Church.

Washington, D.C., African Methodism

Methodism in what is now Washington, D.C., can be traced to October 1772 and a sermon preached by circuit rider Robert Williams (c. 1745–75). The present Dumbarton Oaks United Methodist Church traces its beginning to the original Georgetown meetings, which gathered in a cooper's shop, then on Montgomery Street (now Twenty-eighth Street) near M Street, west of Rock Creek. Washington/Georgetown was a stop on the Frederick (Maryland) Circuit until 1805. At the end of the year, it reported sixty-one White and twenty-five African members. At this time Washington had approximately 14,000 residents of which 3,200 were slaves and 800 free Blacks.[33]

Problems with growth flared as early as 1812. On January 12 of the following year, the Dumbarton trustees purchased a lot that extended between Twenty-sixth and Twenty-seventh Streets just south of P Street from a William Morgan for two hundred dollars. Subsequently, some 125 African American members of the Georgetown church, including Polly Hill, William Crusor, William Trumwell, Shadrack Nugent, Thomas Mason, and Tamar Green, formed a separate congregation. As was the common practice, the new Mt. Zion congregation remained formally under the supervision of the older Dumbarton church.

Mt. Zion was born in traumatic times. War against England was formally declared on June 28, 1812. By the end of the year, the British Royal Navy had instituted a blockade of Chesapeake Bay. Battles would be fought on a number of fronts over the next two years, climaxing in August of 1814 in the invasion and burning of Washington. Peace would be restored only in

February of the next year, when attention would turn to the rebuilding of the city.

Beginning in 1816, Mt. Zion grew steadily, doubling over the next two decades, from 417 members in 1816 to 850 in 1838. Meanwhile a second Methodist congregation had been organized at Greenleaf's Point (south of the Capitol building) in 1801. In 1802, William Watters was assigned to lead the congregation, which then met in a home at South Capitol and N Streets, SW. In 1811, this group became Ebenezer Methodist Church and met at a building on Fourth Street, SE. & W. M Street.

Very early in its history, prior to the separation of Black and White members, rules against slavery in the Methodist Episcopal Church came to bear on the deliberations at Ebenezer. White historian W. M. Ferguson recalled that the very first official meeting at the church was called to deal with two members who owned slaves and to consider what would happen to them. In both cases, the church members dictated the slave's future.[34]

Ferguson also took note of the large African American contingent attending Ebenezer as the nineteenth century began. Though segregated in the galleries, they were well known for the life they injected into the worship services through their active participation in the music and prayers. "Sometimes, too, their swaying bodies and upturned faces made a weird accompaniment to the more decorous worship of the whites, and their leaping suggested the danger of a descent upon the heads of those who were on the lower floor."[35]

By 1825 there were a number of all-Black classes filled by the two hundred members. For several years, Ebenezer had been given two pastors, one specifically assigned to work full-time with the Black members. Then in 1825, the Baltimore Conference named Joseph Cartwright, a local preacher from Mt. Zion, as the first African American supply pastor to be placed on salary and appointed to lead one of its Black congregations. The following year he would become the first African American to be ordained as an elder, though, again, not admitted into the conference of traveling ministers.

We do not know a lot about Cartwright, though he must have been an extraordinary man to have been selected as the first Black elder in the MEC.[36] We do know that his wife had been a slave and that he had purchased her freedom in 1823. He would spend the next decade collecting the money to purchase his children's freedom.[37] During his tenure at Ebenezer, the Black members began meeting as a separate congregation. Adopting the name "Little Ebenezer," the congregation was finally able to erect its own chapel at Fourth and D Streets, SE, in 1838, which subsequently housed the first public school for Black children in Washington. Today, this congregation is known as Ebenezer United Methodist Church.

In 1814, Henry Foxall, a prominent layman, gave the money for the building of the third church in Washington—Foundry Church, originally located
at Fourteenth and F Streets, NW. As with the Dumbarton and Ebenezer
churches, membership was mixed, though the common rules defining Black
and White relations were never challenged. Blacks and Whites sat separately
at worship, in this case, Blacks in the gallery. Whites led the all-Black classes,
and interestingly, it would not be until 1833 that the first Black member, Eli
(or Ely) Nugent, was granted an exhorter's license.

Through the 1820s, membership at Foundry exploded, going from 196
White and 60 Black members to 650 White and 163 Black. Black membership increased to 313 by 1836. In 1929, Rev. John F. Cook, an African Presbyterian minister, founded the Asbury Sunday School, which met at the
John F. Cook building (Fourteenth and H Streets). Benjamin M. McCoy, a
member of Asbury, was the superintendent. As early as 1833, given the continued growth of the congregation, discussions were held concerning the
founding of a separate Black congregation. It was noted in a quarterly conference session that it would cost some fifteen thousand dollars to erect a new
building. That sum not withstanding, on June 24, a number of the members,
under Nugent's leadership, met at the home of Israel Lawrence and decided
that their own house of worship should become a reality.

However, before their plans could be realized, they had to deal with the riots of August 1835, provoked by the presence of one of Rev. Cook's students,
one Arthur Bowen, in the residence of Mrs. Anna Maria Thornton, a proper
White lady. Bowen's mother was Thornton's personal servant. Word circulated that the inebriated Bowen had entered Thornton's bedroom wielding
an axe and was ultimately forced out the back door of the house. The story
inflamed White fears of violence from the Black community, the Nat Turner
incident still in their minds. A gathering crowd turned its anger toward abolitionists and free Blacks, eventually focusing it at Beverly Snow, a mulatto
who ran a popular restaurant, the Epicurean Eating House. The crowd attacked his restaurant and destroyed all the furniture, though Snow escaped
any harm.[38]

The next target was Cook's school, but the prudent minister had already
left town for Pennsylvania. The rioters vandalized the school, inflicting significant damage to the building, and then partially dispersed into smaller
bands, looking for any free Blacks or abolitionists they could find. The
evening ended in the burning of some residences and breaking some windows
in a church. The imprudent Arthur Bowen was later tried and sentenced to
be hung.

By the beginning of 1836, the tension level caused by the riots and trials
had dropped. And the members of Foundry Church who desired to open an

independent church were ready to act. They took their first step on January 15 by forming the Asbury Aid Society. Then they rented an unoccupied schoolhouse at Fourteenth and H Streets, N.W., where the original nucleus of the future Asbury Methodist church began to hold services. On October 5, 1836, the Foundry Church appointed seven trustees to purchase the land upon which a church for the African members could be built. Once the land was secured, the Black leaders moved quickly to erect the three-story Asbury Chapel, also known as the Asbury Methodist Episcopal Church.

Shortly after the church was organized, Benjamin M. McCoy returned to Washington from Lancaster County, Pennsylvania, where he had been teaching, and organized the choir, which he would continue to direct for the next twenty years. The choir had among its members Joseph Ambush and Thomas Bell, famous singers of the era. While Rev. Cook repaired his school, he initially continued his work at the new Asbury church. In 1837, McCoy also opened a school using the church facilities, which he operated for the next twelve years.

Samuel Brison, a White minister officially appointed to Foundry, became the church's first pastor. Asbury's continued ties to Foundry were further illustrated by the pastor-in-charge coming to Foundry every Thursday evening to preach, and the appointment of White members from Foundry to lead the ten classes. Nugent emerged as the church's local elder, eventually being ordained. There were in addition two local preachers (Steven Clarke and Plato Hutt, ordained as deacons in 1845 and 1848, respectively) and two exhorters (Arnold Bowie and Isaac Mason), who held prayer meetings and conducted worship in the absence of the White preacher. Asbury continued to be reported as part of Foundry's membership.

In 1841, Asbury petitioned to become a separate charge with its own full-time minister. Foundry's senior minister, Thomas C. Thornton, appointed James M. Hanson to take charge. Over the next two years, under Hanson's leadership two additional classes were organized and Black class leaders began to assume the roles formerly limited to Whites. In 1843, the ministerial appointments to Foundry specifically mentioned Rev. Wesley Rohr being assigned as the assistant pastor to labor among the "coloured People." By 1845, the appointment read to "Foundry and Asbury."

In spite of continued growth, petitions from Asbury for separation went unheeded. As the Baltimore Conference delayed any action, in 1848, two Asbury members, John Brent and John Ingram, led their families and others out to form an independent congregation, the John Wesley AMEZ Church. This church was not the first break within the ranks of Washington's Black Methodists. By this time, the AMEZ already supported three congregations in Washington. In 1837 Little Ebenezer had experienced a major loss when an exhorter and thirteen class leaders (including Enoch Ambush) would walk out and form the independent Zion Wesley Church, which quickly affiliated with the AMEZ. This church would in turn develop a mission, called the Galbraith church (after the minister who originally organized Zion Wesley). Then in 1844, a second group withdrew from Mt. Zion and established the Union Wesley church.

Even before the AMEZ congregations were founded, however, in 1821 David Smith, the former member of Sharp Street Church in Baltimore who had aligned with Daniel Coker and the AME Church, was assigned to respond to a request for assistance of a few people in Georgetown. Upon his arrival, he received a harsh welcome from the members of Mt. Zion church, but persevered and started his work at an old schoolhouse. He immediately began drawing members away from Mt. Zion. Among the early members of what became Israel African Methodist Episcopal Church were Scipio Beans (later to become the first missionary to Haiti), George Simms, Peter Schureman (later to become a minister), George Hicks, Dora Bowen, William Costin, William Datcher, William Warren, and George Bell. George Bell and Enoch Ambush (then still a member of Little Ebenezer) would form a school that for many years met at the Israel church's building.[39]

In 1822, Smith reported forty-five members. It would host the AME's Baltimore Conference for the first time in 1834, the first of a number of occasions. Over the next few decades, Israel would employ some of the most outstanding men in the AME ministerial ranks, including William Cornish, James A. Shorter, Daniel A. Payne, Alexander W. Wayman, and Henry McNeal Turner.[40]

Wilmington and the First Independent Black Denomination

Wilmington, Delaware, emerged as a prominent center for Methodism rather early. Soon after his initial visit to Philadelphia, Methodist lay preacher Captain Thomas Webb (1724–96) also visited and preached in Wilmington, possibly in the winter of 1766–67. His sermon was delivered while standing under some trees at what is now King and Eighth Streets. He returned several years later and preached a second sermon on November 4, 1769.

It is estimated that by the eve of the American Revolution, some 650 African Americans lived in New Castle County, and there is every reason to believe that, as in almost every other center in which Methodism developed at this time, Black people were among the early auditors of Webb's sermons and among the early members of the original society. However, very little is known of the slowly developing work until 1789 when a parcel of land was purchased and the first church building erected. Bishop Asbury dedicated the building on October 10, 1789. At this time, the society's membership consisted of forty-three Whites and nineteen Blacks. The new church had a gallery, into which the Black members were segregated, and those in the gallery were always the last to take communion.[41]

The continued slow growth was indicated by the changing status of the Wilmington church (later to be named Asbury), alternating between being a station with its own full-time minister and being placed as one charge on a circuit, through the rest of the century.

Delaware had been an early center of Quaker abolitionist activity, which has been credited with leading to a number of manumissions. In 1790, however, the census still reported 8,887 slaves and only 3,899 free Blacks, many of the latter having moved to Philadelphia. By this time two anti-slavery societies were active, the Delaware Society for Promoting the Abolition of Slavery and the Delaware Society for the Gradual Abolition of Slavery, both formed at the end of the 1780s. The number of slaves in the state decreased steadily year by year but as late as 1860 there were still more than a thousand in the state, overwhelmingly located in the more rural southern half of the state. Meanwhile, Wilmington had emerged as the center of the state's free Black community.

Formation of Ezion[42]

By the time Ezion Church, the African Methodist church in Wilmington, was formed, at least four other independent Black Methodist congregations were in existence in Baltimore and Philadelphia, each occasioned by the raising of a slightly different issue between the Whites and Blacks in a formerly racially mixed congregation. In Wilmington, a set of issues grew around the segregated gallery, and by the beginning of 1805, the Black members had decided it was time to form a separate congregation. On February 6, 1805, they caused a notice to be printed in the *Mirror of Times*, a Wilmington newspaper:

African Church.

The people of color, of this Borough being desirous of building a house of worship, but not possessing funds sufficient, contemplate soliciting donations to assist them in the undertaking. For this purpose subscription papers will be shortly presented to the public whose generous aid they respectfully solicit to enable them to accomplish this laudable purpose.[43]

The present Ezion–Mt. Carmel United Methodist Church continues the original Ezion Methodist Episcopal Church founded in 1805.

Among the particular issues that had surfaced at Wilmington, one centered on the class meetings. As the congregation grew, the membership was divided into a number of classes along gender and racial lines. These classes, smaller and more intimate than the Sunday congregational preaching services, were the heart of Methodist life at the time. During these meetings there would be time for members to testify to their progress in the Christian life in a celebrative mood with lively singing, hand clapping, foot stomping, and even dancing.

Several of Wilmington's classes met at the church building, some of them being too big for any private home. It was evident that the White members considered that they were offering the Black members a great privilege by allowing their class meeting to be on the main floor of the church rather than in the gallery, where they normally sat on Sunday. Thus they were noticeably upset when the celebrative element of the Black members' class meeting occasionally got out of hand; as they moved about responding to the music, the Black members occasionally broke benches and other items in the church. Thus it was that on June 19, 1805, the church's board of trustees passed the following resolution:

> Whereas. In consequence of meeting the classes of the black people on the lower seats of this church, a number of the benches have been broken, and the house so defiled by dirt, &c., as to render it unfit to meet in, and if any longer tolerated, more injury may be sustained, wherefore it was
>
> Resolved, That no black classes shall hereafter meet in the lower floor of Asbury Church and if they refuse to meet in the gallery, the sexton inform them that the door will not be opened for their reception, and furthermore, the leaders of the same are requested to respect this resolution and govern themselves accordingly.[44]

The African members soon found land at Ninth and French Streets and erected what became known as the Old Stone Church. While we know the names of a few of the members at this time, the leading member was Jacob Pindergrass, a licensed preacher who was placed in charge of the new congregation. The White minister assigned to Wilmington preached and served the sacraments at both Asbury and Ezion, as the African church was named, but Pindergrass operated as the regular spiritual leader for Ezion's members.

Through the next few years, Pindergrass was joined in his leadership role by Peter Spencer (1779–1843). Spencer had been born into slavery, but he was freed when his master died. He subsequently moved from his home in southern Delaware to Wilmington, where he joined the Asbury Church and subsequently became a charter member of Ezion. In the years after Ezion was established, Spencer began to raise issues about the management of the church. Among other items, he was upset that Ezion did not have charge of its own temporal affairs, which remained in the hands of the White leadership at Asbury, or any word in the selection of its minister, which was sent by the conference.

As Spencer and others pressed their concerns through 1812 and into 1813, some of his followers were expelled from the church. In May 1813, Spencer and those loyal to him withdrew. They rented a building, quite visible from the Old Stone Church, on French Street between Eighth and Ninth Streets. They held their first worship service on June 1, 1813, and subsequently organized in a more formal manner. In September they set Spencer apart as their pastor. They then formally organized as the African Union Church and recorded their action at the state capital. In the meantime, the Old Stone Church became the subject of a lawsuit between Spencer's followers, who made up the majority of the Ezion congregation, and Asbury.

As the adjudication continued, those members who did not wish to join the African Union Church were left out, as the court ordered the church building closed until the suit was resolved. They temporarily worshipped at Asbury. The lawsuit was finally resolved in their favor, and they reestablished their presence in the building and continued as the Ezion congregation. With the assistance of the White minister at Asbury, the congregation, now reduced to thirty-nine members, was reconstituted, and two trustees, Michael Stirling and Ralph Harding, selected. These same men, along with Pindergrass, were named the church's three stewards.

Father Pindergrass resumed his role as the church's spiritual leader. He continued in his role until his death, seemingly in the 1820s.[45] Pindergrass was succeeded in leadership by Joseph Whittington, another licensed lay preacher.

Ezion grew through the years and in 1844 had to enlarge its building. That enlargement came none too soon as the church was now facing new competition. In the early 1840s, representatives of the African Methodist Episcopal Church arrived in Wilmington to begin the work of raising up an AME congregation. Enough members were found that in 1846 it was formally organized and a church building dedicated the next year.[46]

Once the lawsuit was settled, Spencer emerged as head of the first independent Methodist church for African Americans, a most important landmark for the African American community. Three years later, he would travel to Philadelphia and at Richard Allen's invitation participate in the conference at which the African Methodist Episcopal Church was founded. He decided, for reasons not altogether clear, to refrain from joining his work with Allen's.[47] That the church he founded did not have bishops is likely part of the story. Spencer would subsequently make the territory in a fifty-mile radius of Wilmington his primary field of activity. In 1815 he founded congregations in Christiana and New Castle, Delaware. The next year, he moved into New Jersey and formed a congregation at Marshalltown, immediately across the Delaware River from Wilmington and north of Salem.[48] During the remaining years of his life he would found some thirty-one congregations that would together form what is now known as the African Union First Colored Methodist Protestant Church.[49] Included would be churches in Welsh Tract and Summit, Delaware; Baileytown, New Jersey; and Chester, Philadelphia, and Pennsboro, Pennsylvania. By the time of Spencer's death in 1843, congregations had been founded as far away as Connecticut and Rhode Island.[50]

Among Spencer's unique contributions was the organization of an annual cultural festival in Wilmington, generally called the Big Quarterly. Originally held to commemorate the founding of the African Union Church, it early on took on the appearance of a camp meeting complete with outdoor preaching, singing, shouting, and dancing. As it evolved, it took on a political dimension, as Wilmington became a stop on the underground railroad. It also became a major Black socio-cultural event that brought together slaves and free Blacks and drew participants from the neighboring states. Though the lawsuit got the AUC and continuing Ezion members off to a bad start, over the years the Ezion members became active participants in the Big Quarterly, which continues to be held to the present.[51]

As with the other African churches that decided to remain in affiliation with the Methodist Episcopal Church, Ezion's struggle became one of attaining equality with the White congregations relative to its responsibilities as a congregation and the status of its minister(s).[52] Through the 1830s, Ezion continued to be reported as an integral part of the Asbury church in the Philadelphia Conference records. In 1838, Asbury was reported as having 110 Black members. In 1840, that number had grown to 136.[53]

Notes

1. Frederick Douglass, *Narrative of the Life of Frederick Douglass, an American Slave. Written by Himself* (Boston: Anti-Slavery Office, 1845), 34.

2. Summarized earlier in chapter 2. For the complete story, see Donald G. Matthews, *Slavery and Methodism: A Chapter in American Morality, 1780–1845* (Princeton, NJ: Princeton University Press, 1965).

3. The dating of Allen's walkout in Philadelphia has been challenged in recent years following the discovery that the changes in the seating arrangement at St. George's that provoked the problem did not occur until 1792. Dating the problem to June 1792 also fits the incident into other related occurrences. See Milton C. Sernett, *Black Religion and American Evangelicalism: White Protestants, Plantation Missions, and the Flowering of Negro Christianity* (Metuchen, NJ: Scarecrow Press, 1975), and Dee E. Andrews, *The Methodists and Revolutionary America, 1760–1800.* (Princeton, NJ: Princeton University Press, 2000).

4. In 1801, for the sum of eight hundred seventy dollars, Jacob Gillard and Richard Russell purchased land at Forrest Lane and Conwago Street for the use of the African Methodist Episcopal church, the term "African" being the designation for all the local Black members of the Baltimore Methodist community. It appears that this purchase was a venture in real estate speculation, the purchasers hoping to resell the land at a later date for a profit.

5. Josephus R. Coan, "Daniel Coker: 19th Century Black Church Organizer," *Journal of the Interdenominational Theological Center* 3, 1 (Fall 1975), 17–31.

6. Little information is actually available on Coker from 1801 until he reemerges in 1808 and is ordained by Asbury. At some point in this period, probably closer to 1802 than 1808, he was able to surface and become the school's primary instructor. See Leroy Graham, *Baltimore: The Nineteenth Century Black Capital* (Lanham, MD: University Press of America, 1982), 63–77.

7. Daniel Coker, *A Dialogue between a Virginian and an African Minister* (Baltimore: Benjamin Edes, 1810). Text reproduced in Dorothy Porter, comp. & ed., *Negro Protest Pamphlets; a Compendium* (New York, Arno Press, 1969), and Richard Newman and Patrick Rael, eds. *Pamphlets of Protest: an Anthology of Early African-American Protest Literature, 1790–1860* (New York: Routledge, 2001).

8. [David Smith], *Biography of the Rev. David Smith, of the A. M. E. Church Being a Complete History, Embracing Over Sixty Year's Labor in the Advancement of the Redeemer's Kingdom on Earth Including "The History of the Origin and Development of Wilberforce University."* (Xenia, OH: Xenia Gazette Office, 1881).

9. Smith is slightly off on his chronology. If his birth date, 1784, is correct, he would have been a little older when he joined the Methodists. Nasey Schin (Asa Shinn, 1781–1853), later a leader of the Methodist Protestant Church, joined the Baltimore Conference in 1801, and Sharp Street was not established until 1802. Thus he would have been closer to sixteen when he joined the church.

10. Smith, *Biography of the Rev. David Smith*, 15.

11. Larry G. Murphy, J. Gordon Melton, and Gary L. Ward., eds., *Encyclopedia of African American Religions* (New York: Garland Publishing, 1993), 827.

12. Graham, *Baltimore*, 71.

13. Coker's father-in-law. See Graham, *Baltimore*, 72.

14. This account by J. A. Handy was reprinted by Benjamin W. Arnett in the *Centennial Budget* (1887), 272–73. Handy was a prominent member of the African

Methodist Episcopal Church and a member of its Baltimore Conference. A more expanded account of these events is found in Handy's *Scraps of African Methodist Episcopal History* (Philadelphia: A. M. E. Book Concern, 1902).

15. Fortie also ran a school for African children at Bethel AME Church. See Carter Godwin Woodson, *The Education Of The Negro Prior To 1861* (New York: Putnam's, 1915. Rpt., New York: Ayer Co., 1968), 141.

16. A copy of a list of the classes and leadership of the Black members in Baltimore in 1815 has survived. It indicates that of six local preachers, three (including Coker) left, as did two of the ten exhorters and but a single class leader.

17. Harden would later become an AME minister in New York City.

18. Harden, Pierce, Waters, and Williams, along with David Smith, constituted the core of the soon to be organized Baltimore Conference of the AME Church.

19. There has been much speculation about why Coker refused the bishop's chair. Some have attributed his decision to his relatively light skin, others to his perception that it was Allen's right as the instigator of the national organizational effort. See Christopher Phillips, *Freedom's Port: The African American Community of Baltimore, 1790–1860* (Champaign, IL: University of Illinois Press, 1997); Carol V. R. George, *Segregated Sabbaths: Richard Allen and the Rise of Independent Black Churches, 1760–1840* (New York: Oxford University Press, 1973), 88; Graham, *Baltimore*, 73.

20. Cited in Phillips, *Freedom's Port*, 125, and Graham, *Baltimore*, 74–75.

21. Leading in the founding of the Orchard Street Methodist Church was Truman Le Pratt, a former slave in the service of the aging John Eager Howard (1752–1827), Revolutionary War hero and former governor of Maryland (1789–91). In 1837 the members erected a building which survives today (as the headquarters of the Urban League) as the oldest standing structure built by African Americans in the city of Baltimore.

22. While still in Baltimore, Watkins published her first book of poems, *Autumn Leaves*, in 1845. Though this book went through several editions, no copies are known to have survived.

23. "Local Preachers Ordained in the Baltimore-Washington Conference & Vicinity, 1800–1960," *Third Century Methodism* 37, 3 (February 1998): 2–3. In addition to the ordained preachers at Sharp Street, several preachers were also ordained over the years for the other Black churches in Baltimore including Joseph Fortie (1938) and Joseph Carter (1856).

24. P. J. Staudenraus, *The African Colonization Movement* (New York: Columbia University Press, 1961).

25. Daniel Coker, *Journal of Daniel Coker, a descendant of Africa, from the time of leaving New York, in the ship Elizabeth, Capt. Sebor, on a voyage for Sherbro, in Africa, in company with three agents, and about ninety persons of colour. . .* ([Baltimore]: Edward J. Coale, supported by the Maryland Auxiliary Colonization Society, 1820).

26. As early as 1812, Paul Cuffe was in Baltimore, where he met with Coker and other Black leaders about his immigration plans; thus Coker had a number of years to give to consideration of its possibilities. The meeting is cited by Julie Winch, A

Gentleman of Color: The Life of James Forten (New York: Oxford University Press, 2002), 182.

27. Coker's relationship to the church is somewhat obscure for the next few years. In 1817, he was not given an appointment as a preacher by the Baltimore Conference because of "rumors" about his conduct. He was expelled from the church in 1818. He was readmitted to the church and then to the ministry in 1819, but was still in obvious tension with the leadership. See Daniel Alexander Payne, *A History of the African Methodist Episcopal Church*. Ed. by Charles Spencer Smith (Nashville, TN: Publishing House of the A. M. E. Sunday School Union, 1891), 28–29, and *First Conference Minutes of the A.M.E. Connexion composed by Richard Allen in the City of Baltimore, 1818* (Baltimore: Henry Shields, n.d.).

28. See Smith, *Biography of the Rev. David Smith*.

29. David Walker, *Walker's Appeal in Four Articles; Together with a Preamble, To the Coloured Citizens of the World, but in Particular, and Very Expressly, to Those of the United States of America*. Third and Last Edition, with Additional Notes, Corrections, &c. (Boston: Revised and Published by David Walker, 1830). For a more complete discussion of Walker, see chapter 7.

30. Watkins had met Garrison in 1828 when he had come to Baltimore to visit with Quaker anti-slavery leader Benjamin Lundy. Watkins subsequently became a regular contributor to *The Liberator*.

31. Watkins continued as a leader at Sharp Street into the 1840s, but around 1844 he was caught up in the Millerite enthusiasm concerning the predicted end of the world. He was dropped from the role of preacher at Sharp Street and gradually faded into obscurity. (See letter from Isaac P. Cook to T. E. Bond, February 20, 1844, copy in the Lovely Lane Museum in Baltimore, Maryland.) In 1852 Watkins moved to Canada and died there in 1858. Watkins' eventual fate may be one reason that he was largely forgotten in later years at Sharp Street. See Graham, *Baltimore*, 93–146.

32. John Jamison Moore, *History of the A. M. E. Zion Church in America. Founded in 1796, in the City of New York*. (York, PA: Teachers' Journal Office, 1884), 130–31; Payne, *History of the African Methodist Episcopal Church*, 208–10.

33. A most helpful item on Washington's antebellum African American Methodists is John W. Cromwell, "The First Negro Churches in the District of Columbia," *Journal of Negro History* 7, 1 (January 1922), 64–106. Posted at: http://docsouth.unc.edu/church/phoebus/menu.html. See also Nina Honemond Clarke, *History of the Nineteenth-Century Black Churches in Maryland & Washington, D.C.* (Los Angeles: Vantage Press, 1983).

34. W. M. Ferguson, *Methodism in Washington, District of Colombia* . . . (Baltimore: The Methodist Book Concern, 1892), 36–37.

35. Ferguson, *Methodism in Washington*, 65–66.

36. "Local Preachers Ordained in the Baltimore-Washington Conference & Vicinity, 1800–1960," *Third Century Methodism* 37, 3 (February 1998), 2–3. It would be over a decade before additional preachers from the Washington area churches would receive ordination. Deacons named prior to the Civil War include Pompy

Tenny (1837), Plato Hutt (1848), Stephen Clark (1845), William Hicks (1856), Noah Jones (1856), Thomas Mason (1957), and Levi Collins (1858).

37. Edwin Schell, "A Heritage and a Future: Ebenezer 3/19/200." Unpublished typescript, 2000.

38. Jefferson Morley, "The 'Snow Riot,'" *Washington Post* (February 6, 2005). Posted at www.washingtonpost.com/wp-dyn/articles/A55082-2005Feb1.html. Accessed April 15, 2006.

39. See Smith, *Biography of the Rev. David Smith*, 44–55.

40. In an interesting move, the Israel congregation would eventually affiliate with the CME Church after the Civil War.

41. General sources on Methodism and its African membership in Delaware include Robert W. Todd, *Methodism of the Peninsula* (Philadelphia: Methodist Episcopal Book Rooms, 1886), and William Henry Williams, *The Garden of American Methodism: The Delmarva Peninsula, 1769–1820* (Wilmington, DE: The Peninsula Conference of the United Methodist Church, 1984).

42. Much of this history of Ezion is derived from Joseph R. Waters, "Ezion Methodist Episcopal Church," in John D. C. Hanna, ed., *The Centennial Services of Asbury Methodist Episcopal Church, Wilmington, Delaware, October 13–20, 1889* (Wilmington, DE: Delaware Printing Company, 1889), 172–75.

43. Ezion–Mt. Carmel United Methodist Church, "History." Posted at www.gbgm-umc.org/ezion-mtcarmel/history.html. Accessed October 1, 2005.

44. Quoted in John D. Hanna, ed., *The Centennial Services of Asbury Methodist Episcopal Church, Wilmington, Delaware, October 13–20, 1889* (Wilmington, DE: Delaware Printing Company, 1889).

45. At Asbury's centennial in 1887, George S. Hagany, at the time Asbury's oldest member, reported having seen Pindergrass during the last days of his life and attending his funeral, which he said was the largest that he had ever seen. Unfortunately, the record of the year of his funeral was not included in his account.

46. A brief entry on Wilmington, Delaware's AME church can be found in Richard R. Wright, Jr., *Encyclopedia of African Methodism* (Philadelphia: Book Concern of the A. M. E. Church, 1947), 535.

47. The African Union Church differed in a number of respects from the AMEC, most noticeably on the issue of bishops.

48. David James Russell, *History of the African Union Methodist Protestant Church* (Philadelphia: Union Star Book and Job Printing and Publishing House, 1920), 66.

49. For a more complete account of Spencer and the African Union Church see Lewis V. Baldwin, *Invisible Strands in African Methodism: A History of the African Union Methodist Protestant and Union American Methodist Episcopal Churches, 1805–1980* (Methuen, NJ: Scarecrow Press, 1983) and *The Mark of a Man: Peter Spencer and the African Union Methodist Tradition* (Lanham, MD: University Press of America, 1987).

50. Baldwin, *Invisible Strands*, 55–56.

51. On the Big Quarterly, see Alice Dunbar-Nelson, *Big Quarterly in Wilmington* (Wilmington, DE: The Author, 1932).

52. Colonization did not seem to be as major an issue in Wilmington as it had been in Philadelphia and Baltimore. The Wilmington Union Colonization Society, an affiliate of the American Colonization Society, was formed at a meeting at the city's Episcopal Church on September 30, 1823, some years after the first wave of enthusiasm for colonization had passed. It existed for several decades and contributed to the national colonization effort. In 1831 Peter Spencer became the co-author of a statement denouncing the colonization cause. A prominent element of the argument declared free Blacks were Americans, not Africans.

53. Ezion would become one of the primary stations to be served by the Delaware Conference beginning in 1864 (see chapter 8). Today it survives as the Ezion–Mt. Carmel United Methodist Church.

CHAPTER FOUR

~

Emerging Centers of Black Methodism: Philadelphia, New York City, and Brooklyn

African Methodist Struggles in Philadelphia

Prior mention has been made of the beginning of Methodism in Philadelphia and the conversion of Peter Dennis. This isolated incident was followed in 1767 by the arrival of Captain Thomas Webb, a British soldier and Methodist lay evangelist, whose preaching led to the formation of St. George's, the first Methodist congregation in the city. Dennis would later join the small group of Africans who became charter members of St. George's. The presence of Black people in the church in Philadelphia was immediately noticed by Joseph Pilmore, following his arrival in the colonies in 1769.

The African membership of St. George's always included a mixture of slaves and free Blacks, but free Blacks seem to have been the dominant element from the beginning.[1] Interestingly, it was from one of the enslaved members in Philadelphia that the first bit of writing (that has survived) by an African American Methodist comes. In his journal Pilmore recorded having received a letter from a female slave on November 10, 1771. The letter highlights the problems the early African members had to overcome just to be part of the church fellowship:

Dear Sir. These are to acquaint you, that my bondage is such that I cannot possibly attend with the rest of the Class to receive my ticket therefore beg you will send it—I wanted much to come to church at the Watch-night, but could not get leave; but, I bless God that night I was greatly favored with the spirit of prayer, and enjoyed much of His Divine Presence—I find the enemy of my soul continually striving to throw me off the foundation, but I have that within me which bids defiance to his delusive snare—I beg an interest in your prayers that I may be enabled to bear up under all my difficulties with patient resignation to the will of God.[2]

Several years later, Thomas Rankin would note that although many slaves had been converted by the Methodists, their masters would not allow them to become members of the society, much less meet the weekly class meetings, the unique small groups to which all members were expected to belong and regularly attend.

The Philadelphia congregation was thoroughly disrupted during the American Revolution. First, the British confiscated their building as headquarters for the cavalry units, forcing meetings into private homes. Then, many of the Black members left with the British when they withdrew. Paul Burall, who had migrated to Philadelphia from England just after the war, described the congregation as consisting of only about one hundred members, the majority of attendees being Africans.[3] The post-war years would be a hopeful time for Africans, as Pennsylvania passed a law for the gradual elimination of slavery in the state in 1780. Within a decade, of slightly more than 2,000 Black people residing in the city, about 90 percent (1,850) were free. Most congregated in Southwark near the wharves and just outside the city limits to the north in the Northern Liberties (a.k.a. Campingtown).

Even before the Christmas Conference, St. George's had granted the now free Richard Allen (1760–1831) a license to preach,[4] and following the conference he settled in Philadelphia as part of the developing free Black constituency in the congregation. Among his early actions was the formation of a prayer band at St. George's in 1786 that included some forty-two Africans. Members included two other African members who would become important to the Philadelphia story—Absalom Jones (1746–1818) and Lunar Brown (d. 1836).

Beginning in 1787, Brown and Jones would work together closely in the organization and development of the Free African Society (FAS), a self-help benevolent organization serving the Black community and a sign of the increasing role of free Blacks in the city. The FAS would become the crucible in which Allen would be forced to make the important decisions about his life among the Methodists, as the organization moved to create a nondenominational Black church. Allen, who saw Methodism as the best place for Africans (and himself), would for a period be expelled from its membership.

Richard Allen, the first bishop of the African Methodist Episcopal Church.

As that process was proceeding, Allen, Jones, and Brown were greatly affected by some seemingly minor changes at St. George's. In the winter of 1791–92, St. George's added galleries to provide additional seating for an expanding membership. In June 1792, racial antagonisms rooted in White opposition to developments in the FAS and now heightened by the anti-Black prejudices held by the current presiding elder for the Philadelphia area, John McClaskey (1756–1814), set the stage for a confrontation between the Black members and some of the lay leadership at St. George's. As a result, many of the Black members left the church and began meeting on their own.[5] Of course, not all of the Black members left. As late as 1794 there are three Black classes at St. George's, two of which met at the church itself and one in the home of a Black class leader, Jonathan Yorks.[6] Of course, while most Whites understood the separation into different congregations that was occurring, the leadership did not draw the same sharp distinctions as they saw but one Methodist church in Philadelphia whose members and classes happen to meet in different locations.

However, the three men who had emerged as the prominent leaders of the Black constituency of St. George's would now go in different directions, each with long-term implications. Absalom Jones would take leadership of the congregation that grew out of the FAS and lead its transformation into St. Thomas Episcopal Church. In 1793, he would be ordained as an Episcopal deacon. Richard Allen would organize the remaining Methodists who lived in Philadelphia proper, especially those in the southern part of the city, as the Bethel Methodist Episcopal Church. He would personally see to the erection of an initial meeting place, and on June 29, 1794, Bishop Asbury would sanctify all that occurred by preaching at the service at which the building was dedicated. In June 1799, Asbury would ordain Allen as a deacon in the Methodist Episcopal Church, the first African American so recognized.

At the time of the dedication of Bethel, there were two classes meeting there. Blades Wildgoose's class, which met on Monday evening, included Richard Allen, Benjamin Clark, William Hogen, Flora Allen, Eli Sans, Sarah Bass (the future Sarah Allen), Jonathan Trusty, Esther Trusty, Daniel Smith, John []en, Ro[]e Ford, Dieleh Johnson, Charles Wansley, Elihu Samons, and Jane Anderson. John Clinton's class included James Gibbs, David Jackson, Peter Petekin, Jupiter White, Hill, Solomon Brittanham, Stephen Miller, Francis Spires, Eliz[th] Claypoole, Saborah Morris, Pricilla Perkins, Cynthia Bell, Esther Freeman, Sabrina Miller, Lucy White, Jane Gebron, and Mary Spires.[7]

Lunar Brown and Zoar

Shortly after the Black members left St. George's, Lunar Brown and those members who resided some blocks north of St. George's and Bethel, just outside the city limits in the Northern Liberties, organized a prayer meeting that met in several members' homes. Brown, who had been married in 1790 at St. George's to Hester Vandergrief, was the head of a large family residing on Brown Street. He had prospered as a carter and a sweep master. When he died around 1836 as a well-to-do property owner, he left a solid estate to his children and grandchildren.[8]

Lunar Brown differed from both Allen and Jones in that he was a layman who, it appears, never had a call to preach. He was not one who stood in front, and his leadership role was largely forgotten even in the Northern Liberties congregation that he helped found and that would eventually take the name Zoar (a reference to the city to which Lot and his wife were heading in the wake of the destruction of Sodom and Gomorrah). He seems to have arranged for the first meeting place of the congregation, an abandoned butcher shop adjacent to his home.

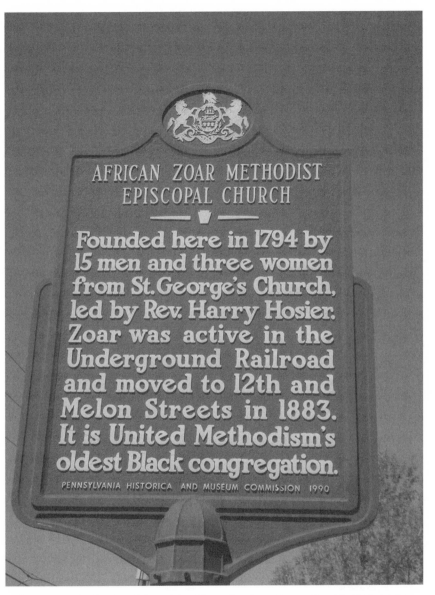

AFRICAN ZOAR METHODIST
EPISCOPAL CHURCH

Founded here in 1794 by
15 men and three women
from St. George's Church,
led by Rev. Harry Hosier.
Zoar was active in the
Underground Railroad
and moved to 12th and
Melon Streets in 1883.
It is United Methodism's
oldest Black congregation.

PENNSYLVANIA HISTORICA AND MUSEUM COMMISSION 1990

This sign marks the site of the original Zoar church on Brown Street in Philadelphia.

After meeting informally for two years, the future members of Zoar formally withdrew in 1794. The building that Brown provided for the congregation was dedicated by Bishop Asbury and John Dickens on August 4, 1796. Asbury recorded the occasion in his journal: "I was called upon by the African society in Campington to open their new house, which I did, on Romans 1:16–18 and had an unwieldy congregation of whites and blacks. Brother Dickens gave a lively exhortation on the new birth." Henry Manley,[9] a member of St. George's, owned the land and would in 1804 sell the small plot to the Zoar congregation. Brown's name is prominent on the deed of conveyance as he was one of the trustees.[10]

Brown originally emerged out of obscurity in 1799 when he joined with other Black leaders in the city (including Jones and Allen) in an effort to stop the slave trade. The effort culminated in a petition, sent to the president and members of the United States Senate and House of Representatives, to halt the African Slave Trade. The innovative petition was symbolically signed right at the end of the old century (December 30) and sent to government leaders so to arrive as an initial consideration for the new century. As we can see, from this and other documents, Brown had not learned to read and write.[11]

The names of the original members (eighteen men and three women) who joined Brown in the founding of Zoar have been lost, and discovering a list of the charter members is a prized goal of current members seeking to reconstruct the story of the early congregation. The earliest record we have of members is from 1800, in which the White ministers assigned to St. George's noted that they had overseen the acceptance on trial of five members.[12] An additional set of sixteen members were accepted later that year, with twenty-five additional members in 1801 and thirteen in 1802.[13] While this is the earliest reference to Zoar's members, those listed were obviously not members in the 1790s. However, there is every reason to believe that Brown, his wife Hester, his sons Lunar, Jr., and Robert, and his daughter, Nancy, were among the original members. It is also likely that the other trustees of 1804—Adam Hall, Elisha Todd, Peter Gray, Cambridge Nixon, James Caldwell, James Daniel, and Daniel Farrow—and their wives were also charter members of the congregation.

As the new century began in Philadelphia, Methodists were organized into five congregations. There were usually two White elders assigned to the city. Also, Philadelphia was, until 1804, the site of the Methodist publishing business, which was headed for most of its years there by John Dickens, a prominent minister. With the presiding elder resident in the city, on most Sundays there were four White elders available for preaching. It was noted in

The present Mother Zoar United Methodist Church continues the original congregation founded in 1794.

1802 that each of the five churches held three preaching services on Sunday, at 10:30 a.m., 3 p.m., and in the evening. In addition each church held services on two evenings each week—Bethel's evening services were on Tuesdays and Thursdays, and Zoar's on Wednesdays and Fridays. The Lord's Supper (at which one of the elders had to be present) was held monthly at each church. Bethel's service was on the second Sunday and Zoar's on the fourth.

In 1796, Ezekiel Cooper (1763–1847) and Richard Allen hammered out a set of "Articles of Association," which were to guide the relationship of Bethel to the larger community of Philadelphia Methodists.[14] While the interpretation of these articles would later be a matter of intense controversy, it is can be assumed that the agreement Allen reached with Cooper operated at least informally for Zoar. Among the key provisions of the Articles was the clear statement of the trust clause noting that Bethel's trustees would hold the congregation's property "in trust for the religious use of Ministers and Preachers of the MEC who are in connexion with the general conference of said [Methodist Episcopal] Church."[15] At issue for Allen at the time was protecting Bethel as a center of African life. All of the trustees were to be

Africans (as would the membership and classes). The trustees were to have charge of the temporal affairs of the church, while all the ecclesiastical affairs at Bethel were to be in accord with the beliefs and practice of the MEC.

The elder in charge of Philadelphia was assigned oversight of Bethel (as he had oversight of all of the White Philadelphia churches) and was to work with the trustees on a matter of intense concern to Bethel's leaders: the discipline of church members. It was the duty of the elder to preside over a sacramental service monthly and see to the appointment of Black preachers, exhorters, and class leaders.[16] He was also to preach once on Sunday and at one of the evening services during the week at Bethel.

The Articles assumed that Bethel would remain within the Methodist Episcopal Church and looked forward to Blacks entering into ministerial orders. As noted in Article XI, "if either of the said colored brethren shall graduate into holy orders, it shall be done in such manner and way as the general conference shall direct." Such graduation appeared to be imminent as Allen was ordained as a deacon just three years later in 1799. But then only in 1809 were two additional Philadelphians ordained: Jacob Tapsico and James Champion.[17] They shared duties at Bethel and Zoar.[18] It appears that in 1804 Harry Hosier retired from traveling (his last assignment being to New Jersey in 1803). He would be available for preaching though his health was failing. He died in 1806, and was buried in the cemetery in Kensington, an area north and east of the Northern Liberties.[19]

In the wake of their formation and the signing of the Articles of Association, both Bethel and Zoar had assumed their normal duties as ME congregations. In 1798, both participated in a revival that swept the city's Methodists. Allen wrote to Ezekiel Copper that the evening meetings were continuing late into the night and that all five churches were crowded. Both Blacks and Whites were experiencing the revival and claiming conversion. He singled out Henry Manley (who sold the property to the Zoar trustees) for his labors during the revival.[20] Thus the first decade of the new arrangement seemed to have been to everyone's benefit.

In the last years of the century, William Colbert was a frequent visitor in Philadelphia and regularly stayed in Allen's home. On February 17, 1797, for example, he noted, "Dined with my good black friend—Richard Allen's wife. I believe that if there is a Christian in Philadelphia this black woman is one." Three years later, on January 19, 1800, he was in the city, where he again "went to Richard Allens and at night preached at Bethel on Heb. 4:7. Bro. Allen gave an exhortation. Here they appear to be lively. We lodged at Allens." Bethel's years as an MEC congregation, however, were fraught with problems, many traced to the itinerant system, which brought new White

An artist's rendition of the original Bethel AME Church.

preachers to Philadelphia every year. Some of these preachers were strongly opposed to the independence allowed Bethel (beyond the provisions of the Articles of Association) and periodically asserted by Allen. Some were simply tactless. Thus, while Allen had the friendship and respect of many of the White Methodist leaders, including Asbury, like Colbert a regular guest in Allen's home, sporadically the traveling ministers assigned to Philadelphia caused problems at the very time a sense of comradeship was developing among the leaders of the several all-Black congregations that had appeared in Baltimore, Wilmington, and New York.

Bethel started small, with 32 people, but membership grew rapidly, bolstered by the 1798 revival, and by the end of the century surpassed the 200 mark. Early in the new century Bethel surpassed St. Thomas and by 1804 counted 457 members. The next year was a real time of celebration for the Bethel congregation as a new brick building went up to replace the former wooden one. Over the next years, membership rose steadily, reaching 1,272 in 1813.

The new building appears to have been the real cause for setting off James Smith,[21] a conservative Virginian and the White minister who (along with Colbert) was assigned to Philadelphia in 1805, though the controversy bedeviling Bethel was actually occasioned by Bethel's expulsion of a female member. In several steps, a territorial war of words ensued. Colbert noted several meetings through the conference year with Bethel's trustees, which by the spring of 1806 had become frustrating. On April 8, he "spent almost half the night at Richard Allen's with trustees of Bethel Church, laboring, if possible, to get them more united with the trustees of St. George's who they think have not been friendly disposed toward." The following evening he was back at it and was "kept up half the night with the trustees of St. George's."

Colbert was moved at the 1806 conference, but Smith stayed on in the city for another year. His issues with Allen culminated in his demanding that Allen turn over Bethel's keys and record books. He forbade Allen to hold any meetings without his concurrence; Allen, asserting the congregation's ownership of the church and property, refused to comply. The harsh words continued until Smith moved on the next year.

Smith, of course, simply asserted the Methodist conference's own understanding of church ownership in a connectional system—a system that included Bethel. Allen seems to have not fully understood Smith's claims and eventually sought out a lawyer, who explained to him that the wording of the trust clause in the Articles of Association verified Smith's position. With Allen reeling from the setback, the lawyer also pointed out what might be a useful fallback position. Article XIII of the 1796 agreement provided a means of amending the Articles by vote of two-thirds of Bethel's male members. Allen subsequently drew up a new set of amended articles, popularly termed the "African Supplement," and quietly submitted them to the courts. The Supreme Court of the Commonwealth of Pennsylvania approved them on March 16, 1807. The Amended Articles did not deal directly with the property dispute (and Smith was by this time in the last days of his Philadelphia appointment). The New Articles did, however, assert Bethel's position relative to the current issue (the disfellowshipping of a wayward member) and redefined the relationship of Bethel relative to the White ministers. The key sentences provided for a Black preacher to take charge of the love feast or quarterly conference should the minister in charge in Philadelphia not attend to his agreed upon duties.[22]

Relieved that no schism had occurred and that Bethel wished to remain under the Methodist Episcopal Church's rules, Asbury chose not to respond to Bethel's latest assertion of its independence. Periodically over the next several years, the White ministers would argue with Allen about the African Supplement, none more vehemently than Stephen G. Roszel (1770–1841), who was stationed there in 1811. Allen's strong asset was the growing Bethel congregation, which surpassed in size not only St. Thomas but St. George's as well. Asbury, in the city for the annual conference in May, called for union in his several sermons, but relative to the local problems merely recorded, "I shall throw all the troubles of the times, the Church, and the conference, into shades; nor will I record these tales of woe."[23]

As of the beginning of 1814, Allen does not appear to have decided to break with the Methodist Episcopal Church, though the events in Wilmington must have been on his mind, including the lawsuit over the Wilmington church's property and the formation of additional congregations affiliated with the African Union Church, but the process in which he would now become entwined would lead him to take Bethel on an independent course.[24]

First, a disciplinary case that had been heard against a prominent member, Robert Green, led to his being disfellowshipped. Green, a former trustee, was among the signers of both the 1796 Articles and the later African Articles. Green had appealed his fate both to the White elder in charge and then to the courts. His court case was heard on July 30, 1814. In January 1815, the court issued its ruling in Green's favor, citing a technical defect in the manner of his expulsion. Second, just weeks before the court's ruling, on July 7, 1814, John Emory (1789–1835), a young White minister and a rising force in the church, issued a public statement labeling the Bethel members as un-Methodist due to their continuing to operate under the African Supplement. Emory's statement grew out of Bethel's withholding funds Emory believed it should be contributing to the common budget for the Philadelphia churches from which the ministers' salaries were paid. Bethel raised two issues—the amount the economically poorer Black members should be expected to pay and the recent neglect by the White ministers of their duties at Bethel. As the rhetoric intensified, Emory suggested disciplinary action against Allen, while Allen questioned Emory's ability to point to any clause of the *Discipline* he might have violated.

In the spring of 1815, Emory's colleague that year on the Philadelphia charge, Robert R. Roberts (1778–1843), stepped into the fray and announced his intention of preaching at Bethel. This announcement startled many as it followed several years during which the White elders had discontinued attending Bethel for services. Jacob Tapsico was in the pulpit when Roberts walked into the church. He refused to concede the pulpit to Roberts, and the members blocked Roberts' access to the front of the sanctuary. Roberts finally gave up and left.

A number of things could possibly have salvaged the situation, including Bishop Asbury's intervention and mediation, but then on June 12, 1815, as a consequence of the court's ruling in the Green case, the sheriff stepped in and held a public auction of Bethel's property. Allen was forced to use a considerable sum of his own money to repurchase Bethel. There is every reason to believe that this incident occasioned the beginning of his decision to break with the MEC, though there would be one more incident of note. In December 1815, the new elder in charge of Philadelphia, Robert Burch (d. 1854), would again try to preach at Bethel. He used the court-reinstated Robert Green as his host. Again the members blocked access to the pulpit. Burch appealed to the courts, but they refused to back him. Allen's repurchase of Bethel's property, and the court ruling upholding the African Supplement, appear to have provided Allen with the legal go-ahead to declare the congregation's ownership of Bethel's property quite apart from any claim now made by representatives of the Methodist Episcopal Church. Thus, the congregation could assert its independence and keep its land and building.

Most certainly, in the months following the auction Allen began thinking seriously of ending the on-going conflict with the White Methodists. What we do know is that it was early in 1816 when he issued the letters of invitation to the Black Methodist leaders outside of Philadelphia about coming to Philadelphia in April 1816 to consider their situation.[25]

Zoar's Early Decades

While Allen was battling the White ministers, Zoar's life was far from entirely peaceful. For reasons lost to history, an internal dispute broke out at

The present Mother Bethel AME Church continues the original congregation founded in 1792.

Zoar in 1809, which caused eighteen of its members to leave and found a new church, the Union Methodist Episcopal Church, which found facilities just a few blocks away from Zoar.

Then, on November 13, 1813, a Black man in the Northern Liberties shot a White man, an action that allowed racial prejudices, never too deeply submerged, to surface. The Zoar Church, a high-profile Black institution, proved a ready target for White anger and in an ensuing riot was severely damaged, in fact, almost totally destroyed. In this case, the leadership at St. George's came to the support of the African members and backed efforts to prosecute the rioters. Zoar's situation would become a matter of on-going concern, and in January 1814, St. George's appointed an attorney to represent Zoar. It appears he was able to work out a financial deal by which the rioters made some recompense to the congregation. This issue would not, however, go away. Thus we find that the authorities in the Northern Liberties had to pass a resolution in 1822 sanctioning anyone who disturbed the life of any worshipping community in the township.

As the situation with the riot was being adjudicated, attention would be directed elsewhere. The country was at war, and things were not going very well. On August 24–25, 1814, Washington, D.C., was captured and burned. The British then marched on Baltimore. In response, Philadelphia's most prominent Black leader, Episcopal businessman James Forten (1766–1842), issued a call for volunteers from among the African residents to defend the city against a possible future British invasion.[26] Some 2,500 men, most certainly including members of Zoar and Bethel, responded and worked to fortify Philadelphia against an invasion and a fate similar to Washington, D.C.[27] In the end, the war did not reach Philadelphia and the events in the city were only briefly disturbed.

Toward an African Church

The conflict at Bethel culminated in April 1816 when the leaders of several separate Black congregations met at Bethel and proceeded to organize the African Methodist Episcopal Church. The Zion congregation in New York, which had been invited to this meeting, did not attend. Peter Spencer and members of the breakaway church in Wilmington attended but decided not to align with Allen. Among those churches that did align with his new effort was the Bethel church in Baltimore led by Daniel Coker and the Union Church that had broken away from Zoar. Jeffrey Beulah,[28] who led the organization of Union, went on to become a prominent leader in the AME Church, and Michael Parker, another of its original members, became an AME minister. But Zoar, like Spencer's African Union Church, chose not to align with Allen. Also aligning with the new denomination was the church at Attleborough, Pennsylvania, a short distance from the city, and a group from the Mt. Hope Church in Salem, New Jersey, some thirty miles down the Delaware River from Philadelphia.[29] This meeting would prove to be a significant watershed not only in Black Methodist history but for the African American community as a whole.

The formation of the AME Church, and the host of issues it brought to the Philadelphia free Black community, often obscures the fact that just as it was solidifying its organization, the whole Black community was hit with possibly the major issue of the decade, the organization of the American Colonization Society (ACS).

Philadelphia stands in contrast with Baltimore, where support for the ACS was vigorously debated, with both MEC and AME leaders prominent on both sides. Home to the most prosperous free Black community in America, Philadelphia never seriously considered supporting the ACS. Here, colonization was denounced though some entertained the notion of an alternative plan, which came to be called "emigration." In 1815, Blacks in Philadelphia under the leadership of James Forten had offered their full support to Paul Cuffe and his plans to "colonize" Africa. Forten's support included his having an account of Cuffe's first voyage read to the congregation at Bethel.[30] There is little doubt that Cuffe's successful voyage partially inspired the creation of the ACS. In 1817, however, the African community in Philadelphia, again with Forten taking the lead, immediately spoke in unison against the ACS' schemes.[31] In January 1817, just one month after the Colonization Society announced its plans, Richard Allen backed Forten in the organization of an anti-colonization rally that brought together some three thousand Philadelphians. At that rally, held at Bethel, Allen took the lead in drafting a letter protesting the idea of colonization, which the signers viewed as merely an attempt to strengthen slavery, hiding under the illusion of ameliorating the burdens on African Americans in general. There is little reason to doubt that members from Zoar were present alongside those from the Bethel and Union Churches at the massive 1817 rally against the ACS.[32]

Allen, who stood with Forten in denouncing the ACS, would within a few years emerge as the major advocate of the emigration plan. Allen emphasized community opposition to any "colonization" scheme advocated by Whites motivated simply by the goal of pushing Black people out of America while at the same time suggesting that if some members of the Black community wished to leave the country in order to uplift themselves, the Black community would support them. Such an opportunity appeared in 1824 when the president of Haiti (where slaves had recently revolted and taken control of the government) invited American Blacks to come help build a free country in the Caribbean. Following meetings at Bethel on June 29 and July 4, Allen organized the Haitian Emigration Society. The first group of fifty-eight people sailed for Haiti on August 23. Allen's son John accompanied the group and delivered a letter from his father to the Haitian president that noted, "My heart burns affectionately in acknowledging the kind offers you have made to these poor oppressed people here in the United States, by offering them an asylum where they can enjoy liberty and equality." Again in 1830, Allen chaired the first national convention of Black people called to consider plans for emigration to Canada.[33]

The struggle with colonization would not be the only obstacle confronting Allen as he attempted to build the AME Church. In 1819, about a dozen members of Bethel left and formed an independent African Methodist church that they called the Wesleyan Society. They obtained property just ninety feet from Bethel and erected a building. Then they contacted Abraham Thompson, a preacher in the newly independent Zion Church in New York City, and made an initial inquiry about joining together. Early in December, Thompson and William Miller arrived in Philadelphia to explore further the new Philadelphia congregation's desire to unite with the Zionists. The Wesleyan Society also threw its support behind the Zion Church's plan to approach the MEC's Philadelphia Conference about developing a semi-autonomous African Conference under the sponsorship of the MEC but with its own elders and, eventually, bishops.[34]

When some of the White Methodists balked at the proposal, the Wesleyan Society was the most vocal congregation in the emerging denomination for pushing ahead with the formation of an independent denomination, later to be known as the African Methodist Episcopal Zion Church. At the forming conference in 1821, the Philadelphia congregation would report three hundred members under the leadership of five preachers: Simon Murray, Edward Johnson, Durham Stephens, Daniel Pernal, and Arthur Landford. Simon Murray was quickly moved up from deacon to elder and placed in charge of the church. In 1822, when the episcopal orders for the AMEZ Church were set in place, Edward Johnson was ordained as a deacon and elder and placed in charge of the congregation.

Work would grow in the Philadelphia area, so that in 1829 the AMEZ Church could form a Philadelphia Conference, the first session of which was held at the Wesleyan Church. The Wesleyan Church would remain one of the important AMEZ churches throughout the remainder of the antebellum era.

Through the 1830s, Union AME Church, situated in the Northern Liberties, operated with the same pastoral appointments as Bethel; however, its membership (approximately two hundred) being but one-tenth of Bethel's, the ministers in Philadelphia tended to neglect it. On several occasions, Union petitioned the Philadelphia Conference for recognition as a separate congregation with a minister assigned specifically as its pastor. That was finally done in 1843, but Union lacked a separate board of trustees and the Bethel trustees refused to allow the conference's action to take place.[35] This confrontation would herald a major controversy about to overtake the AME Church. The church needed to revise its regulations that assigned extra authority to local boards of trustees, regulations that harkened back to the experience of Bethel's struggle with the MEC conference.

A New Direction for Zoar

With the establishment of the AME and AMEZ Churches, Zoar's decision to remain in connection with the MEC now set its path for the next half century. Whereas the struggle in which Allen engaged was built around gaining *autonomy* for himself and the African membership, Zoar's leadership would join with the other Black ME congregations in a struggle to gain *equality*. This struggle would focus in two main arenas: the gaining of equal rights and responsibilities for Black congregations relative to predominantly White congregations, the issue of controlling the congregation's money being a prominent measure of success; and the obtaining of equal status alongside their White colleagues for Black ministers, the issue of ordination and conference membership being the primary gauge. These goals aimed at realizing the vision of the interracial community inherent in the Methodist Church's original self-understanding.

For Zoar, the first step in this new direction was taken in 1822 when the church petitioned the Philadelphia Conference for the privilege of handling its own temporal business by retaining the offerings at Zoar, rather than throwing them into the common pot for all the Philadelphia congregations. Now independent financially, in 1826 the church founded two self-help societies, the Beneficial Philanthropic Sons of Zoar and the Female Beneficial Philanthropic Society of Zoar, organizations not unlike the African Free Society of a generation earlier. The church continued to grow, and in 1829 expanded its facilities onto the property immediately adjacent to its original land.

In 1832, reflecting what was also occurring in Baltimore, a plan of separation, the "Covenant of Assumption," was instituted that would over the next three years establish Zoar as a completely separate charge in the Philadelphia Conference, hence organizationally independent of St. George's. This would create a problem of leadership, as the elder in Philadelphia would no longer be in charge of Zoar, nor would he be available for the sacraments. However, like the Baltimore Conference, the Philadelphia Conference had made provision for the ordination of Black preachers (without offering them the parallel membership in the conference with the White traveling ministers). The first pastor, Perry Tilghman,[36] a Black lay preacher, was appointed to Zoar by the conference. He would remain at Zoar for almost a decade and serve a congregation of more than four hundred members. In the meantime several other Black congregations in Pennsylvania, New Jersey, and Delaware were reorganized similarly.[37] Once the Covenant of Assumption had been fully implemented, in 1837 Zoar adopted a constitution and applied for and received a charter from the Commonwealth of Pennsylvania.[38] The constitution spelled out a relationship with the Methodist Episcopal Church relative to the appointment of the pastor and the holding of property (that now included a cemetery) in trust. It placed the concerns of the congregation in the hands of the adult male membership.[39]

During Tilghman's pastorate, in 1838, in an attempt to expand its facilities, the church appealed to the public for financial support. This occurred just one year after the formation of John Wesley Chapel,[40] a new Black congregation in southern Philadelphia (in direct competition to Bethel), which drew some African American members that resided in south Philadelphia and that had not joined Bethel or the Wesleyan church away from Zoar.[41] Public response to the solicitation was quite poor, and expansion plans had to be abandoned for the moment.

In spite of the financial limitations, Zoar proved itself socially active on behalf of the Black community, nowhere more visibly demonstrated than in its hosting a 1838 meeting to raise funds for the Vigilant Association and Committee. This is its first recorded connection with what was emerging as the Underground Railroad, the committee's unspoken job being to aid and assist slaves fleeing north.

Through the 1830s, Zoar had accomplished the first of several steps needed to gain some equality within the Methodist Episcopal Church. It had become an autonomous unit relative to local church finances and it existed as a separate charge within the Philadelphia Conference with its own pastor. In the next decades it would actively pursue the additional goals of conference membership and ordination for its pastor.

Zion Methodism in New York City

In the oft-told story, Philip Embry, a carpenter and Irish Methodist local preacher, emigrated to New York in 1760. For the next six years he lived a pious life but did no preaching. Then toward the middle of the decade, the Heck family joined a group of Methodists from Ireland that settled in New York. A crisis was reached one evening when Barbara Heck found some of the Methodists' playing cards and threw them into the fire. She then turned to Embry and demanded that he begin preaching to them. An initial class, including Heck's African servant Betty, was organized.

From the original six, the number of attendees at Embry's preaching grew slowly but steadily. In 1767 the group moved into a rigging loft on Horse and Cart Street (now William Street). Here they were joined by Captain Thomas Webb (1724–1796), a British officer and enthusiastic Methodist lay preacher, and Peter Williams, Sr., (175?-1823), later the church's sexton, at the time a slave. The following year, the congregation having outgrown their facilities, plans were initiated to erect a chapel on land obtained on John Street.[42] Subscriptions were taken to underwrite the cost. Among the subscribers were Rachel and Margaret, two young African girls who had been hired to take care of the house reserved for the use of the preacher (their names appearing elsewhere showing the salary paid for their services).[43] The members, both Black and White, joined together in erecting Wesley Chapel, a stone building measuring sixty by forty-two feet. A short time after its dedication on October 30, 1768, they added a gallery, reached via a ladder, which would be reserved for the Black members and the young unmarried White males. The chapel was furnished plainly with no backs to the benches. Later, stairs facilitated movement to and from the gallery.

Richard Boardman, the first of the preachers sent by Wesley to assist the emerging Methodist community, wrote Wesley soon after his arrival and noted the way people were packed in for preaching services. "Our house contains about seventeen hundred hearers. . . . About a third of those who attend the preaching get in, the rest are glad to hear without. There appears such a willingness in the Americans to hear the Word as I never saw before." He went on to note the new phenomenon he encountered, the presence of Africans in the service: "The number of blacks that attend the preaching affects me much. One of them came to tell me she could neither eat nor sleep, because her master would not suffer her to come to hear the word. She wept exceedingly, saying, 'I told my master I would do more work than ever I used to do if he would but let me come; nay, that I would do everything in my power to be a good servant.'"[44]

Joseph Pilmore added his reflections the next year. "Our congregations are large and we have the pious of most congregations to hear us, which makes the Presbyterian bigots mad." He also noted, "We have a number of black women who meet together every week; many of whom are happy in the love of God. This evinces the truth that 'God is no respecter of persons but in every nation he that feareth God and worketh righteousness is accepted of Him.' The society here consists of about a hundred members besides probationers; and I trust it will soon increase much more abundantly."[45]

One notes that hundreds, many being members of other churches, showed up to listen to the British preachers; however, only the actual members could participate in the more intimate love feasts, at which attendees testified to the work of God in their souls. Pilmore reflected on one such event in 1771: "In the Evening we had our Quarterly Love Feast, which was a special season of love to the believers in general. They spoke freely of the goodness of god, while a profound awe and divine reverence seemed to sit upon every countenance. One of the poor negroes declared her heart was so full of divine love that she could not express it, and many more of them were exceedingly glad in their minds. If the people who keep them in a state of slavery would take pains to have them instructed in the Religion of Jesus, it would be some compensation for the loss of their liberty; but this, alas! is too much neglected/ Yet there are a goodly number of Masters in America who are glad to do all in their power for them."[46] Thomas Rankin had a similar experience several years later: "Many declared with great freedom of speech, what God had done for their souls. Some of the poor black people spoke with power and pungency of the loving-kindness of the Lord. If the rich of this society were as much devoted to God as the poor are, we should see wonders done in this city."[47]

New York, commonly the northernmost stop for the preachers traveling in the territory between it and Baltimore, proved a favorite stopping place, as the John Street Church maintained what were possibly the best facilities to house them while they were in town. The preacher's house, as it was known, was kept clean and ready to receive the preachers by several African women, originally by the two young women, Margaret and Rachel, but after 1778 by Molly Williams (d. 1821), the wife of Peter Williams (d. 1823), the sexton. The Williams worked for the church for many years and their names frequently appear in records concerning the African members.[48] The church hired Peter Williams as sexton in 1778, and he continued in his post for the rest of his life, even after developing a successful tobacco business. Because of his position, he became one of the best-documented Methodists, Black or White, of the period.

There is a certain hiatus of information on American Methodism in general during the period of the Revolutionary War. The Methodist leadership had a reputation of being pro-British (Wesley was a Tory), and the small church assumed a low profile during the years of the war. At the close of the war, a number of the Black members who had assisted the British forces joined the Loyalist exodus and migrated to Nova Scotia where the British, who had not expected to lose the war, had hastily commandeered land upon which they could settle.[49]

Those who remained in New York in the years after the war, however, were ready to complete the transformation of Methodism from a revitalization movement into a new evangelistic denomination. As the new Methodist Episcopal Church began keeping records of Black members separately from those of Whites, in the first annual report John Street reported 178 White members and 25 Black members. Over the next generation, additional congregations were established in New York, but as in Baltimore and Philadelphia, leadership would see the city as but one charge with various meeting places; thus only the total membership for the city would be reported. The first of the new churches, the one on Second Street (later Forsyth Street), opened in 1789. Also the New York minister assumed the care of the small group of Methodists in Brooklyn, across the East River.

The Black membership grew steadily during the first decade of the MEC, from 25 to 151 as reported in 1895 (a 500 percent growth).[50] Two Black female classes emerged quite early, and by 1795 the Black members had divided themselves into eight classes, of which two were male and six female, the early majority of females among the Black membership having continued. Class number 31, led by Cornelius Warner, is the most memorable of these classes, in that James Varick (c. 1750–1827), Abraham Thompson (d. 1827),[51] William Miller (1775–1845), and others later to become the founders of the African Methodist Episcopal Zion Church were members. The other Black male class was number 28, in which Peter Williams was a member. On his visit that year, Asbury met with all the classes and took time to speak to almost every member individually.

In 1796, when Asbury made his regular visit to New York, he was petitioned by some the Black leadership (primarily the members in class 31) for his sanction to hold meetings on Sunday afternoon at a site in the section of town where most Black people resided. Having obtained his approval of the idea, in October they rented a house on Cross Street around the corner from James Varick's residence (4 Orange Street). William Miller, a cabinet maker, also had his home and shop nearby at 36 Mulberry Street. The renting of the Cross Street house appears to have been motivated both by a desire to evangelize in the Black community and to create an opportunity for the emergence of leadership among the Black members. As was common among Methodists at this time, Sunday was largely spent in religious exercises, and the Black members attended John Street in the morning and evening and held services on Sunday afternoon at Cross Street.

The Cross Street meeting place was a former stable being used by William Miller as a cabinet-maker's shop, but once refurbished it provided ample space at which members could listen to the Black local preachers and exhorters. With several skilled artisans among them, the members quickly fitted the new meeting hall with seats, a pulpit, and a gallery. Besides the Sunday afternoon gathering, on Wednesday evening they conducted preaching and exhorting meetings led by a local licensed preacher and exhorter. At this time there were three licensed preachers—Abraham Thompson, June Scott, and Thomas Miller—and one exhorter, William Miller. On occasion, a visiting preacher (such as Harry Hosier) would arrive from out of town.

Cross Street served admirably for some five years and met with the approval of both Black and White members. Then, by the end of the year, the growth of membership put considerable pressure on the facilities at John Street. Thus it came about, without the necessity of any particular incident or complaint about the treatment of the African members, that a proposal to build a third New York church, for the African members, was produced and received a consensus approval. And to this end, the Africans met together with some of the Black religious leaders in New York on the best manner to proceed.

By the time the winter weather broke in the spring of 1800, the African members were advertising for support to erect their new church building. On March 21 they received the backing of at least one of the New York newspapers for their effort.[52] When the Methodist General Conference met in Baltimore in May, it received the petition from the Black members concerning the process in which they were involved. Jesse Lee, Ezekiel Cooper, and Philip Bruce (1755–1826) drafted a response on behalf of the conference. They advised the African Brethren in New York to follow the pattern previously followed by Richard Allen for Bethel Church in Philadelphia, or its equivalent under New York Laws, using the name African Methodist Episcopal Church.[53]

The group moved quickly, and a few weeks later, the local newspaper reported, "On Wednesday next at 4 o'clock in the afternoon, the Corner Stone of the Church of the African Society, at the corner of Leonard and Church Streets, will be laid, and a Sermon preached on the ground, suited to the occasion."[54] In the meantime, the Black members had appointed trustees with Francis Jacobs as Chairman; Thomas Miller, Treasurer; and George Collins, Secretary. The trustees purchased the land, two plots at the corner of Church and Leonard Streets. By the end of October of 1800, a framed building thirty-five by forty-five feet had been erected. John McClaskey, one of the elders stationed at New York by the MEC, assisted the Black members in drawing up the instrument of incorporation for the new church, to be named Zion.

On March 9, 1801, the Articles of Incorporation of what was called the "African Methodist Episcopal Church of New York" were filed. Peter Williams assumed a leading role in completing the incorporation process. The Charter was recorded in February 1801, and the Articles of Incorporation the next month. The substance of the text follows the Articles drawn up earlier for Bethel Church in Philadelphia.[55]

Around the same time, the members also negotiated with McClaskey regarding his duties at Zion. It was agreed that a White elder (one of those then appointed to New York) would preach at Zion Church on Sunday afternoons and on Wednesday nights each week. The exception would be the monthly service at the Lord's Supper, which was to be administered in the morning service on the second Sunday of each month, for which the elder would be present. At this point in time, there were 131 Black members in New York, and Zion was one of five Methodist churches for which the elders were responsible. By the end of the decade, Zion reported 490 members.

The Tumultuous Decade

The first decade of the new century proved to be one of relative unity and spectacular growth; however, the second decade would be marked by a series of disturbances that would profoundly alter the shape and structure of New York Black Methodism. The initial trouble began with John Edwards, a former Quaker, who oversaw the construction of a building in which he hoped to house an independent Black congregation. The building included living space for a resident preacher, and he offered the job to Abraham Thompson. Thompson jumped at the opportunity, and then persuaded June Scott to assist him in founding the Union Society. As the pair tried to lure Zion's members away, Zion's leaders countered by excommunicating anyone who participated in the schismatic venture. Just before being excommunicated, Thompson repented of what he had begun and returned to Zion. Scott, left alone but now in charge, persisted in the Union Society, though in the end he was unable to make a go of it.

Then in 1813, while the Union Church was still struggling along, a former Zion trustee who had been expelled from the church, Thomas Sipkins, conspired with William Miller about forming a second Black Methodist church in the city. He had discovered an abandoned church building on Elizabeth Street, and the two obtained possession of it. They also persuaded some of Zion's members to help form the new Asbury congregation. Unlike the Union Church, Asbury proved more substantial, Miller being a man of some ability. It prospered beside Zion and once established, it applied for and was received into the Methodist Episcopal Church.

The formation and development of the Zion and Asbury Churches oc-curred within a significantly changing environment. Beginning at the end of the eighteenth century, legal changes were transforming the whole of the Black community. An initial law, passed in 1799, mandated the freeing of all those henceforth born in slavery—women when they reached the age of twenty-five and men at the age of twenty-eight. Then in 1808 the legislature passed several laws that were designed to prevent the return of people once freed to a state of slavery and forbade the further importation of slaves into the state. Finally, in 1817 New Yorkers agreed that all Black people would be-come free no later than July 4, 1827. The number of slaves dropped measur-ably after the 1817 law was passed, and by 1820, the Black Methodist com-munity in New York included very few members who were slaves.

As in other cities the colonization issue arose in New York, though as in Philadelphia, almost no New Yorkers supported the White-led effort to de-port African Americans back to Africa. As early as 1812, as the American-British relationship was declining into war, Paul Cuffe had toured the coun-try on behalf of his immigration schemes and in New York recruited Peter Williams and William Hamilton to the cause. In 1814 Williams would take the lead in forming a society to communicate with the like organization in Philadelphia, as well as the Sierra Leone Friendly Society and the African In-stitution, the two British groups working to establish a beachhead of African Americans on the West African coast. The British hoped that Christianity could spread from Sierra Leone across the continent. Williams would emerge as the secretary of the New York African Institution that worked with Cuffe through the rest of the decade. By 1820, the distinction between immigra-tion and colonization had been blurred for many New Yorkers, and it is not surprising that the initial ship of colonists for Sierra Leone that carried, among others, Baltimore minister Daniel Coker sailed from New York City.[56] Later in the 1820s, while Williams opposed Allen's establishing an AME congregation in New York, he would support Allen's scheme to set up a colony in Haiti. In this regard, in 1824, he himself took a fact-finding tour of the Caribbean island.[57]

In 1827, Williams and Varick lent their name to the support of the new E. F. Hughes School for Coloured Children recently opened in the city.[58] No-tice of the school would appear in another accomplishment to which Williams (and William Hamilton) contributed. The pair worked with Pres-byterian minister Samuel Cornish in the founding of *Freedom's Journal*, the first newspaper founded by African Americans as an instrument of promot-ing and defending the community. Cornish would be succeeded by John B. Russworm, one of the first African Americans with a college degree. Almost

every issue carried news of happenings at the Zion Church, not the least being the celebration of the ending of slavery in New York state on July 4,
1827, at which William Hamilton delivered the main address. The *Journal*
was originally opposed to colonization, but in 1829, just two years from its
founding, Russworm, now editor of the unstable periodical, announced his
conversion to the idea of colonization. His support for colonization would
doom the newspaper.

Brooklyn's Parallel Emergence

Very soon after the organization of Methodism in New York City, it began to
spread across the river to Long Island. As early as April 11, 1768, Thomas
Taylor, a member of the John Street Church, wrote a letter to John Wesley
in which he spoke of the activity of Thomas Webb, who had begun preaching near his home in Jamaica on Long Island in the fall of 1767. Taylor noted
that during this time, "about twenty four persons received justifying grace,
nearly half of them whites, the rest negroes."[59]

By 1790, Brooklyn had become a regular stop on the Long Island Circuit.
The Brooklyn Church was formally organized in 1794, and members erected
and dedicated the church building on Sands Street before the year was out.
In 1795, Asbury visited and found twelve Black members in Brooklyn and
thirty-one on the Long Island circuit.[60]

The register of members at Sands Street for 1798 lists the following "col-
ored" members: Abraham Anthony, Susannah Anthony, Peter Anthony,
William Thompson, Hannah Thompson, Thos. Hartley, Harvey Anderson,
Thomas Bristol, Caty Jackson, Dinah Benson, Susannah Thomas, Adam
Francis, Bethany Stewart, Mary Dolph, Frances, John Grace, Isaac Minix,
Thomas Peterson, Philip Leonard, Cornelius Anderson, Caty Anderson, Ti-
tus, Nancy, Sarah, John Graw, Nelly.[61]

Brooklyn Church was largely unaffected by the troubles in New York in
1813, but would begin to feel its own tensions as the Black membership
expanded over the following five years. During this time the African population in Brooklyn was growing and a steady increase was shown at Sands
Street, so much so that the Whites became concerned. To stem the
growth, church officials began to charge the African members a kind of
tax, ten dollars per quarter, to continue their affiliation. The members
bore the offense, but when in 1818 the new pastor, who had a reputation
for being supportive of slavery, published a pamphlet, *Slavery Defended
from Scripture*, the Black members revolted. As a body they withdrew and
began to hold private services in their homes. Having heard of the formation of the AME Church, they sent representatives to Philadelphia in

search of a minister and another Methodist community with whom to affiliate.

They formed a board of trustees and incorporated according to the laws of New York State as the First African Wesleyan Methodist Episcopal Church (AWME). They imposed a tax upon themselves equal to fifty cents a month per member. With that income, they purchased land on High Street, where they proceeded to construct a church building.[62] There were approximately one hundred members, the majority women, who met in four classes, two male and two female.

Leading in the formation of the AWME were Benjamin Croger and his brother Peter, two licensed exhorters who had joined the MEC around 1808. The group voted unanimously to leave the MEC on July 30, 1820. On August 10, the church leaders met with Henry Harden, the minister in charge of the AME work in New York City, and became formally incorporated into the African Methodist Episcopal Church. The Crogers were later ordained as AME ministers. It would be some years later before an MEC presence in Brooklyn would reemerge.[63]

Schism in New York City

The next problem for Zion centered on William Lambert, a lay member of Asbury Church. Lambert had expressed his desire to preach, but the leadership at both Zion and Asbury had discouraged him. Frustrated, he moved to Philadelphia and applied to Bishop Allen for some recognition. Allen licensed him to preach, and then sent him back to New York to organize an AME Church in the city. Lambert rented a schoolhouse on Mott Street as a base upon which to build a new Methodist congregation. George White, a deacon at Zion, found his way to Mott Street and offered to assist Lambert. Henry Harden, an AME elder from Baltimore, soon arrived to supplement their fledgling efforts. At that time, Zion Church was undergoing an extensive rebuilding as the congregation had grown too large for the older facilities, and the church leadership had had difficulty securing adequate worship facilities while the renovation was proceeding. The leadership at Zion and Asbury became quite upset that Allen had sent people to New York at that particular moment, a fact that led to some bad feeling between the two groups. In July 1820, Allen himself arrived in New York to dedicate the new church.[64]

If their problems with Allen were not sufficient, a week prior to Allen's visit, on July 16 William M. Stilwell (d. 1851), the White MEC minister assigned general oversight of the Zion and Asbury Churches, informed their leadership that he and several hundred of the White members had withdrawn from the Methodist Episcopal Church. He charged the MEC's General Conference with attempting to assert more centralized control over the local churches in financial and property matters. Stillwell's announcement alarmed the Black members, who, while they felt that they had no particular issue with their White brothers and sisters at the moment, saw the possibility of future conflict that could threaten their ownership of their church property. The began to discuss the possibility of distancing themselves from the MEC, its bishops, and the conferences.

Events now began to move swiftly. A few days later, Zion and Asbury were informed by church leaders that Stillwell had withdrawn from the MEC, and thus had no continuing responsibility over the two Black churches. When asked what they intended to do, the Zion and Asbury leaders acknowledged their awareness of the situation and informed all that they intended to give it serious consideration. Over the next weeks they consulted with a variety of people and investigated the actions of the recent General Conference that had so upset Stillwell. Deliberation continued through the rest of the month and resulted in a consensus within the membership. They decided to continue in relationship with Stillwell, and they questioned the propriety of the General Conference's action, which they saw as a power and property grab. The move, at least temporarily, separated them from the MEC. As they were finding their way, and while the issues were still resolvable, some members began to favor an alignment with Bishop Allen and the AMEs.

Wishing to block the loss of members to the AMEs, the leadership now entered into negotiations with the MEC leaders. The group also opened conversation with the local Episcopal bishop. In the end, they decided that Zion and Asbury would, for the moment, go it alone and in effect form a new denomination. This decision immediately presented them with an obstacle in that while the church had several deacons it had no elders. They saw the presence of elders as necessary if they were to be properly constituted. As a first step over the barrier they had encountered, the members selected James Varick and Abraham Thompson to seek ordination as elders. Also, they accepted Stillwell's analysis of the situation, and considered Varick and Thompson already empowered to act as elders until such time they could receive a proper ordination.

These actions carried them through the winter of 1820–21. Meanwhile, during these months, a group in Philadelphia withdrew from the AME church and aligned with the Zion and Asbury church.

In March 1821, the New York leaders approached the New York and Philadelphia MEC Conferences with a very serious proposal. They clearly laid out their situation, concerns, and hopes, and did not forget to mention some long-standing grievances, especially about the non-ordination of African American ministers. Along the way they pointed out their lack of any desire to join the AMEs. They then proposed the establishment of a semi-autonomous African conference that would work within the Black community but under the guidance and auspices of the MEC. They also explained their need to elect elders, as they wanted to keep the sacraments regularly in the life of the members. To that end, they planned to hold a conference on June 14, 1821.

The Philadelphia Conference, meeting in March, responded quite favorably and passed a lengthy resolution that suggested one of the bishops attend the June 14 meeting, oversee the formation of the separate conference, and see that deacons and elders orders are passed to the church through their agency. The New York Conference, meeting shortly thereafter, seemed to like the idea but balked at agreeing with the Philadelphia action on jurisdictional grounds. They noted that the establishment of such a conference as the Zion and Asbury Churches requested, would need the action of the General Conference and hence was not the sole prerogative of any one or two annual conferences. Given its desire not to usurp the power of the General Conference, New York recommended that no bishop cooperate with the coming meeting in June, especially concerning the ordination of any ministers.

The action of the New York Conference left the brethren at Zion with some major decisions on how to proceed. The next MEC General Conference would not be held until 1824. Some suggested waiting for its possible favorable action. It was the Wesleyan group in Philadelphia that had withdrawn from the AMEs that now became the strongest voice urging immediate independent organization and ordinations. Consensus was reached following a meeting with Bishop McKendree and his refusal to act apart from the General Conference.

In May 1822, the second conference of those churches now connected with the Zion Church gathered in Philadelphia. With the ordination issue still in question, that conference had adjourned to meet later. Meanwhile, the brethren in New York found three Methodist elders willing to act as a presbytery to conduct the ordinations—William Stillwell, his uncle Samuel Stilwell, and James Covell. At a service held at Zion Church on June 17, 1822, the three ordained Abraham Thompson, James Varick, and Leven Smith as elders. With the ordination issue settled, on July 18, 1822, the adjourned conference reconvened and selected Varick as the group's first superintendent (bishop). He was consecrated to his office on Sunday morning, July 23. He then, with Thompson and Leven assisting him, consecrated six deacons—Christopher Rush (1777–1873), James Smith, James Anderson, William Carman, Edward Johnson, and Tilman Cornish. In the afternoon, the same six received their elder's orders. The first set of appointments for what was now a new denomination (though not officially adopting the name African Methodist Episcopal Zion Church until the 1840s) included Abraham Thompson to Zion Church; Christopher Rush to Newark and the surrounding territory; Leven Smith as a missionary to New England; James Smith and William Carman to Long Island; Edward Johnson to the Wesleyan Church at Philadelphia; and James Anderson to New Haven, Connecticut.

The church faced some immediate ups and downs, The Asbury Church withdrew and realigned with the AMEs. The Wesleyan group in Philadelphia did not attend the 1823 conference in protest, but soon reconnected and became one of the strongest Zionist congregations. Meanwhile growth was seen in New England (Providence, Rhode Island; Middletown, Connecticut) and several new proto-congregations emerged on Long Island. By the end of the decade, growth justified the setting off of the Philadelphia Conference from that in New York. In 1828, Christopher Rush, who was elected bishop following Varick's death, would initiate a quarter century of leadership and expansion.

Unlike in Baltimore and Philadelphia, the formation of the Zionist fellowship, and the accompanying movement of the AMEs into the city, claimed virtually all of the African American Methodists in New York. Virtually no Black members remained attached to the MEC. While a few African members later found their way to John Street, it would not be until after the Civil War a predominantly African American MEC congregation would emerge in the city. What is now St. Mark's United Methodist Church was founded in 1871, when William F. Butler left the AMEZ Church and gathered a new congregation in facilities on Broadway, between Thirty-seventh and Thirty-eighth Streets.[65]

Notes

1. By 1790, there were twice as many free Blacks as slaves in the Philadelphia African community, which numbered approximately ten thousand. Through the first decades of the nineteenth century, the percentage of slaves would steadily and relatively quickly decline.

2. [Joseph Pilmore], *The Journal of Joseph Pilmore: Methodist Itinerant*, ed. by Frederick E. Maser and Howard T. Maag (Philadelphia, PA: Historical Society of the Philadelphia Annual Conference of the United Methodist Church, 1969).

3. *Cornwall to America in 1783 From the Journal of Paul Burall (1755–1826), ed, by his great-great-great niece* (London: Fenland Press, 1923), 13. Quoted in Francis H. Tees, *History of Old St. George's* (Philadelphia: The Author, n.d. [1934]), 37.

4. According to the records at the church. See the church's historical material on its website, posted at www.historicstgeorges.org/historic_site/historic_timeline/.

5. Dee E. Andrews, *The Methodists and Revolutionary America, 1760–1800*, herself citing the earlier work by Milton C. Sernett, *Black Religion and American Evangelicalism: White Protestants, Plantation Missions, and the Flowering of Negro Christianity, 1787–1865* (Metuchen, NJ: Scarecrow Press, 1975), makes a good case for dating the break at St. George's in 1792 rather than 1787, a date used in most earlier discussions of the incident. Allen does not date it in his autobiography, the earlier account of the events: *Life, Experience, Etc., of the Rt. Rev. Richard Allen* (Philadelphia: Martin & Boden, Printers, 1833). Dating the break in 1792 clears up a significant number of problems in ordering the sequence of events, including the seeming time lag between the break and the founding of the Bethel and Zoar congregations.

6. The membership of the classes as listed in the records of St. George's is cited in Doris Andrews, "The African Methodists of Philadelphia, 1794–1802," in Russell E. Richey, Kenneth E. Rowe, and Jean Miller Schmidt, eds. *Perspectives on American Methodism: Interpretive Essays* (Nashville, TN: Kingswood Books, 1993), 145–55. Among the members of York's class at St. George's was Robert Green, who would twenty years later cause so much trouble for Allen at Bethel.

7. Andrews, "African Methodists of Philadelphia."

8. We are very much hindered in putting together the story of Zoar in that apart from some very partial records in the archives at St. George's, very few contemporaneous records of events at Zoar have survived. Thus we are left primarily with several legal documents and other secular records of various members that survived.

9. Henry Manley, it will be remembered, was the White member of St. George's who pulled Absalom Jones from his knees while praying, the event that occasioned the Blacks leaving the White church.

10. The story of Lunar Brown has been assembled from the several unpublished papers on Zoar cited in footnote 1 earlier. Copies are now filed at the Institute for the Study of American Religion in Santa Barbara, California. These histories include Historical Committee, "Historical Sketch of African Zoar Methodist Church," undated [1964], 7 pp.; Joshua E. Licorish, "History of Zoar United Methodist Church (African Zoar Methodist Episcopal), Founded 1794, Campingtown, Pennsylvania," 1968, 9 pp.; Janet Harrison Shannon, "Faith of Our Mothers and Fathers: Resurrecting the History of an Early Black Church, Zoar, 1794-1848," 1988, 11 pp.; Ralph E. Banks, "A History of Mother African Zoar United Methodist Church," 1994, 6 pp.; "Mother African Zoar United Methodist Church, 1794–1989," presented at the 203rd Anniversary Luncheon, November 22, 1997, 15 pp.

11. The petition was reprinted in Sidney Kaplan, *The Black Presence in the Era of the American Revolution* (Greenwich, CT: National Portrait Gallery, 1973), 338, and Charles Sullivan, ed., *Children of Promise: African American Literature and Art for Young People* (New York: Henry N. Abrams, 1991).

12. Lunar Broon (probably Lunar Brown's eldest son), Phebe Clouds, Hagate Necolson, Elizabeth Farier, and Rachel Cook.

13. The list of new members may be found in Andrews, "African Methodists of Philadelphia."

14. For a discussion of the Articles, see Will B. Gravely, "African Methodism and the Rise of Black Denominations," in Russell E. Richey, Kenneth E. Rowe, and Jean Miller Schmidt, *Perspectives on American Methodism: Interpretive Essays* (Nashville, TN: Kingswood Books, 1993), 108–26. The complete text of the "Articles of Association" is reprinted in Richard R. Wright, Jr., *Encyclopedia of African Methodism* (Philadelphia: Book Concern of the A. M. E. Church, 1947), 330–32.

15. Allen would later state that he did not understand that this clause had the effect of passing ownership of Bethel to the Methodist Episcopal Church.

16. At this time, Zoar had two classes, one for males and one for females, both led by Whites.

17. Asbury ordained the pair on April 9 during his visit to Philadelphia.

18. Both Tapsico and Champion would later become charter members of and ministers in the African Methodist Episcopal Church.

19. We know of Hosier's last days from William Colbert, a White circuit rider who was in Philadelphia occasionally in 1805–06. He visited Hosier on several occasions and was present at his funeral. Present members consider Hosier their "patron preacher."

20. Given Manley's role in Allen's break with St. George's, it is interesting to see him singled out for praise just a few years later.

21. While having a good career in the traveling ministry, Smith would in 1839 be expelled from the ministry and church.

22. For a full text of the 1807 "African Supplement," see Wright, *Encyclopedia of African Methodism*, 332–34.

23. Francis Asbury, *The Journal and Letters of Francis Asbury*. 3 vols. (Nashville, TN: Abingdon Press; London: Epworth Press, 1958), II:729. Asbury would be in Philadelphia in 1814 and briefly in 1815, but made no reference to the Bethel problems.

24. The most complete discussion of the events forcing Allen out of the MEC is to be found in Will B. Gravely, "African Methodisms."

25. According to the account by J. A. Handy of the founding of the Bethel Church in Baltimore as reprinted by Benjamin W. Arnett in the *Centennial Budget* (1887), p. 272–73.

26. Julie Winch, *A Gentleman of Color: The Life of James Forten* (New York: Oxford University Press, 2002).

27. For an account of Black participation in the War of 1812, see John Hope Franklin and Alfred A. Moss, Jr., *From Slavery to Freedom: A History of Negro Americans* (New York: McGraw Hill, 1988), 99–101.

28. On April 10, 1806, William Colbert performed the marriage ceremony for Jeffrey Beulah's daughter.

29. On the Mt. Zion Church see chapter 4.

30. Winch, *A Gentleman of Color*, 187.

31. Winch, *A Gentleman of Color*, 190–91. E. Franklin Frazier notes that the 1817 meeting in Philadelphia was the first "important organized dissatisfaction" of free

Blacks to take the form of a convention. See E. Franklin Frazier, *The Negro in the United States* (New York: Macmillan Company, 1857), 79.

32. For a brief discussion of this issue in Philadelphia, see Franklin and Moss, *From Slavery to Freedom*, 154–57.

33. Charles H. Wesley, *Richard Allen: Apostle of Freedom*. (Washington, DC: Associated Publishers, 1935), 218ff.

34. Gary B. Nash, *Forging Freedom: The Formation of Philadelphia's Black Community, 1720–1840* (Cambridge, MA: Harvard University Press, 1988), 263.

35. Daniel Alexander Payne, *A History of the African Methodist Episcopal Church*, ed. by Charles Spencer Smith (Nashville, TN: Publishing House of the A. M. E. Sunday School Union, 1891), 158.

36. Tilghman was among the first of the ministers in the Philadelphia Conference to be ordained as an elder in the years leading up to the formation of the Delaware Conference in 1864. Others included Isaac Henson, Philip Scott, James Davis, Samuel Dale, John G. Manluff, and Harrison Smith.

37. The other congregations were Salem, Ebenezer (in Washington, D.C.), and Nazareth.

38. At the time of the charter, the Trustees were Perry Warren, Cyrus B. Miller, Henry Wiles, Richard Crofford, Asbury Layton, Benjamin Jackson, George Junior, John Armstrong, and William Williams.

39. This provision for male leadership of the congregation, like that of organizing classes and forming benevolent societies along gender lines, raises another issue yet to be considered: the role of gender in determining the life of Black Methodists during the period under consideration.

40. John Wesley Chapel continues today as the Tindley Memorial United Methodist Church.

41. The formation of John Wesley Chapel seems to have been due to reemerging problems at St. George's, where some of the Black members in Philadelphia proper who did not go to Bethel attended services. In 1839, St. George's passed a resolution that confirmed their policy relegating Black members to the gallery.

42. About this time a book for the keeping of a record of the emerging congregation was started. This "Old Book," as it came to be called, has become a primary source for the early history of New York. Selections from this book have been published in various histories of New York Methodism.

43. J. B. Wakeley, *Lost Chapters Recovered from the Early History of American Methodism* (New York: Wilbur B. Ketcham, 1889), 102–3.

44. Letter from Boardman to John Wesley, November 4, 1769, reproduced in Atkinson, *Beginnings of the Wesleyan Movement in America*, 248–49.

45. Originally printed in 1784 in the *Arminian Magazine*, the Methodist magazine printed in London, and was reprinted in Atkinson, *Beginnings of the Wesleyan Movement in America*, 192–93.

46. [Joseph Pilmore], *The Journal of Joseph Pilmore: Methodist Itinerant*, ed. by Frederick E. Maser and Howard T. Maag (Philadelphia, PA: Historical Society of the Philadelphia Annual Conference of the United Methodist Church, 1969), 69.

47. Rankin's unpublished *Journal* is located in the library at Garrett-Evangelical Theological Seminary. At about the same time, Francis Asbury, soon to emerge as the leader of the America Methodists, had a similar reflection during a communion service: "At the table I was greatly affected with the sight of the poor Negroes, seeing their sable faces at the table of the Lord. In the evening I had a full house and much Divine assistance." Asbury, *Journals* I, 42–43.

48. Wakeley, *Lost Chapters,* 227; Kenneth Holcomb Dunshee, *As You Pass By* (New York: Hastings House, 1952), 106–7.

49. These Black Loyalists would form the first classes and societies in Nova Scotia and then many of them would leave for Freetown, Sierra Leone, where they would found the first African Methodist churches.

50. From this point, the history in New York (and to a lesser extent in Brooklyn) is covered in the several histories of the AMEZ Church. See especially James Walker Hood, *One Hundred Years of the African Methodist Episcopal Zion Church; or, The Centennial of African Methodism* (New York: A.M.E. Zion Book Concern, 1895); John Jamison Moore, *History of the A. M. E. Zion Church in America. Founded in 1796, in the City of New York* (York, PA: Teachers' Journal Office, 1884); Christopher Rush, *A Short Account of the Rise and Progress of the African Methodist Episcopal Church in America* (New York: The Author, 1843); and William J. Walls, *The African Methodist Episcopal Zion Church: Reality of the Black Church* (Charlotte, NC: A.M.E. Zion Publishing House, 1974).

51. A memorial obituary to Thompson was published in the first issue of *Freedom's Journal* 1, 1 (March 26, 1827): 2, posted at www.wisconsinhistory.org/libraryarchives/ aanp/freedom/volume1.asp.

52. This notice appeared on March 21, 1800, in the *American Citizen and General Advertiser.* It is quoted in I. N. Phelps Stokes, *The Iconography of Manhattan Island,* Vol. 5, p. 1376, and in Walls, *African Methodist Episcopal Zion Church,* 53.

53. Quoted in Leroy M. Lee, *The Life and Times of Jesse Lee* (Richmond, VA: John Early, 1848), 380.

54. *American Citizen and General Advertiser* (New York), July 29, 1800. Quoted by Walls, *African Methodist Episcopal Zion Church,* 56.

55. The complete text of the "Articles of Agreement" is to be found in Walls, *The African Methodist Episcopal Zion Church,* 59–62. It is to be noted how much of this text follows that of the "Articles of Agreement" drawn up just a few years earlier with the Bethel Church in Philadelphia. It contains much of the same language and all of the key clauses concerning the trust into which the property is placed and the role of the elder assigned to the city.

56. Winch, *A Gentleman of Color,* 182ff.

57. Winch, *A Gentleman of Color,* 217.

58. Cited in *Freedom's Journal* 1, 1 (March 16, 1827): 4, posted at www.wisconsin history.org/libraryarchives/aanp/freedom/volume1.asp. Subsequent issues of *Freedom's Journal* made frequent mention of activities of various prominent New York Methodists, and this publication stands as an important source of information on the progress of the church during the last years of the 1820s.

59. Quoted in Nathan Bangs, *History of the Methodist Episcopal Church* (New York: T. Mason and G. Lane, 1839–1842), Vol. 1, chapter 2, posted at www.ccel.org/ccel/bangs/history1.ii.ii.ii.html.

60. Asbury, *Journal*, II, 55.

61. This list was reprinted in Edwin Warriner, *Old Sands Street Methodist Episcopal Church of Brooklyn, N.Y.* (New York: Phillips & Hunt, 1885), 13.

62. Clarence Taylor, *Black Churches of Brooklyn* (New York: Columbia University Press, 1994).

63. In the summer of 1823, the Brooklyn church hosted AME evangelist Jarena Lee, and one of the Croger brothers and "Father" [Abraham] Thompson accompanied her to stops on Long Island. Jarena Lee, *Religious Experience and Journal of Mrs. Jarena Lee, Giving an Account of her Call to Preach the Gospel. Revised and corrected from the Original Manuscript, Written by Herself* (Philadelphia: The Author, 1849), 29–30.

64. The founding of the New York AME Church is covered quite differently in AMEZ and AME sources. On the AME perspective, see Payne, *History of the African Methodist Episcopal Church*, 31–39.

65. See the history of St. Mark's posted at its webpage, www.nycago.org/Organs/NYC/html/StMarkMeth.html. Accessed April 15, 2006.

CHAPTER FIVE

African Methodism
Away from the Cities

Plantation Culture and the Methodist Presence

While developing an early and notable presence in America's urban centers, Methodism made its most impressive gains in the small towns, farms, and all-important plantations. And it is in the rural areas that the great majority of Africans came into their initial contact with the preachers who were making it their responsibility to share the Christian faith with any and all who would listen. While the response widely varied from community to community, Africans constituted the largest distinguishable group responding to the Methodist message, with the largest percentage being those living in slavery.

By 1800, Methodism had had a full generation to establish itself. At that time, of the church's 64,894 members, 13,452, or approximately 20 percent, were African. Most Methodists resided in Virginia or Maryland, reporting 13,390 and 12,046 members, respectively. However, while Black-White percentages in Virginia reflected those of the church as a whole (with 2,531 African members), Maryland had more than twice that number. Its 5,497 African members represented about 46 percent of the total membership. In some places African members were in the majority.

Impressive African pluralities emerged in Calvert (814 to 399), Prince Georges (680 to 153), and Queen Annes (565 to 496) Counties, while pluralities and near pluralities were found throughout the Eastern Shore counties. In Virginia, Black membership was concentrated in the southeast corner of the state, with a matching concentration of Black members in North Carolina on the Camden Circuit in the northeast corner of the state. None of these areas at the time were home to any significant urban centers, the closest being Baltimore with over twenty-six thousand residents and Washington/Georgetown with a whopping six thousand.

The Methodist preachers entered the rather confined existence of the slave as outsiders who brought new options into the slaves' life of long hours of more-or-less hard labor, always subject to the arbitrary whims of their owners. Considered somewhat less than fully human, slaves had little redress to whatever conditions under which they were forced to live. The Methodists were the only group to systematically approach Africans and invite them into membership, and, at least through the eighteenth century, they wedded their message of Christian salvation to an attack upon the institution of slavery. They demanded their preachers rid themselves of slaves and strongly encouraged their laypeople to do the same. Part of the early loyalty of Africans to the church was their perception of its having played a role in their attaining their freedom or their looking to it as the best hope for future freedom.

To those living on plantations, above and beyond the message of salvation that the Methodist preachers saw as their major offering to their audiences, Methodism provided those caught in slavery a number of practical advantages in their participation in church activities, not the least being the entertainment and diversion from their daily routine that worship services and class meetings represented. Here they, not their masters, became the center of the spoken words, and an atmosphere of spontaneity allowed them some freedom to express their religious sentiments, which were never far removed from their feeling and thoughts in general.

Once Africans became involved in the movement, Methodism provided opportunities for leadership development. And lack of education was no barrier to full participation. Many, if not most, of the White preachers were also void of any formal schooling and progress was possible to anyone, even those unable to read or write, as long as they manifested a life of piety and demonstrated some talents for public speaking. Even slaves could be and were assigned formal positions of responsibility as class leaders, exhorters, and preachers.

The classes promoted new levels of intimacy, the meetings allowing time for each to share their personal struggles. The classes, the music, the worship, all culminating in the occasional love feasts, also provided members with a shared experience which set them above and apart from non–churchgoers. The church offered the slave preachers some opportunity to move about the countryside and, with a master's permission, speak throughout the neighborhood. Talented preachers would often be allowed to travel around the circuit supplementing the work of the circuit rider, especially at times when he was necessarily absent from his charge.

Most of what we know of the reception of Methodism in this first generation comes from the diaries and journals of the White circuit riders. While there is a relative lack of material offering a direct voice of African believers in the earlier decades of the American Methodist movement, the circuit rider reports offer much detail and for the time present remarkably vivid insights. For example, in 1772, Joseph Pilmore was in the Tidewater area of Virginian, where on August 5 he noted:

Wednesday—I returned [to Portsmouth] and preached to a pretty congregation with largeness of heart on the nature of free justification through the Righteousness of Christ; After preaching two poor slaves came to me and begged I would instruct them in the way of salvation, so I gave them a short and plain account of the Plan of the Gospel, and showed them how sinners may come to god and be saved. We then joined in singing and prayer, and they expressed great thankfulness for what they had heard, and seemed determined to be Christians.[1]

Several days later he had moved a short distance down the road where on Sunday, August 9, he preached

in the evening at Norfolk. As the ground was wet, they persuaded me to try to preach within and appointed men to stand at the doors to keep all the Negroes out till the white persons were got in, but the house would not near hold them; however, I went into the pulpit, and began but presently a plank gave way and the stage to which the pulpit was fixed began to sink down at one side, which so terrified the people that they cried out amain. As I perceived it would be impossible to quiet the people, I slipped out, ordered a table and began singing in the large plain adjoining the house; this happened to be the very thing, the people drew out of the house, and had a noble congregation of white and black, to whom I freely declared the whole counsel of God, and prepared them to obey the word of the Lord.[2]

Pilmore's time in Norfolk illustrates both the preachers' attempts to reach out to the slaves and the slaves' almost immediate response, while at the same time they acknowledged and accepted most of the social gaps that existed between Africans and the White majority. In spite of the obstacles, the slaves chose to spend their time at Pilmore's meetings. On August 16 he recorded:

Sunday. . . . I was in time to preach at Norfolk in the evening. Just before preaching we had a thunder shower that kept some of the delicate ones from the preaching, yet we had the house perfectly [full] of white people, and a vast multitude of black people stood around about the outside. As I was much fatigued before I began I was afraid I should not be able to preach to the great congregation so as to be heard, but God was better to me than all my fears, and his word like a sharp two-edged sword piercing into the hearts of sinners.[3]

William Bennett noted that before long, an initial building was erected in Norfolk on Fen Church Street. Built off the ground to keep it above water, the plain wooden building seated four hundred people with a gallery for the slaves.[4] Pilmore preached frequently in Virginia's Tidewater Area. In April of 1773 he noted traveling to a plantation owned by a Captain Connors where he preached on a Monday afternoon to an all-White congregation, the Black people all attending to their chores. However, before the next work day began, he noted, "In the morning all the Negroes were called in, and I expounded a Chapter and prayed; then set off for Norfolk again."[5]

James L. Smith, a slave in Northumberland County, learned to be a shoemaker and was hired out to a master in the town of Heathsville. He attended the Fairfield Methodist Church where he found religion and became active in the "underground" slave culture of the area. He mentions all-night prayer meetings which would break up at dawn, just in time for the attendees to return to their place of work and grab an hour's sleep before beginning the day's labors. What drew him to these meetings? He remembered that "the way in which we worshipped is almost indescribable. The singing was accompanied by a certain ecstasy of motion, clapping of hands, tossing of heads, which would continue without cessation about half an hour; one would lead off a kind of recitative style, others joining in the chorus. The old house partook of ecstasy; it rang with their jubilant shouts, and shook in all its joints."[6]

One of the first all-Black Methodist churches in Virginia emerged in Winchester, about sixty miles northwest of Washington. As early as 1786, Asbury notes riding leisurely into the town and speaking under a spreading tree to many White and Black people. Out of the travels of the Methodist preachers in the area, the Market Street Church emerged. In 1802, when first listed separately in the General Minutes, it reported 280 White and 128 Black members, and though it was in Virginia it was assigned to the Baltimore Conference. By 1830 there were 731 White and 225 Black members. Around 1833, African American members formed the John Mann MEC, originally meeting in a log cabin, which was later replaced with a brick structure (1858).[7]

Simultaneously with Methodism's move into Virginia, slaves in Maryland were having their first experience with the visiting circuit riders. On December 7, 1772, Asbury notes speaking to some "poor Negroes" who he hoped "took some notice of what he said." The next day, he was in George-town (now Galena, Kent County, and not to be confused with the George-town section of Washington, D.C.), later to become a favorite stopping place. He found a night's sleep with a Quaker family. In the evening before heading to bed, the Africans came into the home and Asbury spoke to them. The following day, he was at the home of John Randall, where Robert Straw-bridge had preached the first sermon on Maryland's Eastern Shore, and spoke to many people, rich and poor.[8] Over the next years, a Georgetown society was formed, and on June 9, 1775, Thomas Rankin led a love feast at the home of a Brother Hynson. Rankin noted that, according to Mrs. Hynson, a most blessed work had occurred among the African members. The change was manifest in that the many incidents of theft by the slaves had ceased al-together.

The most famous story of this era concerns the slaves of Harry Dorsey Gough (d. 1808). Gough owned Perry Hall, a large estate about twelve miles north of Baltimore, and seems to have been converted to Methodism about 1775. The territory in and around Gough's plantation had been one of the first areas where Methodism had spread among Africans. As the story goes, Gough originally took the phenomenon of Methodism very lightly. At one point, he and some inebriated friends decided to go to a service at which As-bury was preaching just for the diversion of it. However, at the service he was so affected by Asbury that it took all of the pleasure out of his other activi-ties. He did not convert immediately, but did enter a period of spiritual strug-gle, seemingly at one point contemplating suicide.[9] It was not long afterward that Gough was riding around his vast holdings when he heard some noises with a familiar ring from that night with Asbury. Approaching the sounds on foot, he observed an African preacher from a neighboring plantation praying for his slaves. It was a prayer of thanksgiving for the goodness of God. Gough was most struck with the contrast between his own lack of gratitude and the attitude displayed by the poorer than poor slave preacher with barely enough to survive.[10]

This incident became the catalyst for his entering a time of prayer and fasting a few days later and ultimately finding a consciousness of pardon and peace—the Methodist blessing, as he put it. Thomas Rankin, who visited Perry Hall in July 1775, a short time after Gough's conversion, was among the first to encounter the changed owner. He now encouraged the slaves to meet with Rankin, and Rankin moved quickly to organize what he termed a "little congregation" composed of the Gough family and the African ser-vants. Two years later, John Littlejohn was present for morning prayer at which some forty Black servants were present.[11]

Gough had a chapel erected adjacent to the mansion house, and a bell called all on the estate to morning and evening worship, White and Black worshipping together. At this time, Methodist preachers routinely demanded that masters invite servants to family worship and tended to resist holding any family devotions if the greater part of an estate's dwellers were out and about at their work (this practice would change over time). The Gough chapel became a regular preaching point on the local circuit, and the traveling preacher arrived every two weeks, usually on a weekday. As local preachers emerged, they led the estate in worship every other Sabbath. Daily worship continued on the estate even after Gough died. If no White male was present to lead worship, the widow Gough would read a chapter from the Bible, line out a hymn, which the Africans were quick to pick up and sing, and lead a prayer.

The Methodist preachers looked for and prayed for those occasional outbreaks of religious enthusiasm known as revivals, one consequence being the growth of the movement. In the summer of 1776, one such revival broke out in Amelia and the surrounding counties in south central Virginia. Typical of events, Thomas Rankin, its main instigator, recorded his preaching on the morning of July 7 to a overflow crowd at White's Chapel. "Numbers of white and black were bathed in tears, and some went aloud, crying for the mercy of God in Christ Jesus." Then in the evening, he "spent an hour in exhortation and prayer with some hundreds of white and black; and great was the glorying in Christ Our Savior."[12] Such scenes would be repeated many times as the church spread through the countryside.

The institution of slavery, of course, often placed the religious slave in an uncomfortable position. Thomas H. Jones, a slave in Wilmington, North Carolina, where Methodism was quite strong, tells of the troubles he encountered because his master was opposed to religion and opposed to his slaves engaging in any religious activities. He was beaten on a number of occasions for attending Sunday services, going to class meetings, or simply praying. After a week that included several beatings due to his religious inclination, and with a back still bearing open wounds, "on the next Friday evening, I went to the prayer meeting. Jack Cammon [the free Black class leader] was there, and opened the meeting with prayer. Then Binney Pennison [another free Black member] gave out the sweet hymn, which begins in these words:

> Come ye sinners, poor and needy,
> Weak and wounded, sick and sore.

I felt that it all applied most sweetly to my condition, and I said in my heart, *I will come now to Jesus, and trust in him.*"[13]

Greensburg Washington Offley, who was born on the Eastern Shore of Maryland, tells of a fellow slave called Praying Jacob. Jacob ordered his life to pray thrice daily at a set time. His master opposed his interrupting his work schedule for such frivolity, and on one occasion stood with gun in hand ready to shoot Jacob if he did not cease his prayer. Jacob finished and then explained that "death would be welcomed as he would go and meet his heavenly master. His body belonged to his earthly master, and his soul to Jesus."[14]

Slaves noticed Methodist ministers and members who increasingly tended to own slaves and the contradictions between their Christian profession and their unchristian actions toward slaves, including violations of the sanctity of marriage and family. Henry Bibb could hardly contain his anger at his Kentucky Methodist brethren: "In 1836 'Bro.' Albert G. Sibley, of Bedford, Kentucky, sold me for $850 to 'Bro.' John Sibley; and in the same year he sold me to 'Bro.' Wm. Gatewood of Bedford, for $850. . . . A. Sibley was a Methodist exhorter of the M. E. Church in good standing. J. Sibley was a class-leader in the same church; and Wm. Gatewood was also an acceptable member of the same church."[15] After fleeing to Canada, Bibb complained bitterly in letters to his former masters about their treatment of his wife and children. Quoting the Bible freely, he laid bare the gap between their professions and their actions.[16]

African Methodists at Worship

The attraction felt by African Americans toward Methodism has frequently been attributed to a certain resonance between the experiences of Methodist worship and their prior life in Africa, coupled with a certain openness to innovation in the worship contexts. Methodism came to the British colonies as a form of Christianity shorn of much prior theological sophistication (though John Wesley had provided the movement with a sound theological foundation). At the same time, from Charles Wesley, the movement possessed a large number of lively songs using the popular tunes of the era. He went far beyond Isaac Watts, who had initially broken the hold of the biblical Psalms as the exclusive source of Protestant hymnody and focused attention on New Testament themes of Christ and salvation. Methodists also appreciated, even encouraged, outward emotive expressions of individual religious sentiments.

As Methodism initially spread, the great majority of Africans were largely untouched by Christianity. What religion they possessed had traveled with them from Africa. Though losing much in the Middle Passage, Africans retained some of their previous culture. The most distinctive form of religious expression harking back to life before slavery was the ring shout,[17] best described as a sacred dance that takes the form of a circular movement around a central object—a person, an altar, or as later, the platform at a camp meeting. The term "shout" is somewhat misleading, as in this case, it derives from an African-Arabic term, *saut*, describing the movement of Muslim believers during the circumambulation of the Kaaba in Mecca. However, when White people first saw the ring, they also heard people cry out or shout, and thus the practice was associated with the loud exuberance that came to be associated with Methodist meetings in general. The ring shout emerged everywhere plantation culture dominated, from Maryland and Delaware to Texas. Numerous mentions and several descriptions of rings from the antebellum era have survived, most of the substantive accounts from rather late in the period. For example, a former slave, Silvia King, described what she had seen in the 1850s in Texas: "De black folks gits off down in de bottom and shouts and sings and prays. Dey gits in de ring dance. It am jes' a kind of shuffle, den it git faster and faster and dey gits warmed up and moans and shouts and claps and dances. Some gits 'xhausted and drops out and de ring gits closer. Sometimes dey sings and shouts all night, but come break of day, de nigger got to git to he cabin. Old Marse got to tell dem de tasks of de day."[18]

An earlier account was written by Sir Charles Lyell in 1845, by which time the plantation missions had spread along the major river systems of South Carolina and Georgia. In McIntosh County, Georgia, not far from the Butler plantation visited by Fanny Kemble, he noted that "at the Methodist prayer-meetings, they are permitted to move round rapidly in a ring, joining hands in a token of brotherly love, presenting first the right hand and then the left, in which manoeuvre, I am told, they sometimes contrive to take enough exercise to serve as a substitute for the dance, it being, in fact, a kind of spiritual *boulanger,* while the singing of psalms, in and out of chapel, compensates in no small degree for the songs they have been required to renounce."[19]

By far the most famous account was recorded in South Carolina in 1862 by Thomas Wentworth Higginson, who commanded one of the companies of African American soldiers during the Civil War. The shouts were held in small structures constructed by the troops out of palm leaves. An evening's meeting would begin with the rhythm set by hand clapping and foot stomping and the repetitious and (to Higginson) monotonous "Methodist" chants the men began to sang. As the evening progressed, "men begin to quiver and dance, others join, a circle forms, winding monotonously round some one in the centre; some 'heel and toe' tumultuously, others merely tremble and stagger on, others stoop and rise, others whirl, others caper sideways, all keep steadily circling like dervishes; spectators applaud special strokes of skill." Still later, "the circle enlarges, louder grows the singing, rousing shouts of encouragement come in, half baccahanalian, half devout, 'Wake 'em, brudder!,' 'Stan' up to 'em, brudder!'—and still the ceaseless drumming and clapping, in perfect cadence, goes steadily on."[20]

How did their African past affect African Americans' appropriation of Christianity in general and Methodism in particular? It is helpful to remember that through the antebellum period the great majority of African Americans were not Christians and (to Whites) did not appear to have any religion. It was, in fact, the absence of any visible religion, coupled with the often self-destructive activities slaves pursued during any leisure time, that inspired men like Henry Evans and Henry Bibb to become preachers to their fellow slaves. For the great majority of African Americans, through the antebellum era, what religion they had came from the surviving African practices.

Activities like the ring shout, originally an act of acknowledgment of the supreme deity of the traditional African religions, actually carried little if any specific theological content, and thus possessed an inherent capacity for adaptation to a specifically Christian context, being easily transformed into a similar act in praise of the Christian deity. As shouts continued to be held, largely unnoticed by the plantation owners and even the White missionaries who developed Christian churches among the slaves, they were everywhere present on the fringe of church life, usually as a part of the private life of slaves in their free time after dark and on Sundays. First noticed in the eighteenth century, they would continue through the nineteenth century to the late twentieth century, when they experienced a marked revival.

Given the ubiquity of the practice, one would be surprised if it did not enter into the life of African American Christians. Prior to the Civil War, the most likely places that a White person would see a ring shout would be at a camp meeting. These large gatherings, which would be organized periodically through the summer and fall across the land, found their focus in the preaching platforms. Generally, seating would be segregated with the Whites in front and Blacks behind the platform. Seating areas were commonly separated by a partition. The ring shout would appear in two contexts, most notably in the late evening as an activity among Black attendees. Second, there are some reports of camp meetings ending with the Blacks tearing down the dividing partition and circling around the whole gathering.[21] In this case, the ring shout became a variation on the marches that Whites had introduced into the camp meeting context.

The ring shout, as perpetuated in the rural plantation culture, by its very nature tended to be excluded from the regularly scheduled Methodist worship services and class meetings. In spite of Lyell's observation noted earlier, Methodist worship was largely directed by Whites following patterns derived from England. At the same time, it appears that the many expressive elements (both body movements and locutions) that so characterized African American worship were injected into Methodism from the ring shout. By the nineteenth century, when the camp meeting spread through America, many of the expressive forms first observed by the early circuit riders among the African members had come to characterize all Methodists in general. Many Whites freely offered vocal expressions of their religious ecstasy; adopted various movements, some seemingly beyond their immediate control, termed the jerks; and participated in worship with ejaculations of praise and encouragement to the preacher during his sermon.[22] By the early nineteenth century, the difference between Blacks and Whites seemed to be the degree to which they gave visible expression to their spirituality with vocalizations and body movements. While African Americans were everywhere more demonstrative in their worship than their White counterparts, in both cases, the urbanized Methodists tended to be more sedate than those residing in rural areas.

Then, through the nineteenth century, as Methodism grew and became successful, both Black and White Methodists became more orderly and less spontaneous. But as gaps developed and persisted between the levels of expressiveness, so the two groups found separate worship more to their liking, an added motive in establishing separate African American congregations.

Throughout the church, but especially in the South once the plantation slave missions were launched, ministers moved to suppress any heightened degree of expressiveness in worship and especially any elements they understood to be remaining elements of "African superstition." Within the all-African Methodist churches, one could also discern a move away from the more uninhibited forms of worship so noticeable early in the nineteenth century. AME bishop and scholar Daniel Payne raised some ire by discouraging the continuation of the ring shout among African Methodists and as late as the 1880s was complaining about its persistence even as far north as Pennsylvania.[23]

The ring shout provided some continuity between the African past and the slave's new existence at a time before English was acquired and African Americans still found communication of any kind, even with fellow slaves who usually spoke another African language, a struggle. After English replaced the African languages for the second and third generation African Americans, a burst of creativity can be documented as slaves began to generate work songs that served to ease the drudgery of life on the plantation, give expression to their present condition, and offer some hope for a better future. As Christianity spread among the slaves, its themes would become the subject of a new set of songs that came to be known as spirituals. With simple and repetitive lyrics, the spirituals would be sung to tunes adapted to African rhythms.

Meanwhile, as Africans encountered Methodism, they would also be introduced to a very different hymnody. The Wesleyan hymns, written through the mid-eighteenth century, were published in a series of volumes, the first edition circulating in America being one reprinted by George Whitefield. Generally, only a few people in any given congregation (including the traveling minister) would own a copy of the hymnbook. Singing was done by a process called "lining out" the hymn. The song leader, the one with the hymnbook, would sing a line or two in a relatively fast tempo, and the group repeated the lines, usually at a slightly slower tempo. In the pause at the end of the phrase, the next lines would then be rendered by the leader. Over time, this process had a number of consequences. First, the congregation came to memorize a variety of hymns which came to be for each individual their own personal prayer book and theology text. Quite apart from their literacy or the availability of religious texts, they could learn the faith through the songs and carry their knowledge around with them every hour of the day.

Second, the process of lining out the hymns resonated with the call-response pattern that permeates African (and became ubiquitous in African American) culture. In their utilization of this method of spreading their hymnody, the Methodists were unknowingly affirming the African roots of their Black converts.

Third, the auditory transmission and teaching of the hymns allowed both the song leader and the congregation to introduce changes in the way the song was sung. The hymnbook of the time printed only the words to the hymn, the introduction of music being largely a late nineteenth-century innovation. Thus Africans could take a perfectly good Wesleyan hymn and alter its rhythm and even the tune, thus gaining some ownership over a small aspect of their church life.

This process of absorbing and transforming the Wesleyan hymns was noted in the poetry of George Moses Horton (c. 1797–1883). During his teen years, Horton began to compose his own poetry, deriving his meter from the Wesleyan hymns he had learned. Around 1815, he developed contacts with the students and faculty at the newly formed University of North Carolina. Impressed with his efforts, the students began to copy his poems, a first volume of which was published in 1828. They also facilitated his learning to read and write. In return, he composed (and sold) love poems for the students to present to their girlfriends.[24]

With the coming of the camp meeting, a new burst of hymn writing not unlike what was occurring on the fields of the plantation occurred. Attendees anonymously wrote and circulated new hymns that over a season could travel great distances and be subject to addition and revision. There is every reason to believe that African Americans participated in this production of new hymns for the whole of the camp meeting community.

Through the nineteenth century, African Methodists developed their own hymnody by melding the various traditions—the spirituals from the slave culture, the new music from the camp meetings, and the traditional Wesleyan hymns. A first effort in developing a uniquely African American Methodist hymnody was made by Richard Allen in *A Collection of Spiritual Songs and Hymns from Various Authors*, an assemblage of fifty-four hymns initially published in 1801.[25] There is every reason to believe that his hymnal was intended to be a supplementary volume for the Bethel congregation, and that it included a set of hymns which Allen personally liked and felt would be good for his congregation to know and use. Of the hymns in the collection, the authors of approximately half can be identified, including multiple titles by Isaac Watts (1674–1748), Charles Wesley, and John Newton (1725–1807) (former slave trader and author of "Amazing Grace"). There is also one hymn by Allen himself.

The remaining hymns are the most interesting, in that they appear to be from those anonymously written hymns then circulating in revivalist circles. They are full of the vivid imagery of spiritual warfare, crossing the Jordan River, and the need to respond to Christ. The hymnal stands at the beginning of a new set of hymnals that would appear over the next decade that reflect the post-Revolutionary popular religion of what would become the camp meeting movement.[26] As an integral part of the MEC, Bethel members would still be using the same hymnals that were being employed in the White Methodist congregations. And while Allen had arguments with the discriminatory policies of some of the White ministers, he also presented himself as an exemplar of the faith to which he had devoted his life.

Allen's 1801 hymnal stands in stark contrast to the first AME hymnal, brought out in 1818. By this time he was ready to replace the hymnals in use in the White churches, and thus the new hymnal included the songs with which Allen and the African American Church members had become familiar and that they could continue to use without having to reference the hymnbook of the church out of which they had recently come.

Hymnody was not at issue in the establishment of the independent Black churches, but all would in time issue their own hymnals. Peter Spencer produced the *African Union Hymn Book* in 1822 and the first AMEZ hymnbook, *Hymns for the Use of the African Methodist Episcopal Zion Church in America*, appeared in 1838. These hymnals reflected a desire to assert Methodist credentials while at the same time these churches took their place among mainstream Protestant denominations. This desire would also be reflected in the attention of the African American Methodist churches to the Ecumenical Methodist conferences that began to be held in the decades after the Civil War and their quickness to participate in the Federal Council of Churches.

William Colbert in Maryland

For more than three decades William Colbert (1764–1835) traveled as a Methodist itinerant through Maryland, Pennsylvania, and the surrounding states, and kept a rather detailed journal of his work. That journal now rivals Asbury's for the information it offers concerning African American Methodists in the years immediately after the formation of the Methodist Episcopal Church. The record begins in 1790 when Colbert first rode the Calvert Circuit, where he would find over a thousand Black members brought into the church by his predecessors.

Colbert's movement on the circuit reveals the patterns in a preacher's life. At most stops, he met with the White people in the afternoons and with the Black members in the evening after working hours. In the absence of churches or spaces specifically set aside for religious activity, meetings took place in the homes of White members, a plantation building, or, weather permitting, out-of-doors. In most places, Colbert's predecessors had already organized members into a class with whom he now met on most visits. When both Blacks and Whites assembled for worship, a variety of patterns for segregating the races were used. Amid an account of a somewhat humorous incident, Colbert reveals the typical conditions that accompanied his preaching. On April 5 he was preaching at the Scrivinor residence to what he termed a hardened congregation. "I stood at the door of a partition," he notes, "the black people were behind me and the white before—I wanted to see a move among them, therefore I exerted myself, and sure enough, there was a move, for the blacks behind began to shout aloud jump and fall—the whites to look wild and go off. I am sorry that prejudice moved so many to day. A young woman among them that went off said that she would come no more and that she believed that I should kill myself."

Loud responsive manifestations were the order of the day at preaching services, and Colbert was obviously happy to be able to report, as he did on April 12, that a large audience of Black people were "much in the spirit of shouting," and again on May 10, "they shout aloud and may be heard afar off." On July 4, he was at the Hollowing Point meeting house where James Higgin preached and Colbert exhorted, during which "the black people began to shout and jump about in such a manner that brother Higgin said the devil was among them, and told the people to go out from among them."

The following year, Colbert traveled the Harford circuit (halfway between Baltimore and Wilmington), and reported much the same phenomena, especially the meeting with classes in the evening. Then in 1794, he rode the Montgomery circuit that covered Montgomery and Prince Georges Counties. At Oxen Hill he did not have to meet in a home or public building, as he encountered a small congregation of free Black people that had erected a meeting house. As he put it, the little chapel was built by some Black people who had "obtained their freedom and embraced religion." They attributed their good situation to the Methodists, and manifested their gratitude with the building.[27] They also took the lead in evangelizing their neighbors. Colbert had nothing but praise for them:

> God has blessed their labour in an extraordinary manner, their society is very numerous, and very orderly, and to their great credit with pleasure I assert, that I have never found a white class so regular in giving in their Quarterage, as these poor people are, and the greater part of them slaves, of whom never request anything. But they will enquire when the Quarterly meetings are from time to time, and by the last time the preacher comes around before the Quarterly meeting they will have five dollars in silver tied up for him: as they are so numerous the circuit preacher cannot meet them all, there are two leading characters among them, that fill their station with dignity. They not only have their class meetings, but their days of examination in order to find out anything that may be amiss among them and if they can settle it among themselves they will, if not, as the Elders of Israel brought matters which they conceived were of too great importance for them to decide on before Moses, so would these people bring matters of the greatest moment before the preacher.

He visited Oxen Hill approximately every four weeks through the year, and his diary entries were always upbeat about his meeting with those whom he came to describe as his friends there.[28]

**Table 5.1.   African American Methodist Congregations,
The First Generation, 1790–1810**

Date Formed	Present Name	Location	Founded As
1791	St. Paul UMC	Oxen Hill, MD	Oxen Hill MEC
1792	Mother Bethel AME	Philadelphia	Bethel MEC
1794	Zoar UMC	Philadelphia	Zoar MEC
1796	Zion AMEZ Church	New York City	Cross Street MEC
1790s?	Evans Memorial AMEZ	Fayetteville, NC	Evans Chapel
1800	Bryan UMC, Grasonville	Queenstown, MD	Bryan Chapel MEC
1800/1802	Mt. Hope UMC	Salem, NJ	Mt Hope MEC
1801	Centennial UMC	Baltimore	Dallas Street MEC
1801	St. Luke AMEZ	Wilmington, NC	Andrew's Chapel
1801	St. Stephens AME	Wilmington, NC	Andrew's Chapel
1802	St. Peter's AMEZ	New Bern, NC	Andrew Chapel
1803	Smith Chapel UMC	Belton, NC	Gum Swamp MEC
1805	Ezion–Mt. Carmel UMC	Wilmington, DE	Ezion MEC
1808	Bethel AME	Pittsburgh	African Church
1810	Asbury	New York City	Asbury MEC
1810	Christ UMC	Baltimore	Asbury MEC

Hope Memorial United Methodist Church is one of a number of antebellum African Methodist congregations still existing in rural Maryland.

Actually, Colbert was not the first circuit rider to preach to this congregation. Three years earlier, in October 1791, Ezekiel Cooper recorded in his journal, "The record shows that in October, 1791 . . .Thursday 10 went over the Potomac and preached in Oxenhill [sic] in a small preaching house which has been built by a number of religious black people. I had considerable satisfaction among them. I preached at 12 o'clock again at night. The dear black people seem to be alive to God having their hearts placed on things above. I lodged at Mr. Beans—none of the family, except black people, are in the ways of religion, but they are a friendly, kind people. I had much satisfaction with them. O that God may give them His grace."[29]

Though some congregational discontinuity occurred during the later years of slavery, the present St. Paul UMC continues that congregation encountered by Cooper and Colbert, thus making it the first African American Methodist congregation, predating both Bethel in Philadelphia and Sharp Street in Baltimore.

When the circuit rider records such as Colbert's (and Cooper's) are brought together with the *Journal* of Francis Asbury, a picture of the devel-

The present St. Paul United Methodist Church continues the original congregation founded in 1791.

opment of African Methodism, at least around the Chesapeake and along the Potomac River Valley in the quarter century after the launching of the movement in America, begins to emerge. The whole of Maryland (the eastern portion of which was in the Philadelphia Conference) was laid out in a set of circuits, each of which would take a circuit rider upwards of four weeks to travel. Most stops were at the homes of White Methodists, or Methodist sympathizers, and at most stops an abundance of Africans were to be found. As a whole, their acceptance of Methodism did not have an immediate effect upon their status as slaves, but appears to have had an ameliorating effect upon their life (with some notable exceptions). At the very least, the Methodist worship services and class meetings provided a break and rest from their daily routine and in the singing and shouting, as well as the one-on-one conversations with the visiting preachers, some release of pent-up emotions.

Most meetings were out-of-doors (weather permitting), in people's homes, or occasionally in multi-purpose buildings. Where members had enough discretionary income, meeting houses were erected, but these were gathering places for proto-congregations, with administrative organization being limited to the circuit-wide quarterly conferences rather than the type of local church organization seen in the cities. Where Blacks predominated, organization was further stymied as they were not invited to be part of any local lay structure that did arise. However, on the circuits, at this time, organization remained rather informal. One finds repeated accounts of churches being organized on the Eastern Shore of Maryland at or nearby sites where believers had gathered for many years—decades. By the 1790s, there were few places in Maryland more than an hour or two away from a Methodist meeting site. In Maryland, especially, one would be hard pressed to find any Methodist meeting place whose gatherings were exclusively Black or White. In this respect, places such as Oxen Hill were notable exceptions, because of both its African American origins and its predominantly free Black membership. African Americans founded additional churches like Oxen Hill through the first half of the nineteenth century as the number of free Blacks grew.

Dorchester County

Methodism spread to Dorchester County toward the end of the 1770s,[30] and became infamous in Methodist lore after circuit rider Freeborn Garretson was arrested and put into the jail at Cambridge in 1780. Garrettson was renowned for his anti-slavery stance, and as early as 1782, Dorchester Methodists were freeing their slaves. Asbury was caught up in a most interesting local incident during his 1784 visit. A slave, known only as George, a member of the Methodist society, had run afoul of the law. Tried for a theft that had occurred before his conversion, he was sentenced to death. Asbury arrived in Cambridge just before his scheduled hanging on October 14. During his stay, George was reprieved, and Asbury added, "a merchant, who cursed the Negro for praying, died in horror."[31]

Henry Boehm traveled the Dorchester Circuit in 1801 and noted that while in Cambridge, in the evening he met the Black class of some forty members. He became aware that "some of the blacks have stood 20 years," that is, they had been converted in the early 1780s.[32]

On his annual visit to Cambridge in 1802, Asbury praised the church members for the new church building, the original Zion MEC (now UMC). Black members, both slave and free, contributed to its construction. Growth and nurture of the membership were aided by the annual camp meetings, the most attended being the ones on Taylor's Island and at Ennalls' Springs. Boehm observed some four thousand attendees at the Ennalls' Spring meeting in August 1802.

Early in the nineteenth century, Cambridge attracted many of the county's free Blacks. By 1826, their community's size and prosperity prompted the formation of a separate congregation. The White members donated land and the new church would be named for Methodist Bishop Beverly Waugh (1789–1858), later known for his anti-slavery stance. Jasper Cornish, a free Black, led a Sunday school for Black children for a few years until such activity was prohibited.[33]

Leading the Cambridge church was Benjamin Jenifer, a slave married to a free woman. His wife owned their residence, located adjacent to the church. His master was Josiah Bayly, Sr., prominent lawyer, attorney general of the state (in the 1830s), and an Episcopalian. Jenifer served as a local preacher at Waugh and throughout the county for many decades.

Waugh MEC was founded by freedmen. The existence of a relatively large number of freedmen is amply demonstrated by the inroads of the AME Church on the Eastern Shore, which within a few years of its existence had a circuit of churches centered on Denton (Caroline County) and Easton (Talbot County). One of the largest appointments in the AME Church, in 1824 the Eastern Shore Circuit reported 543 members divided between eight locations. Already in 1817, the AMEs had sent a minister into Cecil County. The next year, Shadrack Bassett pioneered the work in Denton and Easton.[34]

As early as 1830, AME ministers came to Dorchester. Rumors circulating through the county tying them to a slave insurrection were serious enough that the local newspapers felt compelled to refute them. Apparently, their attempts to organize the free Blacks had been interpreted as an incitement to rebel. Local opposition blunted their initial recruitment attempts.

In the 1820s, approximately five thousand slaves resided in Dorchester County.[35] One center for Blacks was Bucktown, located about ten miles south and slightly east of Cambridge on the east side of the Transquaking River. Early circuit riders stopped here and in 1812 Scott Chapel was established about a half mile north of Bucktown. At an unknown date, an all-Black congregation began to meet in Bucktown that later would be reorganized as Bazzel's Chapel MEC.

The churches in and around Bucktown take on a special significance as the places where the family of Harriet Tubman worshipped.[36] Tubman was born Araminta Ross around 1820, most likely on the Broades Plantation near Bucktown, the daughter of Harriet Green and Benjamin Ross. (Unknown to her as she grew up, another slave later to take the name Frederick Douglass was growing up not thirty miles north of her near Easton, in Talbot County.) Tubman seems to have reached maturity on the farm of young Edward Brodess, then just starting out on his own, his father having died when he was a child. Most likely, the Ross children worshipped at Scott's Chapel and may have also attended services among the group that would later form Bazzel's Chapel. Descendents of the Ross family (Tubman's siblings) are active in Bazzel's UMC to the present. At the age of twenty-five, Araminta married a free Black man, John Tubman. Then in 1848, she seized an opportunity to escape her condition and made her way to Philadelphia. She would then devote the remaining years until the Civil War to the Underground Railroad (to be discussed in a later chapter).

Frederick Douglass, Tubman's later compatriot in the struggle for emancipation, was born in Tuckahoe, near Hillsborough, at the northeast corner of Talbot County around 1817–18. He spent some time at St. Michaels, on the shore of Chesapeake Bay, and when around the age of seven was sent to Baltimore. During his years in Baltimore he lived near the Fell's Point (Wilk Street) Church. He found his first religious awakening from hearing a White Methodist minister, James Hanson (1783–1860), who taught him that God was his friend. He was nurtured by a kindly and pious Black man named Lawson with whom he would meet for prayer and singing and with whom he attended prayer meetings. Meanwhile, his owner's wife attended the Wilk Street Church and was assigned to the class led by future bishop Beverly Waugh.[37]

In 1832, he returned to St. Michaels. Here he became subject to a most cruel master, Thomas Auld. While Methodism had ameliorated the condition of many slaves, even leading to some being freed, Douglass would experience a quite opposite reality.[38] In August 1832, Auld had a conversion experience at a Methodist camp meeting. Douglass then noted that rather than acting more kindly, getting religion merely gave him a new sanction for cruelty. Among White people, he was a model of piety, much engaged in prayer. He became a Methodist class leader and a licensed exhorter. But in his everyday life, Auld would beat his slaves and quote scripture to justify his actions. At one point he and fellow class leaders had broken up a Sunday School where slaves were being taught to read. He regularly entertained the ministers in his home, but they never seemed to pick up on the dark side of his life.[39]

At one point Auld hired Douglass out to Edward Covey, renowned for breaking the spirit of young slaves who might resist their master's orders. Covey was also a "pious" Methodist class leader, who always began and ended the day with prayer. Douglass was invited to the family's devotions, in part because of his singing voice. Douglass recalled, "The exercises of his family devotions were always commenced with singing; and, as he was a very poor singer himself, the duty of raising the hymn generally came upon me." Douglass would at times toy with Covey and not pick up the hymn, which would leave his tone deaf master in some confusion. He concluded of his years around Auld and Covey that "of all slaveholders with whom I have ever met, religious slaveholders are the worst. I have ever found them the meanest and basest, the most cruel and cowardly, of all others."

In 1834, he went to live with a new master, William Freeland. Here, on his Sundays, Douglass formed a Sunday school and taught his fellow slaves to read and write. The school operated clandestinely out of the home of a free Black man. The next year, Douglass was discovered plotting the escape of himself and several of his cohorts. He was sent back to Baltimore and from there finally in 1838 he made his escape. Once in a safe space, he took the name Frederick Douglass. He eventually settled in New Bedford, Massachusetts, and began to reorient his life as a freeman, which would soon lead to his new career as an activist in the abolitionist cause.

In New Bedford, Douglass initially attended the Elm Street MEC, but was eventually led to the AMEZ church that met on Second Street. The pastor, William Sarrington, brought him into the church. On a visit in 1840, Bishop Rush presented Douglass with his exhorter's license.

While Douglass saw and recorded one part of the reality that was slavery, it was also the case that many slaves and former slaves found a place in the church, and their loyalty to it bespoke a different reality. Across Maryland and Virginia, the church could not have operated as it did had it not been for the many African men, most forgotten and their names lost to history, who themselves filled the posts of class leader, exhorter, and preacher. One Dorchester Methodist who rose above the common anonymity of such tasks was Samuel Green. Green was born into slavery around 1802 at East New Market. He became active in the Methodist church and was licensed as a preacher. He married and as his wife was a slave, so were his two children, Samuel, Jr. (b. 1829), and Susan (b. 1832). He lived the life of a slave but was able to learn to read and master a trade, blacksmithing. Before his owner died in 1831, he had made provision for Green to purchase his freedom. Once that was accomplished he purchased his wife Catherine's freedom, though thwarted in efforts on behalf of his children. From his blacksmithing, he was able to purchase a farm and preached throughout the county. Relatively quiet through the 1830s and '40s, in the 1850s he became involved in the Underground Railroad, which lifted him from obscurity.

In the early 1840s, several Black congregations, separate points on the Dorchester circuit, began to acquire buildings. A church emerged in East New Market (1843),[40] to be followed by Vienna (1845), Church Creek (1847), and Salem (1848). An AME Church at Cambridge finally appeared in 1847. While disturbing many Whites, Tubman's activity in the Underground Railroad did little to affect the overall growth of African American Methodism, and additional new churches, such as Dickerson Chapel, located about four miles outside of Cambridge, continue to materialize through the 1850s.

Nat Turner

While the Underground Railroad did not seem to inhibit the spread of Methodism among African Americans, growth was momentarily checked by the slave insurrection in Southampton County, Virginia, led by Nat Turner. In August of 1831, Turner and a small band of co-conspirators killed his present owners and then moved through the county, where additional deaths occurred. Turner hoped that his action would cause a spontaneous uprising of the slaves. That uprising did not occur, but by the time the rebellion was suppressed, some fifty White people had died. The Virginia militia captured or killed those who followed Turner and eventually tracked down their leader. Turner and a number of his followers were tried and executed.[41]

Nat Turner (1800–1831) grew up on the plantation of Benjamin Turner, a Methodist, who had built a chapel on his Southampton plantation for the use of itinerating ministers. Turner would change hands several times as Benjamin Turner died in 1810 and Samuel Turner in 1822. Following the latter's death, Turner was sold to Thomas Moore of Cross Keys, Virginia, and thus escaped being sent into the Deep South. Meanwhile, Turner, who experienced a variety of mystical experiences as he was coming of age, developed a sense of chosenness. He would lead his people out of slavery. He had also believed that his Methodist owner would free him, a hope that was dashed in 1822. Moore died in 1828, and his widow married Joseph Travis, also a resident of Southampton County. Thus Turner's ownership passed again.

The actual decision to go ahead with the rebellion was occasioned by a solar eclipse that occurred on February 12, 1831, which Turner interpreted as a sign to act. The delays in putting the plan together caused Turner and his original seven associates to wait until August 21 to begin. But before the killing began, Turner delivered an impromptu sermon to a Black audience outside of the Barnes MEC, located near the North Carolina state line, on August 14.

Some seventy-five people joined Turner in his rebellion, and as that force began to meet opposition, suddenly Turner disappeared. An army was raised to pursue him. He was apprehended on October 30 (seventy days after his disappearance). Following a hasty trial, he was hung on November 11. Of those tried as his co-conspirators, sixteen were hung, twelve placed on the auction block, and eight discharged. However, in further retaliation, angry and anxiety-ridden Whites killed more than a hundred Black people who were not involved in the insurrection.

Far more than the Denmark Vesey incident in South Carolina in 1822, in which no one died except those few charged with planning the reputed rebellion, the Turner insurrection sent out a wave of panic through the slaveholding states, especially Maryland and North Carolina. A series of laws were passed over the next few years that introduced measures designed to prevent any further such events. The most severe had to do with schooling, and legislation against enabling slaves to learn to read and write became pervasive from Maryland to Louisiana and remained in place until the 1860s.

After an initial wave of legislation, in 1832 Virginia added regulations forbidding Blacks from preaching and denying them the right of assembly unless one or more White persons were present. For Methodists, these laws most affected the meeting of Black-led classes. Some churches, such as the Central MEC in Staunton, Virginia, reacted to the new laws by reintegrating local Blacks into their fellowship, at least in a limited manner. By 1860, the 550-member church included some 200 Blacks.[42]

Several African Americans who lived through the era left their memories of the Turner incident. Writing toward the end of the decade, James Williams[43] noted that his brother, a preacher in Richmond, had not been allowed to preach since the insurrection. Another Virginian, James L. Smith, remembered that "When Nat Turner's insurrection broke out, the colored people were forbidden to hold meetings among themselves." He then described one particularly moving incident:

> Notwithstanding our difficulties, we used to steal away to some of the quarters to have our meetings. One Sabbath I went on a plantation about five miles off, where a slave woman had lost a child the day before, and as it was to be buried that day, we went to the 'great house' to get permission from the master if we could have the funeral then. He sent back word for us to bury the child without any funeral services. The child was deposited in the ground, and that night we went off nearly a mile to a lonely cabin on Griffin Furshee's plantation, where we assembled about fifty or seventy of us in number; we were so happy that we had to give vent to the feelings of our hearts, and were making more noise than we realized. The master, whose name was Griffin Furshee, had gone to bed, and being awakened by the noise, took his cane and his servant boy and came where the sound directed him. While I was exhorting, all at once the door opened and behold there he stood, with his white face looking in upon us. As soon as I saw the face I stopped suddenly, without even waiting to say amen.[44]

Fortunately, Furshee was merely curious about the noise and just wanted to know what was happening.

In neighboring North Carolina, Harriet Jacobs experienced an opposite reaction.

> After the alarm caused by Nat Turner's insurrection had subsided, the slave-holders came to the conclusion that it would be well to give the slaves enough of religious instruction to keep them from murdering their masters. The Episcopal clergyman offered to hold a separate service on Sundays for their benefit. His colored members were very few, and also very respectable—a fact which I presume had some weight with him. The difficulty was to decide on a suitable place for them to worship. The Methodist and Baptist churches admitted them in the afternoon, but their carpets and cushions were not so costly as those at the Episcopal church. It was at last decided that they should meet at the house of a free colored man, who was a member.[45]

On a larger scale, however, the Turner insurrection would have some effect on the new plantation missions being developed in South Carolina and Georgia, the effort having just been launched two years earlier. It proved an additional obstacle to the mission's initial acceptance in some places, as it reignited the debate over whether religion helped or hindered the operation of the plantation. Slowly, however, plantation owners began to act in the hope that religion would serve as a preventative to any additional Turner-like events.

Meanwhile, back in Virginia, the Norfolk MEC Quarterly Conference re-acted to the post-Turner situation by refusing to renew the preaching license of three Black slave preachers who had previously been licensed to work on the circuit. The action was not taken without significant opposition and led to the submission of a memorial to the Virginia Annual Conference of 1832, and then to the 1832 General Conference. In December 1831, the Norfolk Quarterly Conference met and renewed the licenses of local preachers Beverly Wilson and Lewis Sheppard, both free Blacks. It then refused to renew the licenses of two exhorters who were slaves. The conference adjourned briefly, and when it reconvened, it dealt with a resolution from the White minister in charge to the effect that the licenses of all the Black preachers be reconsidered and that in light of the laws of the state it adopt a policy that the church will "for the present neither license or renew the license of any Coloured man (either Freeman or Slave) who does not give us satisfactory assurances of his determination & ability to remove to some other state or Country before the time of the session of our next Quarterly meeting for this station, where he will probably be at liberty to exercise the ministerial authority unmolested." This resolution passed and remained operative through the Civil War. The memorial by those who opposed the resolution was approved by neither the Virginia Conference nor the General Conference.[46]

Much has been made of the problem of the development of the African American Church following the Turner incident, but overall, the post-Turner anxieties seemed to have most affected education. Relative to Methodism, its effect was mostly local, that is in Virginia (especially the Tidewater Area) and adjacent states, and negative effects declined sharply through the decade. The ongoing needs of the church did not lead to the repeal of the new laws, but certainly led to their widespread non-enforcement. The church at Norfolk, for example, never again renewed the licenses of the Black preachers and exhorters, but they appeared to continue functioning just as they had previously. Meanwhile, across the South, proponents actually incorporated the incident into their arguments for the spread of the plantation missions.

Possibly more important in the long run for the development of African American churches in Virginia, given the key role of free Blacks in the founding and leadership of African American congregations, was the law passed by the Virginia legislature that any slave manumitted after 1836 had to obtain the permission of a county court to remain legally in the state for more than a year after his/her manumission. The law drove many free Blacks north. Though some large congregations developed in Virginia, no churches approaching the importance of Sharp Street in Maryland or Bethel in Philadelphia emerged there, nor proportionately did the same number of separate African American congregations emerge there as occurred, for example, just to the north in Maryland.

Notes

1. Frederick E. Maser and Howard T. Maag, ed., *The Journal of Joseph Pilmore: Methodist Itinerant* (Philadelphia, PA: Historical Society of the Philadelphia Annual Conference of the United Methodist Church, 1969): 149.

2. Maser and Maag, *Journal of Joseph Pilmore*, 149–50.

3. Maser and Maag, *Journal of Joseph Pilmore*, 150.

4. William Bennett, *Memorials of Methodism in Virginia* (Richmond: The Author, 1871), 68.

5. Maser and Maag, *Journal of Joseph Pilmore*, 194.

6. [James L. Smith], *Autobiography of James L. Smith, Including Also Reminiscences of Slave Life, Recollections of the War, Education of Freedmen, Causes of the Exodus, Etc.* (Norwich, CT: Bulletin Company, 1881), 27.

7. Jon Greenstone, "Ante Bellum Methodism in Winchester, Virginia, and the Great Schism," posted at www.emmitsburg.net/archive_list/articles/thoughtful/vicar_john/methodism_in_winchester.htm.

8. Francis Asbury, *The Journal and Letters of Francis Asbury*. 3 vols. (Nashville, TN: Abingdon Press; London: Epworth Press, 1958), I:56–57.

9. This account of Gough is taken from John Lednum, *A History of the Rise of Methodism in America* (Philadelphia, PA: The Author, 1859). Gough is also mentioned frequently in Asbury's *Journal*.

10. Lednum, *History of the Rise of Methodism*, 153–56

11. John Littlejohn, *Journal of John Littlejohn*. (Typescript. Nashville, The Upper Room, n.d.), 72.

12. Thomas Rankin, *Journal*, entry for July 9, 1776.

13. [Thomas H. Jones], *The Experiences of Thomas H. Jones, Who Was a Slave for Forty-Three Years. Written by a Friend, as Related to Him by Brother Jones* (Boston: Bazin & Chandler, 1861), chapter 1.

14. Greensburg Washington Offley, *A Narrative of the Life and Labors of the Rev., G. W. Offley, a Colored Man, and Local Preacher and Missionary, Who Lived Twenty-seven Years at the South and Twenty-three at the North; Who Never Went to School a Day in his Life and Only Commenced to Learn his Letters When Nineteen Years and Eight Months Old; the Emancipation of His Mother and Her Three Children; How He Learned to Read While Living in a Slave State, and Supported Himself From the Time He Was Nine Years Old Until He was Twenty-one* (Hartford, CT: n.p., 1859), 15.

15. Henry Bibb, *Narrative of the Life and Adventures of Henry Bibb, An American Slave, Written by Himself* (New York: The Author, 1849), 203.

16. The correspondence is reprinted in John W. Blassingame, ed., *Slave Testimony: Two Centuries of Letters, Speeches, Interviews, and Autobiographies* (Baton Rouge, LA: Louisiana State University Press, 1977), 48–57.

17. A large literature has now been accumulated on the ring shout and its significance, though with a concentration on its contemporary survival on the Sea Islands in Georgia: see Janet D. Cornelius, "Shout Because You're Free: The African American Ring Shout Tradition in Coastal Georgia," *Journal of Southern History* 66, 4 (November 1, 2000): 865; Jonathan C. David, "Shout because You're Free: The African American Ring Shout Tradition in Coastal Georgia," *Journal of American Folklore* 112, 446 (December 31, 1999): 565–67; Samuel A. Floyd, Jr., "Ring Shout! Literary Studies, Historical Studies, and Black Music Inquiry." *Black Music Research Journal* 11, 2 (1991): 265–87; and Art Rosenbaum and Johann S. Buis, *Shout Because You're Free: The African American Ring Shout Tradition in Coastal Georgia* (Athens, GA: University of Georgia Press, 1998).

18. Taken from her 1936 interview as part of the WPA program to interview still-living former slaves in the mid-1930s, posted at http://memory.loc.gov/cgi-bin/ampage?collId=mesn&fileName=162/mesn162.db&recNum=294&itemLink=S?ammem/mesnbib:@field(AUTHOR+@od1(King,+Silvia)).

19. Charles Lyell, *A Second Visit to the United States of North America* (New York: Harper & Brothers, 1849), 270.

20. Thomas Wentworth Higginson, *Army Life in a Black Regiment and Other Writings* (New York: Penguin Group, 1997), 13–14.

21. Mark P. Bangert, "The Gospel about Gospel—the Power of the Ring," *Currents in Theology and Mission* (August 2004), posted at www.findarticles.com/p/articles/mi_m0MDO/is_4_31/ai_n6150717/pg_9.

22. As observed by Jonathan Edwards in the 1740s in New England, Whites were on occasion capable of a spectrum of bodily expressions of religious exuberance quite apart from any African American influence. See his *A Treatise Concerning Religious Affections* (1746; Rpt.: New Haven, CT: Yale University Press, 1959). However, as noted in George Whitefield's *Journal,* Blacks were regular participants in the activities of the Great Awakening of 1740–43.

23. Daniel Alexander Payne, *Recollections of Seventy Years* (Nashville: A. M. E. Sunday School Union, 1888), 253. Recently, Jonathan Comly David documented the ring shout's survival in Delaware and Maryland's Eastern Shore and the continuance of the very Methodist Singing and Prayer Bands about which Payne complained. See Jonathan Comly David, *In One Accord: Community, Musicality, and Spirit among the Singing and Praying Bands of Tidewater Maryland and Delaware* (Philadelphia: University of Pennsylvania, Ph.D. dissertation, 1994).

24. Joan R. Sherman, ed., *The Black Bard of North Carolina: George Moses Horton and his Poetry* (Chapel Hill: University of North Carolina Press, 1997); Benjamin

Griffith Brawley, "Three Negro Poets: Horton, Mrs. Harper and Whitman," *Journal of Negro History* 2 (1917), 384–92. Horton's own publications have survived and are now available online: George Moses Horton, *The Hope of Liberty. Containing a Number of Poetical Pieces* (Raleigh: J. Gales & Son, 1829); *Life of George M. Horton. The Colored Bard of North Carolina from "The Poetical Works of George M. Horton, the Colored Bard of North Carolina, to which is Prefixed the Life of the Author, written by himself"* (Hillsborough, NC: Heartt, 1845); and *Poems by a Slave* ([Philadelphia]: [s.n.], [1837]).

25. Richard Allen, *A Collection of Spiritual Songs and Hymns from Various Authors* (Philadelphia: T. L. Plowman, 1801). A second edition titled simply *A Collection of Hymns and Spiritual Songs* appeared later that same year. The revised hymnal was reprinted by Mother Bethel African Methodist Episcopal Church in Philadelphia in 1987.

26. J. Roland Braithwaite, "Introduction" in Richard Allen, *A Collection of Hymns and Spiritual Songs* (Philadelphia: Mother Bethel African Methodist Episcopal Church in Philadelphia, 1987), ix–xlvii.

27. This building was possibly erected in 1792 or 1793. Asbury notes passing through Oxen Hill in 1791 on his way to Alexandria, Virginia, and makes no mention of any Methodist meeting house there.

28. Oxen Hill was one of the first places selected by the newly formed African Methodist Episcopal Church as a site for a possible church, and in 1817 Peter Schureman was sent there as a missionary. The town does not reappear, however, as an appointment in succeeding years.

29. Quoted in "The History of St. Paul United Methodist Church," posted at www.stpumcmd.org/history.htm.

30. Asbury had first ventured there in 1779.

31. Asbury, *Journal*, I, 469.

32. Boehm Journal transcript, 50. Henry Boehm, *Reminiscences of Rev. Henry Boehm* (New York: Carlton & Porter, 1865). Boehm discusses his ventures in Dorchester County in chapter 6, 22–26, concluding his discussion with reflections upon the Black members.

33. The Cambridge Black church burned in 1836 and was rebuilt and opened for worship again the next year.

34. James A Handy, *Scraps of African Methodist Episcopal History* (Philadelphia: A. M. E. Book Concern, 1902), 28.

35. Kay Najiyyah McElvey's dissertation on Dorchester, *Early Black Dorchester, 1776–1870* (College Park, MD: University of Maryland, Ph.D. dissertation, 1991), includes a detailed history of the development of African American Methodism throughout the county.

36. On Tubman see Catherine Clinton, *Harriet Tubman: the Road to Freedom* (New York: Back Bay Books, 2004), or Earl Conrad, *Harriet Tubman* (Washington, DC: Associated Publishers, 1943).

37. Douglass gives slightly different accounts of his Baltimore years in the several editions of his autobiography. I am grateful to Ed Schell at the Baltimore Conference Historical Society for helping identify some of the Methodist ministers to whom Douglass refers.

38. On Douglass see William S. McFeely, *Frederick Douglass* (New York: W. W. Norton, 1991); Charles Waddell Chesnutt and Ernestine Williams Pickens, *Frederick Douglass* (Atlanta, GA: Clark Atlanta University Press, 2001); Eric J. Sundquist, ed., *Frederick Douglass: New Literary and Historical Essays* (Cambridge: Cambridge University Press, 1991); and Frederick Douglass, *Narrative of the Life of Frederick Douglass, an American Slave. Written by Himself.* (Boston: Anti-Slavery Office, 1845), posted at http://docsouth.unc.edu/douglass/douglass.html. Douglass revised and expanded his autobiography twice during his life. All three versions have been reprinted in recent years and are posted on the Internet.

39. Douglass remembered kindly one minister who came by, George Cookman (1800–1841), who was a hero to the slaves because of his convincing the owner of a neighboring plantation to give up his slaves. Cookman was born in England and had a fruitful ministry in America, rudely interrupted by a shipwreck on his way back to England for a visit to his family.

40. This church survives as the Mt. Zion Church in present-day New Market, Maryland, and was possibly the church regularly attended by Samuel Green.

41. There is now an extensive literature on the Turner insurrection, discussing not only the incident itself but the problems of understanding it and Nat Turner's own consciousness about what occurred, due to the White overlay on all of the documents, including Turner's autobiographical account taken down during his confinement. See William Sidney Drewry, *Slave Insurrections in Virginia (1830–1865)* (Washington, DC: The Neal Company, 1900); Herbert Aptheker, *Nat Turner's Slave Rebellion* (New York: Grove Press, 1966); Henry Irving Tragle, *The Southampton Slave Revolt of 1831: A Compilation of Source Material* (Amherst: University of Massachusetts Press, 1971); Kenneth S. Greenberg, ed., *The Confessions of Nat Turner and Related Documents* (Boston: Bedford Books/St. Martin's Press, 1996); and Kenneth S. Greenberg, ed., *Nat Turner: A Slave Rebellion in History and Memory* (New York: Oxford University Press, 2001).

42. "History of Augusta Street United Methodist Church," Posted at www.iath .virginia.edu/staunton/harvest/church/asmeth.html.

43. James Williams, *Narrative of James Williams, a American Slave, Who Was for Several years a Driver on a Cotton Plantation in Alabama* (New York: American Anti-Slavery Society/ Boston: Isaac Knapp, 1838).

44. James L. Smith, *Autobiography of James L. Smith, Including Also Reminiscences of Slave Life, Recollections of the War, Education of Freedmen, Causes of the Exodus, Etc.* (Norwich, CT: Bulletin Company, 1881), posted at http://docsouth.unc.edu/neh/ smithj/smithj.html.

45. [Harriett Jacobs], *Incidents in the Life of a Slave Girl. Written by Herself*. Edited by L. Maria Child. (Boston: For the Author, 1861), posted at http://gcclearn.gcc.cc .va.us/adams/hjhome.htm.

46. The memorials are quoted in full in Reginald F. Hildebrand, "'An Imperious Sense of Duty': Documents Illustrating an Episode in the Methodist Reaction to the Nat Turner Revolt," *Methodist History* 19, 3 (April 1981): 155–74.

CHAPTER SIX

The Push into the South

The Unique Way of African Methodism in Charleston

In the generation after the formation of the Methodist Episcopal Church, Charleston became its major urban home in the South. A relatively large free Black population (between 12 and 16 percent of a Black population that in turn constituted slightly more than half of the entire population) resided in the city. While the free Black community formed a distinct social class above that of the slave population, it was itself divided, the upper crust being formed by a group of mulattos, a relatively wealthy group that due to their parentage had some close ties to the White community. White friends and (publicly unacknowledged) relatives often provided protection and assisted in business endeavors. Methodism found a response from all levels of the African community.[1]

Immediately after the 1784 Christmas Conference, Asbury, accompanied by Jesse Lee and Henry Willis, headed south. They arrived in Charleston on the weekend of February 26–27, 1785. They found a local ally in the person of Edgar Wells and a place to hold preaching services in an abandoned Baptist church. Asbury noted that from the beginning the primary response came from the Africans who attended.[2] The then youthful Rachel Wells (d. 1849), Edgar Wells' servant, was the first Black convert in Charleston. She would live a long life as a Methodist, and had a reputation for piety among both Blacks and Whites. She is included in 1830 on the list of the city's free Black heads of households. She passed away near mid-century, the oldest member of the Trinity Church.

At the first session of the South Carolina Annual Conference, in 1787, 141 Black members were reported, of which 53 were in Charleston. That same year the first Methodist church in Charleston, the Cumberland Street Church, was completed and dedicated, thus ending the necessity of movement from place to place as the membership increased. A second congregation, Bethel, was launched in 1793, by which time there were 50 White members and 169 Africans.[3]

The growth that allowed the formation of Bethel had come in spite of the 1791 split in the Cumberland Street Church led by William Hammett, an Irish Methodist minister who founded the independent Trinity Primitive Methodist Church. A short time later, he also opened a second affiliated congregation, St. James Church. In 1813, following Hammett's death, both congregations reunited with the Methodist Episcopal Church, giving the Methodists four congregations in the city through the remaining decades until the Civil War. Black members were scattered among the four congregations.

Leadership among Charleston's African American Methodists came into its own during the tenure of the young minister assigned to the city in 1810. William Capers yearned to evangelize the plantations that surrounded the city but found himself unable to move about freely in the area just outside the city where previously some response to Methodism had been noted. As early as 1793, Ezekiel Cooper, the preacher in charge, had visited John's Island, where he preached primarily to a Black audience. Cooper believed a large work could be developed there, but there had been little follow-up in subsequent years.

Capers spotted some capable and articulate men as he got to know his congregants, some of whom, like Castile Selby and Richard Holloway, were already serving as class leaders. His initial cadre included Amos Baxter, Thomas Smith, Peter Simpson, Smart Simpson, Aleck Harlston, and Harry Bull. Licensed as local preachers, they moved out as evangelists to the plantations around the city—St. John Island, St. James Island, Goose Creek, and elsewhere. Their success gave the evangelists a special role among the Black members and contributed to Capers' own thinking about mobilizing the church to evangelize the plantations, a plan he would put into effect at the end of the 1820s.

In 1814, the Hammett churches realigned with the MEC and brought additional Black members with them. About this same time the Charleston churches developed a unique structure, a separate quarterly meeting just for the African members, now over a thousand in number. With no thought given to forming a separate congregation for the African American members, the new structure did provide recognition of the leadership and talent being demonstrated among them. Thus, the Black members were able to meet separately from the White conference each quarter, collect money and create their own separate budget for charitable purposes, and take charge over the discipline of wayward members. The conference placed considerable power into the hands of those local preachers, exhorters, and class leaders who had seized the opportunity during Capers' tenure in the city.

Among the several people who stepped forward at this time, few would be as prominent as Richard Holloway. A light-skinned mulatto, Holloway had previously demonstrated both his leadership and faith when in 1803 he joined with some colleagues to form the Minors' Moralist Society to educate orphaned and/or indigent Black children. Future African Methodist bishop Daniel Payne remembered Holloway very kindly, as he had been one of the children the Society supported. Then shortly before his thirteenth birthday, Payne was apprenticed to Richard Holloway's son James (who had married Payne's older sister), from whom he learned the carpenter's trade. Payne also remembers Holloway from the late 1820s and the events that were to have such an effect on his life: "Religion among the members of Cumberland Street Church had waxed very cold, and Brother Holloway called a special meeting of all classes, and inquired what might be done for the revival of God's work. It was decided to meet every Sunday between the morning and evening service in Mr. Bonneau's school room to pray for revival. In this place we met Sunday after Sunday. God heard our songs of praise, our prayers of faith, poured out his awakening and converting power upon his waiting children, and many souls were converted and sanctified by it. Of this number I was one."[4] Payne subsequently attended the Cumberland Street Church.

Very different in both temperament and manner was Castile Selby. While Whites remembered Holloway primarily as intelligent and zealous (occasionally suggesting that his zealousness distorted his judgment), Selby was thought of as an exemplar of piety, humility, and simplicity. He became a class leader in 1801 and remained faithful in that task into the 1850s, for a number of years as the leader of class no. 4 at Trinity Church. William Wightman was present in 1830 when Capers fell seriously ill, and Selby stopped to visit. Capers entreated Selby, "You find me near my end, but kneel down and turn your face to the wall, and pray for me; and all of you pray." Wightman described the prayer as "full of humble submission to the Divine Will and at the same time anchored in a mighty faith in the great mediator." The prayer also seemed to have some instantaneous results. Capers noted immediate improvement, and dated the recovery of his health from that moment.[5]

The first time of testing for the relative autonomy of Charleston's African Methodist leadership came in 1815. Anthony Senter, the White preacher in charge, accused the Africans' quarterly conference of corruption. The essence of the charge revolved around the use of the charitable funds, a portion of which, he discovered, was being siphoned off to purchase the freedom of some of the church members still in slavery. Angered at this use of the church's revenue, Senter discontinued the quarterly conference structure, returned control of the money to the White leadership, and demanded that the White minister-in-charge be present whenever Black members faced disciplinary proceedings (church trials).

Senter's action prompted a dramatic response, though it would be several years before most of the Whites were aware of what was occurring. Secretly, a group of the Black members, led by Morris Brown and Henry Drayton, built on the discontent over the loss of their autonomy by laying plans for an independent congregation. In 1816, having heard of the formation of the AME Church in Philadelphia, they saw alignment with it as a possibility, but Brown was unable to travel to Philadelphia for the organizing meeting due to travel restrictions on free Blacks in Charleston at the time. Accompanied by Henry Drayton, he did travel to Philadelphia in 1817, at which time he was admitted on trial[6] and the church was accepted into the connection. The new Emmanuel AME Church had only a few hundred members at this point. But that would soon change.[7]

Through 1817 the new church met in several different locations and laid plans to erect a building at Reid and Hanover in the far northwest of Charleston. Technically operating against the law, in December the church was raided and 469 arrested for disorderly conduct. Authorities charged that the church leaders had "bought the lot, erected a building and engaged therein in a species of worship which the neighborhood found a nuisance." There was no trial, however, and the church leaders were soon released.

Then early in 1818, the Black members of the four MEC congregations dropped their bomb. All at once, 4,367 (of 5,690) Black members withdrew, using as their excuse their protest against the Whites having arbitrarily erected a hearse house on their burial plot on Pitt Street.[8] Interestingly, of the core of licensed preachers, only Harry Bull and Smart Simpson left with the majority. Holloway, Castile, and the others remained with the loyal minority. Other members who left included Charles Corr, Amos Cruckshank, Marcus Brown, Stewart Simpson, John B. Matthews, James Eden, London Turpin, and Aleck Harlston. Though unable to attend the 1818 AME conference in Philadelphia, Brown and Drayton were received into full connection, the former as an elder and the latter as a deacon. Emmanuel Church reported 1,848 members, making it the second largest congregation in the new denomination.[9] Brown was able to leave Charleston and participate in the 1819 conference in Philadelphia.

Meanwhile, the remaining Black MEC membership reorganized. While the 1,323 remaining members seems a large number (still twice as large as the number of White members), it meant that some of the three Sunday services at each of the four Methodist churches in Charleston were held with empty galleries, and the silence from on high was more than noticeable. The number of class meetings dropped considerably. The new record book created in 1820 lists some forty-nine classes, with a number of the class leaders having to do double duty. Selby, for example, led classes 4 and 5 and Holloway classes 36 and 37.

Most, but by no means all, who left the MEC joined the new African Church. Their leaders, all free Blacks, adopted a policy of admitting no slaves to membership without the permission of their masters, many regular attendees not receiving such permission. Those who did join or attend also faced the continual harassment of the authorities, who made a second raid on the church in June of 1818, charging those arrested with holding an anti-slavery meeting. Eight of the ministers were sentenced to pay a fine of five dollars or receive five lashes of the whip. Morris Brown and four of his ministers were sentenced to a month's imprisonment if they did not leave the state. They chose to stay, and languished in jail.

Knowing that their meetings were illegal, church leaders tried to mollify authorities. Soon after the church was organized, they petitioned the state legislature for an exception to the law against their assembling. In their petition they promised to keep the church doors open on all occasions, to invite local White ministers to officiate whenever they were available, and provide separate seating for any Whites who chose to attend the worship services and observe the morals and deportment of the members. In addition they promised not to allow any Black minister who resided outside of South Carolina to officiate at the church. The petition was rejected, but the church continued to meet. Amos Cruckshank, Henry Drayton, Smart Simpson, and Aleck Harlston were ordained as AME elders, though apart from any direct contact with Bishop Allen and the church in Philadelphia.

By 1820, local sentiment against the new church and its building had mounted. Whites saw it as an evil within the Black community and claimed that it had been built with funds from anti-slavery societies in the North. They decried the fact that Brown had been allowed to travel to the North for ordination. The state responded to the growing list of charges (most unsubstantiated) by passing a new law against free Blacks entering the state. The city responded more directly and had the new building dismantled.

The destruction of the church building did not stop the Emmanuel Church; it continued meeting at its other locations for two more years. In 1822, the church reported some three thousand members, just slightly fewer than the church in Philadelphia. Morris Brown was noted as the continuing elder in charge; Henry Drayton, Amos Cruckshank, and Marcus Brown were named as ordained deacons and Charles Corr, Smart Simpson, Harry Bull, John B. Matthews, James Eden, London Turpin, and Aleck Harlston as local ministers.

Such was the situation when the storm of the Vesey conspiracy broke upon the church. Denmark Vesey was a class leader at Emmanuel who was charged with organizing what would have been the largest slave revolt in United States history. The story began to unravel in May when a slave, Peter Desverneys, revealed the plot to his master, who in turn told the authorities. Officials were skeptical of the account related by William Paul, the first person arrested, but later confirmed part of his story after sending a spy to investigate the alleged plot. On June 16 the militia was called out and further arrests ensued. Denmark Vesey was arrested on June 22 and was among the first executed on July 2. Interrogations of suspects produced a number of confessions that included many contradictions and statements of fact that seemed completely unbelievable even to the somewhat panicky Whites who recorded them.

Later testimony singled out the now deceased Vesey as the ringleader and pointed to Emmanuel Church as the center where the conspirators hatched their plot. The proceedings led to the execution of thirty-five people, of which sixteen were members of the African church. Morris Brown was arrested under the 1820 statute against free Blacks entering the city from out of state (a reference to his 1819 trip to Philadelphia), and given fifteen days to leave. He left for Philadelphia accompanied by Amos Cruckshank, Henry Drayton, and Charles Corr. The latter two became members of the newly organized New York Conference of the AME Church. Eventually Brown was elected to the AME episcopacy. The Emmanuel Church was disbanded, though some members continued to meet clandestinely for a number of years. White Methodist leaders touted the fact that no one of the Africans who had stayed with the White church had been implicated in the plot.[10]

Those affiliated with Emmanuel found their way to other churches. Some joined the Scots Church (Presbyterian) and the Baptist church, but most eventually returned to one of the four MEC congregations. As African membership figures from the South Carolina Conference show, it took over five years to recover from the original loss of members in Charleston.

**Table 6.1. South Carolina
Conference Membership, 1816–1827**

1816	16,789
1818 (Jan)	11,714
1818 (Dec)	11,587
1820	11,748
1821	12,485
1822	12,906
1823	13,895
1824	14,766
1825	15,293
1826	15,708
1827	16,552

During the late 1820s, the African membership grew spectacularly in Charleston, and by 1829, even with three services every Sunday, the galleries at the four churches could not contain the members. At Bethel, some of the Africans began to occupy vacant seats in the rear of the main sanctuary. To accommodate the situation, the White members set apart some space near the doors by means of a panel, the area being termed "the Boxes." In general, the wealthier free mulatto members and a few of the older and infirm members claimed these seats. However, even this expedient proved inadequate. As the Black attendance increased, a few began moving into additional empty seats in the rear of the White seating area. Those who occupied these seats tended to be among the most faithful attendees at Sunday worship.

By 1830, the White segment of the congregation had grown to the point that occasionally on Sunday they filled the designated White seating area, but now found some of the seats occupied by Black members who were resistant to giving up seats that they had regularly occupied for several years. To keep the necessary order and decorum of the Sunday worship intact, that is, to force the Black members back behind the panel, Bethel appointed a couple of young men to act as sergeants of arms.

This arrangement worked well enough for several years, but in 1833, William Capers was again appointed to Charleston. A gifted speaker, Capers drew increasingly larger crowds to the Sunday worship and suddenly the demands of both Blacks and Whites for seating became a much more intense issue. Toward the end of 1833, the quarterly conference appointed a committee, mostly of young males, to resolve the problem. Several weeks later, when a large White audience showed up at Bethel church, the young men forcefully ejected those Black members seated in the officially White seating area from the church. This action was repeated the following Sunday. The action of the young men led to a resolution introduced at the next quarterly conference to have the trustees remove the partition and reclaim the area of "the Boxes" for White seating.

The conference's action made a significant disagreement within the congregation visible. Some joined Capers in siding with the Black members, while the majority of White members favored the alteration to the seating arrangements. Their efforts were continually foiled. Some leading laymen accused Capers of using his seemingly autocratic authority to override the wishes of the White members.

The Black members, not being part of the several congregational boards controlling local affairs, were largely shut out of any direct participation in these deliberations. However, more informally, several of the leading Black members, Richard Holloway and William B. Clark, reminded Capers of the significant support provided the congregation by the Black members. They more than hinted that it was in their power to simply leave the church altogether.

In the end, those members who wanted to remove the Black members from the main sanctuary accused Capers and his supporters of backing the African members because the church was at that moment in debt over previous building improvements and needed the contributions of the wealthier mulatto members to rid themselves of that burden.[11]

As the quarrel continued, some of the younger members challenged the church's *Discipline*. Called to account in a church trial, nine members were expelled. Showing their support, 165 White members of the Bethel congregation withdrew and reorganized as a congregation of the Methodist Protestant Church.[12] Those who withdrew did not leave quietly. They aired their grievances in a pamphlet to which Capers, the other preachers in Charleston, and Bishop John Emory (1789–1835),[13] who had attempted at one point to mediate the issue, printed a reply, the result of which was a second pamphlet by the former members.[14]

When the immediate issue subsided, the Charleston churches (still tied together as a single Charleston charge) made several attempts to deal with what was an ongoing seating problem. First, the leadership created a fifth congregation, called Asbury Chapel (which only lasted a few years). Then, seeking a more permanent solution, they decided to enlarge the Cumberland Church Street, and in 1838 they pulled down the old building to make way for a new brick sanctuary. However, before it could be completed, disaster struck. A major fire swept through central Charleston, which destroyed not only the new Cumberland structure, but also Trinity Church. The fire necessitated a complete, if temporary, reorganization of Methodism in

Charleston for the next years. White members were accommodated at St. Philip's Episcopal Church while Black members were provided with separate facilities in a building called the "old circus" located at Queen and Friend Streets. The new buildings, complete with the now standard galleries, were dedicated in the summer of 1839.

The new buildings prompted discussions about separating the churches in Charleston into four separate charges. Voted down in 1840, the idea was finally accepted two years later. Henceforth, a single preacher would be appointed to each one of the four churches. At this time there were a total of 535 White members and 3,500 African members in the city. This division came just prior to the dividing of American Methodism into the MEC and MEC,S, a change that had little immediate relevance to Africans in the South. They were much more affected by the 1848 ordinance passed by the city that demanded all free Blacks wear a visible medallion indicating their status.

The next opportunity for the Black members to assert themselves came in 1853 when the White members at Bethel erected a new sanctuary adjacent to the old building. The new sanctuary included a spacious gallery for the 1,400 Black members. As the old building was about to be demolished, the Black members stepped forward with a request. They asked that instead of occupying the new gallery, they be given the old building. This idea seemed to please everyone, though the Whites soon registered complaints about the noise coming from the old Bethel building. Again, an amicable solution was quickly found—members moved Old Bethel across the street to its present location.[15] For the first time in twenty-five years, the Black members had their own separate congregational facilities, of which they would become most possessive.

In 1857, a new class membership book for the Charleston Black Methodists was started at Trinity Church. It gives a snapshot picture of the church at the time. There are forty-two classes mentioned. Among the class leaders are some familiar names from the new generation of leaders—Charles Holloway (who had assumed the leadership passed down from his father Richard), Samuel Weston, and Moses H. Vanderhorst. Missing from the list, of course, is Castile Selby, who had passed away by this time. The new leadership would carry the church through the war and into the post-slavery era during which time it would assert itself in a new and unique manner.

African Methodism from Georgia to Texas

Even as Charleston was developing, North Carolina was beginning to take its place in Methodist history, with ministers riding three circuits by 1779. In the first report of members in 1786, the Bertie Circuit had the largest number of African American members with 58. Membership growth in North Carolina was spectacular in the last years of the 1790s, going from 1,288 (1796) to 2,096 just four years later, and more than half of that growth came from the movement of many Blacks into the church at New Bern and Camden. (It was not until around 1800 that the work that had been accomplished by Henry Evans at Fayetteville was discovered and included in the statistics.)

Paralleling Evans' work was that of William Meredith, an independent British preacher who moved to Charleston from the West Indies to work with William Hammitt. After falling out with Hammett, he moved to Wilmington, where he devoted himself to ministering to the Black residents. Overcoming initial suspicion and opposition (which included a time in jail and the burning of his first church building), he built an independent Methodist congregation, which he eventually turned over to Asbury. In 1801 it pops up in the annual report with 60 White and 360 Black members.[16]

Rivaling Fayetteville and Wilmington as the home of the oldest African American Methodist church in the state is Bolton, located about twenty-five miles west of Wilmington. There in 1803, the Gum Swamp MEC was founded, and members erected a log cabin church. It continues today as Smith Chapel UMC.[17]

New Bern (the former state capital) is one of the oldest centers of Methodism in the state (Asbury having originally stopped there in 1795), though the church was not organized formally until 1802, at which time the members purchased a lot upon which a chapel was erected. This chapel apparently served both Black and White members until 1843, at which time, following a very successful set of revival meetings, the White membership constructed a new building (now Centenary UMC) and left the older building (Andrew Chapel) to the Black members.

A few of the North Carolina Black preachers (apart from those who came from the Fayetteville church) that rise above the seemingly destined anonymity of their colleagues hailed from the Camden circuit. In the early decades of the nineteenth century, Currituck County was home to Robert Simmons (d. 1857) and Gabriel Whitehurst (d.c.1871), both slaves who were licensed by the MEC,S. Simmons' son, Abel M. Ferebee, also became a preacher and after the war joined the AMEZ as an active minister, at which work he persisted for many years.[18]

By 1813 the major centers of African American Methodists in North Carolina were visible, though church leaders parceled out the state among three conferences. Roanoke, Tar River, New Bern, and Beaufort were in districts attached to the South Carolina Conference, and Camden, Fayetteville, and

Wilmington went to the Virginia Conference. These churches/circuits would remain the primary centers of African membership through the antebellum period (though the location of churches on any given circuit frequently changed as the movement spread). If for example we look at 1840, membership is reported as follows: Washington (from Tar River) (367), New Bern (660), Beaufort (132), Trent/Newport (near Beaufort) (339), Camden (540), Fayetteville (263), Wilmington (590). In addition, large African American congregations had also been developed at Rockingham (422) and Brunswick (615). The AMEZ and AME Churches would make all of these larger churches objects of intense proselytization beginning in 1863. In addition, the first Black congregation in Raleigh formed in 1847 from the Edenton Street Church. It erected a building in 1853, and then aligned with the AME after the war.

The expected spread of Methodism in Georgia was delayed somewhat by the early formation of several African Baptist congregations in Savannah. Thus, the large African following so characteristic of Charleston never materialized. The first Methodist circuit riders were not well received and were on several occasions driven out by angry mobs, and only in 1807 was Jesse Lee finally able to form a Savannah class of four people, though some work developed in other towns.

In 1812, when a building was finally erected, the minister James Russell could report five members, two of whom were Black. One of these two, York Minis, is remembered as having "contributed eight dollars to aid the building, and loaning his quarto family Bible for service until the Church could procure one. His piety is undoubted by all who were acquainted with him. His master, an Israelite of the old stock, relates a number of anecdotes highly honorable to his character as a pious man. He died in peace."[19] In the first year after the building went up, membership shot up to fifty-two, of whom twenty-five were Black.

The building in Savannah was additionally important as one of Hammett's preachers, Adam C. Cloud, had moved to town in 1800 and quickly erected a building. Also, in 1802 the erratic Methodist preacher Lorenzo Dow came to Savannah and spoke at both the Hammett church and the First African Baptist Church.[20]

William Capers, assigned to Savannah in 1819, opined,

From the beginning, my congregations in Savannah were very large; and after a short time, the church might have been filled had it been half again as large as it was. Strikingly, in contrast with the church in Wilmington (North Carolina) in 1813, there were very few negroes who attended Methodist preaching;

the policy of the place allowing them separate churches, and the economy and doctrines of the Baptist Church pleasing them better than ours. There was but one side of the gallery appropriated to their use, and it was always the most thinly seated part of the church; while there were two respectably large colored churches in the city, with their pastors, and deacons, and sacraments, and discipline, all their own. I had therefore, little access to this portion of the people, and could do but little for them.[21]

As in Charleston, however, the Black membership picked up and during Caper's years outdistanced the White (ninety-five to fifty-two). African American membership increased dramatically at the end of the 1820s, but many of these were located on the plantations just outside the city. When the reporting of these members was fully transferred to the slave mission in the mid-1830s, only about a hundred Black members were reported in Savannah proper.

Membership growth at Trinity (the White congregation) called for a new larger building in the mid-1840s and occasioned the creation of a separate congregation for the African American members in 1845. The latter church was named after Bishop J. O. Andrew, who had formerly served in Savannah, but ironically, whose ownership of slaves had just split the church. Following the completion and dedication of the new Trinity, in 1849, a corporation was created for Savannah's three White Methodist churches, with a separate board of trustees being named for Andrew Chapel.[22] This situation would remain stable into the 1860s. Serving the chapel as local preachers were William Bentley, C. L. Bradwell, William Gaines, and Glascow Taylor, whose son Robert was a class leader in the congregation. Bentley and Bradwell were both freedmen.[23]

Augusta competes with Savannah as the cradle of Georgia Methodism. In the 1830s Black members came to outnumber Whites (305 to 268) at St. John's Church, and in 1840 a separate Black church, Trinity MEC, was organized. Around 1850, the members at St. John purchased the freedom of James Harris, a preacher from Athens, Georgia, who served as the Trinity Church's pastor. Ned West, who served the church through the war years, succeeded Harris.[24]

Modern Atlanta emerged from the village of Marthasville in the 1840s. At the same time Atlanta became an independent appointment (1850), the Black members began worshiping separately under the leadership of an African American preacher named Payne. He would be succeeded by Joseph Woods, one of several local preachers, who pastored during the war years.

Methodism came to Tennessee in 1783 and four years later circuit rider Benjamin Ogden reported four Africans among the sixty-three members on the Cumberland circuit.[25] In 1807, Jacob Young reported hearing one of the early Black preachers in Tennessee whom he met at a place near Fishing Creek. Young recalled,

> There was a Methodist society in the neighborhood, the preacher of which was a colored man, by the name of "Jacob." I believe every member had been awakened under his preaching; and, by the assistance of Mr. Chappel's daughters (White women), he had organized them into a class. One of the girls made out a class-paper, and they appointed Jacob leader. He was both preacher and leader; and, although he could not read a word, he could preach a pretty good sermon. He had a kind master, who would read for him Saturday evenings, and when a text was read that suited Jacob, he would ask his master to read it again, memorize the text, book, chapter, and verse; then he was ready for his work.[26]

Nashville Methodism began early in the new century and around 1817, a separate Black church was organized. At the end of the 1828–29 conference year the Nashville station received an additional second preacher to serve "the African Church situated not far from Sulphur Spring; here there was erected, for the colored people, a commodious brick house that was thronged with anxious hearers from Sabbath to Sabbath." After the building of this church, the Black members came to far outnumber the White.[27] Over the next several years, the African work outside the city would be integrated into the larger Tennessee African Mission and the figures and location of the work relative to districts would change erratically. In 1834, for example, James Gwen, the African missionary, would report only 450 Black members, as his work was now limited to Nashville proper.[28] Then in 1836–37, Nashville's African Mission was placed in the Cumberland District, with some 710 members being reported, an increase of about 100 for the year.[29] The work continued to fluctuate over the next decades.

In 1850, the General Conference approved a petition from the McKendree congregation to separate it from the African Mission. As a result, the older African church was sold and replaced with a large brick building located near the Nashville-Chattanooga Depot. White minister John B. M'-Ferrin preached the dedication sermon at the new Capers MEC,S on December 25, 1853.[30] Five years later, a second smaller church, Andrew Chapel, also opened to serve African believers.[31]

James Thomas (1827–1913) saw downtown Nashville filled with dressed-up African Americans every Sunday, with many mingling on the street outside the Capers Church in the afternoon. Meanwhile, inside,

> The opening of the service would be mild and orderly. When in the midst of the sermon the spirit would be working alike on the preacher and his hearers, the brothers and sisters would be partaking of the spiritual feeling with the zeal peculiar to their nature. The laughs, jerks, hand shaking, shouting, at times it took two or three persons to hold one little woman. Finally, she would lay exhausted and unconscious on the floor. The close of the sermon, the hymns following, and the several prayers were all such as to increase ardor of the members. At times two or three would burst out in prayer. It was hard to tell which of the trio or quartette would be allowed to say the prayers. The same would be the case with the hymns.[32]

When the White minister was absent, one of several Black local preachers officiated. The lengthy afternoon service would be followed by an evening service. Bishop Andrew remembered the city's African members as fine singers and musicians.[33]

Methodism spread to Alabama in 1808 with the arrival of Matthew P. Studivant. In 1810 he reported the formation of a lengthy circuit along the Tombigbee River with some seventy-one White and fifteen Black members. As the African membership grew, few documents recording their presence survived, apart from the regularly collected statistics. Among those few records that have survived, however, are those of the quarterly conferences at Tuscaloosa, where in the 1830s the Black members (most slaves) outnumbered the Whites, in this case 229 to 195. Blacks and Whites shared the same building, but met for religious services at different hours. The church's register for 1831 listed York Fontaine, Robin Smith, Peter Banks, and Webster Banks as local preachers; Jack Dearing as an exhorter; and David Collier and Jack Guild as class leaders.

Historian Anson West noted that more Black than White members had been expelled at one time or another. It was easier to apply the disciplinary rules to them, as they could put up less resistance to the Whites who ruled the church. Also, Black members had less privacy, resulting in less facility in covering up any offenses; hence more were caught. Primary offenses listed in the records were sexual immorality (seemingly the leading offense for both Black and White members throughout the church), intemperance, fighting, stealing, and lying. West also notes that the great majority of Black members exemplified the primary traits for which all the church members strove—honesty, temperance, purity, and piety.[34]

Among the more interesting churches in the state is the Cedar Hill congregation, founded in 1830 by Moses Hampton (d. 1885), a devout
Methodist and slave on the plantation of Robert B. Hampton (d. 1846).
Both Black and White attended the church he built, and as a licensed
preacher, Moses was valued as an assistant at the local camp meetings. A
skilled builder of cotton gins, by around 1860 he made enough money to purchase his freedom. As the first Methodist church in the county, the congregation soon became dominated by the Whites who attended and was integrated into the local circuit served by White ministers.[35]

Methodism's introduction to Mississippi followed the organization of the
Mississippi Territory in 1798. in 1799 Tobias Gibson (1771–1804) was appointed as a missionary to Natchez, and he organized the first congregation
at Washington, a small town near Natchez. During the organizational meeting, Gibson called together the eight original members, six White people
whose names have been recorded and remembered, and two Black people, remembered only as "a colored man and his wife, both slaves." Mississippi historian John Jones noted that the nearest Methodist church was, at the time,
over four hundred miles away. He also remembered having known the six
original White members but not the Black couple.[36] The work prospered and
in 1805 counted seventy-four White members and sixty-two Black.[37]

Several years later Gibson led in the erection of the first Methodist church
building, assisted by his "godly colored servant Caesar."[38] Though opposed to
slavery, Gibson had inherited slaves. Finding it inconsistent with his beliefs
to either sell them or simply give them away, he made it his business to spend
time with each, instructing them in Christianity and then freeing them.[39]

A church was established in Natchez proper and in 1827 when it became
a station, it reported eighty White and fifty-two Black members, while Washington had around two hundred White members and a few more Black members. In 1815, Robert Dobbins visited Natchez just as a camp meeting was beginning. He found the arrangement of the grounds peculiar, in that
two-thirds lay in front of the preaching stand and one-third, reserved for the
African attendees, in its rear. A high fence divided the two areas. Dobbins'
biographer noted that during his sermon to the assembled crowd, he turned
to the rear and addressed the Black people, "and with thrilling effect pointed
them to that better land where the distinction between slave and master was
unknown—exhorted them to be obedient to their masters, and above all to
'walk humbly with God.' The burning thoughts and glowing fervor of the
preacher were too much for those hopeful sons and daughters of Ham, and as
might have been expected, their cups ran over, and a shout of joy arose like
a tempest from these ebony worshipers, so that the noise was heard afar off."[40]

Work in Arkansas began in 1814 with two local preachers, William Stevenson and Eli Lindsay. Stevenson would join the traveling ministry in 1815 and later become a district superintendent. Early Arkansas settlers were split on slavery, and as late as 1823 records survive of a church trial in which the Rev. Joseph Reid was charged with owning a slave against church law. One Arkansas district superintendent, Jesse Haile, is remembered for his rants (popularly referred to as "Haile storms") against slavery that caused a number of Methodists to withdraw from the church and others to move on to Louisiana. Slavery remained a contentious issue in Arkansas Methodism until the 1844 split.

The African American presence in Arkansas developed rather late relative to the rest of the South, most being slaves who had traveled to Arkansas with their masters from the East. The slave population went from 1,617 in 1820 to 20,000 in 1840 and some 111,000 by 1860. Methodism also developed slowly. As the war began there were only about 20,000 White members and 3,100 Black members (plus an additional 1,000 probationers). Through the 1830s, three charges in Arkansas developed a Black majority—Little Rock, Pine Bluff, and Colombia.

The best known of the early Arkansas Black ministers, William Wallace Andrews, resided in Little Rock. Andrews emerged from obscurity as the butler of the Ashleys, a wealthy White family. Following his marriage in 1848 to Caroline Sherman, the Ashleys gave him a place to live at the corner of Fifth Street (now Capitol Avenue) and Broadway. Though still a slave, he had been allowed to receive a relatively good education and granted extra freedoms. His wife Caroline (b. 1829), born a slave in Tennessee, demonstrated an early aptitude for learning; she learned to read and write from secretly listening in on the lessons being taught the White girls in the house where she worked. In 1843, when the family who owned her brought their slaves with them to Arkansas, she relocated a short distance from Little Rock. After she met Andrews, she arranged with her owners to stay in Little Rock and give them a percentage of the wages she earned working.

Andrews became a local preacher in the MEC,S and found in the Ashley family generous patrons. They gave him a plot of ground at the northwest corner of Eighth and Broadway as the site for the first Black Methodist congregation in the state. In 1854, Andrews led in the building of Wesley Chapel.[41] His daughter Charlotte Andrews Stephens remembered, "My father was minister of the Methodist Episcopal church for colored people in what is now English and Broadway. He also has a chapel on the property of Mr. [Chester] Ashley. . . . My father was considered the founder of Wesley Chapel." The Andrews home had previously been the site of prayer meetings, class meetings, and Sunday school sessions. Through the Sunday school, many of the attendees, while receiving their religious instruction, also learned to read and write.[42]

Louisiana Methodism dates to the appointment in 1812 of Lewis Hobbs to New Orleans. While there, he lamented, "I feel like a dry branch cut off and thrown into this place to be burnt with the fire of persecution. . . . The Mayor and corporation of the town forbid my preaching at 7 o'clock because the negroes would come. I told them I did not tell the negroes to come and it was not my business to drive them away—and after they found they could not do anything with me they told me I might preach. I have sold my horse, and I have rented a room to preach in at fifteen dollars per month, and I am here with little money and many enemies."[43] The small group survived through the next decades when appointing ministers to New Orleans was a haphazard affair with the city being neglected more often than not.

William Winans succeeded Hobbs in 1813, and found a congregation of twenty Africans. After Winans' tenure, New Orleans was visited only sporadically, but in 1824 it reported twenty-three White and sixty Black members. Growth in the African American membership eventuated in the opening of Wesley Church, affectionately known as Mother Wesley Church, located on Gravier Street, in 1838.[44] It would appear as a separate appointment in 1842, and later in the 1850s it was grouped with Soule Chapel on Maris Street and Winans' Chapel as a single charge. In 1855, future bishop Holland N. McTyeire would be assigned as the pastor of these churches. After the war, Wesley passed to the Louisiana Conference of the MEC.

Then in 1842, Jordan Winston Early (b. 1814), an AME minister from Missouri, came to New Orleans and while there founded what became St. James AME Church. Interestingly, Early was able to use some Masonic contacts to have a bill passed through the Louisiana legislature that allowed his independent congregation to exist, the primary restrictions being that it cater to free Blacks and meet during the daylight hours. He remained in the city tending to the fledgling flock until 1847 when it was able to obtain a full-time pastor. Charles Doughty, one of its lay members, attended the Indiana Conference that year and was ordained and sent back to the city. St. James continued to function until 1858 when all the city's Black churches were closed until after the war. Reopened, it became the basis of the AME's spread in the state.[45]

The first Methodist (even before Hobbs) to be sent to Louisiana in 1806 had a bad experience in New Orleans, which he saw as a dirty inhospitable place. After several weeks in New Orleans, Elisha W. Bowman turned his back on the city and headed west toward an American settlement he had heard about near Opelousas. Among the scattered settlements of Americans (as opposed to those of the French-speaking Catholics) of the region he set up a circuit and reported an initial seventeen converts, all White.

Bowman's work later emerged as the Attakapas (Opelousas) and Rapides circuits (covering present-day Rapides, Avoyelles, St. Landry, St. Martin, Iberia, Lafayette, and Arcadia parishes). Through the second decade of the century, Black membership doubled that of the Whites. The church's early sentiment against slavery's growth in the new territory heightened the slaves' pre-disposure to like the Methodists. At the same time, the ministers were already aware that their keeping any anti-slavery sentiments to themselves was a necessity if they were to have any access to the slaves.

Daniel De Vinne, who spent two years on the Attakapas Circuit (1818–20), has left behind accounts of encountering non-religious masters and talking them into allowing him access to the slaves. Joseph Travis (in New Orleans in 1836) opined,

> Our colored society was truly a sheep without a shepherd. The abolition fever had been raging high; and great efforts and much caution by the citizens of the place were brought to bear on that subject. I was told that if I preached to the negroes, I would subject myself to imprisonment. But I continued to preach to them. The Committee of Vigilance, so called, heard of it, and appointed a sub-committee of five to go to hear to me. One Sabbath, as I had just read out my text, I noticed five good looking gentlemen step in, whom I had never seen at any church. I knew not who they were. They sat together, and were all attention. As I concluded my sermon, one of them, whom I afterwards ascertained was chairman of the Committee of Vigilance, made me a polite bow. I also learned that they made a favorable report concerning me, believing there was no danger of my instigating the negroes to rebellion—so that I went on uninterruptedly preaching to them throughout the year.[46]

Meantime, Methodism spread around the state. John G. Jones, for example, founded the first Methodist church in Monroe, the first person to step forward to take her membership vows being a Black woman, a slave of a Dr. and Mrs. McGuire, who had become deeply concerned for the welfare of her soul under Jones' preaching. He later expanded work into a circuit up and down the Washita (Oushita) River. In his first year he received 192 White and 23 Black members. As churches developed across the state, Blacks and Whites worshiped together, except in New Orleans where several African American congregations emerged. At the same time, in the rural areas, a number of all Black churches composed entirely of slaves would appear. This phenomenon of all-Black churches would, of course, increase significantly through the 1830s with the spread of the plantation mission.

The last place that Methodism would reach prior to the Civil War would be the vast territory of Texas. William Stevenson moved from Arkansas to became the first Protestant minister to preach in Texas—in 1815 at Pecan Point in what is now Red River County. The Pecan Point Circuit developed slowly and in 1822 reported sixty-six members, one of whom (name unknown), a resident of Bastrup, was the first Black Methodist in Texas.[47] As in Arkansas, almost all African Americans in Texas prior to the Civil War were slaves, brought by migrating masters.

Real growth of Methodism in the state did not begin until after Texas won its independence from Mexico in 1836. The next year, the MEC's Missionary Society established a mission in Texas headed by Martin Ruter (1785–1836). The mission grew rapidly, and an annual conference was organized in 1840, with 1,878 members of which 230 were "colored." Continued rapid growth has been attributed to a relatively large number of local preachers (some 68 by 1845), among whom were some African Americans. James H. McCarty, for example, was originally licensed by the Paris Circuit in the 1840s. That same circuit included two other local preachers listed only as Jesse and Jonathan.[48] Some other local preachers of whom at least mention in circuit records survives include Andrew Burrus (Dallas), Campbell Jackson (Sherman), Caleb Wells and Daniel Mims (Marshall), P. Thompson (Livingston-Woodville), and W. Cowan and M. Green (Mound Prairie).[49] The very first Texas circuit was the San Augustine Circuit, located just across the Sabine River from Louisiana. The circuit records show 140 Black members in 1846, among whom were two licensed local preachers, Jesse Payne and Gideon Greer. In 1848 a Red Lands African Mission was developed as part of the circuit with oversight assigned to a White missioner.[50]

Particularly interesting relative to the work of African Americans were the congregations in Austin and Houston. Austin Methodists built their first church in 1847 on a lot at the northeast corner of Congress and Cedar (now Fourth Street). By 1858 the membership had grown to 231, including 135 Black people. Nace Duval, at the time a slave, emerged as an excellent preacher who led the services for the Black members. He assumed pastoral leadership over the congregation and devoted as much time as possible to leading meetings and visiting the members. He was able to gain the White support necessary to have the first church building for the Black members erected.[51]

When T. O. Summers (1812–82) arrived in Houston in 1840, there was still no church building for the fledgling congregations in Houston and Galveston, which had some sixty-eight members of which twenty-six were Black. He started the building, which was completed under his successor in 1844. Very early a pattern was set, with the White congregation gathering on Sunday mornings and the Black members in the afternoon. Around 1850, Black Methodists erected their own church building immediately behind the White church. The congregation was served by a number of local preachers and exhorters such as Elias Dibble, who often led its baptismal services at the nearby bayou.

This initial Black church for Houston attracted believers across the Protestant perspective for Sunday and weekday worship. After the Civil War, Frank Vance, a prominent lay member of the church, purchased a plot of land at Travis and Bell Streets. The Black members relocated their building there and reorganized as the Trinity MEC.[52]

The Plantation Missions

During the years from 1845 to 1860, the Methodist Episcopal Church, South systematically pursued the plantation mission program directed at the slave population. This effort yielded a Black membership in excess of 200,000 (171,857 members plus 35,909 probationers) by the time the War began.[53]

The idea for the plantation missions originated with William Capers, who out of his early experiences in Charleston and his encounters with William Meredith and Henry Evans had developed a special, if paternalistic, concern for the welfare of African Americans in general and the rural slave population in particular. Slowly he constructed the grand plan to evangelize the Southern plantation populations.

Capers' concern originated following the invention of the cotton gin, which further isolated many Black people on the plantations where they resided. Capers saw thousands of potential Methodist converts being so isolated as to not even get a chance to learn English. On the South Carolina plantations, the slaves developed Gullah, a new language that mixed Bantu and English, and their isolation led to the perpetuation of the "superstitious" practices they had brought with them from Africa. At the same time, Southern Methodists now assumed that slavery was a long-term institution to which they must accommodate if the church was to have any role in the society. Capers' new program allowed some response to the slave culture. The program also partially answered charges from the North (and internationally) that the South represented a moral failure in its acquiescence to slavery. The church would do what it could to ameliorate the situation of the slave.

The plantation mission program began as an experiment on the plantation of Charles Baring, who requested that the circuit rider from the Orangeburg circuit preach to his slaves. Baring was so impressed with the results that he and a fellow plantation owner subsequently asked the South Carolina Conference to send missionaries to their plantations on a regular basis. Then in the fall of 1828, immediately following Capers' return from a trip to England, plantation owner Charles Pinckney asked him to send an exhorter to his plantation on the Santee River. Soon afterwards, two additional plantation owners added their request.

The 1829 South Carolina Conference yielded to Capers' request for a broader program, assigning two ministers to work on the plantations and giving Capers the additional duty of superintending the new mission. The first year the missionaries produced 417 conversions and new members. They proceeded year-by-year under close scrutiny by the skeptical plantation owners, the different denominations already active in the state, and, of course, the Methodists who had to raise the financial support to provide the missionaries' salaries and expenses.

In 1833, Capers helped direct the mission's work by authoring two catechisms for use by the missionaries. The first, designed for use with the plantation's children, *A Catechism for Little Children (and for use on) the Missions to the Slaves in South-Carolina*, would be quickly followed by its adult version for use among those adults who were readying themselves for church membership. The conference immediately printed 250 copies of the children's *Catechism* for its missionaries.[54] In 1832 future bishop James O. Andrew built support for the work with a memorable conference speech contrasting the neglected slaves to converted Black people, whom he pictured as the greatest proof of the efficacy of the gospel to redeem a life. He backed his images with figures—three years, 1,950 converts, 490 catechists. His audience proved responsive to the ever-increasing requests for support for the plantation mission. Five years later seventeen missionaries served 234 plantations and had taken 5,556 slaves into the church, and 2,500 children were learning Capers' catechism. The time invested in the youth would have long-term consequences.

The ministers sold the mission on the benefits it would bring to the plantation owner. The converted slave would be "contented with his lot, cheerful in his labors, submissive for conscience' sake to plantation discipline, happy in life, hopeful in death."[55] A key passage in Capers' catechism would be the Bible verses (to be memorized) which spelled out "The Duty of Servants":

> Servants, be obedient to them that are your masters according to the flesh, with fear and trembling, in singleness of your heart, as unto Christ. Not with eye-service as men pleasers, but as the servants of Christ, doing the will of God from the heart. Ephesians vi, 5, 6.
>
> Let as many servants as are under the yoke count their own masters worthy of all honor, that the name of God, and his doctrine, be not blasphemed. And they that have believing masters, let them not despise them because they are brethren, but rather do them service because they are faithful and beloved, partakers of the benefit. These things teach and exhort. 1 Tim. vi, 1, 2.[56]

Though less than half a page in more than twenty pages of the catechism to be memorized, these paragraphs became crucial to the success of the mission. The planters looked for greater control, manifested in the reduction of theft, tool breakage, and general misbehavior. From their perspective, greater control meant less use of the whip.

A number of the narratives by Methodist slaves refer to incidents built around the sermons and exhortations on Christian servanthood directed especially to African Americans. In North Carolina, Harriett Jacobs heard such a discourse in the local Anglican church in the months following the Nat Turner incident. Following the talk, "the benediction was pronounced. We went home, highly amused at brother Pike's gospel teaching, and we determined to hear him again. I went the next Sabbath evening, and heard pretty much a repetition of the last discourse." Following the next session, she noted, "the slaves left, and went to enjoy a Methodist shout. They never seem so happy as when shouting and singing at religious meetings."[57]

Fanny Kemble, in her descriptions of the slaves she observed in Georgia, noted that when Whites were present, the Black preacher London Cooper exhorted the slaves "not to steal, or lie, or neglect to work well for massa," but otherwise communicated his feelings that all people were equal.[58] White ministers would regularly say a few words on the subject, if plantation owners or staff were present, more to satisfy them than to exhort the slaves.

Of course, the Duty of Servants paragraphs were not the only words spoken to the members of the plantation-based churches. The Christian life was presented to them in such a way as to emphasize those particular Christian virtues that were most desirable for a slave master to see in his/her slaves—humbleness, obedience, and a willingness to serve. They looked for slaves who could like Paul say, "I have in whatsoever state I am, therewith to be content" (Philippians 4:11). Plantation owners would much rather hear sermons drawn from the story of Philemon and his slave Onesimus than, for example, concerning Jesus' mission to set the captives free.

However, we know from numerous accounts of former slaves that they listened to the message of their captors with a discerning ear. It is evident that they heard the whole message of the missionaries and built a workable theology from it. From the readiness to adapt to life as freedmen, and the quickness to choose from the various religious options presented to them immediately after the Civil War, we can assume that they had heard the message of obedience as instruction concerning the role that they must outwardly assume in order to improve their lot in life on the plantation and ease the way for the immediate moment. The façade presented to the White world obscured privately held beliefs often confined to personal cogitation or conversations with the most trusted of friends.

We can today gain some perspective on the difference between what was offered and what was appropriated by the plantation residents. Both agreed with James Andrew that the gospel was for "all men [and women] of all conditions of life, in all stages of civilization."[59] In spite of the manner in which slavery often exhausted the supply of hope upon which some could draw, many Africans nevertheless, in contrast to their masters, saw their condition as temporary. They repeatedly took refuge in images of release from their captive state, be it by escape to a free state, the success of abolitionism, manumission by a repentant master, or an act of God.

Even though they were isolated on rural plantations, often hardly able to understand the commands being given by White overseers, we have come to see the slaves as thinking persons fully capable of weighing alternatives and making self-interested decisions. Why, then, would they choose Methodism—setting aside for the moment consideration of any supernatural qualities of the Christian faith? For those stuck in the drudgery of plantation life, Methodism offered an immediate benefit in its value as entertainment and diversion. While meetings were often just before or after the end of a long day of hard work, the Methodist prayer and class meetings rose above the mundane with their singing, self-expressive bodily movements, and sermons (oratory being the oldest of the arts).

For the slave who had retained some hope, church activities also offered some important tools that would be needed if freedom were attained. While skipping over reading and writing, the Methodist meeting provided times for English to be spoken and heard; the ministers modeled patterns of behavior appropriate to the dominant society; and sermons often inadvertently provided information about the larger world which they hoped one day to see. For the more adept, at least those with good memories, a facility with words, some skill in organization, and a grasp of abstract thought, the church held out the possibility of some rudimentary leadership training as a class leader and licensed exhorter or preacher. Those with speaking skill would occasionally find that calls for their preaching would cut into time otherwise required for work.

Education, at least of a rudimentary kind, took place in the missions. In fact, one of the problems to be confronted by the White missionaries was how to go about teaching without giving instruction in reading and writing, most southern states having adopted laws against providing slaves with literary skills. Methodism was already somewhat adapted to such a situation, being largely an oral as opposed to a literary tradition. It passed the faith through the sermon and the song. There was no Prayer Book to be consulted at worship and no theological text to be passed among the members (though of course such books did exist for the ministers and learned laypeople). In fact, Capers' *Catechisms* revived an old method of passing church teachings used since ancient times. Other church leaders provided their own catechisms, and books with content designed to be shared with slaves were written.[60] In spite of the Protestant emphasis on the written Word, plantation missionaries took solace in the fact that the early church began, grew, and spread without written documents.

Much as been made of the element of simplicity in the presentation of the gospel as an element in attracting Blacks to Methodism. Timothy Hebert, for example, quotes one former Louisianan plantation slave who attributed his conversion to the fact that the Methodist preachers "preached in a grammar so plain that the way-faring man, though a fool, could not err therein."[61] It was probably more correct to say that Methodists presented the essential ideas of Christianity in a practical manner that did not require great theological sophistication, and presented them in a setting that emphasized personal spirituality over literary discourse. This form of presentation appealed to White as well as Black people, and made Methodism the largest religious community in America through the last decades of the antebellum era.

Finally, Christianity came into the slaves' life to replace any religious beliefs and practices that had been brought to America from Africa. Once in America, on the plantation, the slave quickly discovered numerous obstacles to recreating his/her former religious community and the worldview it supported. While African elements certainly survived and remained an active part of many lives, the slaves had lost access to the hierarchy of religious practitioners that would have been available to them in their home setting; they could no longer visit the shrines and sacred places to which they had been introduced as a child; and they no longer had family and fellow villagers with whom to celebrate the religious ceremonies of the year. While the invention of the new was possible and probably occurred, the old was an increasingly distant reality as every year passed.

Methodism entered the slaves' life offering a certain resonance with their African past and became a setting where an Africanized form of Christianity could be constructed in public. Modes of behavior understood by the White ministers merely as manifestations of religious experience, but which mimicked actions appropriate to worship in the African context, could now be carried out in sight of all. In addition, as preachers, exhorters, and class leaders were named, some men, if not their female counterparts, could resume roles as religious functionaries. The plantation mission promoted the development of Black preachers, and by precept and example encouraged their emergence every place to which the mission extended its reach.

The plantation missions led to the development of a new form of the religious life combining elements of Christian beliefs and biblical content chosen as appropriate to the situation of the listeners with surviving African religious practices. Such a synthesis was made possible by common elements shared by the two religions, including a belief in a supreme deity, an affirmation of community life, and music. Methodist missionaries unknowingly offered a place for the continuance of some African forms by encouraging individual vocalizations and bodily movements as expressions of spirituality. The expressiveness of the slaves in the meetings led some preachers to identify elements of what they termed African superstitions, and members soon learned to keep some expressions to times when the Whites were not around. Over time, the missionaries were more or less successful in suppressing the Africanisms, in part by concentrating on training the children and youth.

In the end, it seems amazing that so many who did absorb the teachings did so at such a sophisticated level. It is even more surprising that in the appropriation of Methodism and its adaptation to their situation the new form of the faith the freedmen created was so faithful to the Christianity that had been passed to them. Given the new environment created by the Civil War, they could easily enough have created an array of new religious forms more closely resembling the faiths of their African past.

In any case, as the plantation mission grew, so did Southern Methodism. By the 1840s, many plantations located relatively close to established Methodist congregations became open to the plantation missionary activity, and ministers otherwise serving predominantly White pastoral appointments were able to supplement the plantation missionaries by including a nearby plantation or two in their regular weekly duties. As might be expected, the Georgia Conference, which had only been set off from South Carolina in

1830, was the first to develop similar plantation missions. By 1840, nine such missions operated in the state and could report more than 1,300 members.[62] Meanwhile, the mission created a unique situation in South Carolina, which in 1838 became the only conference in the Methodist Episcopal Church with a majority of African members. It would maintain that uniqueness through the Civil War.

Through the 1830s, plantation missions, somewhat haphazardly, spread to other conferences. In 1830, five members of the Mississippi Conference were appointed to a committee to plan for religious instruction to the African church members. They decided to try catechizing the younger members and actually created a catechism that was used until superseded by Capers' two catechisms published in 1833. Catechetical instruction could be overseen by the average lay leader and the catechisms proved to be especially useful tools on those Sundays when the circuit rider was not available at a particular location.[63]

Among the places that the plantation mission concentrated its activity was along the Tennessee-Alabama border. In 1832, the Tennessee Conference designated two Black missions, centered in the territory just across the state line in North Alabama, one for Madison and Limestone Counties and one for Franklin and Lawrence Counties, and appointed Thomas King and Gilbert D. Taylor to them, respectively.[64] Here they found the ground already prepared for them by a Black preacher, Pompey Moore. Moore's owner, a Methodist minister, itinerated through western North Carolina and Tennessee. Moore learned to read and also studied his master's preaching. He evolved to the point where he could offer helpful observations, even critical ones, on his master's sermons. Rather than receiving rebukes for his growing assertiveness, Pompey received an invitation to preach. After his first sermon, his master gave him his freedom so he could travel about preaching. He married and settled in central Tennessee, eventually moving to McNairy County. From his home he traveled widely through the state, and spoke to large congregations of Africans, while attracting many White listeners as well.

H. H. Montgomery, a White minister, recalled hearing Moore:

> I will never forget the scene I witnessed when he related the circumstances of his awakening, repentance and conversion. There seemed to be scarcely one who was not weeping, and when he described the simplicity of that faith, by which he received pardon and salvation, and the great change of heart and feeling which he realized and every thing was so new, so new that he could hardly realize it was Pompey. There was a burst of glory and praise that went up from many in that congregation.[65]

The year 1844–1845 would bring significant development for the plantation missions, though those most involved in the work hardly felt the change, and many were completely unaware any change had occurred. However, at the national level, the MEC had voted to divide into two separate jurisdictions, north and south, and in 1845 the Methodist Episcopal Church, South met for its organizational conference in Louisville, Kentucky. That same year the Baptists split and the Southern Baptist Convention was organized (the Presbyterians had already divided in 1837). The work among Black people largely fell upon these new ecclesiastical units, as the great majority of African American church members now resided in the states over which they assumed hegemony. The MEC,S signaled its direction in part by electing William Capers to the episcopacy and backing their commitment to the plantation missions with a budget, modest at first, but destined to grow steadily over the next fifteen years.

Meanwhile, Southern churchmen of all denominations faced increasing criticism from their colleagues in the North and in other countries over their seeming support of slavery. Plantation missions offered a partial solution to their problem. In May 1845, an interdenominational group of ministers met in Charleston, South Carolina, to discuss the "Religious Instruction of the Negroes." Capers represented the Methodists at this gathering. They surveyed past efforts at reaching the slave populations and compiled a set of proposals to present before their various judicatories. This meeting resulted in actions by the MEC,S General Conference and other church bodies and the further spread of the South Carolina model.[66]

In spite of the time and energy poured into the missions, few accounts of the work were compiled, the major surviving documents being the annual conference reports. Timothy Hebert has recently tried to correct these lacunae in his history of Methodism, at least for the Bayou region of Louisiana south and west of New Orleans.[67] The Lafourche Mission had initially been supplied in 1832 when Benjamin Coxe traveled the bayou and found forty members, half of whom were African Americans. The Lafourche Circuit would come to stretch from Donalsonville on the Mississippi River south to the new town of Houma and west to Berwick in St. Mary's Parish. The first church building on the circuit was finally erected in 1845 at Houma.

Through the 1840s, Louisiana Methodism included some four thousand Black members, most of them slaves residing on a plantation. Most were brought into the church as the preachers were granted access to the plantations, where the residents welcomed the preachers. Most had not been born in Louisiana, and many had had prior contact with Methodism in their former homes. As was common across the South, Whites and Blacks generally worshipped together, though occupying segregated seating. By 1847, when the Louisiana Conference was formed, eight missions in Louisiana were totally focused on the African population. These missions continued in operation until the end of the Civil War.

In 1849, the Lafourche Colored Mission was formed to reach the slave population in the area covered by the Lafourche Circuit. Lewis A. Reed, the first appointee to the circuit, would stay on the job for four years. He was one of a handful of White ministers who would spend most of their time between 1845 and 1860 in the "colored missions." He liked his job, and both slaves and slave owners liked him. At the end of the first year, the mission reported five hundred new members scattered over thirteen plantations along the two hundred miles of Bayou Lafourche and its tributaries. The Mission centered on the church in Houma. Nearby plantation owners increasingly came to believe that it was their duty to provide religious instruction to the slaves and allowed them to attend Sunday services. By 1850, the Houma church was more than 80 percent Black.

In 1851, a new preacher was assigned to what became known as the Houma/Bayou Black Mission, another long narrow circuit that began at Tigerville, near the Mississippi River in St. John the Baptist Parish, and reached south of Houma. As with the Lafourche Mission, its membership figures went up and down through the decade as plantation owners gave and withdrew access to the plantation residents. In 1853, for example, Lewis Reed noted that during the year he had lost access to five of the twelve plantations he had at one time served. The losses on Reed's circuit meant that membership on his circuit suddenly decreased by 700. In 1854 the Lafourche and Bayou Black Circuit Missions were combined and reported a membership of 50 Whites and 882 Blacks.

N. A. Cravens, who traveled the Lafourche and Bayou Black Circuits for 1858, noted that he had 41 White and 540 Black members, but also had additional attendances of some 1,599 slaves at his preaching services. He lamented that he had been unable to provoke a general revival within the otherwise large and attentive audiences to his sermons. On the brighter side, however, he was able to baptize some 132 slaves in one quarter.

The Civil War would largely end the slave mission as chaos overtook different areas and White preachers were redeployed. Membership figures plummeted, and as elsewhere in the South, Methodism in the Louisiana low country was about to undergo radical change.

Notes

1. For background on Charleston, its African American population, and Methodism in the city, see Rosser H. Taylor, *Antebellum South Carolina: A Social and Cultural History* (New York: Da Capo Press, 1970); William J. Fraser, Jr., *Charleston! Charleston!: The History of a Southern City* (Columbia: University of South Carolina Press, 1989); F. A. Mood, *Methodism in Charleston: A Narrative*, edited by T. O. Summers (Nashville, TN: E. Stevenson & J. E. Evans, 1856); Abel M. Chreitzberg, *Early Methodism in the Carolinas* (Nashville, TN: Publishing House of the Methodist Episcopal Church, South, 1897); Albert M. Shipp, *Methodism in South Carolina* (Nashville, TN: Southern Methodist Publishing House, 1883); Luther P. Jackson, "Religious Instruction of Negroes, 1830–1860, with Special Reference to South Carolina," *Journal of Negro History* 15, 1 (January 1930), 72–114; Leroy F. Beaty, *Work of South Carolina Methodism among the Slaves* (Columbia, SC: Historical Society of the South Carolina Conference, Methodist Episcopal Church, South, 1901); and Jason Poole, "On Borrowed Ground: Free African-American Life in Charleston, South Carolina, 1810–1861," posted at http://etext.virginia.edu/journals/EH/EH36/poole1.html.

2. Francis Asbury, *The Journal and Letters of Francis Asbury*. 3 vols. (Nashville, TN: Abingdon Press; London: Epworth Press, 1958), I:483–85.

3. Ann Taylor Andrus, *The Name Shall be Bethel: The History of Bethel United Methodist Church, 1797–1997* (Charleston, SC: Bethel United Methodist Church, 1997).

4. Daniel Alexander Payne, *Recollections of Seventy Years* (Nashville, TN: A. M. E. Sunday School Union, 1888), 14–18.

5. William M. Wightman, *Life of William Capers, D.D., One of the Bishops of the Methodist Episcopal Church, South* (Nashville, TN: Southern Methodist Publishing House, 1959), 306.

6. The minutes of the 1817 AME conference were lost and no subsequent records survive as to the progress of Morris into the ordained ministry.

7. On the history of Emmanuel A.M. E. Church during its antebellum existence see James A. Holmes, Jr., and Richard Allen Leonard, "Early African Methodism in South Carolina," in *African Methodism in South Carolina: A Bicentennial Focus* (Tappan, NY: Seventh Episcopal District of the African Methodist Episcopal Church, 1987), 25–29; Marina W. Kramanayake, *A World in Shadow: The Free Black in Antebellum South Carolina* (Columbia: University of South Carolina Press, 1973), 113–27; Payne, *History of the African Methodist Episcopal Church*; Mood, *Methodism in Charleston*; and Powers, *Black Charlestonians*, 194–205.

8. This plot, on the southern end of the land owned by the Bethel church, had in 1806 been designated as a burial plot for the Black members.

9. *First Conference Minutes of the A.M.E. Connexion composed by Richard Allen in the City of Baltimore, 1818* (Baltimore: Henry Shields, n.d. [1923]); Payne, *History of the African Methodist Episcopal Church*, 26–27.

10. On Vesey and the revolt associated with him see Douglas R. Egerton, *He Shall Go Out Free* (Madison, WI: Madison House, 2000); Edward A. Pearson, ed., *Designs Against Charleston: The Trial Record of the Denmark Vesey Slave Conspiracy of 1822* (Chapel Hill, NC: University of North Carolina Press, 1999); and David Robertson, *Denmark Vesey* (New York: Alfred A. Knopf, 1999).

11. *An Exposition of the Causes which Led to the Secession from the Methodist Episcopal Church in Charleston, S.C.* (Charleston: Printed by E. J. Van Brunt, 1934), 4.

12. This church existed for a number of years, but finally affiliated with the Lutherans.

13. This is the same John Emory who as a young minister in Philadelphia had in 1815 challenged what he saw as the un-Methodist prerogatives assumed by the Bethel congregation and Richard Allen.

14. William Capers, *An Exposition of the Late Schism in the Methodist Episcopal Church in Charleston, in which the conduct of the schismatics, and the course of the church towards them, are fully set forth, and their complaints against the ministry answered* (Charleston: J. S. Burges, 1834); *A Rejoinder to "An Exposition of the Late Schism in the Methodist Episcopal Church in Charleston"* (Charleston: Printed by W. Riley, 1834).

15. There is some confusion in the records as to exactly when the building was moved to its present location. It appears that it was moved twice, once in 1852 to clear the lot where the new church would be constructed, and again after the Black members took control. Whether it was moved in 1853–54 over the noise issue or in 1880, when the Black congregation finally won control of the building, is unclear.

16. Wightman, *Life of William Capers, D.D.*, 160–64.

17. Linda D. Addo and James H. McCallum, *To Be Faithful to Our Heritage: A History of Black United Methodists in North Carolina* (Raleigh, NC: Western North Carolina Annual Conference, UMC, 1980), 27.

18. L. R. Ferebee, *Brief History of the Slave Life of Rev. L. R. Ferebee, and the Battles of Life, and Four Years of His Ministerial Life. Written from Memory. To 1882* (Raleigh, NC: Edwards, Broughton & Co., Steam Printers, Publishers and Binders, 1882), 5–6, posted at http://docsouth.unc.edu/ferebee/ferebee.html.

19. Ferebee, *Brief History*, 257.

20. Lorenzo Dow, *History of Cosmopolite; or the Four volumes of Lorenzo Dow's Journal* (Wheeling, WV: Joshua Martin, 1848), 124.

21. Wightman, *Life of William Capers, D.D.*, quoted in Albert M. Shipp, *Methodism in South Carolina* (Nashville, TN: Southern Methodist Publishing House, 1883), 406.

22. Haygood S. Bowden, *History of Savannah Methodism: from John Wesley to Silas Johnson* (Macon, GA: Press of the J. W. Burke Company, 1929), 73–74.

23. Wesley J. Gaines, *African Methodism in the South: Twenty-five Years of Freedom* (Atlanta: Franklin Publishing House, 1890; Rpt.: Chicago: Afro-Am Press, 1969), 5; and "Sherman Meets with the Coloured Ministers in Savannah," posted at www.civilwarhome.com/shermanandministers.htm.

24. George Gilman Smith, *A Hundred Years of Methodism in Augusta, Georgia* (Augusta, GA: Richards & Shaver, 1898).

25. John B. M'Ferrin, *Methodism in Tennessee* (Nashville, TN: A. H. Redford, 1875), 1:26.

26. Jacob Young, *Autobiography of a Pioneer* (Cincinnati: Cranston and Curtis, 1857), 90–91.

27. M'Ferrin, *Methodism in Tennessee*, 1:84–85.

28. M'Ferrin, *Methodism in Tennessee*, 1:117.

29. M'Ferrin, *Methodism in Tennessee*, 1:119.

30. M'Ferrin, *Methodism in Tennessee*, 1:148.

31. Bobby L. Lovett, *The African-American History of Nashville, Tennessee, 1780–1830* (Fayetteville: University of Arkansas Press, 1999), 28–29.

32. James Thomas, *From Tennessee Slave to St. Louis Entrepreneur: The Autobiography of James Thomas* (Colombia: University of Missouri Press, 1984), 66–67.

33. James O. Andrew, *Miscellanies: comprising letters, essays, and addresses : to which is added a biographical sketch of Mrs. Ann Amelia Andrew* (Louisville, KY: Morton & Griswold, 1854).

34. Anson West, *A History of Methodism in Alabama* (Nashville, TN: Printed for the Author, Publishing House of the Methodist Episcopal Church, South, 1893), 332–33.

35. Stewart, Mrs. Frank Ross, *The History of Methodism in Alabama: Including Index to Anson West's History.* Vol. 1 (Centre, AL: Stewart University Press [1984]), 20–25

36. John G. Jones, *A Complete History of Methodism in the Mississippi Conference* (Nashville, TN: Southern Methodist Publishing House, 1887), 36–37.

37. Natchez is located upriver from New Orleans, and was on the western border of what was the United States in 1799. The land across the Mississippi River came into the United States' hands in 1804 with the Louisiana Purchase. Natchez would thus become the point of dissemination of Methodism throughout the region.

38. Jones, *Complete History of Methodism*, 79–80.

39. Jones, *Complete History of Methodism*, 105.

40. Charles Caddy, *Life and Times of Rev. Robert Dobbins* (Philadelphia: J. W. Daughaday & Co., 1868), 87–90.

41. Daniel Lester Woodie, *The History of the Negro and Methodism in Arkansas and Oklahoma: The Little Rock-Southwest Conference, 1838–1972* (Little Rock, AR: Little Rock Conference, UMC, 1979), 13.

42. See Adolphine Fletcher Terry, *Charlotte Stephens: Little Rock's First Black Teacher* (Little Rock, AR: Arkansas Academic Press 1973).

43. Quoted in Robert Henry Harper, *Louisiana Methodism* (Washington, DC: Kaufmann Press, 1949), 38.

44. Grant Shockley, *Heritage & Hope: The African American Presence in United Methodism.* (Nashville, TN: Abingdon Press, 1991), 47.

45. Sarah J. Early, *Life and Labors of Rev. Jordan W. Early, One of the Pioneers of African Methodism in the West and South* (Nashville: Publishing House A. M. E. Church Sunday School Union, 1894), 31–36.

46. Joseph Travis, *Autobiography of the Rev. Joseph Travis, a Member of the Methodist Annual Conference. Embracing a Succinct History of the Methodist Episcopal Church, South; Particularly in Part of Western Virginia, the Carolinas, Georgia, Alabama, and Mississippi. With Short Memoirs of Several Local Preachers, and on Address to His Friends.* Ed. by Thomas O. Summers. (Nashville, TN: Stevenson & Owens, for the MECS, 1855).

47. R. F. Curl, *Southwest Texas Methodism* (Dallas: The Inter-Board Council, the Southwest Texas Conference, the Methodist Church, 1951), 86–87.

48. Walter N. Vernon, *Methodism Moves Across North Texas* (Dallas: Historical Society, North Texas Conference, The Methodist Church, 1967), 86–87.

49. Walter N. Vernon, Robert W. Sledge, Robert C. Monk, and Norman W. Spellman, *The Methodist Excitement in Texas: A History* (Dallas: The Texas United Methodist Historical Society, 1984), 86–87.

50. William Warren Sweet, *Religion on the American Frontier, 1783–1840: A Collection of Source Materials.* Vol. IV. *The Methodists* (Chicago: University of Chicago Press, 1964), 567–619.

51. Quoted in W. P. Harrison, *The Gospel Among the Slaves* (Nashville, TN: Publishing House of the Methodist Episcopal Church, South, 1893), 256–7.

52. On the developments in Houston see Mrs. I. M. E. Blandin, *History of Shearn Church* (Houston: Shearn Auxiliary of Woman's Home Mission Society, 1908).

53. For an overview of the plantation missions see Jackson, "Religious Instruction of Negroes"; Thomas Leonard Williams, *The Methodist Mission to the Slaves* (New Haven, CT: Yale University Ph.D. dissertation, 1943); Beaty, *Work of South Carolina Methodism among the Slaves;* and Harrison, *Gospel among the Slaves.*

54. Holland N. McTyeire, *A History of Methodism* (Nashville, TN: Southern Methodist Publishing House, 1884), 584–86.

55. McTyeire, *History of Methodism*, 586.

56. William Capers, *Catechism for the Use of the Methodist Missions.* 3rd ed. (Charleston, SC: Published by John Early, 1853), 21–22.

57. [Harriett Jacobs], *Incidents in the Life of a Slave Girl. Written by Herself.* Edited by L. Maria Child (Boston: For the Author, 1861), chapter 13.

58. Fanny Kemble, *Journal of a Residence on a Georgian Plantation in 1838–1839* (New York: Harper & Brothers, 1863), 114.

59. McTyeire, *History of Methodism*, 586

60. Charles C. Jones, in *The Religious Instruction of the Negroes in the United States* (Savannah, GA: Thomas Purse, 1842), noted a set of catechisms and instructional literature developed in other denominations for use among the slaves, including a catechism he himself had compiled for the Presbyterians.

61. Timothy Hebert, "Methodism Along the Bayou," posted at www.iscuo.org/hist1.htm.

62. On the development of the mission in Georgia see Christopher H. Owen, *The Sacred Flame of Love: Methodism and Society in Nineteenth-Century Georgia* (Athens: University of Georgia Press, 1998), 38–41.

63. John G. Jones, *A Complete History of Methodism in the Mississippi Conference.* Volume II (Nashville, TN: Publishing House of the Methodist Episcopal Church, South, 1908), 442.

64. Anson West, *A History of Methodism in Alabama* (Nashville, TN: Printed for the Author, Publishing House of the Methodist Episcopal Church, South, 1893), 598–99. These two missions were short lived and only picked up later, after the formation of the Alabama Conference, when a large mission was developed in the Tennessee River Valley.

65. M'Ferrin, *Methodism in Tennessee*, III, 387–91; Rpt. in Arnett, Centennial Budget, 303–04.

66. Jackson, "Religious Instruction of Negroes."

67. Hebert, "Methodism Along the Bayou."

CHAPTER SEVEN

Women—the New Force
in Church Life

From the Beginning

Throughout this narrative a number of women have been mentioned for the role they have played in the emergence of African American Methodism. Annie Switzer and Betty, Barbara Heck's servant, certainly nailed down African American claims that they were part and parcel of American Methodism from the very beginning. However, it is also the case that during their first century, in the process of dealing with slavery and racism, African American Methodists rarely challenged the male-dominated structures, which were also pervasive in Protestant communities in general. The all-male leadership that was written into the constituting documents of the Methodist Episcopal Church was simply assumed to be normative in the various African American Methodist denominations. Not until the last half of the twentieth century did Methodists in general begin meaningfully knocking down of the structures of sexism. Thus, in considering the antebellum period, some further attention needs to be given to bring the contributions of female African Americans into the foreground.

Women were equally responsive to Methodism from its beginnings in the 1760s and in some places formed the majority of the members of the movement. New York stands out in this respect. Among the first members of the John Street Church were two Black women, probably working as servants, named Rachel and Margaret. We believe that they were Africans by the fact that only their first names were mentioned in the book that recorded their gifts for the erecting of the new chapel in 1768. They may have been free, as we learn elsewhere that they were later hired by the church to take care of the famous preacher's house that had been set aside for housing the traveling preachers sent from England by Wesley.[1]

The Black women in the New York congregation were singled out by Richard Boardman, the first of the British preachers, in his 1770 letter to Wesley on the New York situation, and Joseph Pilmore took notice of the first African American class consisting of black women.[2] Toward the end of 1771, he was able to report, "We have about twenty black women who meet in one Class, and I think upon the whole they are as happy as any class."[3] Most of the time, whenever he singled out any of the Black members for comment, it would be one of the women. For example, at one point he visited a woman who was gravely ill. In answer to his question about any fear weighing upon her, she responded out of the faith she held so dearly that she had no fear, and added, "I have my blessed Saviour in my heart. I should be glad to die. I want to be gone, that I may be with him forever. I know that He loves me, and I love him with all of my heart." Though remaining anonymous in Pilmore's brief paragraph, this woman was noteworthy for the testimony she shared with those who visited her, many of whom were "astonished" at her faith.[4] Again, he noted on August 1, 1771, "One of the poor negroes declared her heart was so full of divine love that she could not express it, and many more of them were exceedingly glad in their minds."[5]

In 1780, Molly Williams, the wife of Peter Williams, the sexton, took over the duties as housekeeper at the preacher's house.[6] Originally named Mary Durham, she came from the island of St. Christopher's in the West Indies. She was two years older than Peter and described as "beautiful, full of good sense, and distinguished for consistent piety."[7]

It appears that Molly found her way to the Methodist fellowship on her own and it was there that she met her future husband. He was a slave to James Aymar, and within months of his becoming the John Street sexton, he and Molly were forced to flee with Aymar to New Jersey (a result of the Revolutionary War then in full force). They returned to New York in the fall of 1780, and Peter resumed his duties as sexton. It was at this time that Molly became the housekeeper at the preacher's house, and she and Peter resided there. Three years later, when Almar, a Tory, decided to move back to England, the church purchased Peter's freedom.

Molly continued to live at the preacher's house until around 1787. Peter subsequently also launched a very successful tobacco business. Their son, Peter, Jr., learned to read as a youth and kept the books for the family business. He later became an Episcopal priest. The couple also adopted a daughter.

Through the 1790s, Molly moved from the background into complete obscurity. She backed her husband's work that led to the creation of Zion Church, the first African Methodist congregation in the city, and in 1801 participated in the laying of the cornerstone. She was like many women who filled the pews in support of the new autonomous congregation. She died in 1821 just as the Zion Church broke with the MEC. Peter lived two more years and died in 1823.[8]

One finds a similar story across the river in Brooklyn. In 1798, there were twenty-six Black members, of which twelve were women. However, after the turn of the century, the African membership began to grow. By 1808 there were eighty-five, of which the clear majority were women. A decade later, when the Black members broke with the MEC and affiliated with the AME Church, there were about one hundred members, the female majority continuing. They supported two all-female classes that provided the substance to the movement in Brooklyn, though all of the key positions—trustee, exhorter, preacher—were filled by males.[9]

It is safe to say that women constituted a significant element of every Black congregation that emerged in the late 1700s and early 1800s. Where statistics are lacking, other evidence is forthcoming, most important the surviving membership and class records of various congregations. Here we see clearly the exclusively male role as class leaders, exhorters, and preachers. The Black women put their primary energy behind the effort of Black men to gain access to those positions and then to move beyond to ordination as deacons and elders. Given the domestic model into which most women were forced, it is not surprising to find that one of the primary avenues for their exercise of leadership in the church was the formation of women's auxiliary organizations.

It is to be noted that in the African American community, there had been considerable breakdown of the traditional domestic model. Female Black slaves were expected to produce for their owners just as males, and while many were put to work as domestics, many others, especially in rural settings, engaged in hard labor in the fields beside the men. This history of work had an interesting effect as the free Black community emerged in the cities. Black women rarely fell into the exclusive role of housewife; they attained employment in homes, took in washing, or assumed one of the other acceptable occupations. That meant that they had an income and while usually at the bottom of the economic ladder, they could with frugality exert some economic clout. At church, they could provide support not only by their attendance and participation but through their giving.

The most famous incident in which a woman used her financial resources occurred soon after AMEZ bishop J. J. Clinton (1823–81) took office over the Philadelphia and Southern Conferences in 1862. His task as missionary bishop over the states of the Confederacy came with no funding. Clinton soon voiced his discouragement over being assigned an impossible task. He considered resigning his office. At this point, in the fall of 1863, he was awakened in the middle of the night by one Melvina Fletcher, a laywoman who had become increasingly concerned about Clinton's possible resignation. In their late-night confrontation, she promised to raise the money he needed to send missionaries into the South. She had a favored position as governess to the children of Postmaster General Montgomery Blair. She would use her relatively high status among the working African American women of Washington, D.C., to mobilize her acquaintances throughout the city. Within a very short time she raised the three hundred dollars (a considerable sum at the time) that Clinton had indicated he needed to proceed. With the money raised by Fletcher, Clinton commissioned five men and immediately began the spread of the AMEZs through the South.

Organized work by African American Methodist women first appears in the Zion congregation in New York City. The Female Benevolent Society was organized to meet a variety of felt needs, including the visiting of the ill and otherwise distressed, support of orphans, and arrangements for the burial of the deceased. This group came to the support of the entire congregation when it built its first building in 1820 and after the fire of 1838 that destroyed the building.

The New York benevolent society became the seed from which the first denominational organization, the Daughters of Conference, emerged. The Daughters of Conference came into being in 1821 in response to the first AMEZ conference and the felt need to support the growing church. Money was lacking to send the preachers to their appointments in the surrounding states, especially in the cases where they were going into a pioneering situation without a church and guaranteed salary waiting to pick up their support. The organization was founded by a prominent member in the New York congregation, Mary Roberts, who continued to lead the organization for the next four decades.

Roberts was able to recruit women throughout the growing connexion to support the expansion of the church. The group in New England was led by Eliza Ann Gardner in Boston, Mary E. Anderson in Worcester, and Adella Hicks Turner in Providence. Ellen Stevens in New York took the lead in organizing the younger women. This first church-wide lay organization inspired the laymen (who had no direct representation at the annual and general conferences at this time) to also organize Sons of Conference organizations that soon united their work to the women as the Sons and Daughters of Conference in many of the congregations. There were also variations on the Daughters of Conference serving children and the elderly.

The organization of the AMEZ Daughters of Conference and its accomplishments soon came to the attention of the AME women who in 1827 suddenly emerged at the AME's Philadelphia Conference. Their organization was occasioned by the approach of the 1828 General Conference and the expressed concern as to how the expenses of Philadelphia's delegates (one of which would come all the way from Ohio) would be covered. Thus, seemingly without being asked by the men, the women organized a Daughters of Conference chapter, which raised more than 10 percent of the money needed for the upcoming meeting.[10] The Daughters of Conference would be the first lay organization to emerge within the AME Church and led directly to the later Women's Mite Missionary Society organized in 1874. As the work of the Daughters spread through the connection, different units assumed variant names such as the Benevolent Daughters of Conference, the Rising Daughters of Conference, and the United Daughters of Conference, though their primary task of making an annual contribution to the conference budget remained the same.[11]

The existence of the Daughters of Conference across the church allowed Mary Still (1808–89) some resources as she came to the aid of the *Christian Recorder,* the AME periodical, which in 1856 had to suspend publication after a brief two years' existence. She would call her female compatriots (as well as the church's male members) to a consideration of the importance of the journal of the largest Black-led organization in the United States. She promoted a fund drive that called women to assume responsibility for educating the new generation and to show their concern by using their leisure time to raise the money to get the *Recorder* active again, which finally occurred in 1861.[12]

Not to be outdone, the women of the African Union Church responded to the need of support of the ministers, which in the mid-1830s had reached a crisis stage. It is noted that in 1835 a group of women from Woodstown, in southern New Jersey, walked across the state to New York City where a meeting was held in the home of one "Sister Polke," at which an effort to raise money to support the preachers was launched. This meeting became the originating point of the Spencer United Daughters of Conference, the church-wide women's organization, which is credited with saving the connexion by providing funds for destitute ministers and fragile congregations to survive.[13]

The African American women of the MEC came much later to organization than their sisters in the independent Methodist denominations. The relative wealth of the larger White-led church, coupled with the need to open the White Methodists to African American participation, distanced them somewhat from the needs that led to the founding of the Daughters of Conference in the AMEZ and AME Churches.

The Question of Ordination

While most of the women in the several African American Methodist churches were concentrated on the building of the Daughters of Conference, some launched the effort that would continue through the twentieth century to open ministerial ordination to women. The initial questioning of the all-male ministerial leadership, of course, occurred in the context of the establishment of African Americans as deacons, elders, and bishops, and it would be 1894 before the first Black woman would be ordained—Julia Foote, ordained by the AMEZ. However, early in the nineteenth century, the first voices were raised requesting entrance of women into the ordained ministry. The first one of which records survive was Jarena Lee (1783–1851?).[14] Born of free parents at Cape May, New Jersey, she was hired out as a servant at the age of seven and grew up largely void of an outward religious life. But then she had a deep religious experience in 1804, which served to heighten her inner struggles. Shortly after that experience, she moved to Philadelphia where she found her way to St. Paul's Episcopal Church, then pastored by Joseph Pilmore (who had left the Methodists to become an Episcopal priest). Eventually, she found her true religious home at Bethel Church among the Methodists. Here she experienced salvation, but did not attain a satisfactory state until about four years later when she had an experience of Wesleyan sanctification. Several years later, she had a call to preach, which she shared with her pastor, Richard Allen. He refused to grant her a preacher's license. There being no place for female preachers in the MEC, on rare occasions he did allow her to exhort.

Lee initially accepted Allen's judgment. A short time later she married Joseph Lee, who pastored a group of Black Methodists at Snow Hill (an all-Black community across the river from Philadelphia, near Cherry Hill, New Jersey). Then in 1818, her husband died. Shortly thereafter the congregation applied for affiliation with the AMEs. The widow Lee moved back to Philadelphia and Allen gave her permission to lead prayer meetings in her home and to exhort at Bethel. She used the occasion of making an exhortation at Bethel the next year to inform Allen and the congregation of her call to preach. Impressed, Allen subsequently acknowledged her call, and eventually gave her a preaching license.

Prior to Lee's appearance, Allen had encountered at least one other women who wished to preach. In 1803 an English woman, Dorothy Ripley, had come to Philadelphia and requested the privilege of speaking at Bethel. Allen did not allow her to preach, citing the same reasons he had applied to Lee. However, shortly thereafter she attended a service at which Allen spoke, and at the close of the service she was granted a moment to speak. As a result of her spontaneous exhortation on Allen's sermons, she was invited to return the next evening and deliver a discourse. Her words were well received, though interrupted by the actions of a drunken White soldier. Following the completion of her discourse, Allen stood to speak and called attention to the earlier disturbance, branding it a sign of the Devil's attempt to disrupt the peace of the gathered sons and daughters of God.[15]

It would be after Allen's death that another AME woman would claim a call to preach. Her name was Rebecca Cox Jackson (1795–1871). She was the sister of a local preacher at Bethel who cared for her after her mother's death around 1808. In 1833 she had a call to preach and began traveling to that end. However, she met stiff opposition from her brother, her husband, and various AME clergy. She was also accused of preaching heretical ideas, some coming from her lively inner mystical experiences. These became her downfall among the Methodists, and in 1837 she left and joined the Quakers, where she found a welcoming place to exercise her gifts.

Meanwhile Lee had developed a far-flung ministry among Black Methodists. With Allen's initial approval, she began to move about Philadelphia, preaching to small groups in private homes. Her winsome personality and obvious speaking talents generally overcame any opposition of a more theoretical nature against her gender. In 1821 she made her first trip away from Philadelphia to preach, to her hometown of Cape May. Upon her return in 1822, she founded and led a class in Philadelphia.

Then beginning in 1823, she spent most of her time on the road as an independent itinerant evangelist on behalf of the AME Church. Allen aided her efforts by occasionally writing letters introducing and vouching for her. She preached to any who would listen in any facilities that opened to her, frequently in the buildings of Black congregations that remained a part of the MEC. In 1834 she spent six months on the Eastern Shore of Maryland, primarily in Talbot and Caroline Counties, but wandering as far south as Worcester County. As her fame spread, many Whites came to hear her, and a number credited her with being the instrument of their conversion.

In the winter of 1827–28, she traveled to Rochester, New York, and then crossed into Canada at Niagara and preached among the different Black congregations that had emerged in the area. Later in the year she moved on to Ohio, just then being opened up by AME ministers. In her autobiography, she recalled an incident at Columbus that typified her ability to overcome opposition. A leading member of the church from Chillicothe was visiting the congregation. He was opposed to women preachers and as she began her preaching service, he walked out. However, he did not go far and soon returned, but turned down a request that he lead the group in prayer. Lee proceeded to preach. Afterward, the man came to her and confessed his prejudices but also confided that he had been won over by listening to her message. He could now affirm anew that God was no respecter of persons, relative to women preaching.

Lee initially published an account of her life and preaching activity in 1836, and brought out an expanded edition in 1849, shortly before her death.[16] She remained a singular presence in the AME Church and her gifts did little to destroy the overall prejudice against female preachers in the church. It was actually right at the end of Lee's life that the AME Church gave its only other serious consideration of the question of women preachers.

Paralleling Lee's career is that of Zilpha Elaw (c. 1790–1850?).[17] Elaw was born in the countryside not far from Philadelphia. Her parents, both of whom were free, placed her in the care of a Quaker family with whom she lived until her eighteenth birthday. She had already by this time become a Methodist, but possibly more important was having visions. In 1810 she married and the following year moved to Burlington, New Jersey, where her husband got a job working in the making of cloth. Their first child was born in 1812, and the couple lived a relatively sedate life for the next five years.

Then in 1817, Elaw attended her first camp meeting, during which she fell into an ecstatic trance. She came to feel that she had been sanctified, a event occasioning her initial public speaking in the form of prayers for others attending the gathering. The camp meeting setting proved welcoming to her, and in 1819, she ventured to offer her first exhortation. She viewed the positive reception to her words as confirmation of a call to preach she had felt. More important, the pulpit of her home church was opened to her. Burlington reported a relatively small African American membership at the time, 78 Black members compared to 642 Whites. But many White people came to hear her and seemed more impressed than her fellow Black members. She did not pursue her calling immediately, however, due to her husband's opposition.

Her husband's death from tuberculosis in 1823 forced her to go to work, and for a while she taught at a school for Black children that she had formed.

But then around 1825, she closed the school, moved to Philadelphia, and began the life of an independent traveling evangelist. She worked for the next decade in the mid-Atlantic and Northeast, spending 1828 in the Washington, D.C., area, even risking her freedom by venturing across the Potomac into northern Virginia.

In 1840, Elaw went to England and spent the next five years speaking there. The last we hear from her is in 1845 when she announces plans to return to the United States. Following the publication of her *Memoirs* in 1846,[18] she drops from sight, and what eventually happened to her is unknown.

In 1848, the AME Church's General Conference debated the question of licensing women preachers. The debate was prompted by its having received a petition of a group of women calling themselves the Daughters of Zion, an association of some women who had felt themselves called to preach. The conference did not grant them licenses, but it did grant them permission to preach, at least in the short run. The women subsequently indicated that they planned to designate an area in which they might be most useful and begin to make appointments of their members to places to preach. They would operate as an annual conference within the annual conference.

The Philadelphia Conference picked up the issues raised by the Daughters of Zion in 1850 as delegates discussed whether it would be appropriate for the women to follow through on their plans. After a lively debate, it was moved that a committee be appointed to continue the discussion of their proposal. Although the motion passed, it was very quickly reconsidered and abandoned. The organization again approached the General Conference in 1852, this time asking for licenses to preach, as a first step toward full ordination and admittance to the conference. This motion found little support though again a lively debate was held. However, when the vote was taken, it lost by a large majority. The Daughters of Zion fell apart a short time later and it would be the next century before the issue of ordination was again seriously considered.[19]

Not Waiting for Ordination

While some women fought for ordination and recognition in one of the several African American Methodist communities, a few operated quite apart from any official ecclesiastical sanction. Such was the case of a woman known only as Elizabeth (1776–1866), who worked on the edge of the Methodist world in Maryland and Virginia.[20] Elizabeth was born in rural

Maryland just as the American Revolution was beginning and died shortly after the Civil War ended. Her parents were Methodists and taught her the Bible, and she grew up with a sense of God's presence overshadowing her. Her separation from her parents when she was twelve led to an intense religious experience that included a visionary encounter with Jesus and a resulting sense of salvation. Her experience of the presence of God was quite independent of any preaching services or even any religious life whatsoever, neither of which was present in her hometown at the time. She was eventually sold to a Presbyterian minister who after some years of service freed her, around her thirtieth birthday (1806?). During these years she had developed a sense of mission—that she should preach. After gaining her freedom, she began to attend church and occasionally spoke, but in general did not respond to her call to preach. Her limited reading ability and lack of mastery of the Bible held her back.

While wrestling with her calling, Elizabeth spoke to a widow woman who lived in Baltimore, where she now resided, and asked her if she might hold a regular meeting at her house, which happened to be in one of the worst sections of town. The widow responded gladly and called together a small group of her female acquaintances. In this meeting she began to speak regularly. The meeting soon attracted the attention of the neighbors, who complained of the noise, and the authorities forced her to discontinue the gatherings. The leaders of the local Methodists (Sharp Street?) also opposed her until she proposed that a male leader assume control of the meeting, after which the group was able to continue for several more years.

Leading a ladies' prayer meeting was somewhat acceptable, but almost everyone seemed opposed to her exercising her call to preach. Both the local preachers and class leaders told her that it went against the *Discipline*. Finally, an older female lay member of the church opened her home to her for a preaching service. A few came; others who wanted to come stayed away lest they be turned out of the church for attending. Overcoming her own hesitancy and some stage fright, Elizabeth preached and found, as the Methodists termed it, great freedom in her delivery. While the male leaders complained more, she now confidently spoke in different settings. At one of these meetings, she noted the presence of several of the class leaders, who were during the meeting won over and later testified, "Surely the Lord has *revealed* these things to her."[21] Her early success was confirmed in additional revelatory experiences that reiterated her calling.

While church leaders contemplated excommunicating her, she began to receive invitations to preach in different locations around the state and across the Potomac in Virginia, where she barely escaped being imprisoned.

When queried as to the authority for her assuming the role of a preacher, she replied that the Lord had ordained her, and thus she needed nothing else. Through the 1850s she traveled as far away as Michigan and to the Black settlements in Ontario. In Michigan she stayed four years and founded a school for Black orphaned children.

She finally retired in her eighty-seventh year and settled in Philadelphia, where she had made friends among the Quakers. She died on June 11, 1866. She was a hundred years old.

Aunt Jane Lee of Louisiana

In the South, the majority of African American religious leaders have fallen into obscurity, and it is only by a chance occurrence that we know anything about them. Such a person is Jane Lee, who just happened to meet former-slave Charlotte Brooks, simply because Brooks had also been sent from Virginia to Louisiana to work on a sugar cane plantation. One Sunday evening Brooks slipped away from her plantation to the one where Lee resided. Maybe she had some news from home; maybe she even knew some of Brooks' kinfolks. She found the woman in the slave quarters. She did not know any of Brooks' family, but the two women shared an immediate kinship, both having been forced to leave all their family behind.

Even in their initial conversation, Lee inquired about any local religion and churches. Brooks informed her that there was little of the former and none of the latter. Lee was unusual in that she was religious, could read the Bible, and had memorized many hymns. She longed to be able to go to church and participate in the singing and preaching services. As their relationship developed over the next months, Lee read Bible stories to Brooks and taught her the hymns from an old hymnbook she had acquired.

Brooks eventually "got religion" from Lee, and Lee subsequently began holding prayer meetings at Brooks' plantation. However, the owner of her plantation, a Roman Catholic, was quite hostile to religion among his slaves, and on one occasion interrupted their gathering because of the noise the slaves were making. From that time on, Brooks noted, whenever we met, we "would put a big wash-tub full of water in the middle of the floor to catch the sound of our voices when we sung. When we all sung we would march around and shake each other's hands, and we would sing easy and low, so marster could not hear us."[22]

In the absence of Methodist local preachers, Brooks attributed the conversion and Christian nurture of many slaves to the efforts of Aunt Jane, as she came to be known: "We did not have any church to go to, but she would talk to us about old Virginia, how people done there. She said them beads and crosses we saw every body [i.e., Roman Catholics in Louisiana] have was nothing. She said people must give their hearts to God, to love him and keep his commandments; and we believed what she said. I never wanted them beads I saw others have, for I just thought we would pray without any thing, and that God only wanted the heart."[23] Lee was not supposed to leave her plantation, but would slip away in the evening, travel the two miles between her living quarters and Brooks' place, and lead prayer sessions in Brooks' cottage. She was remembered as always having her Bible and hymnbook with her. In the mid-1850s Lee's master left the area, moved to Texas, and took Lee with him. Brooks and Lee never met again. Shortly before departing, Lee asked everyone to meet her in heaven. Subsequently, Brooks and some of the seven women and four men who had regularly attended the meeting tried to assume its leadership for the next several years.

Female Leadership in Other Venues

By the time that the AMEs were responding to the Daughters of Zion, the African American community in general and the Methodist churches in particular were also everywhere responding to the several new crusades challenging the social order, especially the abolitionist movement and the Underground Railroad. Some Black Methodist women looking for a place to exercise their Christian commitments were drawn to these new social movements, along with the emerging women's rights cause, each in need of support and more than willing to accommodate any talented people who would align with them. One immediately thinks of Harriet Tubman (to be discussed more fully later in chapter 8) as the leading figure in the Underground Railroad. At the same time, leaders in the community had reached a general consensus that education was an essential ingredient in whatever the future held for Black Americans, and they poured an enormous amount of energy into promoting, creating, and nurturing schools for Black youth.

Frances Watkins (b. 1825–1911) was born a free Black in Baltimore, Maryland. Orphaned at the age of three, she went to live with her uncle, William Watkins, the Sharp Street Church's preacher-teacher. Her uncle passed to her both his religious and social views (he opposed colonization and supported abolitionism). Upon completing her schooling in her early teens, she obtained employment as a domestic. By this time, however, her poetic talents were manifesting. She published her first poems in the several abolitionist periodicals, including *Frederick Douglass' Paper* and Garrison's *Liberator* (for which her uncle also wrote). Her first book, *Forest Leaves*, appeared in 1845.[24]

In 1850, Harper moved to Ohio to take a position as a teacher at the AME's Union Seminary at Wilberforce. She stayed at Union for two years before moving on to Pennsylvania, where she taught and became involved in the activities of the Underground Railroad. She was greatly affected by a new law passed in 1854 to control the movement of African Americans. It stated that free Black people who came into Maryland from the north were subject to being re-enslaved. This law, which in effect separated her from her family in Baltimore, spurred her into action. Already in agreement with the abolitionist position, she now began to lecture throughout those northern states into which she could still travel. She also picked up themes of women's rights and challenged the privileges ascribed to birth and class. Her poetry made her unique among the abolitionists, and she freely integrated poetry into her talks. About this same time, she published her second book of poetry, *Poems on Miscellaneous Subjects* (1854).

Poems on Miscellaneous Subjects contained several of the poems she used in her abolitionist talks, such as "The Slave Auction."

> The Sale Began—young girls were there,
> Defenseless in their wretchedness,
> Whose stifled sobs of deep despair
> Revealed their anguish and distress.
> . . . .
> And men, whose sole crime was their hue,
> The impress of their Maker's hand
> And frail and shrinking children, too
> Were gathered in that mournful band.[25]

She would return to the injustice of sending one to slavery because of his/her color in her poem "Eliza Harris," which told the story of a mother attempting to get her son to freedom. Harper rhetorically cries out, "How say that the lawless may torture and chase/A woman whose cry is the hue of her face?"[26] Along with the anguish over the lot of her enslaved brothers and sisters, the faith (and hope) passed to her in the years in Baltimore permeates all her work, and is highlighted in several specifically religious poems. "Saved by Faith," for example, retells the story of the woman with an issue of blood who approaches Jesus and is remembered for touching the hem of his garment. Harper closes her account as follows:

> Kindly, gently, Jesus said—
> Words like balm unto her soul—
> "Peace upon thy life be shed!
> Child thy faith has made thee whole!"[27]

Just as the Civil War began, she married Fenton Harper (1860), and their daughter was born two years later. He died in 1863, and after the war, in part to support herself, she again picked up her career as a lecturer and writer of poetry. Her lengthy life would culminate in her election in 1897 as the Vice-President of the National Association of Colored Women. She had recently experienced some success with her novel, *Iola Leroy: On Shadows Uplifted* (1892), which told the story of the marriage of a wealthy slave owner and his African American love. All but forgotten through most of the twentieth century, she was rediscovered in recent years by feminist scholars.[28]

As unique as any of the women permeating African American Methodism was Catherine Harris (1809–1907). Born in Meadville, Pennsylvania, her father was a free Black man and her mother a White woman. Following her marriage in 1828, Harris and her husband moved to Buffalo where she soon become both a mother and a widow. Three years later she and her little daughter became the first Black people to settle in Jamestown, in the southwest corner of New York. Through the decade additional Black people, a few being runaway slaves and their families, began to trickle into Jamestown and settled near the Harris house. Once the Underground Railroad was up and running, Jamestown would prove a popular and convenient stopping point for fugitive slaves heading north from eastern Ohio as they made their way around Lake Erie to Buffalo and Canada.

As African Americans congregated in the town, the White people began to call the area around Harris' house Africa. Her home became the meeting place for an emerging congregation of the AME Zion Church, but more important the central stop (and one of the best documented stops) on the Underground Railroad. Recognizing that such stops usually became a community affair, in which Blacks and abolitionist Whites cooperated in the hiding, feeding, and moving of the refugees, in no way diminishes Harris' role in organizing the effort at her stop when the train moved through carrying passengers. After the war, Harris, now a widow for a second time, continued to live quietly in Jamestown. Her home evolved into the Blackwell Chapel AMEZ Church and still later served as the parsonage for the minister.[29]

Sojourner Truth has a unique place among African American women, possibly the most charismatic and accomplished of any from the nineteenth century.[30] Primarily known as a abolitionist speaker/activist, she transcended labels as an advocate of women's rights and, like Frances Willard who would come after her, became a dabbler in a variety of the century's fads from Spiritualism to various health cults to a Methodist favorite, temperance. She was born in 1797 as Isabella Baumfree, in Hurley, Ulster County, New York. She

Sojourner Truth emerged as an independent voice for Black liberation in the last decades of the antebellum era. Photographer and date unknown, Sojourner Truth Library, State University of New York at New Paltz.

moved several times in her younger years as she was passed from owner to owner.

Along the way, Isabella was married and gave birth to five children. In 1811, her last master, a man named Dumont, had promised to grant her freedom a year before the mandated general freedom for New York slaves (July 4, 1827) as spelled out in the recently passed New York general manumission law. When the time came, however, he refused to honor his promise, so Isabella took her youngest son with her and left the plantation. When her master caught up with her, she was aided by Isaac Van Wagenen, who purchased the last months of her time in slavery and provided her with a place to live. She later changed her name to Isabella Van Wagenen and set about the task of reassembling her family, one of whom Dumont had sold and allowed to be to taken illegally to Alabama.

Her new freedom also provoked a religious awakening. At a point of feeling guilty for having neglected any acknowledgment of God, she had a vision of Jesus, though to that point she had led a life in which religion had been a cursory matter. She had received only cursory religious instruction and had no real knowledge of Christian teachings about Jesus, believing basically that he was a friend who stood between her and an angry God. Only later did she receive a more complete understanding. Meanwhile, in 1827 she affiliated with the newly formed congregation of the Methodist Episcopal Church in Kingston, New York.[31]

Isabella now had a new set of problems. Freed from slavery, she had moved into poverty. Her husband was ill and could do little to assist their situation. She was forced to move to New York City. She took a letter of transfer with her from the Kingston church to the John Street Church in the city. She worshiped there for a short time, but soon discovered the Zion congregation on Church Street and moved her membership there. She expanded her religious life, attending some meetings led by an independent Methodist for whom she worked, and participated in an effort of Methodist women attempting to reform prostitutes. Through the network she developed in these various activities, she was brought into a group headed by a Mr. Pierson, who believed himself a new Elijah commanded to call together believers at a new Mt. Carmel, namely Bowery Hill in New York City. Pierson then merged his group into the followers of Matthias, a prophet from upstate New York who claimed that he had been commanded to take charge of the world for God. She met Matthias when he came to Pierson's house, which Isabella was caring for in his absence. Pierson later concluded that he was Matthias' wayshower and united his following to that of Matthias. Isabella remained with the group a short time, but left as the group became more and more extreme. At one point Matthias was arrested and tried for the murder of Pierson (though found not guilty).[32]

Then in 1843, she took an assessment of her life and felt a calling to become a lecturer and to do what good she could. At this point she changed her name again, emerging as Sojourner Truth. She adopted the life of a wanderer, staying where she could, lecturing to any who would listen, and working for a few days when she needed money. She often paid people to read the scriptures to her and compared what she heard with her own experience. She occasionally spoke to the followers of William Miller (1782–1849), then in the heightened expectation of the impending return of Christ, seeking to calm them from her own prior experience with Matthias.

Out of her first tour through Long Island and New England, she developed an understanding of her calling "to travel up and down the land, showing the people their sins and being a sign unto them." She was naturally drawn to lecturing on the evils of slavery and soon wedded it to her support for the women's rights movement. In 1850, she accepted help to record her life story, which was published as the *Narrative of Sojourner Truth*, to which William Lloyd Garrison wrote a preface. She never learned to read and write, and thus spoke extemporaneously. She was known for her quick wit that always had a comeback for hecklers. Her speeches were also liberally sprinkled with references from the Bible, most of which she had memorized.

Interestingly, her most famous speech was delivered not in an abolitionist context, but at the 1851 Woman's Rights Convention in Akron, Ohio. Having heard a number of speeches declaring women equal, she asserted, "I can carry as much as any man, and can eat as much too, if I can get it." She probably never spoke the famous words attributed her, "Ar'n't I a Woman?"[33] though those words would have been a fitting conclusion to words actually recorded of her: "The Lady [one of the previous speakers] has spoken about Jesus, how he never spurned woman from him, and he was right. . . . And how came Jesus into the world? Through God who created him and a woman who bore Him."[34]

At the time her *Narrative* was published, Sojourner, in her early forties, was just beginning to make a name for herself. She saw the *Narrative* primarily as a means of her gaining added financial support for her chosen career as a lecturer for the associated causes that she advocated. Through the 1850s she would emerge more fully on the national stage as a voice of abolitionism. Once the war began, she used her platform to recruit African Americans into the Union Army. Abraham Lincoln took notice of her work and in 1864 appointed her to serve with the National Freedman's Relief Association. And she continued to follow her calling for the rest of her life, which finally came to an end in 1883.

Women's Rights

In the 1840s, a group of women, primarily White, kept from the platform of the abolitionist movement, used their disappointment in their treatment by the most socially aware elements of society to initiate consideration of the status and role of women in society. Elizabeth Cady Stanton is rightly remembered for her cogent summary of the issues and her making the call for a convention of women to meet and consider the status and role of women in America. Their venue would be the Wesleyan Methodist Chapel at Seneca Falls, New York. The gathering was planned for July 19 and 20, 1848.

The convention considered a broad set of resolutions of importance to women relative to legal proceedings, the making of law, property ownership, divorce, education, and entrance into various professions. It also called for the right to vote. Of twelve resolutions brought before the assembled women, only one fell short of unanimous support—the one calling for women's suffrage. The idea prompted a heated debate. Interestingly enough, it was a male friend of Stanton's, Frederick Douglass, who finally moved the audience.

One of the few males to participate in the convention, Douglass' speech on behalf of women receiving the vote would be credited with being the decisive factor in the resolution's finally passing. From this point on, Douglass would wed abolitionism and women's rights in his thinking. Just a week later, he published an editorial on "The Rights of Women" in the July 28, 1848, edition of his newspaper, the *North Star*. Then on August 2, he met with the women again at the adjourned Women's Rights Convention session held in Rochester (where he resided) and joined with colleagues William C. Nell and William C. Bloss in calling for the emancipation of women from all the confining and hobbling factors in their lives due to "false customs, creeds, and codes." He would continue to work for women's rights as he did for the end of slavery.[35] Douglass would in later life reflect on his support of women's issues:

> Observing woman's agency, devotion, and efficiency in pleading the cause of the slave, gratitude for this high service early moved me to give favorable attention to the subject of what is called "Woman's Rights," and caused me to be denominated a woman's-rights-man. I am glad to say I have never been ashamed to be thus designated. Recognizing not sex, nor physical strength, but moral intelligence and the ability to discern right from wrong, good from evil, and the power to choose between them, as the true basis of Republican government, to which all are alike subject, and bound alike to obey, I was not long in reaching the conclusion that there was no foundation in reason or justice for woman's exclusion from the right of choice in the selection of the persons

who should frame the laws, and thus shape the destiny of all the people, irrespective of sex.[36]

Notes

1. J. B. Wakeley, *Lost Chapters Recovered from the Early History of American Methodism* (New York: Wilbur B. Ketcham, 1889), 102–3.

2. Originally printed in 1784 in the *Arminian Magazine*, the Methodist magazine printed in London, and was reprinted in Atkinson, *Beginnings of the Wesleyan Movement in America*, 192–93.

3. This undated letter is reprinted in John P. Lockwood, *The Western Pioneers; or, Memorials of the Lives and Labours of the Rev. Richard Boardman and the Rev. Joseph Pilmoor* (London: Wesleyan Conference Office, 1881).

4. Quoted in John Atkinson, *The Beginnings of the Wesleyan Movement in America and the Establishment Therein of Methodism* (New York: Hunt & Eaton, 1896), 248–49.

5. Frederick E. Maser and Howard T. Maag, ed., *The Journal of Joseph Pilmore: Methodist Itinerant* (Philadelphia, PA: Historical Society of the Philadelphia Annual Conference of the United Methodist Church, 1969): 96.

6. Wakeley, *Lost Chapters*, 227.

7. Samuel L. Seaman, *A History of Methodism in New York City* (New York: Hunt & Eaton, 1892) 487.

8. A sketch of Molly Williams is found in Kenneth Holcomb Dunshee, *As You Pass By* (New York: Hastings House, 1952), 53.

9. According to Payne, the same was the case of the initial AME congregation in New York: "The membership at that time [1819] amounted to twenty souls, the majority of whom were women." This demographic remained the case through the church's early years. Daniel Alexander Payne, *A History of the African Methodist Episcopal Church*, ed. by Charles Spencer Smith (Nashville, TN: Publishing House of the A. M. E. Sunday School Union, 1891), 35–36.

10. Payne, *History of the African Methodist Episcopal Church*, 56.

11. William J. Walls, *The African Methodist Episcopal Zion Church: Reality of the Black Church* (Charlotte, NC: A.M.E. Zion Publishing House, 1974), 133–37.

12. Mary Still, *An Appeal to the Females of the African Methodist Episcopal Church* (Philadelphia: n.p., 1857), Reprinted in Richard Newman and Patrick Rael, eds. *Pamphlets of Protest: an Anthology of Early African-American Protest Literature, 1790–1860* (New York: Routledge, 2001), 254–60.

13. Baldwin, *Invisible Strands in African Methodism: A History of the African Union Methodist Protestant and Union American Methodist Episcopal Churches, 1805–1980.* (Methuen, NJ: Scarecrow Press, 1983), 57.

14. Elizabeth Elkin Grammer, *Some Wild Visions: Autobiographies by Female Itinerant Evangelists in Nineteenth-Century America* (New York: Oxford University Press, 2003); Marcia Y. Riggs, *Can I Get a Witness?: Prophetic Religious Voices of African American Women: An Anthology* (Maryknoll, NY: Orbis Books, 1997).

15. Charles H. Wesley, *Richard Allen: Apostle of Freedom* (Washington, DC: Associated Publishers, 1935), 114–15.

16. Jarena Lee, *Religious Experience and Journal of Mrs. Jarena Lee, Giving an Account of her Call to Preach the Gospel*. Revised and corrected from the Original Manuscript, Written by Herself (Philadelphia: The Author, 1849).

17. Kimberly Denise Blockett, *Traveling Home/Girls: Movement and Subjectivity in the Texts of Zilpha Elaw, Nella Larsen and Zora Neal Hurston* (Madison: University of Wisconsin, Ph.D. dissertation, 2002); Grammer, *Some Wild Visions*; and Riggs, *Can I Get a Witness?*

18. [Zilpha Elaw], *Memoirs of the Life, Religious Experience, Ministerial Travels and Labours of Mrs. Zilpha Elaw: An American Female of Colour, Together with Some Account of the Great Religious Revivals in America* (London: T. Dudley, 1846).

19. Payne, *History of the African Methodist Episcopal Church*, 237, 301.

20. *Elizabeth, a Colored Minister of the Gospel, Born in Slavery* (Philadelphia: Tract Association of Friends, 1889).

21. *Elizabeth, a Colored Minister of the Gospel, Born in Slavery* (Philadelphia: Tract Association of Friends, 1989), 9.

22. Octavia V. Roberts Albert, *The House of Bondage or Charlotte Brooks and Other Slaves Original and Life-Like, as they Appeared in their Old Plantation and City Slave Life; Together with Pen-Pictures of the Peculiar Institution with Sights and insights into their New Relations as Freedmen, Freemen, and Citizens* (New York: Hunt & Eaton/Cincinnati: Cranston & Stowe, 1890) 12.

23. Octavia V. Roberts Albert, *The House of Bondage or Charlotte Brooks and Other Slaves Original and Life-Like, as they Appeared in their Old Plantation and City Slave Life; Together with Pen-Pictures of the Peculiar Institution with Sights and insights into their New Relations as Freedmen, Freemen, and Citizens* (New York: Hunt & Eaton/Cincinnati: Cranston & Stowe, 1890), 13.

24. No copy of Harper's first book is known. Poems and prose that have survived may be found in the *Complete Poems of Frances Ellen Watkins Harper* (New York: Oxford University Press, 1988) and Frances Ellen Watkins Harper, *A Brighter Coming Day: A Frances Ellen Watkins Harper Reader*, ed. by Frances Smith Foster (New York: Feminist Press, 1990).

25. Harper, *A Brighter Day Coming*, 64.

26. Harper, *A Brighter Day Coming*, 61.

27. Harper, *A Brighter Day Coming*, 69.

28. Frances Ellen Watkins Harper, *A Brighter Coming Day: A Frances Ellen Watkins Harper Reader*, ed. by Frances Smith Foster (New York: Feminist Press. 1990); Patricia Liggins Hill, "Let Me Make the Songs for the People: A Study of Frances Watkins Harper's Poetry," *Black American Literature Forum* 15 (1981): 60–65; Carla L. Peterson, *"Doers of the Word": African American Women Speakers and Writers in the North (1830–1880)* (New York: Oxford University Press, 1995); and Melba Joyce Boyd, *Discarded Legacy: Politics and Poetics in the Life of Frances E. W. Harper, 1825–1911* (Detroit, MI: Wayne State University Press, 1994).

29. "Catherine Harris, Africa, and Some History of Jamestown, NY," posted at www.math.buffalo.edu/~sww/0history/harris.and.jamestown.html.

30. Sojourner Truth has become the object of much attention from contemporary African American and feminist scholars, and her autobiographical *Narrative* has appeared in several new editions. See Sojourner Truth, *Narrative of Sojourner Truth*, ed. by Margaret Washington (New York: Vintage Books, 1993). On Sojourner's life, see also Nell Irvin Painter, *Sojourner Truth: A Life, A Symbol* (New York: W. W. Norton, 1996), and Carleton Mabee with Susan Mabee Newhouse, *Sojourner Truth, Slave, Prophet, Legend* (New York: New York University Press, 1995).

31. Now the Clinton Avenue United Methodist Church.

32. An important independent source on Matthias' career is William L. Stone, *Matthias and his Impostures: or, The Progress of Fanaticism. Illustrated in the Extraordinary Case of Robert Matthews, and Some of his Forerunners and Disciples* . . . (New York, Harper & Brothers, 1835).

33. The "Ar'n't I a woman?" phrase seems to have been ascribed to her some twelve years after the fact by one of her abolitionist-feminist colleagues in the 1860s. See Painter, *Sojourner Truth*, 164–78.

34. Truth, *Narrative*, 118.

35. Though continuing to support women's rights through his life, he split with the leadership of the women's movement for a time when he supported the Fifteenth Amendment to the Constitution (that gave African American men the right to vote while excluding women).

36. Frederick Douglass, *Life and Times of Frederick Douglass, His Early Life as a Slave, His Escape from Bondage, and His Complete History to the Present Time* (Hartford, CT: Park Publishing Co., 1881), 480.

CHAPTER EIGHT

Toward Emancipation

African Methodism Crosses the Alleghenies

Simultaneously with its spread across the Deep South, African American Methodism also swept across the Alleghany Mountains into the Ohio River Valley. Kentucky was set aside as an annual conference in 1820, just as the African American presence in the state took an upswing. The new conference centered on Lexington, its only station, and the Lexington Circuit that united a set of nearby preaching points around the city. Its first year, the station reported 113 White and 70 Black members, while the circuit had 811 White and 317 Black members.

That same year, some of the Black members began to meet separately on Upper Street in a stable. A local preacher, William Smith, led the group in purchasing the stable and surrounding land, upon which a brick building was eventually erected (1826).[1] A second African congregation, Asbury MEC (now Wesley UMC), was begun in 1837, but it was not until 1844, the year of the Methodist split, that the conference appointments initially listed a separate work for African Americans. That year Rev. George B. Peage (a White man) was appointed as the assistant minister in Lexington, his special assignment being to pastor the Negro members, now 835 in number. (Black membership in the conference now reached almost 10,000.)[2] In 1850 Asbury erected its building on Branch Street, and was henceforth popularly known as the Old Branch Church.[3]

An initial Methodist society was organized in Louisville in 1806, and Methodism grew up side by side with the future metropolis. In 1820,

Louisville reported a membership of 100 White and 37 Black members; however, by the mid-1830s the African membership had skyrocketed. The original church on Fourth Street was divided and the new Brock Street and Eighth Street Churches created. All of the Black members, some 485, remained at Fourth Street for a short time, but then were transferred to Brock Street (now Broadway UMC), which at the time held services on Market Street (at least if the weather was favorable). At other times the biracial congregation met in a dining room at Elliott's Tavern on Main Street.

The desires for a better arrangement on the part of both Blacks and Whites led some White members to give the Black members a parcel of land on Jackson Street between Jefferson and Green where they constructed a church, now the R. E. Jones Temple, henceforth one of the main centers of the African American community in Louisville.[4] Meanwhile, though officially slave territory, Louisville proved very receptive to the AME missionary William Paul Quinn, who in the early 1840s founded a congregation. Later called Quinn Chapel, it became the denomination's leading church in the state. The Missouri Conference (whose original territory included all of the slaveholding states in the West and Southwest) was organized there in 1855.[5]

Settling even further to the west was Josiah Henson (1789–1883), who in 1825 moved from Baltimore to Daviess County, where he became a slave on a large plantation owned by one Amos Riley. As the farm's superintendent, he had some leisure time to think about religious questions which had arisen prior to his movement to the West. He was also able to attend camp meetings and church services where he heard both White and Black preachers. He fully converted and trained himself as best he was able from the example of others, and around 1827 was licensed as a preacher by his local circuit's quarterly conference.[6]

Then, in the spring of 1828, his real master (the brother of the owner of the plantation where he resided) ran into financial difficulties and had to sell all of his slaves, Henson and his family being the only exceptions. His witnessing the anguish caused by the capricious sale of his working companions stripped Henson of any loyalty to his master. He set his sights on freedom.

During the summer a White Methodist minister impressed by Henson's abilities conspired with him about gaining his freedom. Henson subsequently obtained a letter allowing him to travel. He went to Cincinnati, where Methodists became enthusiastic over his attempt to gain his liberation. They promoted his speaking in the various Methodist churches. As he accumulated funds to purchase his freedom, he cut a deal with his master in Maryland, only later to discover that his master had taken the money and deceived him. When Henson returned to the plantation, he found his master demanding far more for his freedom than the amount upon which they had previously agreed.

Shortly thereafter he was sent to New Orleans with the plantation owner's son, the intention being to sell him and leave him behind. He was saved by the young man taking sick and needing Henson's care to return home safely. Upon their arrival back in Kentucky and the son's recovery, the immediate expressions of gratitude for what he had done were short lived. Henson now planed his escape to Canada. In September he and his family, with the assistance of his friends in Cincinnati, made their way north into Canada.

Once in Canada, he was able to work, make a home, and place his children in school. He also began to preach. In 1834 he helped develop a Black settlement near the shore of Lake Erie. Over time, he developed a consciousness of the plight of those left behind in slavery and eventually became one of the leading activists of the Underground Railroad, about which more will be said later. In 1842, Henson was ordained as a deacon in the AME's Canadian Conference and was appointed to the Colchester Circuit. He was named an elder two years later.[7]

Similarly to Henson, Henry Bibb (b. 1815) lived on several plantations in Kentucky and became a Methodist. He briefly attended a Sabbath school headed by a Ms. Davis, until it was stopped by local opposition. He was quite aware of the disfavor the church had fallen into by its alignment with the slave owners. He also found a wife who was owned by a Methodist, William Gatewood, to whom he was also eventually sold.

Despairing of ever being freed, Bibb escaped to Canada, but returned to try to bring his wife and family out. In that effort, he was betrayed, recaptured, and returned to his slave state (though now able to share his knowledge of Canada and the route there with other slaves). At the time of his capture,

> they found my certificate from the Methodist E. Church, which had been given me by my classleader, testifying to my worthiness as a member of that church. And what made the matter look more disgraceful to me, many of this mob were members of the M. E. Church, and they were the persons who took away my church ticket, and then robbed me also of fourteen dollars in cash, a silver watch for which I paid ten dollars, a pocket knife for which I paid seventy-five cents, and a Bible for which I paid sixty-two and one half cents. All this they tyrannically robbed me of, and yet my owner, Wm. Gatewood, was a regular member of the same church to which I belonged.[8]

He would attempt to run away on several subsequent occasions. He eventually made his escape north and in the mid-1840s began a career as an anti-slavery lecturer. After the passing of the Fugitive Slave Law, he and his wife would move to Canada, where they published a newspaper, the *Voice of the Fugitive*, and founded several schools for Black children.

The first mention of Black Methodists in Ohio comes from Chillicothe, the state's original capital and a preaching point on the Scioto circuit. Circuit rider Henry B. Bascom recorded in 1807, "March 19 [Chillicothe, Ohio, circuit]. Preached, met a large society, rode to town, and met the black class at night. Met class at nine, preached at eleven, met class at twelve, and one at three o'clock."[9] It appears that four classes operated in the church at Chillicothe, one of which was Black.

Methodism entered Cincinnati as early as 1788 but the first class was not organized until 1802. The church then expanded rapidly. Wesley Chapel, fondly referred to as the Old Stone Church, was erected in 1806. At some point, a gallery was added for the Black members, though it soon proved to be too small to accommodate them.

Added to the problem of cramped space was the growing gap in worship styles between White and Black members. One evening, it seems, one of the Black brothers could hold back his joy no more, and to prevent disturbing the others with his shouting, he grabbed a handkerchief and shoved it into his mouth. He successfully suppressed his self-expression but at the expense of rupturing a blood vessel. He was carried from the sanctuary bleeding.

The next day, the well-spoken Samuel Carrell, the senior African American in the congregation, seized the moment and approached the White leadership to make his case for the Black members having a separate church. He wanted to prevent any reoccurrence of the previous evening's incident and noted that a separate space would allow an enlarged freedom for members to express themselves during the worship hour. Shortly thereafter, the White brothers showed Carrell a plot of land which they were ready to give to the Black members. The Black members gratefully accepted the gift and immediately began to raise money to purchase materials for a building and pay a contractor. They selected one of their own, Joseph Dorcus, a local preacher and a carpenter, as the architect in charge of the project.

Once the house was completed, they turned to one James King, who, though a slave, was allowed to travel between his home in Lexington and the church in Cincinnati, as their minister. For a number of years he made regular trips to Cincinnati, and for his services was given twenty dollars a month. When he was unable to be in Cincinnati, Dorcus and several other local preachers filled in.

After several years, the White lay leader who had given the plot of land upon which the church rested, a Judge Spencer, himself a staunch advocate of the anti-slavery cause, decided it would be best for all if King remained in Cincinnati permanently. Knowing the law, he obtained possession of King's travel pass and then arranged for King's arrest (for being away from home without a pass). When King was brought before the court, Spencer produced the pass and argued that he had come into Ohio, a free state, with his master's consent. Therefore, Spencer argued, King should be declared a free man.

Spencer's beneficence placed King in a moral dilemma. An honorable man, he thought he should honor the trust his master had placed in him by allowing him to travel so freely. At the same time he was a law-abiding person, and so in the end he decided to obey the law and remain in Cincinnati. For the next two years he lived quietly in Judge Spencer's home, and was guarded closely when moving about the city and carrying out his religious duties. His wife, who was already a free woman, also moved to Cincinnati.

All was well until 1823, when events would transpire to take the African congregation out of the Methodist Episcopal Church. The move was occasioned by an incident at a camp meeting attended by King and a local preacher named Philip Brodie. Brodie, a native of Virginia, grew up near Knoxville, Tennessee. Here he joined the Methodists and was eventually licensed as an exhorter and then a preacher. A talented speaker, he began to travel around Tennessee and Kentucky, and eventually settled in Cincinnati. King and Brodie enjoyed the lively preaching at the camp meeting, but then came the time for the sacramental service. As was the common practice, the officiating minister invited all the other ministers to come forward and take the sacrament first. King and Brodie joined their colleagues. However, as they knelt before the table, one of the elders touched their shoulder and told them that they would have to wait until after the White laypeople were served. King later noted that as he rose, all the spirit of the meeting left him. All he had heard about God being no respecter of persons seemed hollow words. As they later watched the Black laypeople receive the sacrament, King would remember thinking that it seemed as if there were two Saviors, one for each race. The consciousness hit them that those making the distinctions between White and Black at that moment were wrong, and were in fact encouraging the broadly held prejudices of the times.

Upon their return to the city, the pair shared their experience with the other church members. About that same time, one of their number, Isaac Jones, traveled to Baltimore for the purpose of taking a wife, who as it turned out was a member of the Bethel AME congregation. Here, he also met and conversed with one of the preachers, Jacob Matthews. He returned to Cincinnati with the tales of a church in which no one had to wait second table for the sacrament, sit in the gallery, or be inhibited in expressing their religious sentiments. King and Brodie and a number of the members were eager to learn of the new church, and what questions Jones could not answer, his wife supplied.

A group decided very quickly to affiliate with the AMEC, and they sent for a minister. Moses Freeman arrived in Cincinnati and on February 4, 1824, organized what became Allen Temple AMEC, the first AME congregation west of the Alleghenies. The congregation subsequently met in various locations, including the cellar of Brodie's home. Brodie went on to become an AME minister and remained in Cincinnati to preach until his death in 1829.[10] It was in late 1829–30 that Jarena Lee, the AME evangelist, visited Cincinnati and left an account of her preaching and visitations among the members.[11]

Not all the Black Methodists joined the AMEs, and those who remained constituted a continuing African American congregation, which in 1840 reported some 245 members.

The John Stewart Saga[12]

As the events in Cincinnati were being played out, a most singular story was unfolding on the other side of the state—the work of John Stewart as a missionary among the native Wyandott people of north central Ohio. Born of free parents in Virginia, as a young man Stewart journeyed to Ohio. The robbery of all his possessions as he made his way to Ohio began a time of drinking and despair that terminated with his conversion at a Methodist camp meeting near Marietta, Ohio, where he had settled. He joined the church and was soon afterwards licensed as an exhorter.

A short time later, he was at private prayer and heard a voice speaking to him, "Thou shalt declare my counsel faithfully"; and he felt a pull toward the northwest direction. He accepted this incident as a call to preach, and he eventually encountered Jonathan Pointer, a Black man who in his youth had been taken prisoner by the Wyandotts, and while among them had learned to speak their language.

With Pointer's reluctant assistance, Stewart settled among the Wyandotts. At first they listened to his faltering attempts to preach out of respect to the stranger among them. But slowly, a few began to respond. He was initially challenged by some White traders who called attention to his lack of any credentials for doing his missionary work. His Native audiences were not as interested in his credentials nearly as much as his insistence that Christianity demanded that they forsake the religion of their people and give up their magical practices. The Wyandott leaders objected. The Great Spirit had given them their practices and they would not abandon them. Stewart countered the particularity of the Great Spirit's words to the Wyandotts with the universal demands of the gospel, a message to all people. His being convinced that he had communicated the gospel to the people completed the first phase of his ministry and he returned to Marietta for the winter of 1816–17. He returned among them in July 1817, and sometime afterward commenced a relationship with Polly Carter, the resident of a village on the Upper Sandusky called Negro Town. The two were wed on Christmas Day, 1818.

Meanwhile, by the Treaty of Fort Meigs (signed on September 29, 1817), the Wyandotts had ceded their traditional lands in Ohio to the United States, for which they received (among other things) some land around the Upper Sandusky, a saw-and-grist mill (built 1820), a blacksmith shop, and a sum of four thousand dollars to be paid annually.

Further attacks on his credentials led Stewart to communicate with the leadership of the Mad River Circuit. They were already aware of his work, and began immediately to take steps to have him licensed as a preacher. In early 1819, a minister from Mad River traveled through the Upper Sandusky and observed Stewart at his work. He also assembled a set of documents to be presented to the next Mad River Quarterly Conference, held in March 1819 at Urbana, Ohio, at which Stewart was presented with his license as a Methodist preacher. At the meeting, several of the local preachers also agreed to assist Stewart in his labors.

The 1819 "Civilization Bill" made available up to ten thousand dollars per year of government money to operate a school for Native Americans. Churches were allowed and even encouraged to apply. This bill encouraged the Ohio Conference to follow through on its vote to support Stewart. Also, that year, with funds raised by Bishop William McKendree, the church purchased a sixty-acre farm for Stewart and his wife immediately adjacent to the Wyandotts' land. In 1821, the Ohio Conference threw its support behind Stewart and sent James B. Finley as a missionary to the Upper Sandusky. For several years the mission founded by Stewart prospered. Findley and Stewart worked together until the fall of 1823, when Stewart took ill. His health steadily declined, and he passed away from tuberculosis in December. Just prior to Stewart's passing, Finley, accompanied by two of the Wyandott chiefs who had converted, and taking Jonathan Pointer along as a translator, left Upper Sandusky on a preaching mission to a group of Shawnee and Wyandotts who lived north of the Grand Reserve.

Stewart's years among the Wyandotts fits as part of the story of the role of African Americans in the development of American Methodism, but has additional import as the real beginning of American Methodist missionary work. He was certainly the first Methodist to give primary attention to Native Americans. Word of his work and its initial successes occurred just as the MEC's Missionary Society was being organized (1819) with the aim of supporting the annual conferences in their outreach. The subsequent publication of the account of Stewart's activity modeled life on the frontier for other missionaries who soon followed his example.

The new mission board targeted Native Americans for evangelism, and in 1820, two years before he visited Stewart in Ohio, Bishop McKendree prioritized the effort to spread the gospel among Native Americans in his Episcopal Address before the General Conference.

Besides its standing as the fountainhead of Methodist missions, there were some direct outgrowths of his work. In 1820, news of Stewart's work was carried to the Wyandotts residing in Canada and later two evangelists raised up in the Ohio mission were sent. They launched a thriving mission in Upper Canada that within a decade saw some two thousand people attending church and some four hundred students enrolled in eleven schools.

In 1824, a stone church was erected, and subsequently a revival broke out among the Wyandotts that spread to other Native peoples in the vicinity. Assuming leadership at this time were four Wyandott chiefs converted by Stewart—Between the Logs, Mononcue, Hiks, and Scuteash. The work continued in Ohio until 1843 when, after many years of negotiation, the Wyandotts moved to Kansas. The church was reestablished among them in their new home.

An interesting follow-up to the story of Stewart and Jonathan Pointer is the tale of Alfred Brunson, who in 1836 began work among the Native people residing near Prairie du Chien, Wisconsin. Brunson's work did not take off until he met a mulatto, a slave belonging to an army officer from Kentucky. The slave had a Methodist background, was married to a Dacotah woman, and spoke their language. The immediate problem was that the officer demanded twelve hundred dollars if he had to give up his slave. Brunson put his case before the readers of the *Western Christian Advocate*, the Methodist newspaper published in Cincinnati. Within a short time the money began to arrive and Brunson was notified that he could make the purchase and present the document of his freedom to his new interpreter.[13]

Beyond Ohio

Individual African Americans were making their way into the land beyond Ohio and Kentucky through the last half of the eighteenth century, and that migration only increased in the first decades of the nineteenth century. In several cases, where families found each other and were able to purchase land, some predominantly Black communities, towns built on a surrounding farm economy, emerged. A number formed across central Indiana in Randolph, Rush, Hamilton, Grant, and Vigo Counties. Other families moved to the emerging metropolitan centers.

In 1830, the AME Church, now led by Morris Brown (1770–1849), formed the Ohio (a.k.a. Western) Conference. By 1833 it had four circuits in Ohio centered on Zanesville, Columbus, Chillicothe, and Hillborough, which together covered the central and southern portions of the state. That same year, William Paul Quinn (c. 1788–1873) was admitted (or readmitted) to the traveling ministry (though not receiving elder's orders until 1838) and transferred to the Ohio Conference. He was assigned as a missionary based in Cincinnati but with his vision directed westward. He initially roamed as far as Indianapolis, where a small AME class already met in the home of a barber, Augustus Turner. Over the next years he started churches in Terre Haute and Richmond, which, along with Indianapolis, became the centers of the three Indiana circuits when the Indiana Conference was established in 1840. He also visited Louisville, where he gathered a small group that eventually evolved into Quinn Chapel. By this time there was also a circuit in Illinois. He was appointed general overseer for the Indiana Conference circuits in 1841. His subsequent travels now took him as far north as Detroit, where he found an independent Colored Methodist Society that had separated from the White Methodists, and Quinn invited them into the Indiana Conference as the city's Bethel AME Church.

When Quinn made his appeal for the churches west of the Alleghenies at the 1844 AME General Conference, he reported seventy-two congregations, of which forty-seven were established churches, some being former MEC congregations which had left to affiliate with the AMEs. Quinn would continue to direct his attention to the West. Based on his awe-inspiring report, he was elected bishop in 1844. He settled in Richmond, Indiana, the Quaker stronghold where he could feel personally safe while resting from his travels, and where he lived the rest of his life.

Africa in Illinois[14]

As European Americans pushed their way into the Indiana and Illinois Territories, both destined to be admitted into the union as free states, relatively

William Paul Quinn, a bishop of the AME Church, founded many of its original congregations in the Midwest.

few African Americans accompanied them, though occasionally stories illustrative of the racial conflicts brought onto the frontier emerge. Such a story is found in Williamson County, Illinois, destined to be the scene of intense Ku Klux Klan activity in the 1920s.

Around 1815, one John McCreery moved to Illinois from Kentucky, bringing his family and a number of slaves with him. Among his first actions once he was settled was to give four slaves to his son Robert. Another son, Allen, stole the four slaves and took them to Missouri with the intent of selling them and pocketing the money. Robert pursued his brother, recovered the slaves, and returned them to Illinois. He then freed them, bought a plot of land from the government in Franklin County, and built homes for his former slaves and other African people. Cornelius Elliott, a mulatto, is credited with bringing the Black people together, thus initiating a settlement which assumed the name Africa.

Meanwhile, in 1818, when Illinois was admitted to the Union as a free state, John McCreery took his family and remaining slaves and moved to Missouri. He died in 1821 and his widow inherited his property. When she died, they then passed to another son, Alexander. In the 1840s, Alexander brought all of the slaves (along with the wife of one of them he had purchased to keep the family unit together) back to Illinois. Here he freed them and settled them at Africa. By this time Franklin County had been divided and Williamson County established. Africa was located in the southeast corner of the new county, a Black town in the midst of a predominantly White state.

The residents of Africa initially attended the Liberty Methodist Church south of Thompsonville. However, in the 1840s as the settlement grew, they built their own church at Africa. The new Locust Grove Church maintained cordial relations with Liberty and followed Liberty into the Methodist Episcopal Church, South. In the 1850s, Southern Illinois was home to many who sympathized with the South, and as the prospect of war grew, a cadre of White men threatened the residents of Africa and demanded that they leave their homes. Some were ready to do just that, before the members of the Liberty Church came to their aid and silenced the threatening voices.

Among the notable members of the Africa church was Richard Inge, one of the slaves brought back from Missouri in the mid-1840s. It was his wife that Alexander McCreery bought to preserve the family. Once freed Inge worked as a shoemaker and paid Alexander back what he and his wife would be worth on the open market. He later purchased an eighty-acre tract of land for himself, and there made a home for his wife and a young boy that they had adopted from a woman who settled in Africa and was too poor to provide for him.

As the African congregation was developing, the AME Church had made its initial presence felt in the area. In the 1830s, an African family named Smith moved to Gallatin County (west of Williamson on the Ohio River). One or two of their number were local AME preachers. At some point prior to the beginning of the Civil War, the Methodist congregation at Africa switched their affiliation to the AME Church and the Locust Grove Church was superseded by what was called Allen Temple. It is not known if the log cabin housing the temple was the original Locust Grove Church building or another building. By this time Africa had also changed its name and it came to be known as Skeleton Town.

According to a letter written by a former resident of Skeleton Town, in 1860 the black residents of neighboring Saline County put up a brush arbor and held a camp meeting, which many from Skeleton Town attended (among them the Inge family). The brush arbor was located near the county line and not far from the residence of George Elliott, likely the son of Cornelius Elliott. At the time there were many more professing the faith in Skeleton Town than in Saline County.

The small church served the community until some point in the early 1870s when it was replaced with a large hewed-log building. Still later, the residents built a large frame church.

Methodist Protestants[15]

In 1828, the Methodist Episcopal Church was shaken by the outward movement of a segment of its membership who protested its episcopal organization and who, upon leaving, formed themselves into a more loosely organized fellowship that was headed by district superintendents elected by a combination of ministers and representatives of the local churches. At the time of its formation, some free Blacks left the MEC and joined the new church and many slaves followed their masters into it. Within a few years, the Methodist Protestant Church (MPC) emerged as a national body, though one decidedly smaller than its parent. The Maryland MPC Conference, which covered the states of Maryland, Pennsylvania, New Jersey, Delaware, South Carolina, and the District of Columbia, was one of its largest and strongest conferences and one in which many of its Black members were located.

Almost from the beginning, the conference included Black congregations, which were given voice but not vote in the conference except on issues directly pertaining to them. An Association of the Colored Churches of the MPC was formed at the beginning of the 1840s and included churches in Philadelphia and Elkton, Pennsylvania; and Glasgow and St. Thomas, Delaware. Several ministers were ordained as elders to provide leadership for these churches.[16]

Work in South Carolina originated from the controversy at Bethel MEC in Charleston, which grew out of a disagreement over the seating of Black members and led to more than a hundred members leaving and founding a Charleston MPC in 1834 (as covered in chapter 5). That same year a Georgia MPC Conference was organized to include congregations in South Carolina, Georgia, and Florida.

The development of African American work was not a significant consideration within the church during the antebellum years and as a whole

Black members attended the White churches, where they were organized in segregated classes and were further segregated during Sunday worship. The Association in the Maryland Conference appears to have been the primary expression of the several Black congregations above the congregational level. This would change with the coming of emancipation.

In 1868, the Maryland Conference set in place a policy of organizing its remaining Black members still in predominantly White churches into new congregations. In the 1870s the MPC as a whole found itself with African American churches in Alabama, Texas, and Tennessee. A single congregation in Charleston was placed in the Maryland Conference. It soon multiplied with the addition of several churches at Berkeley, South Carolina. In 1880, the MPC created several Colored mission conferences, resulting in the formation of the Baltimore Colored Mission (1880), the Colorado Texas Colored Mission (1880), the Spring Creek Colored Mission (1884), the Charleston Colored Mission (1889), and the Alabama Colored Mission (1896). Most of these missions survived until 1939, when they were absorbed into the Central Jurisdiction of the Methodist Church (1939–68).

Boston Methodism and the Origins of Abolitionism

Joseph Pilmore started a Methodist class in Boston as early as 1772, and Freeborn Garrettson and Harry Hosier visited in 1790, but it was twenty years after Pilmore's original effort (1792) before a permanent work developed. This modest society of twelve members, pulled together by Jesse Lee, would grow to become the First Methodist Church of Boston. In 1796, a building was erected on what was termed Methodist Alley (Hanover Avenue), the same year that the first session of the New England Conference met.

Relatively few Africans resided in Boston, even though slaves had been introduced in the previous century, and the practice only outlawed in the 1780s. In Boston in 1790 only 761 Africans (all free people) could be found among its 18,038 citizens. It appears that the first Methodist society was all White, but two years after its founding, four Africans are reported among the forty-nine members. That number doubled over the next three years, but Boston was the only Methodist society in the state at the time with any Black members.

The number of Black members would grow steadily through the next decade, and forty-two would be reported in 1810. Already in 1806, the Methodist Alley church had started a separate African mission on Bromfield Street, but following common practice, the conference listed the several Boston congregations as a single charge. The Bloomfield Street Church attracted many relatively wealthy Blacks, as the new church was located close to their residents on Beacon Hill. In 1818, Samuel Snowden, an African minister then working with the Chestnut Street Church in Portland, Maine, moved to Boston to provide spiritual oversight for Boston's African Methodists.[17] In hiring Snowden, the Whites were able to both meet the needs of the Black members and handle their own problem with the White members' rejection of the exuberant religious expressions of the Black members, who found attempts to make them act more like Whites insulting.

Five years after Snowden's arrival, the Black members petitioned for a separate meeting house, which was opened as a new mission on May Street (now Revere Street), made possible through the generosity of one of the White members, Amos Burney. The building served the congregation for a decade but was eventually replaced with a new brick edifice erected in 1835.[18] The youthful Snowden would have a long ministry and was still shown on the tax assessment records of 1850 as a resident in the Beacon Hill neighborhood.[19]

May Street was the second African church in the city, a Baptist church having opened in 1805. While the Baptist church was the larger of the two, May Street MEC (now Union UMC) served the upper echelons of Black society. It was noted in 1827 that twenty-nine of its eighty-four members were occupied as artisans, professionals, or skilled workers. Among these was one David Walker (1796–1830), who had moved to Boston around 1825 and opened a used-clothing store near the city's wharves.

Walker, though residing in the city for only a few years, was to have a major impact on Boston's Black community and across the nation. Walker had been born free in North Carolina, had moved about the South for several years, and left Charleston for the North in the wake of the Denmark Vesey trials. Soon after his arrival in the city, he participated in the founding of the Massachusetts General Colored Association, established to abolish slavery and generally work for an improvement of living conditions for African Americans. His speech at the first meeting of the Association was published in 1828 and represented a step toward the radicalization of his opinions concerning the state of Black America: "[T]he primary object of this institution is to unite the colored population, so far, through the United States . . . and not [withhold] anything which may have the least tendency to meliorate our miserable condition."[20]

Soon after his settling in Boston, Walker married Eliza Butler, joined the local Masonic Lodge, and in 1827 became the local agent for *Freedom's Journal*. He also became a member of May Street MEC and developed a close friendship with Rev. Snowden. By 1829, through the variety of activities he helped organize and lead, he had become one of Boston's most important African American spokespersons.

Through 1828–29 he worked on the small volume for which he is now universally remembered by African Americans, the *Appeal to the Colored Citizens of the World,* published on September 28, 1829. In the *Appeal* he raised the level of rhetoric as he vented his anger and outrage at all he had seen of the cruelty of the slave system. He spotlighted the un-Christian way that slavery was perpetuated in America and claimed that his fellow Africans were the most degraded and wretched of creatures. Americans were guilty of depriving them of education, religion, and civil liberties. He raged against colonization schemes aimed at driving Africans from the land they had enriched with their blood.

Walker culminated his discourse by charging that Whites had insulted all Africans by denying them membership in the human family. Given the cruelties being enacted upon them, Walker went so far as to suggest that they were justified in rising up and even using violence against the slave owners, supporting his argument with citations from the Declaration of Independence. This most radical notion elevated the *Appeal* to the center of a major controversy while forcing many in the forefront of the anti-slavery struggle to distance themselves from it.

While his readers in the anti-slavery movement were thinking about what to do with his *Appeal,* Walker devised creative ways to circulate it where he believed it would do the most good. He recruited sailors to smuggle it into southern ports, such as Charleston and Savannah, and assisted his cohorts by hiding copies into the linings of clothes he processed and sold. What the *Appeal* lacked in laying out a specific scheme for emancipation, it made up for in the fear it struck in slave owners, already entertaining fears of slave revolts. Within months of its publication, Whites discovered copies in Savannah, and over the next year they surfaced throughout the South. Rewards were offered as high as three thousand dollars for Walker dead and ten thousand dollars should someone be able to bring him to the South alive. Southern states moved on a variety of fronts to suppress the circulation of the *Appeal,* enacting new laws which, for example, forbade the education of black children or barred Black sailors from leaving their ships docked in Charleston. The situation just worsened a year later following the Nat Turner revolt.

Walker did not live to see the public react to his writing. In August 1830, just two months after publishing a third edition of *The Appeal,*[21] he was found dead in his shop. Some ascribed his passing to tuberculosis (or consumption, as it was then termed), from which his daughter had recently died. Others suspected foul play, possibly poisoning by an assassin.[22]

While the main body of the anti-slavery movement rejected Walker's *Appeal*, a new generation of free Blacks and anti-slavery advocates received it as a call to arms, a fresh incentive to abandon outmoded schemes for the gradual elimination of slavery upon which previous deliberations had been largely based. Though not the first call for immediate emancipation, Walker's *Appeal* would soon be seen as the originating point of the new phase of the anti-slavery movement that blossomed in the 1830s: abolitionism. Quite apart from the issue of the use of violence, Walker's denunciation of the gradualist approach would resonate with fellow Bostonian William Lloyd Garrison, who launched the new movement's main periodical, the *Liberator* (1831–65). Garrison picked up Walker's use of the Declaration of Independence as the starting point of the abolitionist position.

The abolitionist movement placed the situation of the slaves before the public with a new urgency. It tossed aside the utopian plans of the colonizers and showed the ineffectiveness of the various schemes for gradual elimination which, after some success in the North, had been unable to prevent the further spread and growth of slavery. Most important, gradualism gave many "good" people the privilege of believing in the wrongness of slavery without compelling them to work to eliminate it.

Among the first people influenced by the sentiments that spread from Walker's *Appeal* was one Hezekiel Grice, a young but relatively wealthy Philadelphian. Grice initiated correspondence with Black leaders across the country, suggesting that a convention be called to discuss the possibility of large-scale emigration to Canada. In response, the first National Negro Convention met for ten days beginning September 15, 1830, at the Bethel African Methodist Church in Philadelphia, with Richard Allen serving as the convention's president. Among the forty black leaders who traveled to Philadelphia for the convention would be the late David Walker's pastor, Samuel Snowden. The attendees fully discussed the Canada proposal, but then allowed their deliberations to range over a variety of additional issues before the African American community. Before they adjourned they founded a new organization, the "American Society of Free People of Colour," whose first annual meeting would occur a year later, this time hosted by the AMEZ congregation in Philadelphia.

Garrison, in making Boston his headquarters, made the city the most radical in the anti-slavery cause. Black leaders gathered in July 1831 at the Baptist meeting house to honor him. By the end of the year, he and his White supporters were organizing the New England Anti-slavery Society, the initial organization of the new abolitionism. Among those who became active in the society was Maria W. Stewart (1803–79), a Baptist who had known Walker and agreed with most of his ideas. His death changed her life, which she now dedicated to Black liberation. Through 1831–32 she spoke wherever she could and wrote articles, later to be published in book form, that Garrison picked up for the *Liberator*.[23] In the immediate support she gave to Garrison, she led in establishing both Black and female voices in the new movement.

Unfortunately, in arguing that Black people should stand up and face off their oppressors, Stewart made an inadvertent but severe tactical error. In her attempt to motivate what she saw as a host of lethargic male Blacks, she challenged their manhood. They reacted harshly against Stewart, forcing her to withdraw to New York, where she assumed a much lower profile. She remained a supporter of Garrison's work, however, and Garrison, remembering Stewart, emerged as a supporter of women's rights in general and their right to air their opinions within the movement in particular.

The radicalizing milieu of Boston would have its effect on the Methodists in two stages. Snowden, the pastor at May Street, had already shown his colors by his support of Walker and his participation in the Black Conventions. However, he could not prevent two movements out of his church in 1838. First, seventeen members of his church withdrew and founded Boston's first AMEZ congregation. Organized in June 13, the congregation soon found a permanent meeting site on Cambridge Street and petitioned for a minister to be sent. Shortly thereafter, Jehiel C. Bemen, who was to have a long and eventful pastorate in the city, joined Snowden in tending for the Black Methodists of Boston. Within two years he had built a congregation of 140 members.[24]

Then, a few months later, Daniel Laing, a layman representing a second group of Boston Methodists, appeared at the New York Conference of the AME Church, bearing a petition that the conference send a preacher to found an AME congregation. After indicating their willingness to provide support to the sum of seventy-five dollars, the conference sent Noah C. W. Cannon (c. 1796–1850). He organized the Boston church and the following year founded one in nearby Providence, Rhode Island.[25] It had become a relatively strong and stable church by the time the New England Conference was founded in 1852.[26]

Second, several years prior to the founding of the AME and AMEZ congregations, one of the more prominent White Methodist ministers, Orange Scott, the presiding elder of the Springfield District of the New England Conference, converted to abolitionism. In 1835, he wrote the first articles on the subject for the conference newspaper, *Zion's Herald*. The bishop responded by removing him from his presiding elder's position and sending him to pastor in Lowell. He responded to the bishop by delivering a rousing speech on abolition at the 1836 General Conference. Henceforth the leading spokesperson for abolitionism in the MEC, he worked within the church until 1842, but unable to move the leadership away from their gradualist position, he then withdrew. Others across the northern states joined him. They came together in 1843 as the Wesleyan Methodist Connexion of America. The Boston congregation was formed by former members of the Bromfield MEC led by Jotham Horton. Other congregations emerged as far west as Michigan. The nine ministers and forty-three laymen that attended the organizing conference held in Andover, Massachusetts, united on two platforms—the denial of legitimacy to slavery and the withdrawal of Christian fellowship from slaveholders.

The establishment of the Wesleyan Church moved the MEC's New England Conference toward the abolitionist camp, and its Boston leadership began to sponsor anti-slavery gatherings. Rhetoric at these gatherings turned to reforming Methodism relative to slavery. It was not surprising then that in 1844, it would be the New England delegation that offered the petition calling for the division of the MEC. They felt unable to continue in fellowship with slaveholders. The division of the church into two jurisdictions was, of course, adopted in 1844 amid heated discussion of Georgia bishop James O. Andrew's slave ownership. By the time those who regretted their initial support for church division reconsidered what they had done, it was set in concrete by action of the southern conferences.

Progress of the AMEZ, AUP, and AME Churches

When the African members in New York finally decided that there was no future in alliance with the MEC, the fellowship included the two churches in New York City and small congregations in New Haven, Connecticut; and Philadelphia and Easton, Pennsylvania. Following the conference structure that had worked so well for the White brethren, the Zionist leadership deployed the ministers in such a fashion as to both maintain the existing congregations and create new ones. Two thrusts became evident: the push into New England and the evangelism of Black communities in Pennsylvania.

New England was virtually virgin territory, there being few MEC congregations and only one Black congregation, in Boston. Growth began in Providence, Rhode Island; and Hartford, Connecticut. By the time the Boston church emerged in 1838, new congregations were being formed across Massachusetts (New Bedford and Nantucket) and Connecticut (Middleton, Stonington, and Bridgeport). Continued growth justified the formation of a New England Conference in 1845.

In 1838, just as the New Bedford church was getting started, Frederick Douglass moved to town and settled in a little house on Elm Street. He had already identified with the Zionist community and now became an active member at Zion Chapel, then served by William Sarrington. Soon after Douglass arrived, however, a new pastor, Thomas James (1804–?) took charge of the small congregation that met in the little schoolhouse on Second Street. During James' pastorate, Douglass became successively a class leader, exhorter, and local preacher. He remained an active member until he sailed for England in 1845. The churches and ministers of the New England Conference became the original abolitionist network, of which Douglass would become such an important member in the 1850s.[27]

From the Wesleyan Church in Philadelphia, the Zionists pushed westward and southward. The first church organized in Washington, D.C., opened in 1837 under the capable hands of George Galbraith, who had previously served in Harrisburg, Pennsylvania. Washington would prove to be a welcoming city and by the beginning of the Civil War, there were four Zionist congregations. At the same time, however, the Potomac River would prove a barrier that would not be crossed until the 1860s. Maryland would have to be the place of growth, and work there began in 1843, in Baltimore. The Maryland and Washington congregations would be set apart as the Southern Conference in 1859.

The real growth would be from Philadelphia westward. Central and western Pennsylvania had numerous communities of free Black people, and Zionist missionaries lost no time in finding them and organizing classes that quickly grew into substantial centers of church life. The growth throughout the state was acknowledged by the formation of the Philadelphia Conference in 1819 and the setting off of the Allegheny Conference in 1849. But here again, the church would run into a barrier—the Allegheny Mountains. While the initial church in Pittsburgh would be opened as early as 1836, the move into Ohio and the Midwest would wait until after the war, not that there was not enough work to do in the territory that had been laid out roughly within the triangle formed by Boston, Washington, and Pittsburgh.

One of the most important areas into which the Zionists pushed through the 1830s was Western New York, and no more important congregation would be founded than the one at Rochester, though the one to the southeast at Auburn would rival it. It would be to Auburn, New York, that Harriet Tubman would repair from her labors on the Underground Railroad.

Upon his return in 1847 from Europe, now a free man, Frederick Douglass settled in Rochester.

The Canadian border proved no barrier to the AMEZs, the first congregation being founded by Hamilton Johnson, a Black preacher from Prescott, Ontario. As additional congregations were organized, they waited to receive any who found their way north.

Thus, by the time of the Civil War, the AME Zion Church was spread from New England to the Potomac River and westward to the Alleghenies. It staunchly aligned itself with the abolitionist movement. That identification led to significant controversy during the 1850s, but became an asset as it claimed support among the freedmen in the decades after the war.

Though rarely mentioned in their churches' histories, the primary competition faced by both the AMEZs and AMEs in the first decades of their existence came from the African Union Church, headquartered in Wilmington, Delaware. It preceded both churches by several years and was centered in the heart of the northern African American Methodist community. The church proved to be highly evangelistic, and reached out through the small towns and countryside in the hundred mile radius of its home base in Wilmington, Delaware. Word of its existence flowed through the Free Black Methodist communities in Eastern Pennsylvania, New Jersey, and Maryland.

In the late 1830s and early 1840s, the AUC pushed into New England (Connecticut and Rhode Island). By 1843, when Spencer died, twenty-one congregations had affiliated with the African Union Church and membership had been organized into three regions including one for New York and New England.

Its impressive growth in its first decades did not hide the fact that the AUC fell significantly behind the AMEs and AMEZs in the 1840s.[28] Its congregational form of church governance soon proved no competition in the face of the more centrally organized episcopal jurisdictions that could deploy ministers for maximum effect. In the end, the Union Church remained a limited regional fellowship that only slightly challenged the boundaries formed by the Potomac and the Alleghenies. The limitations of the congregational system may have been behind the 1850 schism that occurred when a group arose within the church demanding that an episcopal governing system be installed. That group did not prevail and left to form the Union American Methodist Episcopal Church.

In the meantime, in 1849–50, struggles in Bethel Church–Philadelphia and Bethel Church–Baltimore led two groups to leave the AME Church in Maryland. Those who left opposed the actions of ministers appointed to the charges by the conferences. In Baltimore, Nathaniel Peck, a local preacher, led the withdrawal and subsequently organized the people who followed him as the First Colored Methodist Protestant Church. Soon afterwards, the much larger group that left in Philadelphia adhered to the new church.[29] That church would in the 1860s merge with the African Union Church to form the African Union First Colored Methodist Protestant Church. Its congregations are now primarily concentrated in New York, New Jersey, Delaware, Maryland, and Washington, D.C.

Following its organizational conference in 1816, the new African Methodist Episcopal Church began a systematic attempt to reach African American Methodists in the area around Philadelphia and Baltimore, next in the other major metropolitan areas, and then westward all the way to the Mississippi River. Attending the original gathering were, among others, four of the deacons that Bishop Asbury had ordained—Richard Allen, Jacob Tapsico, and James Champion from Philadelphia, and Daniel Coker from Baltimore. They were joined by some preachers from Attleborough (now Langhorne), Pennsylvania, and Reuben Cuff from Mt. Hope MEC in Salem, New Jersey.

From Asbury's early visits, Salem had become a strong Methodist center. An active Quaker presence throughout southern New Jersey led many residents to manumit their slaves in the decades after the Revolution, and by the first decade of the new century, free Blacks outnumbered slaves almost two to one. Founded in 1801, Mount Hope Church in Salem was the first separate Black Methodist congregation in the state, and would later become the focus of a lengthy dispute as supporters of the MEC and AME struggled for control of the property.

The preachers assigned to Salem by Bishop Allen beginning in 1816 had the support of Reuben Cuff and others, but ran into the trust clause in the local church deed. They were unable to claim the church property from those congregants who remained loyal to the MEC. Finally, in 1825, the AME group separated and began worshiping in a log cabin. As they retained hope of eventually gaining control of the Mt. Hope building, they delayed erecting a new church. Finally, in 1841 they laid the foundation for what would be the Mt. Pisgah AME Church, but only after arson had taken the original Mount Hope building, leaving both factions homeless.[30]

Apart from Salem, the AME Church made significant gains in New Jersey during its first decade. It formed congregations successively at Trenton, Gouldtown, Rahway, Mt. Holly, Snow Hill, and New Brunswick. Gouldtown, located in Cumberland County, has attained some fame as one of the oldest Black settlements in the state.[31] It would be one stop on the Salem Circuit that was served for many years by Reuben Cuff and later by members of his family. Founded in 1818, the congregation raised their building in

Mt. Zion United Methodist Church at Salem is the oldest African American Methodist congregation in New Jersey. Photo courtesy of Frank L. Greenagel.

Mt. Pisgah African Methodist Episcopal Church was founded by former members of the Mt. Zion Methodist Episcopal Church in Salem, New Jersey. Photo courtesy of Frank L. Greenagel.

1825. Many of the town's founding Gould family were members, including Theodore Gould, who had a notable career as an AME minister.[32]

While the leadership at the Zion church in New York were deciding whether to break with the MEC, Black members at the Sands Street Church in Brooklyn had walked out in 1818 after a pro-slavery pastor was assigned to the church. Under the leadership of Benjamin and Peter Croger, they formed

Trinity African Methodist Episcopal Church houses the original congregation serving the all-Black community of Gouldtown, New Jersey. Photo courtesy of Frank L. Greenagel.

the First African Wesleyan Methodist Episcopal Church and in 1820 formally requested alignment with Allen's work in Philadelphia. Following the opening of the AME Church in New York City (see chapter 3) a third AME church was founded in Rahway, New Jersey. Towns north of New York City were brought together in the White Plains Circuit. Also, an early and singular New England church was founded in New Bedford, Massachusetts.

Very early in the church's history, the Philadelphia and Baltimore Conferences were gradually distinguished from each other, and each negotiated hegemony over new territory that was being opened up. Early decisions had to be made relative to Washington, D.C., western Pennsylvania (to the Philadelphia Conference), and the Eastern Shore of Maryland (to the Baltimore conference). The New York Conference was organized in 1822. Work on the Eastern Shore of Maryland initially appeared as the Easton Circuit in 1823. It included 543 members scattered through Talbot and Caroline Counties. A Kent County Mission Circuit was established in 1847.

In 1824 the Philadelphia Conference assigned three ministers to Ohio, largely in response to the group that had left the MEC in Cincinnati, but strategically placed Jeremiah Miller in Chillicothe and Noah C. W. Cannon in Steubenville.[33] Philip Brodie organized the first church, in Cincinnati, and by 1830, the year that the Ohio Conference was formed, their work had spread as far north as Cleveland.

In Ohio, the church attempted its most ambitious pre–Civil War project, the erection of Union Seminary, a ministerial training school. As that project proceeded, the Cincinnati Conference of the Methodist Episcopal Church entertained the idea of setting up a combined high school and college, which came into being as Wilberforce University in 1856. Both schools closed during the Civil War. But in 1863, Daniel Payne (by this time a bishop) arranged to purchase the property of Wilberforce University and reopened the school. Union Seminary was absorbed into Wilberforce, which continues today as the oldest AME institution of higher learning.

After settling Ohio, the church continued to push west wherever African Americans were to be found and the laws did not forbid the existence of such independent Black-led institutions. We have elsewhere spoken of the exploits of William Paul Quinn in pioneering the work in Indiana and Illinois, which led to the formation of the Indiana Conference in 1840. Appointed to roam the West in 1840, Quinn would push into Missouri (where the first church was organized in 1841), Michigan, and Kentucky. He would note in his legendary report to the General Conference of 1844 that even though Missouri and Kentucky were slave states, a friendly atmosphere existed toward the AME Church and thus a congregation had been established at St. Louis (1841) and Louisville.[34] In 1855, the Missouri Conference was carved out of the Indiana Conference and was assigned as its territory all of the slaveholding states of the West and Southwest. This designation in effect included southern Illinois, western Kentucky, and the states of Missouri, Tennessee, Alabama, Mississippi, and Louisiana.[35] Interestingly, the first move into the Deep South had come as a result of an invitation from the MEC,S asking the AME Indiana Conference to take over its African American work in New Orleans. The conference responded by ordaining Charles Doughty as a deacon and sending him as the pastor in charge of its "Louisiana Mission," later known as St. James AME Church.[36]

While the push west dominated the attention of the church, more quietly, work was being established across New England. By 1840, the year the New York Conference appointed a missionary to roam across the region, over a thousand members could be found. A New England Conference was organized in 1852.

In 1852, the AME Church also made an important adjustment to its organization. It designated three Episcopal districts and assigned one of its bishops to each: First District, embracing the Philadelphia and New England Conferences and their territory, to which Bishop D. A. Payne was assigned; Second District, embracing the Baltimore and New York Conferences with their territory, under Bishop Willis Nazrey; and Third District, embracing the Indiana and Canada Conferences with their territory, under Bishop Quinn. When Indiana was divided and the Missouri Conference set off, it was added to the third Episcopal district.

The Canadian Heaven

Canada had both an actual and symbolic place among African Americans, and a number of Black Methodists had made their way to Canada during and after the American Revolution. Barbara Heck moved to Montreal in 1778, where her long-time servant Betty joined her in founding an initial Methodist class. In 1785 she would move on to Augusta (near Brockville), Ontario, where they founded the first class in Upper Canada. Betty was among around 2,000 Blacks who left for Canada as a result of the Revolution.

Then, at the close of the war, some 3,500 former slaves who had supported the British were transported to Nova Scotia and New Brunswick. In 1783, William Black, an independent Wesleyan preacher, began traveling through Nova Scotia on his own and encountered the recently arrived settlers, including many former members of the John Street Church in New York. Overwhelmed by the numbers, he appealed directly to John Wesley and was directed to the American preachers. With the help of the likes of Freeborn Garrettson and James Oliver Cromwell, the work expanded rapidly throughout the Maritime Provinces.[37]

In 1793, Upper Canada introduced a law for the gradual elimination of slavery in the province. By this time slavery was already on the wane and by the beginning of the new century had all but disappeared among the Loyalist settlers. Through the first two decades of the nineteenth century, Methodism spread throughout Upper Canada and in those places where there were enough Black members, Black classes and even congregations emerged.

Toward the end of the 1820s, African Canadian Methodists began to seek a relationship with the expanding African Methodist churches in the States. In May 1827, the Philadelphia Conference of the AME Church forwarded a petition from Canada asking that a preacher be sent from the New York Conference. Within a year there were congregations formed at Malden, Gambia, Niagara, and Fort Erie. In the mid-1830s, Richard Williams was sent out to further expand the Canadian work, and he established societies at Niagara, St. Davids, and St. Catherines, all in the same region west of Buffalo. By 1840, the work had grown enough to justify its organization as a separate Upper Canada Conference.[38]

The AME Zion Church dates its Canadian work to May 1829 and the arrival of Hamilton Johnson, a Black preacher from Prescott, Ontario, who came to New York. The work grew slowly and the New England Conference eventually assumed responsibility for it. By 1860 five Zionist preachers worked in Canada.

On August 28, 1833, the British Parliament abolished slavery throughout the British colonies. By this time Canada had already become a symbolic entity as the place where escaping slaves could finally relax and know that they had reached a safe haven from those who would hunt them and take them back to their former bondage (though a few incidents of slave hunters operating in Canada have been documented). Religiously minded slaves could easily collapse their yearnings into an eschatological vision in which Canada symbolized the heaven where aspirations for freedom (salvation) in this life could be realized. Canada was the land beyond the river (usually the Ohio River) that marked the boundary of the slave states. It was no surprise that in his scheme to liberate African Americans, Philadelphian Hezekiel Grice had immediately thought of Canada, where he himself eventually moved.

The average slave knew little or nothing about the route or the path markers along the way to heaven; they knew that it lay in the north and that their pilgrimage could be kept in the right direction by the *North Star* (the name of Frederick Douglass' periodical). One of the few bits of wisdom passed around the slave community was the relation of the easily spotted Big Dipper to the North Star. When they escaped they knew to follow the Drinking Gourd (one name of the Big Dipper), which no matter how far they might have wandered off course, always pointed them toward their goal. As Josiah Henson, talking of his escape, noted, "I knew the North Star—blessed be God for setting it in the heavens! Like the Star of Bethlehem, it announced where my salvation lay."[39]

The African Methodist literature contains numerous stories of slaves who found their way to Canada. Thomas H. Jones was such a person.[40] A slave for over forty years in North Carolina, as a young man, he had had a conversion experience, become a Methodist, and subsequently won over his hostile master as to the benefits of his church involvement. He married and fathered several children, but lost contact with them after his family was carried off to Alabama. He later remarried, and saved the money to purchase his new wife's freedom. Responding to a rumor that his wife might be re-enslaved, he took the money set aside to purchase his own freedom and sent her to New York. Then, at the first opportunity, he made his escape north.

Once he contacted his wife, he found a new career among the Methodists as he began to speak in the church, initially as a means of raising funds to put more distance between him and those who sought to return him to North Carolina. In Boston, he would, for example, speak successively at the May Street Church, the Zion Church, and the AME Church. He subsequently found his greatest aid from the Wesleyan Methodist minister in Boston and began to move in Wesleyan circles, eventually becoming a Wesleyan preacher and pastor of their church in Salem, Massachusetts.

The passing of the Fugitive Slave Act in 1850 significantly destabilized the fugitive community in the Northern states and convinced many that they needed to move further north. Jones relocated to Canada and spent the next decades lecturing in Canada, New England, and at one point, England.

In 1830, Josiah Henson had made his way to Canada. Earlier he had gained some knowledge of the lay of the land and some sense of how to avoid Northerners sympathetic to the South. It took him two weeks to reach Cincinnati. Heading north to the shore of Lake Erie took him through new territory, his greatest luck being his stumbling upon a friendly boat captain who carried him and his family to Buffalo, and even gave him the money to take the ferry to Ontario.

He soon found work and prospered. After rumors spread that he was a preacher, he consented to hold services for the other Africans in the neighborhood. His son Tom was able to go to school and learned to read. Tom then cajoled his father into learning to read.

He also began to organize his neighbors in a program of economic self-improvement, and he established a collective settlement near Colchester, south of Windsor. His preaching and lecturing on the obligation of the African Canadians to those still enslaved led to his meeting a man whose family was still in Kentucky. The attempt to free the man's family began Henson's career as a "conductor" on what was to become known as the Underground Railroad. His first trip involved working with a group of some thirty people in

Kentucky whom he brought out to Cincinnati, and then north through Richmond, Indiana, to Toledo and then across Lake Erie to Colchester. On his second trip, he brought out the man's family from Maysville.

Organizing to Subvert the System (The Underground Railroad)

The beginning of the Abolitionist Movement was one marker of change for the black community and the passing of the Fugitive Slave Law in 1850 another. Each upped the ante in the political game that African American leaders at every level were playing and each altered the actions of many, some in quite radical ways. The call for action by David Walker and the subsequent response from Garrison changed the status of the debate and certainly called for new responses, the Black Conventions being just one of them. Possibly as important as any was the gradual creation of an organized system of civil disobedience structured to attack and subvert the whole system of slavery and destroy the tentacles it wrapped around the free Black community to keep it docile and ineffective.

Josiah Henson's story is a key to understanding how the Underground Railroad developed.[41] He escaped slavery with the barest of information and assurance of support. Having never made such a journey before, he led his family on a trip through hostile territory to Cincinnati, where he luckily discovered his former acquaintances to be true friends. However, they did not accompany him north; rather they gave him a set of vague instructions. His arrival in Canada included not just his willingness to make the trip but the fortunate helpers he found along the way. One wonders about others who after escaping approached the wrong people for assistance and wound up back in the South and sold down the river to oblivion.

On his first trips into the South, Henson had the knowledge of routes northward, but always remained dependent on his instinct for finding the right people who would help him at crucial moments—a Quaker, a boatman with an integrated crew, and so on. As the number of people attempting an escape to Canada increased, the information on places to hide and the names of people willing to risk their property and even their freedom to help fugitive slaves became exceedingly valuable knowledge, as was the ability of those who emerged as regular leaders of the fugitives not to give away knowledge of who their allies were.

In encountering stories of the events surrounding the Underground Railroad, frequently romanticized in modern retellings, it is important not to forget that the apparatus for assisting slaves making the journey from the southern states to Canada operated completely outside of the law. For various

reasons, the northern states were moving, however slowly, toward the abolition of slavery, but the majority of Whites still thought in terms of the infe-
riority of Black people and maintained a set of restrictive laws indicative of
an unwillingness to integrate Blacks into mainstream society. They also
demonstrated a hostile attitude toward any who worked for Black liberation.
All who participated in the Underground Railroad faced the severest of consequences if caught in the act.

At the same time, the stakes were high. Anxieties about loved ones made
for hard choices about steps to be taken to save them from slavery itself and
from the added evils of loss of family ties when threatened with the oblivion
of movement to a distant location. The anxiety that could at any moment
seize even the seemingly most secure free Black resident is no better illustrated than in what became known as the Pearl Incident, instigated by some
members of Asbury Methodist Episcopal Church in Washington, D.C.

In 1848, market changes had created a perceived overabundance of slaves
in the Washington–Baltimore region. Whites openly talked about the need
to sell a number of slaves to the Deep South. Filled with fear, Paul Edmonson, a free Black man whose wife Emily and children were still slaves, conspired with Daniel Bell, also a free man married to a slave wife, and Paul Jennings. They constructed an escape plan to move their families and other
slave acquaintances away from any would-be mass sale of slaves. With money
raised in part from other members of the Asbury church, the men hired a
ship, the *Pearl*, to pick up a group of seventy-seven African Americans and
take them further north. Unfortunately, soon after the *Pearl* sailed, it was discovered, and as it moved into Chesapeake Bay was overtaken. All those on
board, including the six Edmonson children, were sold and sent south. Paul
Edmonson would spend the rest of his life trying to locate his children and
buy their freedom.[42]

It would be people like Edmonson, overcome with the desire to assist family and friends caught in the entanglements of slavery and a need to act on
their behalf even at risk of their own life and liberty, who would fill out the
various positions both great and small in the Underground Railroad. They
would be joined by many Whites who were ready to do their little bit to bring
down the great evil that polluted the country. Christians from a spectrum of
denominations were drawn to the cause. Without forgetting the many Quakers, Presbyterians, Congregationalists, and others (most of whom will never
be known by name) who united to fight the system, as this is a book about
African American Methodists, we shall concentrate on their contributions
to the work. And, of course, we have already been introduced to three of the

most prominent leaders—Harriet Tubman, Frederick Douglass, and Samuel Green—whose lives intertwined through the 1850s.

Araminta Ross seemed destined to live her life out in Dorchester County, Maryland. In the midst of a rough life as a slave, in 1844, she married a free Black man, John Tubman. They probably resided for a while in Caroline County on the property of Anthony Thompson, who had married into the family of Araminta's ultimate owner, Edward Brodess. During the first years of her marriage she had a lawyer investigate her status, who discovered that in all likelihood, her mother should have been free by the time of her birth, and therefore she should be free. But her mother's status had not been acknowledged. The knowledge seems to have thrown her into a spiritual struggle. She began to pray for Brodess in the hope that he would convert and acknowledge that she was really a free woman. Then in 1849, having heard a rumor that he planned to sell her into the Deep South, she altered her prayer somewhat. She asked God to either convert him or kill him. He died a short time later. She felt some guilt over the coincidence, but soon rebounded and turned her attention to what her future would be.

After mulling over her situation for several years she decided to try an escape. She considered all the obstacles—lack of knowledge, resources, and assistance. Soon after departing her home in September of 1849, Tubman made initial contact with a friendly White woman (possibly a local acquaintance), who gave her two names and some directions. The instructions led her to a family, and a wagon that carried her the next step. She then journeyed by foot north following the Choptank River, already a popular route for fugitive slaves. She traveled by night, looking to the North Star when local landmarks proved insufficient.

Though she lived a long life, she never spoke much about the particulars of the trip between her entrance into Kent County, Delaware, and her eventual arrival in Philadelphia. Here she found the relatively large community of free Blacks and White sympathizers who had organized to assist fugitive slaves. Included in this community was the spectrum of Methodist churches—MEC, AME, and AMEZ—and the Vigilance committee that had held one of its organizational meetings at the Zoar Church. However, most importantly, Tubman came into contact with William Sill, the key leader in the Underground Railroad nexus that was Philadelphia. Tubman remained in Philadelphia for the next year.

It would be the coincidence of the passing of the Fugitive Slave Act and receiving word that her niece Kizzy was up for sale that led her to act toward the end of December 1850. She decided to return to Dorchester County and effect a rescue. A plan was put together and communicated to Kizzy's husband, who got her across Chesapeake Bay in a boat and into Tubman's hands in Baltimore. On her second trip Tubman got her brother out. Over the next decade she averaged one trip annually, usually late in the fall. She would try to arrive in Canada by Christmas and stay in St. Catherines during January and February. She would then take a job to raise money to support her next venture, each one of which added to her growing legend on both sides of the Mason-Dixon line. To the abolitionists she was both an enigma (a Black woman acing as a guide for fugitives) and a heroine. To the slaves, especially in Eastern Maryland, she was a savior figure, a female Moses. To the slave owners, she was an effective outlaw who was measurably hurting them, and they posted a large reward for her capture.

But she was never captured. She learned the arts of espionage and often covered her trail disguised as an old woman singing the "harmless" religious ditties of the slave culture. Stories generated from among those she led to freedom frequently told of her seemingly supernatural awareness of danger awaiting them on her pre-selected route, danger averted by her sudden decision to go another way.

Meanwhile as Tubman made the transition from slave to rescuer of slaves, her neighbor from Talbot County, Maryland, Frederick Douglass, was beginning his career in both the African American struggle and the women's movement. He had married and become a father. Following the publication of his autobiography in 1845, he found it convenient to begin a lecture tour in England, not returning until his status as a free man had been permanently secured. Upon his return, he settled in Rochester, New York, and became active in the local AME Zion church.[43]

The church derived from the initial effort of Austin Steward, a businessman and activist, who opened a Sunday school on Favor Street for his fellow African Americans in 1818. That Sunday school became the organization from which the church evolved in 1827. Thomas James (b. 1804), one of the school's early pupils, experienced a call and by the late 1820s was actively preaching. He later purchased a lot, also on Favor Street, upon which the first building of what later became Memorial AME Zion Church was erected. The church would become a focal point of the Rochester African American community, while James would go on to be ordained as an Zionist minister (1833) and have an outstanding career.[44] Among his early pastoral appointments would be New Bedford, Massachusetts, where he met Frederick Douglass.[45]

James was not the only tie to Rochester Douglass forged. In 1845 he met Susan B. Anthony, also a Rochester resident. He would join her in attending the July 19, 1848, meeting at the Wesleyan Chapel of Seneca Falls, New York, remembered as the first Women's Rights Convention in American history. By this time he had already founded his own abolitionist newspaper, the *North Star*, its very title declaring his solidarity with the fugitive slaves.[46] He backed the announcement of his work for the Underground Railroad in the first issue with action, and through the 1850s Rochester was one of the most welcoming stops for fleeing slaves. Douglass became aware of Tubman's work long before they met, but early in her career, he noted her courage and shrewdness, and predicted that "she may yet render even more important service to the Cause."[47]

There is every reason to believe that Tubman knew, or at the very least knew of, Samuel Green in the years prior to her escape. He had a rather high profile among the African American Methodists of Dorchester County.[48] Born around 1801, he lived for thirty years a slave, but was freed in 1831. Before the clampdown on education, he had learned to read and write and was a capable blacksmith. He was also a leader in the church, having become a local preacher. Shortly after he was freed, he put together the money to purchase his wife and free her, but his children remained slaves. The sale of his daughter into slavery in Missouri and the loss of contact with her may have influenced his reestablishing contact with Tubman, who led his son to Canada in 1854.

Late in 1856, Green visited his son in Canada, an action that was to have some unplanned consequences. While he was away, in November 1856, Tubman made her annual foray onto the area and escorted five people back to Canada. Then in March 1857, a man from Bucktown, where Harriet had previously lived, got word that he was headed for the auction block. Taking the situation in his own hands, he organized a group of his comrades and left the county. A reward was placed on their heads immediately, and near Dover, Delaware, they were betrayed by a White man. They were taken to the jail in Dover, but escaped while waiting to be transported back home. This time they made it to Philadelphia and safety.

Green returned home from Canada seemingly oblivious to the rage affecting Dorchester County over the Dover Eight, as the escapees had been dubbed. Green, already suspect for his son's escape, proved a ready target with his reappearance in the county at the wrong moment. He was soon arrested and his home searched. Nothing was found to tie him to the Dover Eight, but the authorities did find a copy of *Uncle Tom's Cabin*, the runaway bestselling novel attacking the institution of slavery. In the eyes of many, the book fell under the provisions of a 1841 Maryland law that forbade African Americans from knowingly possessing any abolitionist literature—literature

that might tend to stir up discontent or rebellion among the slave population. Violation of the law carried a penalty of ten to twenty years in the state
penitentiary.

In addition to the hated novel, Green had a map of Canada, schedules de-
tailing transportation services north, and a letter from his son. The letter detailed in somewhat coded language his escape to Canada and concluded with
a request that he tell certain other slaves to come on. This letter may have
ultimately been the item that sealed Green's fate. The persons named in the
letter had in fact earlier fled the county.

Tried two weeks after his arrest, Green was convicted and sentenced to
ten years in prison. That Green had lived an exemplary life caused a few of
his White supporters to write the governor on his behalf. But others claimed
that the number of slaves taking leave of the county created a problem for
land owners. But even before the letter arrived on the governor's desk, another group of slaves left Cambridge for the North, and rumors pictured
Green masterminding their escape from his prison cell. The slaves, it seemed,
would have to pass by Green's home on the way out of the county.

Among those who had actually assisted the Dover Eight was Ben Ross,
Tubman's father. Thus, Tubman prepared to make an off-season trip back
home, while all the attention remained on Green, the Cambridge jail, and the
governor. To everyone's surprise, she pulled off the snatch successfully, carrying her now aging mother and father by wagon to Wilmington and then on
to Philadelphia by train. Several weeks later they arrived in St. Catherines,
and her family was finally reunited. Green's story did not have such a positive
ending. He was sentenced to prison, where he would languish until 1862.[49]

During her activist years, Tubman encountered a number of Methodists
who worked the Underground Railroad, and while space does not allow most
to be mentioned, we would be remiss if we failed to mention Jemain Wesley
Loguen (1813–72).[50] Born in slavery in Tennessee, Loguen escaped from a
brutal early life and in his twenty-first year made his way to Hamilton, Ontario. Here he learned to read, educated himself, and was even able to gain
two years of formal education as a young adult at the Oneida Institute. In
1841 he settled in Syracuse and started an independent church. Shortly
thereafter he encountered the AMEZs and following his ordination was assigned duties at their church in Bath, New York. It was on a tour to raise
money for his church that he encountered the abolitionist movement. From
that time he became more and more involved in the effort to eradicate slavery. In 1846, he moved back to Syracuse, henceforth his headquarters. He
eventually turned his home into a major depot for fugitive slaves and, along
with Luther Lee (1800–89) and the city's Wesleyan Methodists, helped

transform it into an open city. By local law, Syracuse protected fugitive slaves and allowed them to live openly in its city limits without fear of arrest.

Loguen is best remembered for his role in the so-called "Jerry Rescue" case that began in 1851 with his snatching a fugitive from the marshal who had taken him into custody. Loguen saw to his escape into Canada, for which he was arrested and put on trial in Albany. Previously, Loguen had announced the formation of a committee specifically designed to thwart the intent of the 1850 Fugitive Slave Act. Now his defiance would be put to the test. The trial resulted in a hung jury. When the case was retried, the same result ensued. The drawn out proceeding and the inability of the prosecutors to get a verdict against Loguen and fellow defendants provided a significant obstacle to the enforcement of the Fugitive Slave Act in northern New York.

Then in 1857, the entire African American community reeled from the *Dred Scott* decision, which not only reinforced the Fugitive Slave Act but in effect transformed African Americans into non-citizens and further declared unconstitutional all congressional laws prohibiting slavery in the western territories. Once again the ante had been raised for those trapped in slavery. For the abolitionists, the decision again raised the issue of the necessary use of violence to further their cause. A White man, John Brown, would lay the issue at Tubman's and Douglass' front door.

Tubman had every reason to stay away from Brown. She had accomplished the reunion of her family and in 1858 had been given a home in Auburn, New York, another town with an active abolitionist cadre centered on the local Presbyterian seminary. However, Tubman had met Brown in April 1858, and he shared with her the plot to take over the arsenal at Harpers Ferry, Virginia (now West Virginia), and arm the slaves with the weapons stored there. Brown's plan resonated with Tubman's activist soul. It would not take much to move her from the clandestine escapes (which to date had involved no violent encounters or the deaths of anyone), to taking up arms against an institution that seemed to be growing stronger day by day. She initially showed her support by assisting Brown in the recruitment of additional conspirators.

Douglass first met John Brown in 1847 and was impressed with his passion. He still had hope that some positive action could bring down slavery. Brown shared with Douglass his entire plan for creating an independent slave-free state, for which he drafted a new constitution, written during the three weeks he stayed with Douglass in Rochester. While Douglass had spoken and written in fiery language full of violent metaphors, he had never acted violently. And now, faced with Brown's plan, Douglass hesitated and then backed off. Like most with whom Brown shared his plan, Douglass concluded that in the end it was doomed to failure.

Tubman met up with Brown at the end of 1858 in Boston. She would remain there to raise money for him, and then later join him when he was ready to act. Meanwhile she addressed the July 4 (1859) gathering in Framingham and an August 1 meeting of the New England Colored Citizens' Convention in Boston.

In August Brown had his last meeting with Douglass in Chambersburg, Pennsylvania, and again failed to recruit his further help. After Brown revealed the target—Harpers Ferry—Douglass was even more opposed to the scheme. Brown would be walking into a trap and would be crushed.

As Brown planned to move, he called for Tubman to come and join him. However, she had disappeared. He did not know that she had taken ill and was in New Bedford in bed.

Brown moved on October 16, and as many of his supporters had predicted, his attack proved a disaster. In the end Brown was arrested and, after a quick trial, on November 2 was sentenced to death. He was hung a month later, and quickly turned into a martyr for the cause. Tubman returned to her home in Auburn. Her career was far from over, but in the new year a new era was about to open for the African American community and a new phase in the life of Tubman, Douglass, and the Underground Railroad activists.

Notes

1. William Henry Perrin, *History of Fayette County, Kentucky* (Easley, SC: Southern Historical Press, [1979])

2. Much of the Lexington story is drawn from the account in David Morris Jordan, Sr., *The Lexington Conference and Negro Migration* (N.p.: 1957), an informally published mimeographed report.

3. "A History of Wesley United Methodist Church," posted at www.gbgm-umc .org/wesley-lexky/history.htm.

4. Records from Indiana indicate that a preacher from this church, George W. Clark, spoke at the North Indiana Conference in 1853 and in addition asked for financial assistance to purchase his freedom. A collection was taken up and $53.70 turned over to him. H. N. Herrick and William Warren Sweet, *A History of the North Indiana Conference of the Methodist Episcopal Church* (Indianapolis: W. K. Stewart Company, 1917), 42.

5. Daniel Alexander Payne, *A History of the African Methodist Episcopal Church*, ed. by Charles Spencer Smith. (Nashville, TN: Publishing House of the A. M. E. Sunday School Union, 1891), 171, 327.

6. Henson first issued his autobiography in 1849, and it was subsequently updated, retitled, and reissued on several occasions through his life, one edition making reference to the belief that he was the model for Harriet Beecher Stowe's fictional character, Uncle Tom. *The Life of Josiah Henson, formerly a Slave, now an Inhabitant of*

Canada, as Narrated by Himself (Boston: Arthur D. Phelphs, 1849); *Truth Stranger Than Fiction. Father Henson's Story of His Own Life* (Boston: John J. Jewett and Company, 1858); and"*Uncle Tom's Story of His Life*": *An Autobiography of the Rev. Josiah Henson (Mrs. Harriet Beecher Stowe's "Uncle Tom"). From 1789 to 1876* (London: Christian Age, 1877), posted at http://docsouth.unc.edu/neh/henson/henson.html.

7. Payne, *History of the African Methodist Episcopal Church*, 144, 178.

8. Henry Bibb, *Narrative of the Life and Adventures of Henry Bibb, An American Slave, Written by Himself* (New York: The Author, 1849), 87.

9. M. M. Henkle, *The Life of Henry Bidleman Bascom* (Louisville, KY: Morton & Griswold, 1854), 58.

10. On the church in Cincinnati, see James A. Handy, *Scraps of African Methodist Episcopal History* (Philadelphia: A. M. E. Book Concern, 1902), 83; Arnett, *The Centennial Budget*, 296–301; and Payne, *History of the African Methodist Episcopal Church*, 61–62.

11. Jarena Lee, *Religious Experience and Journal of Mrs. Jarena Lee, Giving an Account of her Call to Preach the Gospel*. Revised and corrected from the Original Manuscript, Written by Herself. (Philadelphia: The Author, 1849), 56–57.

12. The account of Stewart is taken from *The Missionary Pioneer, or A Brief Memoir of the Life, Labors, and Death of John Stewart (Man of Colour,) Founder, Under God of the Mission among the Wyandotts at Upper Sandusky, Ohio* (New York: The Author, 1827); J. H. Fitzwater, "John Stewart," in I. L. Thomas, ed., *Methodism and the Negro* (New York: Eaton & Mains/Cincinnati: Jennings & Graham, 1910), 28–33; and the account of Stewart in Wade Crawford Barclay, *History of Methodist Missions*. Vol. I (New York: Board of Missions and Church Extension of the Methodist Church, 1950), 203–5.

13. Alfred Brunson, *A Western Pioneer: or, Incidents in the Life and Times* (Cincinnati, OH: Jennings and Pye, 1880), II, 62–64.

14. I am totally reliant for the story of Africa, Illinois, on information supplied to me by local historian Jon Musgrave, to whom I express my deepest gratitude. His documents included a letter written May 18, 1944, by John L. Patton to J. T. Bean. Patton was then an elderly and long-time former resident of Skeleton Town. He also posted the article by Chloe McNeill, "Africa, Illinois," on his website, www.illinois history.com/africa.html. Accessed August 2, 2006.

15. Information on African Americans in the MPC is derived from various issues of the *Journal* of the Maryland Conference and the journals of the several colored mission conferences. For the overview of MPC conference structures see Albea Godbold, John H. Ness, Jr., Ed. Schell, *Table of United Methodist Church Annual Conferences, 1796–1997* ([Madison, NJ]: General Commission on Archives and History, the United Methodist Church, 1998).

16. This association and the Black churches associated with the White-led Methodist Protestant Church should not be confused with the Colored Methodist Protestant Church founded in Philadelphia and Baltimore by former members of the AMEC in 1848–49 and discussed in the next chapter.

17. Snowden had previously been preaching in Cape Elizabeth, Maine, near Portland. See Steven Allen and W. H. Pilsbury, *History of Methodism in Maine, 1793–1886*. Vol. 1 (Augusta, ME: Press of Charles E. Nash, 1887), 289.

18. Pat Thompson, "A Brief Overview of African American History in the New England Conference," posted at www.neumc.org/Conf-2002/Conf-02-Af-Am-History.htm. Accessed May 16, 2003.

19. Cf. "Tax Assessment Records for "Colored" Citizens, 1850," posted at www.primaryresearch.org/bh/db/bcabrowse.php.

20. Quoted in "David Walker (c. 1785–1830)," posted at "Boston African American National Historic Site," www.nps.gov/boaf/davidwalker.htm. Accessed June 15, 2004.

21. David Walker, *Walker's Appeal in Four Articles; Together with a Preamble, To the Coloured Citizens of the World, but in Particular, and Very Expressly, to Those of the United States of America*. Third and Last Edition, with Additional Notes, Corrections, &c. (Boston: Revised and Published by David Walker, 1830).

22. On Walker, see Peter Hinks, *To Awaken My Afflicted Brethren: David Walker and the Problem of Antebellum Slave Resistance* (University Park: The Pennsylvania State University Press, 1997).

23. Maria W. Stewart, *Religion and the Pure Principles of Morality, etc.* (Boston: Friends of Freedom and Virtue, 1835) and *Productions of Mrs. Maria W. Stewart Presented to the First Baptist Church and Society* (Boston: Friends of Freedom and Virtue, 1835). A variety of Stewart's works have been posted at http://afroamhistory.about .com/library/blmaria_stewart_index.htm. Accessed August 2, 2006.

24. William J. Walls, *The African Methodist Episcopal Zion Church: Reality of the Black Church* (Charlotte, NC: A.M.E. Zion Publishing House, 1974), 128–29. The original Boston congregation is now known as the Columbus Avenue AME Zion Church.

25. The sources on the founding of the Boston church are contradictory, but the article by John T. Jenifer, "Has African Methodism been a Success in New England?" included by Benjamin W. Arnett in the *Centennial Budget*, 210–19, seem to be most authoritative.

26. The progress of the Boston church is covered in snippets as part of the coverage of the New York Conference's annual meetings in Payne.

27. William S. McFeely, *Frederick Douglass* (New York: W. W. Norton, 1991), 81–82.

28. Lewis V. Baldwin, *Invisible Strands in African Methodism: A History of the African Union Methodist Protestant and Union American Methodist Episcopal Churches, 1805–1980* (Methuen, NJ: Scarecrow Press, 1983), 55–61.

29. Payne, *History of the African Methodist Episcopal Church*, 230–32.

30. Joseph H. Morgan, *Morgan's History of the New Jersey Conference of the A. M. E. Church, from 1872 to 1887* (Camden, NJ: S. Chew, 1887), 91–93.

31. William Steward, *Gouldtown: A Very Remarkable Settlement of Ancient Date* (Philadelphia: J. P. Lippencott, 1913).

32. Morgan, *Morgan's History*, 58, 73.

33. Payne, *History of the African Methodist Episcopal Church*, 44.

34. Payne, *History of the African Methodist Episcopal Church*, 171

35. In 1851, the First Colored Methodist Church in Sacramento, California, petitioned the Indiana Conference to be received as an AME congregation. That petition was accepted.

36. Payne, *History of the African Methodist Episcopal Church*, 222.

37. Many of the Black Methodists in Nova Scotia would soon move to Freetown, Nova Scotia, on ships supplied by William Wilberforce and British abolitionists. They would thus become the founders of African Methodism. On their story see Charles Marke, *Origin of Wesleyan Methodism in Sierra Leone and History of Its Missions* (London: Charles H. Kelly, 1913).

38. For a variety of reasons, the AMEs found it expedient to separate their Canadian Conference and grant it autonomous status. It reorganized in 1856 as the British Methodist Episcopal Church of Canada and continues cordial relations with its parent organization.

39. Henson, *Truth Stranger than Fiction*, 102–3.

40. *The Experiences of Thomas H. Jones, Who Was a Slave for Forty-Three Years*. Written by a Friend, as Related to Him by Brother Jones (Boston: Bazin & Chandler, 1861).

41. Henson, *Life of Josiah Henson*. Like Frederick Douglass, Henson revised and expanded his story twice during his life.

42. The Edmonson family story is told in John H. Paynter, *Fugitives of the Pearl* (Washington DC: Associated Publishers 1930) and summarized in Mary Kay Ricks, "A Passage to Freedom," *Washington Post Magazine* (February 17, 2002), 21–36, posted at www.washingtonpost.com/wp-srv/national/horizon/aug98/pearl.htm. See also John H. Paynter, "The Fugitives of the Pearl," *Journal of Negro History* 1 (July 1916), 243–64; and Daniel Drayton, *Personal Memoir of Daniel Drayton, for Four Years and Four Months a Prisoner in Washington Jail. Including a Narrative of the Voyage and Capture of the Schooner "Pearl"* (Boston: B. Marsh; New York: American and Foreign Anti-slavery Society, 1855).

43. On Douglass' Rochester years see McFeely, *Frederick Douglass*, 151ff.

44. On Rochester and Thomas James, see Norman Coombs, "History of African Americans in Rochester, NY," posted at www.rit.edu/~nrcgsh/arts/rochester.htm; and Walls, *African Methodist Episcopal Zion Church*, 148.

45. McFeely, *Frederick Douglass*, 81–82.

46. Douglass' paper changed names in 1851, becoming *Frederick Douglass' Paper*, which he continued to publish until 1860.

47. Walls, *African Methodist Episcopal Zion Church*, 151.

48. On Green and his career see John Dixon Long, *Pictures of Slavery in Church and State; including Personal Reminiscences, biographical; Sketches, Anecdotes, Etc., Etc., with and Appendix containing the Views of John Wesley and Richard Watson on Slavery* (Philadelphia: The Author, 1857), 398–400; Brian Beaubein, "Samuel Green,"

paper posted at www.mc.cc.md.us/Departments/hpolscrv/beaubien.htm. Accessed August 2, 2006.

49. Green was released on the condition that he leave the country and not return to Dorchester County. He moved to Canada to be with his family.

50. *The Rev. J. W. Loguen, as a Slave and as a Freeman, a Narrative of Real Life* (Syracuse, NY: J. G. K. Truair & Co., 1859); Fergus M. Bordewich, *Bound for Canaan: The Epic Story of the Underground Railroad, America's First Civil Rights Movement* (New York: Amistad/HarperCollins, 2005), 126–46, 334–43, 406–13.

CHAPTER NINE

Emancipation and Its Transitions

The Development of African American Conferences (MEC)

In a struggle paralleling that of the entire Black community, the African American congregations within the Methodist Episcopal Church worked for equality within the White-controlled denomination. As described in earlier chapters these congregations had arisen in most of the urban centers, with those in the older Methodist strongholds assuming a leading role among Black Methodists as a whole. By the 1840s, most of the effort was focused around the one issue of the obtaining of equal status alongside their White colleagues for Black ministers, which meant admission to ministerial orders and membership in an annual conference.

As discussed in chapter 3, a set of all-Black congregations had appeared in the major urban centers. Additionally, a number of congregations now dotted the countryside, some serving the large concentrations of Black members in what was primarily slave territory, such as the Eastern Shore of Maryland, and others serving independent-minded free Blacks, as were found across New Jersey.[1] The first independent Black church on the Eastern Shore was Bryan Chapel, founded in 1800 outside Queenstown (now Grasonville), Maryland. It would be followed by Waugh Church, founded by freedmen in Cambridge (1826), Asbury Church in Easton (1836), John Wesley Church in Salisbury (1837), and Joshua Chapel in Chestertown (1839). The number of such churches on the Eastern Shore and adjacent Delaware, territory then in the Philadelphia Conference, would more than double through the 1840s and 1850s.

Meanwhile, similar congregations would emerge in southern New Jersey where a concentration of free Blacks could be found, the first in Salem, where Methodism had developed as early as 1774. By 1789, the Salem Circuit, that covered a large part of southwest New Jersey had more than 700 members, though only 24 African Americans. Eleven years later, when Mount Hope, the African church, was founded, there were still just 61 members; however, now growth would be quick, to 159 (1809) and 238 members (1813). A group led by Reuben Cuff would leave in 1816 to form the first AME Church (Mount Pisgah), but the Mount Hope congregation survived the loss.[2] The MEC would encourage the formation of additional Black congregations in New Jersey in the 1850s in anticipation of the formation of the Delaware Conference, the first African American annual conference.

As was noted in chapter 4, a modest number of Black preachers had been ordained as deacons and elders and subsequently appointed (hired) as the minister (supply pastor) of one of the several African American churches, especially in the Baltimore, New Jersey, and Philadelphia Conferences. Through the 1840s, a network of these supply pastors (and others who aspired to their status) emerged across these conferences. Those serving as supply pastors would, in a manner similar to the traveling preachers, be assigned for several years to a particular church and then moved about much as the White preachers were but gained no real status nor conference membership to which they could relate. These ministers had moved from being amateur and semi-professional preachers to salaried pastors who worked full-time at their calling. Bishops and presiding elders kept records of the ordained and otherwise available local preachers in their conference and annually appointed them to one of the several Black churches as needs arose.

This informal structure of the Black pastorate led in 1844 to a meeting of the Black preachers in Eastern Maryland and Delaware, who then petitioned the members (ministers) of the Philadelphia Conference to petition the General Conference to authorize the bishops to hold an annual gathering of traveling colored preachers. The conference did not act on the petition, but two years later, Zoar Church and John Wesley Chapel jointly petitioned the Philadelphia Conference to allow the preachers serving the two churches permission to travel throughout the conference to raise money for their ministry.

Eventually, in reaction to the failure of petitions to the annual conference, Black Methodists from the Sharp Street and Asbury Churches in Baltimore, beginning in 1848, began to lobby for the organization of an all-Black conference to include the congregations in the bounds of the Baltimore Conference. Addressing the General Conference, they noted that the Black preachers had done much good, but were limited by, among other factors, their receiving no remuneration for their efforts. If employed in the Baltimore Conference, it would prepare some for further service, for example, in Africa. An all-Black annual conference within the Baltimore Conference could be held under the oversight of White bishops. The 1848 petition was signed on behalf of sixty of the Baltimore members by John Fortie, Thomas Watkins, Benjamin Brown, David F. Jones, and Richard J. Chew.[3]

In 1852, the General Conference acted favorably on a petition to form an annual "meeting" of the Black preachers of the Philadelphia and New Jersey Annual Conferences. The General Conference's action also mandated the attendance of the presiding elders whose districts contained such churches, along with one or more bishops. The first such gathering took place in Philadelphia at the Zoar MEC on August 23, 1852, as the Convention of Colored Local Preachers and Laymen, a kind of proto-annual conference.

Those ministers in attendance included Isaac Henson (New Jersey), Ely Nugent (Washington), Jacob Nelson (Port Deposit, Maryland), David Tilghman (Zoar Church, Philadelphia), Peter Wise (Philadelphia), Noah Fisher (Philadelphia), Richard Crawford (Philadelphia), and James Davis (Philadelphia). Listed as not present were King Still and Philip Hacket. Arriving late were Henry Thomas, Harrison Smith, Isaac Cannon, and Henry Dobson. Ely Nugent was elected the convention's president and presided at its opening sessions. Most of the first convention was taken up with organizational matters, with the idea that another convention would be held the following year and that money would need to be raised to support it. To this end Richard Crawford was selected as a missionary to travel among the Black congregations. While the conference adjourned on August 27 in a atmosphere of hope, there was no immediate follow-up.[4]

In 1856, John A. Collins, a delegate to the General Conference from Baltimore, presented a petition from the Sharp Street and Asbury Churches asking permission to form a separate quarterly conference for Baltimore's African American churches (apart from the White churches in the city). The conference responded favorably, and also suggested that the Baltimore Conference could, as was already occurring in the Philadelphia Conference, employ "colored" preachers to travel and preach where their services seemed necessary.[5]

At that same conference, another petition was presented, which led it to authorize the calling of an annual conference of the Black preachers for the purpose of "conferring with them with respects to the wants of the work among our colored people."[6] Again, Zoar was chosen to host a "Conference of Colored Local Preachers" from Eastern Pennsylvania, New Jersey,

Delaware, and the Eastern Shore of Maryland. This conference was formally called by Bishop Levi Scott, who attended and presided.

In this conference, one can more clearly see the development of what would become an annual conference structure. A list of churches ready to receive Methodist ministers was assembled and those in attendance asked if they were willing to devote themselves to the work and receive appointments to the churches and circuits. A rudimentary plan for the further education of the ministers was also adopted.

On the final day of the conference, Bishop Scott announced a set of appointments for the following year.

North Philadelphia District
  Zoar, John Wesley, and Centreville, Isaac Henson
Wilmington (DE) District
  East Zion and New Castle, Philip Scott
Odessa Circuit (Zoar, St. Paul's, and Zion) Samuel Dale
  Easton (DE) District
    Smyrna Circuit (Lee's Chapel, Friendship, Keys Cross Roads, and Smyrna), James Davis
    Dover Circuit (Dover, Thomas' Chapel, Jones' Neck, Gum Swamp, and Muddy Branch), Rodger O. Adams
    Milford Circuit (Milford, Slaughter Neck, Barratt's Chapel, Purnell's, Williamsville, Laws, and Wesley Chapel), To be supplied
Snow Hill (MD/DE) District
  Georgetown Circuit, S. Medcap, R. Crawford
Burlington (NJ) District
  Zion Circuit, W. P. Gibson
Bridgeton (NJ) District
  Springtown District, H. Smith
  Bay Shore Circuit, To be supplied

A relatively small number of African American churches were brought into this new arrangement, and only a limited number of the many Black preachers participated in it. These were exceptional churches ready to exist on their own, disconnected from nearby White congregations, and wealthy enough to give a pastor a salary, if paltry by comparison to his White colleagues, for his full-time services. The ministers who stepped forward were willing to work full-time and to go through some education and examination to attain one of these appointments to a parish or circuit.

At this time, the greater number of Black members remained in congregations that included both Black and White members, or in Black churches integrated on circuits with predominantly White churches. These Black members were served by White elders and local (unsalaried) Black preachers and exhorters. These churches were located primarily in areas where there was a concentration of Black members and where the great majority of the Black community had attained freedom. Thus there were, for example, no churches from the Chesapeake District of the Philadelphia Conference, which included a large concentration of Black members, but where the majority of members were still enslaved.

The "Conference of the Colored Local Preachers" met annually each August for the next six years. It acted like an annual conference—examining the ministers on their work, passing on new ministerial members, adding new appointments, and developing a budget to defray the cost of the meeting. Bishop Scott continued to chair the annual sessions.

The fourth conference, in August 1860, is notable in that for the first time in answering the roll call, the members were listed as belonging to one of three groups—elders, deacons, and (unordained) preachers. The seven elders included men who had many years' experience as preachers and had been ordained as local elders by the Philadelphia Conference: Isaac Henson, Philip Scott, James Davis, David Tilghman, Samuel Dale, John G. Manluff, and Harrison Smith. Henson, Davis, and Tilghman had been present at the original convention eight years earlier. Those who had been previously ordained as deacons were Alexander Lee, Isaiah Broughton, Nathan Young, Jehu Pierce, Wilmore S. Elsey, Joshua Brinkley, Peter Wise, and Richard Moore. Local preachers included Simon Taylor, Silas W. Murray, Jacob Ivans, Wilson Gross, Samuel Laws, Robert Price, Henry P. Gray, Sherry E. Adams, Daniel Oney, and William Polk.

The last of the seven conferences, and the first since the Emancipation Proclamation, met at Ezion Church in Wilmington, Delaware, in 1863. It reported care over twelve charges (only two more than was reported for the first convention) and 1,989 members, thus representing only a small minority of African American members of the Philadelphia Conference, which reported an additional 6,423 Black members, mostly in Eastern Maryland. There were seventeen "Colored" charges in the Snow Hill District alone with 2,941 members. However, the importance of these seven conventions should not be underestimated. They joined with the history of what had occurred in Liberia in preparing the whole of the MEC for the new social reality being created by the Civil War. The eighth Colored Conference would gather as the organizational conference for the new Delaware Conference, the first of the new conference structures created to welcome the freedmen to a new level of participation in the MEC.[7]

The Black churches in the Baltimore Conference continued to push for a structure like that serving the Philadelphia and New Jersey Conferences. By 1864 there were sixteen separate Black churches in the bounds of the Baltimore Conference—five in Baltimore; three in Washington, D.C.; one each in Annapolis, Frederick, Hagerstown, Sandy Spring,[8] Patapsco, Calvert, and Prince Georges, Maryland; and one in Alexandria, Virginia. Early in 1864, Benjamin Brown, then pastor of the Sharp Street Church in Baltimore, called a meeting of the pastors of the sixteen churches, who then conferred with the Baltimore Conference leadership on petitioning for the creation of a new annual conference to cover Maryland (apart from the Eastern Shore), Washington, D.C., and Northern Virginia. The General Conference accepted the petition and passed the enabling legislation for the formation of the Washington Conference.

The action of the 1864 General Conference was preceded by and based upon a series of changes during the Lincoln administration. First, in 1862, slavery was abolished in the District of Columbia. Then, on January 1, 1863, Abraham Lincoln publicly proclaimed the Emancipation Proclamation, by which those African American living in slavery in the Confederate States were declared free. Maryland then moved to abolish slavery in 1864.

Following the General Conference, two African American annual conferences formed.[9] The first session of the Delaware Conference convened on July 28, 1864, at John Wesley Chapel in Philadelphia with Bishop Edmund S. Janes in the chair. Janes' first action was to receive the recommendations from the presiding elders of the Philadelphia and New Jersey Conferences of those preachers to be received as the charter members of the conference, the prime requirement being that they had already served as a full-time employed minister for at least two years. Ten names were presented and admitted: Isaac Henson, James Davis, Harrison Smith, Isaac Broughton, John G. Manluff, Samuel Dale, Wilmore S. Elsey, John H. Pierce, Nathan Young, and Joshua Brinkley. In addition, three deacons were recommended for elder's orders and seven preachers selected for deacon's orders. Two districts were designated, and Isaac Henson named presiding elder of the Delaware River District and James Davis of the Odessa District.[10]

Among the preachers ordained as elders at this first session of the Delaware Conference was Frost Pollet (b. 1787), then seventy-six years old, well past retirement age. Pollet had for many years preached in Somerset and nearby counties prior to emancipation. He had purchased his freedom in

1840 and had wandered through the area of the Philadelphia Conference in the succeeding years, and been ordained by the conference as a local deacon. At the same time, his son, Charles Pollet (b. 1817), was ordained as a deacon and admitted on trial.[11]

The first session of the Washington Conference convened at Sharp Street Church on October 27, 1864, with Bishop Levi Scott in the chair. Four elders—Benjamin Brown, James Peck, James H. Harper, and Elijah Grissem—were received as the first members of the conference. Additional deacons were recognized and ordained as elders. The seventeen churches (stations) and circuits were arranged in two districts. The conference completed its work on October 31, 1864, the last day that slavery was legal in the state of Maryland.

Among those freed that day was Stephen P. Whittington (b. 1814), who had just been admitted on trial into the new Delaware Conference. Whittington had been born and raised in Somerset County, Maryland. He had been converted at a camp meeting as a young man and eventually became a Methodist local preacher. Following his becoming a Christian, his master, who was only slightly older than his slave companion, had agreed that should he die, Whittington would be freed. However, he died without leaving a will, and the family would not honor the verbal agreement. Whittington spent most of the next decades trying to purchase his own and his family's freedom while having to stop at odd moments to prevent the sale of family members and their resultant scattering around the country. In 1864 he began life as a Methodist itinerant with no formal education and little by way of literary skills; however, he completed his working years successfully as a salaried minister.[12]

The Emancipation Proclamation was operative in that area of Northern Virginia traditionally included in the Baltimore Conference. Like the remaining borderland of the Confederacy, Northern Virginia was very much contested territory. In 1858, the John Mann MEC in Winchester had finally been able to replace its old log cabin with a new brick church, complete with gas lighting for its many evening meetings. A relatively strong congregation, it had nine local preachers and three exhorters. It was also located in an area occupied by Union troops relatively early, in the spring of 1862, and on March 15, African Americans openly celebrated their arrival as a sign of their freedom. That evening, the Methodists gathered at their church and passed a resolution that "no White man should preach to them who did not go in for President Lincoln and the war for the liberty of the slaves!"

Unfortunately, their enthusiasm proved premature, as the local White residents complained to the Union officer in charge that there was widespread

Black insubordination. He agreed to halt further meetings at the Black church in order to prevent any trouble. The church remained shut until the Emancipation Proclamation was publicized. However, as soon as the Washington Conference was set up, the Winchester congregation was accepted into it. By this time, the AMEs were in the field, and one of John Mann's ministers, Robert Armsted (1832–1904), adhered to the new church. He would in 1870 become the pastor of the Winchester AME congregation. The John Mann Church, however, stayed with the MEC. It initially held the allegiance of only a minority of its former members, reporting but 67 in 1865, but seemed to win them back over the next years and by 1871 reported 209. Beginning in 1862, the AMEs would vigorously recruit among the many MEC local preachers in Virginia as the Union forces successively occupied various parts of the state. However, the MEC was able to maintain strong congregations in the Shenandoah Valley at Staunton, Winchester, and Berkeley (West Virginia).[13]

Meanwhile, in the border state of Kentucky, some White congregations rejected association with the Methodist Episcopal Church, South (MEC,S) and declared their allegiance to the Methodist Episcopal Church (MEC). In 1852, the MEC supporters organized a new Kentucky Conference. Its membership was exclusively White, and only in 1866, with slavery no longer a factor, did it admit five Black preachers. Following their acceptance, their work was immediately organized into a "Colored Mission District," under a White presiding elder. That district grew to include thirty-five hundred members by 1869, when the Kentucky Conference split along racial lines and the new Lexington Conference was created as an all-Black structure. That conference was steadily enlarged by the addition of African American congregations in Ohio and Indiana (1872), Illinois (1876), and eventually Michigan, Minnesota, and Wisconsin. The Lexington Conference was the largest MEC conference, geographically, until the organization of the Central West Conference in 1928.

In Lexington proper, the two African American congregations went their separate ways. The church on Upper Street asserted its independence in 1865 and in 1866 joined the AME's Ohio Conference. The Asbury Church, however, went on to become a part of the MEC's Kentucky Conference. It became the largest congregation of the future Lexington Conference. The Louisville congregations continued as adherents of the MEC and AME Church respectively. As the war drew to a close, Louisville became the site of intense competition between the four churches wishing to build an African Methodist constituency. As early as 1864, the AMEZ sent a missionary, William F. Butler, to Louisville. He secured the support of the largest of the Black Methodist congregations, the Center Street Church, and there on June 6, 1866, the AMEZ Kentucky Conference would be organized.[14]

That same year, the MEC,S began to move on setting up separate Black conferences, looking toward the formation of the Colored Methodist Episcopal Church. The key to its work in the state was William H. Miles (1828–92), a former slave who had been licensed to preach in 1857 and then was ordained a deacon by Bishop Andrew in 1857 (one of the very few MEC,S ordinations of a Black person). Miles joined the Center Street Church and became a minister in the AMEZ church when it was organized. He became pastor of Center Street in 1867. The next year he was appointed as a missionary to organize work across the state. However, Miles was attached to the MEC,S, and having now perceived what it was doing, he left the AMEZ, returned to the MEC,S, and led in the organization of its new Kentucky Colored Conference. In the meantime, the MEC,S went to court and won back the property of the Center Street Church, which hosted the third (and last) conference of the MEC,S' Kentucky Colored Conference. Miles was elected as an alternate delegate to the organizing conference of the CME Church, at which he was chosen one of the new church's bishops.[15]

Both the AME and MEC advocated their case in the Louisville's Black community, the former from Quinn Chapel, almost twenty-five years old by the end of the war. The MEC church proved quite successful in attracting members and by the time the Lexington Conference was organized in the early 1870s it had four African American congregations in the city.

Liberia's Role in Securing Ordination

African Americans had largely rejected plans for Liberian colonization; however, the issue persisted and occasionally claimed some modest support. One advocate was "Aunty Roberts," a widow and free Black parent of three sons, John W., Henry J., and Joseph J. Roberts. In 1829, she led her family to Liberia with support from the American Colonization Society chapter in Petersburg, Virginia. Both Joseph and Henry became Methodist local preachers, and Joseph went on to become Liberia's first president. Liberia also appears to have lain behind a unique event, the ordination of David Payne, an African American free man, as a deacon by the Virginia Conference in 1824. Conference historian William Bennett described him as "pious, intelligent and useful" and noted that he later migrated to Liberia.[16]

With some struggle, as the inability of White men sent to Africa to cope with the climate was a constant obstacle, Methodism in Liberia began to take shape. Finally, in the 1830s it seemed to be time for an annual conference to be formed. In preparation, in 1833, an African, Anthony D. Williams, traveled to New York and was ordained an elder at the meeting of the Oneida Conference. The next year he joined two White missionaries in forming the Liberia Mission Conference, which was given full authorization to exist by the 1836 General Conference. Like Williams, other ministers in the conference had to return to America for ordination. Such was the case of Beverley R. Wilson (d. 1864), previously a local preacher in the church at Norfolk. In the wake of reactions to Nat Turner, he initially traveled to Liberia in 1832 and returned to New York in 1835, where he was ordained as an elder for the Liberia Conference.[17]

In 1834, African American Francis Burns (1809–63) moved to Liberia and in 1838 joined the Liberia Conference. Born free at Albany, New York, he had been raised by a Methodist farmer as an indentured servant until his twenty-first birthday. During his teen years, he was converted, experienced a call to the ministry, and became a local preacher. He was encouraged to begin thinking about Liberia.

Burns would be present when Bishop Levi Scott traveled to Africa and while in Liberia (1853) presided over an ordination service at which eight men became elders and five more deacons. One of those ordinands was Edward D. Taylor, who had migrated to Liberia from Mobile, Alabama.[18] By this time the work in Liberia had grown considerably. In his letters back home, former Virginian Abram Blackford described a great revival that spread through the Methodist churches in 1844.[19]

In spite of the leadership provided by the African elders, the Liberia Conference remained without episcopal leadership through the 1840s. Finally, in 1856, the MEC General Conference created a new office in the church— missionary bishop. Allowed a choice, the Liberia Conference picked Francis Burns, who sailed for America and, at the meeting of the Genesee Conference in 1858, was consecrated to his office by Bishops Edmund Janes and Osmon Baker (1812–71).

After Burns died in 1863, the Conference chose John Wright Roberts (1812–75) as his successor. Roberts had became an elder in 1841 and in the 1850s was named presiding elder of the Monrovia District. As the president of the Liberia Conference, he held the space of the recently deceased Bishop Burns, until his own consecration in 1866 in New York.

The Liberia Conference embodied all for which the African American members of the MEC were asking. However, the White leadership, in the face of strong anti-Black prejudices, were unwilling to establish similar structures in the United States. Only in slow hesitating steps did the church allow one small proto-conference to evolve gradually. What they could not deny, however, was the effectiveness of the Liberian ministers and bishop, whose successes took away almost all of the arguments against organizing Black conferences in America.

The AME Church to War's End

Through the 1840s and 1850s, the AME Church steadily extended its boundaries across the northern States, eventually reaching from Maine to Missouri and even planting several pioneering congregations in California. However, at the same time, internally, it struggled with an old problem. The AME Church was formed out of a struggle between the board of trustees at Bethel (and the preachers they acknowledged) and the White minister placed over them by the MEC's Philadelphia Conference. The Whites saw this as a struggle over the connexional system, while the members at Bethel saw themselves as engaging in a struggle over equality—gaining the prerogatives of the trustees of a White congregation and pushing for African American ordained ministers.

In the end, that battle would be settled by a set of technicalities, and the repurchase of the Bethel property by Allen using his own funds. In establishing the AME Church, Bishop Allen retained all of the MEC's ecclesiastical structures, including the episcopal leadership and the centralized ownership of property that had been operative in the MEC. However, memory of Bethel's struggle led to one change. The AMEs assigned significant extra powers to local church trustees. Over time, the power assigned to the trustees came back to haunt the church. Daniel Payne, in reflecting on the seriousness of the situation, observed that powers were assigned to the trustees to prevent the local church's being arbitrarily abused by the ministers; however, in exercising their power, trustees had "become in turn the oppressors both of the ministry and the people, and had produced in many sections of our Connection the most violent commotions and riots, ending in several instances in bloodshed and the rending asunder of whole congregations."[20] As a result, in 1844, the AME General conference moved to redefine and limit the trustees' power.

In 1848 an intense struggle between trustees and pastors broke out at Mother Bethel in Philadelphia. The conflict surfaced when the pastor, John Cornish, accused the trustees of a laundry list of charges. In anticipation of a negative ruling as their church trial proceeded, the trustees withdrew their previously offered welcome to Cornish and declared the pulpit of the church empty. They subsequently selected a local deacon, Shadrack Bassett, as the new pastor, without consulting either the Philadelphia Conference or the church's membership. As expected, the trial concluded with a verdict against the trustees, and Cornish notified them that they had been removed from their office. Refusing to step down, the trustees barricaded the church against Cornish and the matter went to the secular courts, which in February 1850 ruled in favor of Cornish and the conference.

Meanwhile, in Baltimore, the existence of two local churches controlled by the single board of trustees at the Bethel Church troubled Daniel Payne's ministry there. He finally worked out an arrangement whereby the smaller Ebenezer Church would be cut free of the larger Bethel church. The action included forgiving a large debt owed by Ebenezer. The refusal of the trustees to accept the plan led to their trial. Their expected conviction led to open conflict during which Payne was physically attacked and the police summoned. Again, the matter ended in the courts.

The conflicts in Philadelphia and Baltimore caused a number of members to leave; some were expelled, others withdrew. The former members made common cause and formed the Colored Methodist Protestant Church (MPC). Under the leadership of the Revs. Nathaniel Peck, Adam S. Driver, and John S. Scar, an initial Maryland State Convention of Colored Methodist Protestants was held on October 13, 1849, in Baltimore at the Israel Methodist Church. It issued a call for a national convention to be held in Philadelphia in June 1850.[21] The Colored MPC would later merge with the African Union Church to create the present African Union First Methodist Protestant Church.

The problem that led to the formation of the Colored MPC behind them, the AME Church expanded steadily through the 1850s and entered the war period with some anticipation of the possibilities that peace might bring. Those new opportunities would be realized soon after the issuance of the Emancipation Proclamation. In April 1863, C. C. Lynch, an officer with the National Freedmen's Bureau (and an MEC minister), asked Bishop Payne to select two missionaries to work among the freedmen in the areas of South Carolina then under Union control. In Charleston and elsewhere, the White ministers had abandoned their Black members. Payne jumped at the opportunity and selected James Lynch (1839–72) from the Baltimore Conference and James D. S. Hall of New York.

Beginning in May, the pair visited Port Royal, Edisto, and Beaufort, South Carolina, with James Lynch expanding operations to Savannah and Charleston as soon as those cities fell to Union control. Subsequently, the first work in North Carolina would focus on Wilmington. Then, in December 1863, Payne headed to Nashville, Tennessee, to initiate work among the members of the Capers Church and Andrew Chapel, both of which he accepted into the AME Church, as St. John's and St. Paul's AME Churches respectively. Already in 1855 the AMEs had assigned their Missouri Conference hegemony over Tennessee, Mississippi, Louisiana, and Alabama. A single struggling congregation, closed in 1858, had been accepted into the conference from New Orleans, but as the Union assumed control of the Mississippi River, new churches were planted between St. Louis (where the St. Paul Church had been organized in 1841) and New Orleans, the first being in Memphis.

Wartime work culminated in Payne's May 1865 trip to Charleston to initiate the South Carolina Conference. A personal triumph, his return reversed his having had to leave when the city had shut down the school and prevented his continuance as a teacher in 1835. He found congregations had been opened along the coast from Savannah to New Bern, North Carolina, with one center inland at Raleigh, North Carolina.

Meanwhile, in the fall of 1863, Alexander Wayman journeyed to Norfolk, Virginia, at the request of the members of St. John's Chapel, the MEC,S church on Butte Street that had been left without pastoral leadership. On May 4, 1863, it voted to discard the *Discipline* of the MEC,S and later that year, the military government assigned the property to the congregation. When Wayman arrived, he found a group of some eight hundred members and nine local preachers, including Peter Shepherd (d. 1907), Richard H. Parker (b. 1808),[22] James Tynes, Americus Woodhouse, and Amos Wilson.[23] After a brief first visit, Wayman returned to Norfolk with Bishop Payne, and the pair also found the North Street MEC,S in nearby Portsmouth ready to affiliate.[24] The separate African American Church in Portsmouth had been founded in 1843 and for several decades was served by a resident White preacher, George M. Bain. When the church building had burned, Bain secured funds for a new brick building on North Street, which would become Emmanuel AME Church under the pastorate of James A. Handy after the war ended.[25]

The AMEZs in the Pre-War North

In 1852, the AMEZ Church experienced a church-wide disturbance relative to the needed expansion of the bishop's office as the church expanded. The very capable Christopher Rush dominated the leadership (1828–52) as the church's only bishop for twenty years. In 1848, George Galbraith (1799–1853) was elected as the assistant bishop, though a growing minority thought Galbraith should be designated as a full bishop. Then in 1852, Rush retired and three equally empowered bishops were elected—Galbraith,

William H. Bishop (1793–1873), and George A. Spywood (1802–75). Galbraith's death the next year set the stage for an intense power struggle between the two remaining bishops.

By 1854, those favoring Spywood held control of the New York and New England Conferences. They called a special session of the General Conference at which they suspended Bishop from office and elected John Tappan as Spywood's assistant. The other faction, which included most of the membership south and west of Philadelphia, held its general conference in 1856. It reelected Bishop and chose Joseph Jackson Clinton (1823–81) as a second bishop. At its 1856 session, the Spywood faction chose James Simmons (1792–1874) as bishop and Solomon T. Scott (1790–1862) as the assistant bishop.

Repeated disputes over church property landed the two factions in court. As the larger group had approved a name change, the court tended to favor the small group. Then, as the first cases were being adjudicated, leadership arose in both factions that worked out a solution to what was seen as an entirely unnecessary and unwanted division. The agreement was solidified before the June 1860 General Conference, and the reunited church selected three equally empowered bishops—William H. Bishop, Peter Ross (1809–90), and Joseph J. Clinton.

Clinton was but thirty-three when elected to office and assigned leadership over the Philadelphia Conference. Two years later he also was given the new Southern Conference, a paper conference into which all the southern states were assigned, Clinton soon became discouraged over being assigned to what appeared an impossible task of evangelizing the South with no budget. Following his making his intention of resigning his office known, Melvina Fletcher, a laywoman raised three hundred dollars, the amount needed to get the effort started. Thus, toward the end of 1863, he commissioned five men, including James Walker Hood (1831–1918), as missionaries.

In January 1864, Hood arrived in New Bern, North Carolina, where he convinced the members of the Andrew's Chapel (MEC,S) to adhere to the AMEZ Church. Renamed St. Peter's Church, it became the first AMEZ church in the former Confederate states . When Bishop Clinton visited in May, he licensed the first AMEZ preachers who had formerly been licensed by MEC,S. Among them would be Jeffrey Overton, who proudly showed Clinton the original preacher's license he had received in 1831. Once given to him, it had never been renewed as the church in the area had stopped renewing licenses following the Nat Turner rebellion.

From New Bern, Hood moved on to Beaufort and Wilmington and added two more churches to the connexion. In the later city, he competed with the

AME missionaries who had already claimed the two Black congregations they had found, but Hood convinced the congregants at St. Luke's Church to withdraw from the AME and affiliate with the AMEZ. By December he had recruited a dozen ministers and some four hundred members, enough to found the North Carolina Conference. That conference would go on to become the largest in the AMEZ Church, though at its founding, it was limited to the area between Wilmington and New Bern plus a single center on Roanoke Island in Dare County.

After organizing the North Carolina Conference, Clinton sailed to New Orleans, then under Union control. On March 13, 1865, he organized the Louisiana Conference with fifteen preachers enrolled. These two actions completed the first stage of the AMEZ's southern strategy developed a year earlier. The idea was to use North Carolina and Louisiana as two bases from which missionaries would penetrate the rest of the South as soon as the war ended.

From MEC,S to the CME Church

Once the Civil War began, African Americans turned their eyes on the South. Hope for an end to slavery blossomed after the Emancipation Proclamation. At the same time, the MEC saw the war as a opportunity to assert the growing opinion that the split of 1844 was not a result of General Conference action, but a schism. The MEC leaders had come to feel that all property of the church in the South belonged to them. They planned to reclaim their property and as many members as possible. The AME and AMEZ churches saw their mission almost entirely as one to the Black members of the MEC,S, which they felt would flock to a church headed by members of their own race now that they could freely choose.

The Methodist Episcopal Church, South, of course, experienced the war quite differently, but hoped as soon as it ended to be able to return to "normal" as soon as possible. The White leadership, of course, took credit for having evangelized southern African Americans and initially hoped that the freedmen would remain loyal. Assisted by the plantation missions, Black membership had gone from 124,811 (1845) to 207,776 members when the war began.

The situation of the Black members was high on the list of priorities at the first post-war General Conference, held in 1866. With more than half the Black members already having abandoned the church, the General Conference quickly discarded any remaining pipe dreams of a return to normal. At the same time, while a majority of former Black MEC,S members had already switched allegiance, a substantial minority, choosing a different path, forwarded their plan to the General Conference. They wished to model their future on the pattern that had led to the creation of the MEC,S in 1845. They requested the formation of a commission representing the continuing Black members to plan a separate church, which would be created by action of the next General Conference in 1870. The delegates favored the proposal. The new commission moved soon after the General Conference to organize several African American annual conferences and begin assessment of the property being used by the Black members.

The completion of the separation process awaited the action of the next General Conference in 1870, which passed all of the enabling legislation for a smooth transition. By May 1870, five new annual conferences existed, but three more appeared during the next few months. Thus, when the organizing General Conference of the African American members was held in Jackson, Tennessee, beginning on December 15, 1870, delegates from eight annual conferences were in attendance.[26]

The delegates, with two MEC,S bishops in the chair, proceeded with the organization of what was to be known as the Colored Methodist Episcopal Church (CME). It adopted the MEC,S *Discipline* in a slightly modified form. The MEC,S turned over to the new church all of the land and buildings currently used by the Black members and assisted in the formation of a publishing house and the initiation of a connexional periodical, *The Christian Index*. The church was divided into nine annual conferences. The conference elected Richard H. Vanderhorst and William Henry Miles to the episcopal office and MEC,S Bishop Robert Paine (1799–1882) was present to consecrate them.

A Uneasy Transition

When the war finally ended with the surrender of Robert E. Lee's army on April 9, 1865, the ME, AME, and AMEZ Churches were ready to move quickly into the states of the former Confederacy and lay claim to the 200,000 African American Methodists. In addition, the MEC wanted to woo White members of the MEC,S back into the fold and to claim ownership of the thousands of buildings and pieces of property which it felt really belonged to it. The far larger and wealthier MEC would be able to field the most personnel for the task, but those sent were almost exclusively White ministers, whom the freedmen found less attractive church leaders than the representatives of the two African churches. Being smaller and possessing less financial resources, the AME and AMEZ churches were slower in covering the same territory now open to them, at least during the first decade. However, they knew where the primary concentrations of Black members could be found. They also attracted many of the unordained preachers, who were quickly offered the ordination they had been previously denied.

Among the first places that the several churches competed for the loyalty of the freedmen was Charleston, South Carolina. Charleston had been a flourishing center of African American Methodism with its thousands of adherents spread among the one MPC and four MEC,S congregations. During the war, the Cumberland Street Church burned down (1861), an early victim of bombardment of the city. Then in the summer of 1863, the Trinity Church was damaged by Union bombardment. During this time there had been a steady migration of Charlestonians from the city. Subsequent to the damage to Trinity, all the White members reorganized and held services at Bethel. Black members were also reorganized into one "City Colored Mission" with several meeting points, though the largest group met at Old Bethel.

The city finally fell in February 1865, and soon after the soldiers established control, T. Willard Lewis, an MEC minister, and James Lynch of the African Methodist Episcopal Church began work in the city. AME bishop Alexander W. Wayman arrived in March and preached at the Zion Presbyterian Church, at which time he called for a meeting of those interested in founding a congregation. At the subsequent meeting he founded, or possibly more properly, reorganized Emmanuel African Methodist Episcopal Church (taking its name from the earlier congregation organized by Morris Brown in 1817).

Emmanuel hosted Bishop Payne in May for the organization of the AME South Carolina Conference. Initially James Lynch and James A. Handy (1826–1911) were the only two ordained ministers present, but they were joined by two itinerant licentiates, Theodore G. Steward and James H. A. Johnson (soon ordained as deacons), and one local preacher, William Bentley. However, before the conference ended three other elders—R. H. Cain, Anthony S. Stanford, and George S. Rue—arrived along with several local preachers from Georgia and the Carolinas, not yet ordained but ready to affiliate with the new church—Charles Bradwell, N. Murphy, Robert Taylor, and Richard Vanderhorst. R. H. Cain would be left in Charleston and lead the Emmanuel congregation in the construction of their own church building.

In the meantime, T. Willard Lewis held a similar meeting of Charleston Methodists in the abandoned Trinity Church building and appealed to its Black members to leave the MEC,S and adhere to the MEC. Almost all in attendance accepted the invitation to return to their "original" church home, which had for the time being taken charge of Trinity's property and designated it as a church for African members. At the same time, members at Old Bethel also adhered to the MEC and brought their property with them.

These initial movements by the former African members of the MEC,S were taken before the return of the White ministers who had fled the city during the last stages of the war. By the end of the summer of 1865, however, they were again active in the city, and in October succeeded in having the Trinity Church property returned to them. Nevertheless, the Black members did not stay. They moved their meeting to a nearby school building and assumed the name Centenary MEC. With the financial help of the American Missionary Association, they purchased a building from the Wentworth Street Baptist Church. An additional group of Black Methodists began to meet at a former military storehouse. Initially taking the name St. James MEC, they met at several locations, changed their name to Wesley MEC, and in 1873 purchased property upon which to build a church.

In 1866, MEC Bishop Osman Baker organized the South Carolina Mission Conference (including parishes in Georgia and Florida) at a meeting in Charleston. The conference counted 1,436 members in its two Charleston congregations—Trinity and Old Bethel Churches, soon to be joined by the St. James/Wesley church. The MEC was, however, unable to find any White support, and its presence in the city would henceforth be centered on its three African congregations. It also found itself fighting for its remaining possessions. The Trinity Church had already lost its building, and now the Old Bethel property was being contested. In addition there was the McKee estate, property that had been bequeathed to the Methodist Episcopal Church in 1831. The MEC,S, as the continuing MEC in the state, contended that both properties belonged to them. The Black members at Old Bethel argued that Bethel Church had given the building to them. MEC representatives claimed that the MEC,S was a breakaway group and that the McKee property, willed to the MEC at a time the MEC,S did not even exist, should be returned to their control. The case dragged on through the period of military control and the Reconstruction era into the 1880s.

As the fight over the Charleston properties continued, the MEC developed its work in the state. Black laypeople, such as Charles Holloway and George Shrewsbury, now moved from simply informally leading the Black community to official roles in their local church structures. Holloway and Shrewsbury also became the MEC's trustees for the McKee property. Former class leader Samuel Weston was welcomed into the traveling ministry and ordained as a member of the new South Carolina Mission Conference. Joseph

A. Sasportas (d. 1898), a butcher and merchant, and one of the better educated lay members, took the lead in founding the Baker Theological Institute (1866) and later Claflin University (1869), and then oversaw the merger of the former into the latter (1871). He also became a minister and presiding elder.

Finally, in the 1880s the MEC and MEC,S settled their litigation. The McKee property was returned to the MEC,S, which in turn agreed to withdraw any claims to Old Bethel. As a result of the changes through and after the war, the Old Bethel building emerged as the oldest Methodist structure in the city.

During the war the MPC church in Charleston was disbanded and the building destroyed. The White congregation did not rebuild, but the Black members did and continued as a MPC congregation attached to the Maryland Conference.

During the decade after the war, what was documented most completely in Charleston, with the several churches competing over the former members of the MEC,S, would be repeated across the South, especially in those areas where the larger Black congregations had been established during the slave era. Through the 1870s, the North Carolina Conference would become the new center of the AMEZ Church nationally. Established first in the cities close to the Atlantic Ocean, the first move into the interior of the state would come in 1866 when Hood moved to Fayetteville where he found what was left of the members of Evans Chapel, some seventy-eight in number, and reorganized them as an AMEZ church. Among its members he discovered Thomas Lomax (1832–1908), a young man who had been able to secure an education. Licensed to preach in 1867, Lomax went on to become an ordained deacon before the year was out. He would have an outstanding career in the AMEZ Church, eventually being elected a bishop in 1876. Also in 1866, Cicero R. Harris (1844–1917), who had been born in Fayetteville but as a child had moved with his family to Ohio, returned to his hometown where he became an active lay worker in Evans Chapel. In 1872, he was licensed to preach and thus began an outstanding career in the ministry that would also lead him to the bishop's office (1888).

Lomax and Harris turned out to be but two of a number of local preachers who either surfaced or were recruited by the small cadre of ministers that were originally sent into North Carolina and that put a significant amount of energy into locating groups of Methodist believers, organizing them into churches, and building the churches into substantive congregations. One such person was Thomas Shirden, a free Black before the war, who around 1855 began preaching throughout Columbus County, in the southeast corner of the state, and raised up several independent churches that in 1865 he brought into the AMEZ Church.

As the war began, the Union Street Church in Petersburg, Virginia, was one of the strongest African churches in the state. It had originated in 1830 when the White Methodists of the city saw to the construction of a separate church for the Black members, then some 160 in number. The Ebenezer Church operated some sixteen years. Meanwhile, in 1846, the Union Street Church, in which the White members met, became the site of the first General Conference of the MEC,S. However, by this time, the White congregation had outgrown their building and had already begun construction of a new sanctuary on High Street. When it was completed, Ebenezer's building was sold and its African American members moved into the Union Street church.

After the war, the AMEZ occupied the church briefly, but was taken to court and had to relinquish control, even though Bishop Hood came to town in 1866 to organize the Virginia Conference in Petersburg. Eventually, the congregation became a part of the CME connexion.[27]

After the Carolinas, Georgia became the important battleground between the AMEs and AMEZs in the South. The AMEs sent James Lynch to Savannah in 1865 and he made contact with C. L. Bradwell, one of the local preachers at Andrew Chapel, the MEC,S congregation, and engaged in the initial negotiations leading to that church's realignment with the AMEs. At the first South Carolina Conference, Bradwell and his colleague William Gaines were recognized as AME ministers. A. L. Stanford was appointed to Savannah and completed the reorganization of the congregation as St. Philip AME Church.[28]

On January 12, 1865, Bradwell, Gaines, the seventy-two-year-old Glasgow Taylor, class leader Robert N. Taylor, and Lynch joined other local Black ministers in a meeting with General George Sherman, who had just completed his march through the state, and U.S. Secretary of War Edwin Stanton. They discussed the situation of the freedmen and ascertained that their freedom was now backed by the U.S. government. They reached a consensus on a variety of matters, save James Lynch, who began to express some of the opinions that would soon lead him to separate from the AME and return to the MEC.[29]

While only a minority of the members of Andrew Chapel refused to join the AMEs, that remnant, under the leadership of layman David Deas, remained together and eventually reestablished their control of their property. They reorganized and in 1871 emerged as the St. Paul CME Church. A few of the members of Andrew Chapel would also align with the MEC and in 1871 found Asbury MEC (now UMC).[30]

William Gaines left Savannah to lead AME development through central Georgia, including Atlanta. There he found Joseph Wood holding the African congregation together and in 1866 invited it into the AME Church. It subsequently emerged as Bethel AME Church, now one of the most prominent congregations in the whole denomination.

Future bishop Henry McNeal Turner spent some time in Georgia, and in 1866 in Macon met Robert Anderson (1819–1902). Anderson had been raised in slavery and had been brought to Macon in 1838. Converted in a protracted meeting in 1839, he joined the Methodists and founded and led a Sunday school through most of the 1840s. In 1849 he was called to preach and finally received a license in 1856. He afterwards preached throughout central Georgia. After the war he brought the African Methodists in Macon into the AME Church, was ordained, and then over the next twelve years founded and led several AME churches in the state. Then in 1882, he defected to the MEC's Savannah Conference, where he would spend the last years of his lengthy ministry.[31]

The AMEZ Church, too late in the field to present either the Savannah or Atlanta congregations with its claims, scored a real victory in Augusta when Hood was able to woo Trinity Church and its one thousand-plus

St. John Christian Methodist Episcopal Church continues the original Andrew Chapel Methodist Episcopal Church, South.

St. Paul Monumental AME Church was founded after the Civil War by former members of Andrew Chapel Methodist Episcopal Church, South.

members into the fold. In June 1867 Bishop Clinton traveled to Augusta and personally organized the church's Georgia Conference in the Trinity Church building, welcoming its pastor Edward West into conference membership. However, several months later, West resigned from the AMEZ and took his church into the MEC. It would now become the lead church of the Georgia Mission Conference, later to evolve into the Savannah Conference. This action by West significantly slowed the AMEZ's hope of making Georgia one of its stronger centers.[32]

Mobile's first African American Methodist church had emerged out of the Pensacola–Mobile Mission in the 1820s and had shown steady growth such that in the early 1840s four congregations suddenly appeared, one being Little Zion (1843). Over the next two decades, the church was served by three local preachers—Ferdinand Smith, Charles Lee, and Battas Dayes (another local preacher, E. D. Taylor, having left for Liberia). J. J. Clinton visited Mobile in 1865 and persuaded the congregation to adhere to the AMEZ Church. He ordained Ferdinand Smith, who became the first pastor of what was renamed Big Zion Church, the lead congregation of the AMEZ's Alabama Conference.

James Lynch, who had helped found the AME work in South Carolina and Georgia, left the church in 1867 and joined the MEC. He moved to Mississippi and helped found the Mississippi Conference in 1869. He combined his ministry with political activity and in 1870, while still a presiding elder, became the Mississippi Secretary of State. His career was then unfortunately cut short by pneumonia, from which he died in 1872.[33] The vacuum caused by Lynch's diversion to politics and premature death was then picked up by John B. Bowen, one of the conference's new presiding elders.[34]

African American Methodism in Nashville had been focused in two churches, the Capers Church and Andrew Chapel. The former operated out of a new brick building that had been erected in 1851 on a lot near the Nashville–Chattanooga Depot. Its location made it a fitting target for the Union Army, which after it occupied the city in 1862, turned the church into a military hospital. Bishop Daniel Payne arrived in Tennessee in December 1863 and initially contacted members of the Capers Church. Shortly thereafter local preacher Napoleon Merry and a group of the laypeople applied for membership in the AME Church. Bishop Payne soon gained control of the property and reconstituted the congregation as the St. John AME Church.

Soon after the war, the MEC,S went to court and regained possession of the Capers Church building, which subsequently became a leading parish in its new Memphis Colored Conference. That conference then became a constituting part of the CME Church in 1870. It continues today as Capers Memorial CME Church. The St. John AME Church continued but had to find alternate facilities until it could erect its own building.

Meanwhile Andrew Chapel was taken over by the MEC, which in 1865 opened a school for freedmen in its facilities. That school moved to the former Confederate gun factory in 1866 and the next year was chartered as Central Tennessee College (now Walden University). Andrew Chapel kept its connection to the school, and as the church grew, it evolved into Clark Memorial United Methodist Church.

As federal troops approached Little Rock, Arkansas, in the early 1860s, the Ashley family, which had been the patron of William Wallace Andrews, the pastor of the city's only Black Methodist church, granted Andrews his freedom and gave him an additional piece of property at the northwest corner of Tenth and Broadway, as his residence. After the Civil War, Andrews and three friends—William Warren, Solomon Winfrey, and Frank Evans, all respected members of antebellum Little Rock's relatively small Black community—purchased the block at Tenth and Broadway and made their homes there. Andrews' daughter Charlotte Stephens later reflected on this time: "Before the break came in the Methodist church [1844], you know, it was all the same, north and south. After the division on account of slavery the Methodist church in the south had the word 'South' attached. For a long time my father did not realize that. In 1863 he and his church went back into the original Methodist church."[35] He was ordained as a minister, and the church was absorbed into the previously existing Missouri and Arkansas Conference. Andrews was named presiding elder of the Arkansas District, which originally included all the African American work in the state.

Immediately after the war, Andrews opened a school in the Wesley Chapel facilities.[36] He also founded MEC congregations in Ft. Smith, Pine Bluff, and Van Buren.[37] His daughter, Charlotte, grew up to attend Oberlin College and then become Little Rock's first African American public school teacher.[38] After Wesley Chapel identified with the MEC, another Little Rock preacher, John Peyton, organized a separate congregation in 1870, which he took into the CME Church. That congregation is now known as Miles Chapel.

The Civil War hit Louisiana as hard as the rest of the South, though it was plainly at the edge of most of the hostilities. This was especially true in the Bayou. While approximately 40 percent of the members of the MEC,S were Black statewide, in much of the Bayou, they made up anywhere from 70 to 90 percent. Leadership also disappeared as the war progressed, many of the White Methodist ministers being detained by the occupying forces.

When the AMEs founded their Louisiana Conference in November 1865, among the first appointments was James Reese to the Thibodeauville Mission. Thus six weeks later when MEC,S minister Robert Hardie, Jr., arrived in Thibodeau he found the church building in the hands of the former Black members, now affiliated with the AME Church. He found the few White members, who still considered themselves members of the MEC,S, and was able to eventually reclaim the property, but the great majority of the members were now part of the two AME congregations that were created out of the former plantation circuit.

Meanwhile, on December 25, 1865, representatives of the MEC organized the Mississippi Mission Conference and appointed Richard King Diossy as the presiding elder of its Opelousas District. Though White, Diossy proved effective in mobilizing African Americans and bringing many into the MEC. To assist him he had the help of William Murrell (b.c. 1814–92). Born a slave in South Carolina, Murrell had as a young man been sold and brought to New Orleans. Here he was purchased by a Rev. Wolbridge, who allowed him to get an education and exercise his preaching skills, which he did in both MEC,S and AME settings. Then in 1865, he joined the MEC and was assigned to the Houma/Thibodeau circuit.

On land purchased by Diossy, Murrell led in the building of Wesley Methodist Church in Houma and Calvary Methodist Church in Thibodeau. Even with time out serving two terms in the state legislature beginning in 1868, he brought more than four hundred people into the MEC during his several years on site. By 1870, the Thibodeau church had over eight hundred members. Murrell's leadership would be supplemented by that of Emperor Williams, who had come to New Orleans in 1839 from Tennessee. He had joined the church in 1845 and become a local preacher.[39] He joined the Mississippi Mission Conference and transferred to the Louisiana Conference at its founding. He presided over the Opelousas District in 1870, when Robert Hodge became the minister of the Thibodeau church. Hodge had been born a slave in 1807 in Virginia. A longtime member of the MEC, he was also a charter member of the Mississippi Mission Conference. Several more African American MEC churches would be founded in the area over the next few years and the area would go on to become an important part of the MEC's Louisiana Conference.

It will be remembered that the AMEZ Church had formed its Louisiana Conference in March 1865 with the understanding that it would be the base from which expansion would be generated east and west. With fifteen ministers, Bishop Clinton built a work that included some fifteen thousand members in a relatively short time. The next years became one of the less talked about eras in AMEZ history, for as Bishop Walls later observed, "His [Clinton's] immediate successor, by neglect and mismanagement, lost nearly all of the 15,000 members."[40] Among the people lost was Henry P. Taylor (1825–77). Born in South Carolina, Taylor was able to get some education in his teen years and converted to Methodism. As a young man he was moved to New Orleans and while there came into contact with the AMEZ Church. He joined their Louisiana Conference but in 1873 left it for the MEC. He would later serve the church in Houma.

Texas Methodists had founded Black congregations in Austin and Houston in the 1850s. The Austin church had been built up by Nace Duval. Receiving his freedom as the war came to an end, he left for San Antonio and there joined the AME Church and founded its San Antonio congregation. The Austin congregation affiliated with the MEC and with the assistance of Isaac Wright, a MEC minister, reorganized as Wesley Chapel Methodist Church and was placed within the Texas Mission Conference.[41]

After the Civil War, the White members of the Houston MEC,S congregation gave the title of the building in which the African American congregation met to its members, with the understanding that they would move it from its location immediately adjacent to the White church to a new parcel of land. Frank Vance, a prominent lay member of the church, purchased a plot of land at Travis and Bell Streets upon which the building could be relocated. The congregation reorganized as the Trinity MEC, and like the Austin church became a member of the Texas Mission Conference.[42]

The first AME Church missionary in Texas, M. M. Clark, arrived in Galveston in 1866. Here he found an African MEC,S congregation originally organized in 1848. He convinced it to affiliate with the AME Church. Subsequently congregations opened in San Antonio and Bryan. An initial meeting to organize an annual conference assembled in Galveston in 1867. Bishop James Shorter arrived in the city to preside over the organization of the Texas Conference on October 22, 1868, which was attended by Houston Reedy, Steven Patton, Emmanuel Hammitt, and Johnson Reed. The MEC went to court to claim the Galveston property, and was initially successful, but in 1874, the property was returned to the AMEs.[43]

An Open Future Beckons

As the Civil War began, African Methodists were divided among four churches. By far the largest number were affiliated with the Methodist Episcopal Church, South, which had a virtual monopoly on Methodism from Virginia to Texas. It reported approximately 208,000 members and probationers, capping a steady growth rate of better than 3 percent per annum through the 1850s. A decade later it had virtually no African American members.

The second largest number of African American Methodists were members of the Methodist Episcopal Church. Through the last half of the 1860s it engaged in a massive evangelism campaign to gather the freedmen into its fold and by 1870 had created a set of conferences that reached across the former Confederacy. Five of the conferences (Lexington, Mississippi, Tennessee, South Carolina, and Texas) were founded as African American bodies. Three others (Alabama, Georgia, and Virginia and North Carolina) were founded as integrated conferences that split along racial lines in the mid-1870s.

The MEC became even more attractive to African Americans from the string of colleges it founded. Very much aware of the need for education among a people who had for a generation or more been denied access even to basic reading and writing skills, the church sponsored new schools scattered from South Carolina to Texas that would become the backbone of higher education for African Americans in the South through the rest of the century (until the Morrill Act extension of 1890 provided state-supported universities that accepted Black students). Schools such as Claflin University, Clarke College, Dillard University, and Wiley College would train generation after generation of African American leaders.

The AME Church had reached across the free states from Boston to St. Louis prior to the war and had the most resources and motivation to throw into the task of claiming the freedmen as the war came to a close. By 1868 it too had formed a dozen conferences that reached across the South and transformed the church into a national body. Of the three "northern" churches that colonized the southern states, it gained the most. Additionally, it picked up members in places like Delaware and the Eastern Shore of Maryland where many former slaves left the MEC.

The AMEZ entered the war as the smaller and more geographically confined of the two African Methodist denominations. According to Bradley, in 1860, after three decades of activity, it had thirty-eight congregations, served by eighty-two elders, fifteen deacons, and eight preachers. The 4,600 members were organized into five conferences. But with the Herculean efforts of men like Bishop Clinton and bishop-to-be Hood, it made monumental strides forward. By 1870, it had formed eleven conferences covering the same territory as its sister denomination, save for Texas, which would not be opened until the mid-1880s. Its loss of strength in Louisiana was made up by its early growth in Mississippi. By 1870 it could report some 125,000 members in 840 churches served by more than a thousand ministers.[44]

The growth of both the AME and AMEZ Churches had been spectacular. Together, they now claimed more members than the MEC,S prior to the war, meaning that they not only claimed some Africans who were Methodists before the war but brought many into the church for the first time, which was not surprising given the status of both churches as longstanding Black-led organizations with impressive credentials in the struggle for freedom.

That being said, the largest single group of former members of the MEC,S, of course, did not go to either the AME or AMEZ, but to the new Colored Methodist Episcopal Church which took shape through the late 1860s and attained formal existence at the end of 1870. It would begin the new era with some 78,000 members and a certain material head start as the recipient of an initial gift of property and buildings from its MEC,S patron. It would be hindered, however, by a perception of its continued relationship with the same White people who had held its members in bondage. As the AME, AMEZ, and CME Churches would turn to the hard task of evangelizing African Americans, the great majority of whom remained unchurched, because of its origin, the CME Church would have to fight for many decades to establish its legitimacy in the new world the war had created.

For over a century, African Americans had exercised their will to choose Methodism. At times the choice was simple, to be a Methodist (or not) in a church headed by White people. After the formation of the AUC, AME, and AMEZ Churches , the choice, at least in part of the country, broadened and became much more complicated. It now involved long-term interracial relationships, both positive and negative, and the strategy and tactics to be used to liberate the African American community as a whole into the promises of both the nation in which African Americans resided and the Christian faith they professed.

As of 1870, a new spectrum of choices were presented to African Americans as to how they could relate to the larger Methodist community. That each of the four communities had its appeal was amply demonstrated by the number of ministers who moved from one communion to another, a few changing allegiance more than once. How they would choose and the paths they would carve through the wilderness of the future is the next chapter of African Americans' as yet still unfinished vision quest.

Notes

1. Joshua E. Licorish, "Delaware Conference," in Nolan B. Harmon, ed. with Albea Godbold & Louise L. Queen, *Encyclopedia of World Methodism* (Nashville, TN: United Methodist Publishing House, 1974): 652.

2. [Joseph H. Morgan], *Morgan's History of the New Jersey Conference of the A. M. E. Church, from 1872 to 1887* (Camden, NJ: S. Chew, 1887): 91–93.

3. Fortie and Watkins were ordained deacons at the Sharp Street Church.

4. Lewis Y. Cox, *Pioneer Footsteps* (Cape May, NJ: Star & Wave Press, 1917), 5–10.

5. James Edward Armstrong, *History of the Old Baltimore Conference from the Planting of Methodism in 1773 to the Division of the Conference in 1857* (Baltimore: The Author, 1907): 305.

6. This was printed in the minutes of the 1856 General Conference of the Methodist Episcopal Church.

7. William C. Jason, Jr., "The Delaware Annual Conference, 1864–1865," *Methodist History* 6, 4 (July 1966): 26–40.

8. The Sharp Street Church in Sandy Springs (named for the Baltimore congregation) was founded in 1822 by some former slaves on land formerly owned by Thomas L. and Sophia Brooke. They designated the plot for a cemetery and a house of worship, the first building being a small log cabin.

9. During the decade beginning in 1864, the MEC formed a set of African American conferences stretching from Delaware to Texas. In 1939, when the MEC merged with the MEC,S and MPC to form the Methodist Church (1939–68), these conferences were set apart in what was termed the Central Jurisdiction. After the 1968

merger that created the United Methodist Church, action began immediately to do away with the Central Jurisdiction and, at least at the annual conference level, merge the African American churches into the contiguous geographic conference.

In anticipation of the 1968 merger, in 1965, the Washington Conference merged into the Baltimore Conference (now known as the Baltimore Washington Conference) and the Delaware Conference merged into the Peninsula Conference, now known as the Peninsula Delaware Conference). The Lexington Conference became involved in a complex series of mergers, also beginning in 1964. at which time work north of the Ohio River merged into the contiguous geographical conferences. The continuing Lexington Conference then merged with African American work in Tennessee to form the short-lived Tennessee-Kentucky Conference. That conference merged into its contiguous geographical conferences in 1968.

10. Cox, *Pioneer Footsteps*, 60–63.

11. Robert W. Todd, *Methodism of the Peninsula* (Philadelphia: Methodist Episcopal Book Rooms, 1886): 187–93; Cox, *Pioneer Footsteps*. 61–63, 74; Jason, "Delaware Annual Conference," 30–31.

12. Todd, *Methodism of the Peninsula*, 292–93.

13. Jon Greenstone, "Ante Bellum Methodism in Winchester, Virginia, and the Great Schism." Posted at www.emmitsburg.net/archive_list/articles/thoughtful/vicar_john/methodism_in_winchester.htm.

14. Walls, *African Methodist Episcopal Zion Church*, 194–96; and Israel L. Butt, *History of African Methodism in Virginia, or Four Decades in the Old Dominion* (Hampton, VA: Hampton Institute Press, 1908), posted at http://docsouth.unc.edu/church/butt/butt.html.

15. C. H. Phillips, *The History of the Colored Methodist Episcopal Church in America, Comprising Its Organization, Subsequent Development and Present Status*. Third edition (Jackson TN: Publishing House C.M.E. Church, 1925): 196–204; and Othal Hawthorne Lakey, *The History of the CME Church* (Memphis: CME Publishing House, 1985. Rev. ed.: Memphis: CME Publishing House, 1996): 155–56.

16. William Bennett, *Memorials of Methodism in Virginia* (Richmond: The Author, 1871): 705.

17. Reginald F. Hildebrand, "'An Imperious Sense of Duty': Documents Illustrating an Episode in the Methodist Reaction to the Nat Turner Revolt," *Methodist History* 19, 3 (April 1981): 172.

18. His August 3, 1853 letter is reprinted in John W. Blassingame, ed., *Slave Testimony: Two Centuries of Letters, Speeches, Interviews, and Autobiographies* (Baton Rouge, LA: Louisiana State University Press, 1977), *Slave Testimony*, 97–98.

19. Blassingame, *Slave Testimony*, 61–65.

20. Daniel Alexander Payne, *A History of the African Methodist Episcopal Church*, ed. by Charles Spencer Smith (Nashville, TN: Publishing House of the A. M. E. Sunday School Union), 1891, 220.

21. "To the Colored Methodist Protestant Churches in the United States." One-page flyer, Baltimore, November 9, 1849.

22. Parker was raised a slave in Norfolk, and in spite of the laws prohibiting it, learned to read and write. He was converted as a result of his clandestine reading to the Bible, joined the Methodists, and became a local preacher. He subsequently became a leading member of the AME's Virginia Conference, organized in 1867. He recounted much of his life in a 1866 interview reprinted in Blassingame, *Slave Testimony*, 465–66.

23. Butt, *History of African Methodism in Virginia*, 32–33.

24. Charles Spencer Smith, *A History of the African Methodist Episcopal Church: Being a Volume Supplemental to A History of the African Methodist Episcopal Church, by Daniel Alexander Payne, D.D., LL.D., Late One of Its Bishops: Chronicling the Principal Events in the Advance of the African Methodist Episcopal Church from 1856 to 1922* (Philadelphia: Book Concern of the A. M. E. Church), 1922, 51–65.

25. James A. Handy, *Scraps of African Methodist Episcopal History* (Philadelphia: A. M. E. Book Concern, 1902), 9.

26. C. H. Phillips, *The History of the Colored Methodist Episcopal Church in America, Comprising Its Organization, Subsequent Development and Present Status*. Third edition (Jackson, TN: Publishing House C. M. E. Church, 1925), 28–29.

27. P. H. Drewry, *The Story of a Church: A History of Washington Street Church at Petersburg, Virginia, 1773–1923* (Petersburg, VA: The Author, 1923).

28. Now St. Philip Monumental AME Church.

29. "Sherman Meets with the Colored Ministers in Savannah," posted at www.civilwarhome.com/shermanandministers.htm. Accessed August 2, 2006.

30. George Gilman Smith, *The History of Methodism in Georgia and Florida from 1785 to 1865* (Macon, GA: Jno. W. Burke & Co., 1877): 456; Wesley J. Gaines, *African Methodism in the South: Twenty-five Years of Freedom* (Atlanta: Franklin Publishing House, 1890): 5–6, 8; Charles J. Elmore, *Savannah, Georgia*. Black Americans Series (Charleston, SC: Arcadia Publishing, 2002); and Whitton B. Johnson, *Black Savannah, 1788–1864* (Fayetteville: University of Arkansas Press, 1996).

31. Robert Anderson, *The Life of Rev. Robert Anderson. Born the 22d Day of February, in the Year of Our Lord 1819, and Joined the Methodist Episcopal Church in 1839* (Macon, GA: The Author, 1892).

32. George Gilman Smith, *A Hundred Years of Methodism in Augusta, Georgia* (Augusta, GA: Richards & Shaver, 1898).

33. Ralph E. Morrow, *Northern Methodism and Reconstruction* (East Lansing, MI: Michigan State University Press, 1956); and Vernon L. Wharton, *The Negro in Mississippi, 1865–1890* (Chapel Hill, NC: University of North Carolina, 1947).

34. J. B. Cain, *Methodism in the Mississippi Conference, 1846–1870* (Jackson, MS: The Hawkins Foundation, Mississippi Conference Historical Society, 1939): 456–57.

35. See Adolphine Fletcher Terry, *Charlotte Stephens: Little Rock's First Black Teacher* (Little Rock: Arkansas Academic Press 1973).

36. Andrews died in 1866. Caroline remarried and continued with her work until her death in 1914.

37. Woodie Daniel Lester, *The History of the Negro and Methodism in Arkansas and Oklahoma: The Little Rock-Southwest Conference, 1838–1972* (Little Rock, AR: Little Rock Conference, UMC, 1979), 15–19.

38. Walter N. Vernon, *Methodism in Arkansas, 1816–1976* (Little Rock: Joint Committee for the History of Arkansas Methodism, 1976): 87–88.

39. Williams would later relate his story in an interview originally published in W. D. Godman, A. H. Dexter Godman, and Inez Godman, *Gilbert Academy and Agricultural College: Winsted, Louisiana Sketches and Incidents: Selections from Journal* (New York: Hunt & Eaton, 1993): 43–49, and partially reprinted in Blassingame, *Slave Testimony*, 621–22.

40. Walls, *African Methodist Episcopal Zion Church*, 194.

41. Quoted in W. P. Harrison, *The Gospel Among the Slaves* (Nashville, TN: Publishing House of the Methodist Episcopal Church, South, 1893): 256–57.

42. On the developments in Houston see Mrs. I. M. E. Blandin, *History of Shearn Church* (Houston: Shearn Auxiliary of Woman's Home Mission Society, 1908).

43. Hightower T. Kealing, *History of African Methodism in Texas* (Waco, TX: C. F. Blanks, Printer and Stationer, 1885).

44. David Henry Bradley, A History of the A. M. E. Zion Church. Vol. 1 (Nashville, Parthenon Press, 1956), 158.

~

A Selected Bibliography
of Antebellum African
American Methodism

A note on the Internet: This volume has been completed contemporaneously with the explosion of the publication of source materials on African American history on the Internet. For example, the Documenting the American South website, sponsored by the University Library of the University of North Carolina at Chapel Hill (http://docsouth.unc.edu/), has now made readily available many of the slave narratives and other items that had been compiled during the research phase of this work. As I have discovered Internet republication of source material, I have added citations below. Doubtless, some titles have been missed, and more will come online in the near future.

Secondary Sources

Addo, Linda D., and James H. McCallum. *To Be Faithful to Our Heritage: A History of Black United Methodists in North Carolina*. Raleigh, NC: Western North Carolina Annual Conference, UMC, 1980. 264 pp.

Allen, Steven, and W. H. Pilsbury. *History of Methodism in Maine, 1793–1886*. 2 vols. Augusta, ME: Press of Charles E. Nash, 1887.

Andrews, Dee E. *The Methodists and Revolutionary America, 1760–1800*. Princeton, NJ: Princeton University Press, 2000. 367 pp.

Andrews, Doris. "The African Methodists of Philadelphia, 1794–1802." In Russell E. Richey, Kenneth E. Rowe, and Jean Miller Schmidt, eds. *Perspectives on American Methodism: Interpretive Essays*. Nashville, TN: Kingswood Books, 1993, pp. 145–55.

Andrews, William L., ed. *Sisters of the Spirit*. Bloomington: Indiana University Press, 1986. 245 pp.

Armstrong, James Edward. *History of the Old Baltimore Conference from the Planting of Methodism in 1773 to the Division of the Conference in 1857.* Baltimore: The Author, 1907. 527 pp.

Asbury United Methodist Church, Annapolis, Maryland. White Plains, NY: Monarch Publishing, 1978. 52 pp.

Atkinson, John. *The Beginnings of the Wesleyan Movement in America and the Establishment Therein of Methodism.* New York: Hunt & Eaton, 1896. 472 pp.

Baldwin, Lewis V. *Resources for the Study of Blacks in Methodism: A Guide to the Garrett-Evangelical and Northwestern University Collections.* Evanston, IL: Institute for Black Religious Research, Garrett-Evangelical Theological Seminary, 1980. 80 pp.

Bangert, Mark P. "The Gospel about Gospel—the Power of the Ring." *Currents in Theology and Mission* (August 2004). Posted at www.findarticles.com/p/articles/mi_m0MDO/is_4_31/ai_n6150717/pg_9.

Bangs, Nathan. *A History of the Methodist Episcopal Church.* 4 vols. New York: Mason and Lane, 1839. Posted at www.ccel.org/b/bangs/history_mec/HMEC1TOC.HTM.

Barclay, William C. *History of Methodist Missions.* Vol. II. New York: Board of Missions and Church Extension in the Methodist Church, 1949, pp. 52–111.

Beaty, Leroy F. *Work of South Carolina Methodism among the Slaves.* Columbia, SC: Historical Society of the South Carolina Conference, Methodist Episcopal Church, South, 1901. 24 pp.

Beaubein, Brian. "Samuel Green." Paper posted at www.mc.cc.md.us/Departments/hpolscrv/beaubien.htm.

Bennett, William. *Memorials of Methodism in Virginia.* Richmond: The Author, 1871. 741 pp.

Berlin, Ira. *Slaves without Masters: the Free Negro in the Antebellum South.* New York: Oxford University Press, 1874. 423 pp.

Bethea, Joseph B. "Black Methodists in North Carolina." In O. Kelly Ingram, ed. *Methodism Alive in North Carolina.* Durham, NC: Divinity School of Duke University/North Carolina Conference and the Western North Carolina Conference of the United Methodist Church, 1976, pp. 87–97.

Betts, Albert Deems. *History of South Carolina Methodism.* Columbia, SC: Advocate Press, 1952. 544 pp.

"A Black History Moment: Harry Hosier's Last Days." *Third Century Methodism* 38, 3 (March 1999): 2.

Blandin, Mrs. I. M. E. *History of Shearn Church.* Houston: Shearn Auxiliary of Woman's Home Mission Society, 1908. 229 pp.

Blassingame, John W., ed. *Slave Testimony: Two Centuries of Letters, Speeches, Interviews, and Autobiographies.* Baton Rouge, LA: Louisiana State University Press, 1977. 777 pp.

Blockett, Kimberly Denise. *Traveling Home/Girls: Movement and Subjectivity in the Texts of Zilpha Elaw, Nella Larsen and Zora Neal Hurston.* Madison, WI: University of Wisconsin, Ph.D. dissertation, 2002. 241 pp.

Bordewich, Fergus M. *Bound for Canaan: The Epic Story of the Underground Railroad, America's First Civil Rights Movement.* New York: Amistad/HarperCollins, 2005. 540 pp.

Bowden, Haygood S. *History of Savannah Methodism, from John Wesley to Silas Johnson.* Macon, GA: L. J. W. Burke Company, 1929. 321 pp.

Boyd, Melba Joyce. *Discarded Legacy: Politics and Poetics in the Life of Frances E.W. Harper, 1825–1911.* Detroit, MI: Wayne State University Press, 1994. 265 pp.

Brawley, Benjamin Griffith. "Three Negro Poets: Horton, Mrs. Harper and Whitman." *Journal of Negro History* 2 (1917): 384–92.

Caddy, Charles. *Life and Times of Rev. Robert Dobbins.* Philadelphia: J. W. Daughaday & Co., 1868. 250 pp.

Cain, J. B. *Methodism in the Mississippi Conference, 1846–1870.* Jackson, MS: The Hawkins Foundation, Mississippi Conference Historical Society, 1939. 519 pp.

Cartmell, Thomas Kemp. *Shenandoah Valley Pioneers and Their Descendants. A History of Frederick County, Virginia from Its Formation in 1733 to 1908 Compiled Mainly from Original Records of Old Frederick County, Now Hampshire, Berkeley, Shenandoah, Jefferson, Hardy, Clarke, Warren, Morgan and Frederick.* Winchester, VA, Eddy Press, 1909. 598 pp. Rpt.: Berryville VA., Va. Book Co. 1963. Bowie, MD: Heritage Books, 1989. 598 pp.

Chesnutt, Charles Waddell, and Ernestine Williams Pickens. *Frederick Douglass.* Boston: Small, Maynard, 1899. Rpt.: Atlanta, GA: Clark Atlanta University Press, 2001. 141 pp.

Chreitzberg, Abel M. *Early Methodism in the Carolinas.* Nashville, TN: Publishing House of the Methodist Episcopal Church, South, 1897. 380 pp.

Clark, Erskine. *Wrestling' Jacob: a Portrait of Religion in Antebellum Georgia and the Carolina Low Country.* Atlanta: John Knox Press, 1979. 207 pp.

Clarke, Nina Honemond. *History of the Nineteenth-Century Black Churches in Maryland & Washington, D.C.* Los Angeles: Vantage Press, 1983. 319 pp.

Clinton, Catherine. *Harriet Tubman: the Road to Freedom.* New York: Back Bay Books, 2004. 272 pp.

Coan, Josephus R. "Daniel Coker: 19th Century Black Church Organizer." *Journal of the Interdenominational Theological Center* 3, 1 (Fall 1975): 17–31.

Connor, Elizabeth. *Methodist Trail Blazer: Philip Gatch 1751–1834. His Life in Maryland, Virginia, and Ohio.* Rutland, VT: Academy Books, 1970. 248 pp.

Conrad, Earl. *Harriet Tubman.* Washington, DC: Associated Publishers, 1943. 248 pp.

Cornelius, Janet D. "Shout Because You're Free: The African American Ring Shout Tradition in Coastal Georgia." *Journal of Southern History* 66, 4 (November 1, 2000): 865.

Cox, Lewis Y. *Pioneer Footsteps.* Cape May, NJ: Star & Wave Press, 1917. 86 pp.

Cromwell, John W. "The First Negro Churches in the District of Columbia." *Journal of Negro History* 7, 1 (January 1922): 64–106. Posted at http://docsouth.unc.edu/church/phoebus/menu.html.

Curl, R. F. *Southwest Texas Methodism*. Dallas: The Inter-Board Council, the Southwest Texas Conference, the Methodist Church, 1951. 154 pp.

Darden, Alveta E. "Mt. Tabor Historical Highlights." In *The Heritage Celebration: 127 Years of Life for Mt. Tabor United Methodist Church, 1858–1985*. Crownsville, MD: Mt. Tabor United Methodist Church, 1986, pp. 1–4.

David, Jonathan Comly. *In One Accord: Community, Musicality, and Spirit among the Singing and Praying Bands of Tidewater Maryland and Delaware*. Philadelphia: University of Pennsylvania, Ph.D. dissertation, 1994. 475 pp.

———. "Shout because You're Free: The African American Ring Shout Tradition in Coastal Georgia." *Journal of American Folklore* 112, 446 (December 31, 1999): 565–67.

Del Pino, Julius E. "Blacks in the United Methodist Church from Its Beginning to 1968." *Methodist History* 19, 1 (October 1980): 3–20.

Drewry, P. H. *The Story of a Church: A History of Washington Street Church (Methodist Episcopal Church , South) at Petersburg, Virginia, 1773–1923*. Petersburg, VA: The Author, 1923. 240 pp.

Dunshee, Kenneth Holcomb. *As You Pass By*. New York: Hastings House, 1952. 270 pp.

Egerton, Douglas R. *He Shall Go Out Free*. Madison, WI: Madison House, 2000. 248 pp.

Ellingsworth, M. Keith. *Chew's Memorial United Methodist Church: A History of the Early Church*. Shady Side, MD: The Author, 1996.

Elmore, Charles J. *Savannah, Georgia*. Black Americans Series. Charleston, SC: Arcadia Publishing, 2002. 127 pp.

Ferguson, W. M. *Methodism in Washington, District of Colombia . . .* Baltimore: The Methodist Book Concern, 1892. 182 pp.

Fitzwater, J. H. "John Stewart." In I. L. Thomas. *Methodism and the Negro*. New York: Eaton & Mains/Cincinnati: Jennings & Graham, 1910, pp. 28–33.

Floyd, Samuel A. "Ring Shout! Literary Studies, Historical Studies, and Black Music Inquiry." *Black Music Research Journal* 11, 2 (1991): 265–87.

"Former Delaware Churches." *The Historical Trail* 2, 4 (1968): 10–14.

Fraser, William J., Jr., *Charleston! Charleston!: The History of a Southern City*. Columbia: University of South Carolina Press, 1989. 542 pp.

Galloway, Charles B. *The Editor-Bishop Linus Parker: His Life and Writings*. Nashville, TN: Southern Methodist Publishing House, 1886. 439 pp.

Godbold, Albea, and John H. Ness, Jr. Rev. by Ed. Schell. *Table of United Methodist Church Annual Conferences, 1796–1997*. [Madison, NJ]: General Commission on Archives and History, the United Methodist Church, 1998. 110 pp.

Godman, W. D., A. H. Dexter Godman, and Inez Godman. *Gilbert Academy and Agricultural College: Winsted, Louisiana Sketches and Incidents: Selections from Journal*. New York: Hunt & Eaton, 1993. 307 pp.

Graham, J. H. *Black United Methodists: Retrospect and Prospect*. New York: Vantage Press, 1979. 162 pp.

Graham, Leroy. *Baltimore: The Nineteenth Century Black Capital.* Lanham, MD: University Press of America, 1982. 335 pp.

Grammer, Elizabeth Elkin. *Some Wild Visions: Autobiographies by Female Itinerant Evangelists in Nineteenth-Century America.* New York: Oxford University Press, 2003. 270 pp.

Gravely, Will B. "African Methodism and the Rise of Black Denominationalism." In Russell E. Richey, Kenneth E. Rowe, and Jean Miller Schmidt, eds. *Perspectives on American Methodism: Interpretive Essays.* Nashville, TN: Kingswood Books, 1993, pp. 108–26.

———. "The Decision of the A.M.E. Leader, James Lynch, to Join the Methodist Episcopal Church: New Evidence at Old St. George's Church, Philadelphia." *Methodist History* 15 (July 1977): 263–69.

———. "Methodism in Black & White." *South Carolina United Methodist Advocate* 135, 11 (March 18, 1971): 8–9, 14.

———. "The Social, Political and Religious Significance of the Formation of the Colored Methodist Episcopal Church (1870)." *Methodist History* 18 (October 1979): 3–25.

———. "The Rise of African Churches: Re-examining the Contexts, 1786–1822," *Journal of Religious Thought* 41 (1984): 58–73.

———. "'. . . many of the poor Affricans are obedient to the faith': Reassessing the Early African-American Presence in Methodism in the US, 1769–1809." In Nathan O. Hatch and John H. Wigger, eds. *Methodism and the Shaping of American Culture.* Nashville, TN: Kingswood Books, 2001, pp. 175–95.

Greenbie, Sydney, and Marjorie Barstow Greenbie. *Hoof Beats to Heaven: A True Chronicle of the Life and Wild Times of Peter Cartwright, Circuit Rider.* Penobscot, ME: Traversity Press, 1955. 623 pp.

Greenstone, Jon. "Ante Bellum Methodism in Winchester, Virginia, and the Great Schism." Posted at www.emmitsburg.net/archive_list/articles/thoughtful/vicar_john/methodism_in_winchester.htm.

Harmon, Nolan B. ed. with Albea Godbold and Louise L. Queen. *Encyclopedia of World Methodism.* 2 vols. Nashville, TN: United Methodist Publishing House, 1974.

Harper, Robert Henry. *Louisiana Methodism.* Washington, DC: Kaufmann Press, 1949. 172 pp.

Harrison, W. P. *The Gospel Among the Slaves.* Nashville: Publishing House of the Methodist Episcopal Church, South, 1893. 394 pp.

Hartzell, J. C. *Methodism and the Negro in the United States.* New York: Hunt & Eaton, 1894. 21 pp. Rpt. in the *Journal of Negro History* 8, 3 (July 1923): 301–15.

Higginson, Thomas Wentworth. *Army Life in a Black Regiment and Other Writings.* New York: Penguin Group, 1997. 336 pp.

Hildebrand, Reginald F. "'An Imperious Sense of Duty': Documents Illustrating an Episode in the Methodist Reaction to the Nat Turner Revolt." *Methodist History* 19, 3 (April 1981): 155–74.

———. "Methodist Episcopal Policy on the Ordination of Black Ministers, 1784–1864." *Methodist History* 20 (April 1982): 124–42.

———. *The Times Were Strange and Stirring: Methodist Preachers and the Crisis of Emancipation.* Durham, NC: Duke University Press, 1995. 189 pp.

Hill, Patricia Liggins. "Let Me Make the Songs for the People: A Study of Frances Watkins Harper's Poetry." *Black American Literature Forum* 15 (1981): 60–65.

Huggins, Nathan Irvin. *Slave and Citizen: the Life of Frederick Douglass.* Boston: Little, Brown, 1980.

Jackson, Luther P. "Religious Instruction of Negroes, 1830–1860, with Special Reference to South Carolina." *Journal of Negro History* 15, 1 (January 1930): 72–114.

Jason, William C., Jr. "The Delaware Annual Conference of the Methodist Church, 1864–1965." *Methodist History* 4 (July 1966): 16–40.

Jenkins, Warren M. *Steps Along the Way: The Origin and Development of the South Carolina Conference of the Central Jurisdiction of the Methodist Church.* Columbia, SC: State Printing, 1967.

Johnson, Whitton B. *Black Savannah, 1788–1864.* Fayetteville: University of Arkansas Press, 1996. 242 pp.

Jones, John G. *A Complete History of Methodism in the Mississippi Conference.* 2 vols. Nashville, TN: Southern Methodist Publishing House, 1887.

Jordan, David Morris, Sr. *The Lexington Conference and Negro Migration.* Evanston, IL: n.p., 1957. 31 pp.

Kramanayake, Marina W. *A World in Shadow: The Free Black in Antebellum South Carolina.* Columbia: University of South Carolina Press, 1973. 237 pp.

Lawson, Elizabeth. *The Gentleman from Mississippi: Our First Negro Congressman, Hiram R. Revels.* New York: n.p., 1960.

Lazenby, Marion E. *History of Methodism in Alabama and West Florida.* N.p.: 1960. 1256 pp.

Lednum, John. *A History of the Rise of Methodism in America.* Philadelphia, PA: The Author, 1859. 434 pp.

Lester, Woodie Daniel. *The History of the Negro and Methodism in Arkansas and Oklahoma: The Little Rock-Southwest Conference, 1838–1972.* Little Rock, AR: Little Rock Conference, UMC, 1979. 144 pp.

Licorish, Joshua E., *Harry Hosier, African Pioneer Preacher, Including [a] Brief History of African Zoar Methodist Church, Founded 1794. Philadelphia, Pennsylvania.* Philadelphia: Afro-American Resources, 1967. 12 pp.

"Local Preachers Ordained in the Baltimore-Washington Conference & Vicinity, 1800–1960." *Third Century Methodism* 37, 3 (February 1998): 2–3.

Loveland, Anne C. *Southern Evangelicals and the Social Order, 1800–1860.* Baton Rouge: Louisiana State University Press, 1980. 293 pp. See chapter 8, "Religious Instruction of the Negroes," pp. 219–66.

Mabee, Carleton, with Susan Mabee Newhouse. *Sojourner Truth, Slave, Prophet, Legend.* New York, New York University Press, 1995. 293 pp.

Maser, Frederick E. *Robert Strawbridge: First American Methodist Circuit Rider.* Rutland, VT: Academy Books/Strawbridge Shrine Association, 1983. 86 pp.

Matthews, Donald G. *Slavery and Methodism: A Chapter in American Morality, 1780–1845*. Princeton, NJ: Princeton University Press, 1965. 329 pp.

McElvey, Kay Najiyyah. *Early Black Dorchester, 1776–1870*. College Park, MD: University of Maryland, Ph.D. dissertation, 1991. 735 pp.

McFeely, William S. *Frederick Douglass*. New York: W. W. Norton, 1991. 465 pp.

McTyeire, Holland N. *A History of Methodism*. Nashville, TN: Southern Methodist Publishing House, 1884. 692 pp.

Melton, J. Gordon Melton. *A Bibliography of Black Methodism*. Evanston, IL: Institute for the Study of American Religion, 1970. 45 pp.

———. "A Footnote to Black Methodist History: The Death of Harry Hosier." *Methodist History* 8, 1 (October 1969): 88–89.

M'Ferrin, John B. *Methodism in Tennessee*. Vols. I–III. Nashville, Southern Methodist Pub. House, 1869–73.

Morley, Jefferson. "The 'Snow Riot.'" *Washington Post* (February 6, 2005). Posted at www.washingtonpost.com/wp-dyn/articles/A55082-2005Feb1.html. Accessed April 15, 2006.

Morrow, Ralph E. *Northern Methodism and Reconstruction*. East Lansing, MI: Michigan State University Press, 1956. 269 pp.

Mt. Zion United Methodist Church 175th Anniversary, 1816–1991. Washington, DC: Mt. Zion United Methodist Church, 1991. 100 pp.

Murphy, Larry G., J. Gordon Melton, and Gary L. Ward., eds. *Encyclopedia of African American Religions*. New York: Garland Publishing, 1993. 926 pp.

Our Heritage. [Baltimore, MD]: Baltimore Washington Conference of the United Methodist Church, 1993. 144 pp.

Owen, Christopher H. *The Sacred Flame of Love: Methodism and Society in Nineteenth-Century Georgia*. Athens: University of Georgia Press, 1998. 290 pp.

Nash, Gary. *Forging Freedom: The Formation of Philadelphia's Black Community, 1720–1840*. Cambridge, MA: Harvard University Press, 1988. 354 pp.

Painter, Nell Irvin. *Sojourner Truth: A Life, A Symbol*. New York: W. W. Norton, 1996. 370 pp.

Paynter, John H. *Fugitives of the Pearl*. Washington, DC: Associated Publishers, 1930. 209 pp.

Pearson, Edward A., ed., *Designs Against Charleston: The Trial Record of the Denmark Vesey Slave Conspiracy of 1822*. Chapel Hill: University of North Carolina Press, 1999.

Peterson, Carla L. *"Doers of the Word": African American Women Speakers and Writers in the North (1830–1880)*. New York: Oxford University Press, 1995. 284 pp.

Phillips, Christopher. *Freedom's Port: The African American Community of Baltimore, 1790–1860*. Champaign, IL: University of Illinois Press, 1997. 350 pp.

Poole, Jason, "On Borrowed Ground: Free African-American Life in Charleston, South Carolina, 1810–1861." Posted at http://etext.virginia.edu/journals/EH/EH36/poole1.html.

Powers, Bernard E., Jr. *Black Charlestonians: A Social History, 1822–1885*. Fayetteville: University of Arkansas Press, 1994. 384 pp.

Raybold, R. A. *Reminiscences of Methodism in West Jersey.* New York: Lane & Scott, 1847. 1202 pp.

Redford, Albert H. *History of Methodism in Kentucky.* 3 vols. Nashville, TN: Southern Methodist Publishing House, 1868–1870.

Richardson, Harry V. *Dark Salvation: The Story of Methodism as it Developed among Blacks in America.* Garden City, NY: Doubleday, 1976. 324 pp.

———. "Early Black Methodist Preachers." *Journal of the Interdenominational Theological Center* 3 (Fall 1975): 1–8.

Ricks, Mary Kay. "A Passage to Freedom." *Washington Post Magazine* (February 17, 2002): 21–36. Posted at www.washingtonpost.com/wp-srv/national/horizon/aug98/pearl.htm.

Riggs, Marcia Y. *Can I Get a Witness?: Prophetic Religious Voices of African American Women: An Anthology.* Maryknoll, NY: Orbis Books, 1997. 250 pp.

Riley, Walter H. *Forty Years in the Lap of Methodism: History of the Lexington Conference of the Methodist Episcopal Church.* Louisville, KY: Mayes Printing Co., 1915. 164 pp.

Roberts, George C. M. *Centenary Pictorial Album: being Contributions of the Early History of Methodism in the State of Maryland.* Baltimore: Printed by J. W. Woods, 1866. 114 pp.

Robertson, David. *Denmark Vesey.* New York: Alfred A. Knopf, 1999. 224 pp.

Rosenbaum, Art, and Johann S. Buis. *Shout Because You're Free: The African American Ring Shout Tradition in Coastal Georgia.* Athens, GA: University of Georgia Press, 1998. 190 pp.

Seaman, Samuel A. *A History of Methodism in New York City.* New York: Hunt & Eaton, 1892. 505 pp.

Schell, Ed. *Background to Conference Merger—1965.* Baltimore: Baltimore Conference Historical Society, 1965. 4 pp.

Shaw, J. Beverly F. *The Negro in the History of Methodism.* Nashville, TN: Parthenon Press, 1954. 234 pp.

Shelton, Arthur E. "The History of Methodism in Warrenton, Virginia," 1959. Posted at www.warrentonumc.org/about.html.

Sherman, Joan R. Sherman, ed. *The Black Bard of North Carolina: George Moses Horton and His Poetry.* Chapel Hill: University of North Carolina Press, 1997. 168 pp.

Shipp, Albert M. *Methodism in South Carolina.* Nashville, TN: Southern Methodist Publishing House, 1883. 648 pp.

Shockley, Grant. *Heritage & Hope: The African American Presence in United Methodism.* Nashville, TN: Abingdon Press, 1991. 350 pp.

———. "Methodism, Society and Black Evangelism in America: Retrospect and Prospect." *A. M. E. Zion Quarterly Review* (July 1974): 145–82.

———. "The Methodist Episcopal Church: Promise and Peril, 1784–1939." In Grant Shockley. *Heritage & Hope: The African American Presence in United Methodism.* Nashville, TN: Abingdon Press, 1991, pp. 39–97.

———. "Negro Leaders in American Methodism." *The Garrett Tower* 12, 1 (December 1966): 3–12.

Small, Clara L. "Abolitionists, Free Blacks, and Runaway Slaves: Surviving Slavery on Maryland's Eastern Shore." Posted at www.udel.edu/BlackHistory/abolitionists .html.

Smith, Edward D. *Climbing Jacob's Ladder: The Rise of Black Churches in Eastern American Cities, 1740-1877.* Washington, DC: Anacostia Museum/Smithsonian Institute Press, 1988. 143 pp.

Smith, George Gilman. *The History of Methodism in Georgia and Florida from 1785 to 1865.* Macon, GA: Jno. W. Burke & Co., 1877. 530 pp.

———. *A Hundred Years of Methodism in Augusta, Georgia.* Augusta, GA: Richards & Shaver, 1898. 59 pp.

Smith, John Abernathy. *Cross and Flame. Two Centuries of United Methodism in Middle Tennessee.* Nashville, TN: Parthenon Press. 1984. 376 pp.

Smith, Warren Thomas. *Harry Hosier: Circuit Rider.* Nashville, TN: Discipleship Resources, 1981. 64 pp.

Staudenraus, P. J. *The African Colonization Movement.* New York: Columbia University Press, 1961. 323 pp.

Steelman, Robert B. *What God Has Wrought: A History of the Southern New Jersey Conference of the United Methodist Church.* Pennington, NJ: Commission on Archives and History, Southern New Jersey Conference, 1986. 352 pp.

Stevens, Abel. *The Women of Methodism: Its Three Foundresses.* New York: Carlton & Porter, 1866. 304 pp.

Stewart, Frank Ross, Mrs. *The History of Methodism in Alabama: Including Index to Anson West's History.* 6 vols. Centre, AL: Stewart University Press [1984].

Sundquist, Eric J., ed. *Frederick Douglass: New Literary and Historical Essays.* Cambridge: Cambridge UP, 1991. 295 pp.

Sweet, William Warren. *Religion on the American Frontier, 1783–1840: A Collection of Source Materials.* Vol. IV. *The Methodists.* Chicago: University of Chicago Press, 1964. 800 pp.

———, ed. *The Rise of Methodism in the West, being the Journal of the Western Conference, 1800–1811.* New York: Abingdon Press/Nashville: Smith & Lamar, 1920. 207 pp.

———. *Virginia Methodism—A History.* Richmond, VA: Whittet & Shepperson, 1955. 427 pp.

Taylor, Clarence. *Black Churches of Brooklyn.* New York: Columbia University Press, 1994. 197 pp.

Taylor, Winston H. "Congregations in Mission: Washington's Asbury." *New World Outlook* (Nov.–Dec. 1986): 21–24.

Taylor, Rosser H. *Antebellum South Carolina: A Social and Cultural History.* New York: Da Capo Press, 1970.

Tees, Francis H. *History of Old St. George's.* Philadelphia: The Author, n.d. [1934]. 115 pp.

Terry, Adolphine Fletcher. *Charlotte Stephens: Little Rock's First Black Teacher.* Little Rock: Arkansas Academic Press, 1973. 129 pp.

Thompson, Julius. *Hiram R. Revels, 1827–1901: A Biography.* New York: Arno Press, 1982.

Todd, Robert W. *Methodism of the Peninsula.* Philadelphia: Methodist Episcopal Book Rooms, 1886. 336 pp.

Upham, Francis Bourne. *The Story of Old John Street Methodist Episcopal Church.* New York: The Author, 1935. 84 pp.

Vernon, Walter N. *Becoming One People: a History of Louisiana Methodism.* Bossier City, LA: United Methodist Church, 1987. 375 pp.

———. *Methodism in Arkansas, 1816–1976.* Little Rock: Joint Committee for the History of Arkansas Methodism, 1976. 490 pp.

———. *Methodism Moves Across North Texas.* Dallas: Historical Society, North Texas Conference, The Methodist Church, 1967. 416 pp.

———, Robert W. Sledge, Robert C. Monk, and Norman W. Spellman. *The Methodist Excitement in Texas: A History.* Dallas: The Texas United Methodist Historical Society, 1984. 443 pp.

Wakeley, J. B. *Lost Chapters Recovered from the Early History of American Methodism.* New York: Wilbur B. Ketcham, 1889. 594 pp.

Warriner, Edwin. *Old Sands Street Methodist Episcopal Church of Brooklyn, N.Y.* New York: Phillips & Hunt, 1885. 520 pp.

Waters, Joseph R. "Ezion Methodist Episcopal Church." In John D. C. Hanna, ed. *The Centennial Services of Asbury Methodist Episcopal Church, Wilmington, Delaware, October 13–20, 1889.* Wilmington, DE: Delaware Printing Company, 1889, pp. 172–77.

West, Anson. *A History of Methodism in Alabama.* Nashville, TN: Printed for the Author, Publishing House of the Methodist Episcopal Church, South, 1893. 755 pp.

Wharton, Vernon L. *The Negro in Mississippi, 1865–1890.* Chapel Hill, NC: University of North Carolina, 1947. 298 pp.

Wightman, William M. *Life of William Capers, D.D., One of the Bishops of the Methodist Episcopal Church, South.* Nashville, TN: Southern Methodist Publishing House, 1959. 516 pp.

Williams, George Washington. *History of the Negro Race in America from 1619 to 1880.* New York: G. P. Putnam, 1883. See Chapter 25, "The Methodist Episcopal Church."

Williams. Thomas Leonard. *The Methodist Mission to the Slaves.* New Haven, CT: Yale University Ph.D. dissertation, 1943. 439 pp.

Williams, William Henry. *The Garden of American Methodism: The Delmarva Peninsula, 1769–1820.* Wilmington, DE: The Peninsula Conference of the United Methodist Church, 1984. 225 pp.

Winch, Julie. *A Gentleman of Color: The Life of James Forten.* New York: Oxford University Press, 2002. 501 pp.

Primary Sources

Albert, Octavia V. Roberts. *The House of Bondage or Charlotte Brooks and Other Slaves Original and Life-Like, as they Appeared in their Old Plantation and City Slave Life; Together with Pen-Pictures of the Peculiar Institution with Sights and insights into their New Relations as Freedmen, Freemen, and Citizens.* New York: Hunt & Eaton/Cincinnati: Cranston & Stowe, 1890. 161 pp.

Allison, William J. *Memoir of Quamino Buccau, a Pious Methodist.* Philadelphia: Henry Longstreth/London: Charles Gilpin, 1851. 30 pp.

Anderson, Robert. *The Life of Rev. Robert Anderson. Born the 22d Day of February, in the Year of Our Lord 1819, and Joined the Methodist Episcopal Church in 1839.* Macon, GA: The Author, 1892. 151 pp. Posted at http://docsouth.unc.edu/neh/andersonr/andersonr.html.

Andrew, James O. *Miscellanies: Comprising Letters, Essays, and Addresses.* Louisville: Morton & Griswold, 1854.

Asbury, Francis. *The Journal and Letters of Francis Asbury.* 3 vols. Nashville, TN: Abingdon Press; London: Epworth Press, 1958. Posted at http://wesley.nnu.edu/holiness_tradition/asbury_journal/.

Bangs, Nathan. *A History of the Methodist Episcopal Church.* 4 vols. New York: T. Mason and G. Lane, 1839–1842.

Bayley, Solomon. *Narrative of Some Remarkable Incidents in the Life of Solomon Bayley, Formerly a Slave in the State of Delaware, North America; Written by Himself, and Published for His Benefit; to Which Are Prefixed, a Few Remarks by Robert Hurnard.* London: Harbey and Darton, 1825. 57 pp. Posted at http://docsouth.unc.edu/neh/bayley/menu.html.

Bibb, Henry. *Narrative of the Life and Adventures of Henry Bibb, An American Slave, Written by Himself.* New York: The Author, 1849. 207 pp. Posted at http://docsouth.unc.edu/neh/bibb/bibb.html.

Black Itinerants of the Gospel: The Narratives of John Jea and George White. Ed. by Graham Russell Hodges. Madison, WI: Madison House, 1993. 208 pp.

Boehm, Henry. *Reminiscences of Rev. Henry Boehm.* New York: Carlton & Porter, 1865. 493 pp.

Bruce, H. C. *The New Man: Twenty-Nine Years a Slave, Twenty Nine Years a Free Man: Recollections of H. C. Bruce.* York, PA: P. Anstadt, 1895. 176 pp. Posted at http://docsouth.unc.edu/bruce/menu.html.

Brunson, Alfred. *A Western Pioneer: or, Incidents in the Life and Times.* 2 vols. Cincinnati, OH: Jennings and Pye, 1880.

Capers, William D. *A Catechism for Little Children (and for use on) the Missions to the Slaves in South-Carolina.* Charleston, SC: Printed by J. S. Barges, 1833. 17 pp.

———. *Catechism for the Use of the Methodist Missions.* 3rd ed.: Charleston, SC: Published by John Early, 1853. 40 pp. Posted at http://docsouth.unc.edu/church/capers/capers.html.

———. *A Short Catechism for the Use of the Colored Members on Trial of the Methodist Episcopal Church in South Carolina.* Charleston, SC: Observer Office Press, 1833.

Cartwright, Peter. *The Autobiography of Peter Cartwright*. New York: Carlton & Porter, 1856. 525 pp. Rpt.: Nashville, TN: Abingdon Press, 1984. 349 pp. Posted at www.hti.umich.edu/cgi/b/bib/bibperm?q1=AFK0444.0001.001.

Coker, Daniel. *A Dialogue between a Virginian and an African Minister*. Baltimore: Benjamin Edes, 1810. 43 pp. Text reproduced in Dorothy Porter, comp. & ed., *Negro Protest Pamphlets; a Compendium*. New York, Arno Press, 1969; and in Richard Newman and Patrick Rael, eds. *Pamphlets of Protest: an Anthology of Early African-American Protest Literature, 1790–1860*. New York: Routledge, 2001, pp. 52–65.

Coker, Daniel. *Journal of Daniel Coker, a descendant of Africa, from the time of leaving New York, in the ship Elizabeth, Capt. Sebor, on a voyage for Sherbro, in Africa, in company with three agents, and about ninety persons of colour* . . . [Baltimore]: Edward J. Coale, supported by the Maryland Auxiliary Colonization Society, 1820. 52 pp.

Delaney, Lucy Ann. *From the Darkness Cometh the Light: Or, Struggles for Freedom*. St. Louis, J. T. Smith, n.d. [1890?]. 64 pp. Posted at http://docsouth.unc.edu/neh/delaney/menu.html.

Douglass, Frederick. *Life and Times of Frederick Douglass, His Early Life as a Slave, His Escape from Bondage, and His Complete History to the Present Time*. Hartford, CT: Park Publishing Co., 1881. 509 pp. Posted at http://docsouth.unc.edu/douglass life/douglass.html.

———. *Narrative of the Life of Frederick Douglass, an American Slave*. Written by Himself. Boston: Anti-Slavery Office, 1845. 125 pp. Posted at http://docsouth.unc.edu/douglass/douglass.html.

———. *My Bondage and My Freedom*. New York: Miller, Orton & Mulligan, 1855. 464 pp. Posted at http://docsouth.unc.edu/neh/douglass55/douglass55.html.

Dow, Lorenzo. *History of Cosmopolite; or the Four Volumes of Lorenzo Dow's Journal*. Wheeling, WV: Joshua Martin, 1848.

Early, Sarah J. *Life and Labors of Rev. Jordan W. Early, One of the Pioneers of African Methodism in the West and South*. Nashville: Publishing House A. M. E. Church Sunday School Union, 1894. 161 pp. Posted at http://docsouth.unc.edu/neh/early/early.html.

[Elaw, Zilpha]. *Memoirs of the Life, Religious Experience, Ministerial Travels and Labours of Mrs. Zilpha Elaw: An American Female of Colour, Together with Some Account of the Great Religious Revivals in America*. London: T. Dudley, 1846. Rpt in William L. Andrews, ed. *Sisters of the Spirit*. Bloomington: Indiana University Press, 1986, pp. 25–52. 49–160.

[Emory, Robert]. *The Life of the Rev. John Emory by His Eldest Son*. New York: George Lane, 1841. 380 pp.

Ffirth, John. *Experience and Gospel Labors of the Rev. Benjamin Abbott*. New York: Phillips & Hunt, 1842. 284 pp.

Finley, James B. *Sketches of Western Methodism: Biographical, Historical, and Miscellaneous*. Cincinnati: Methodist Book Concern, 1854. 551 pp.

[Garrettson, Freeborn.] *American Methodist Pioneer: The Life and Journals of the Rev. Freeborn Garrettson, 1752–1827*. Edited with Introductory Biographical Essay and Notes by Robert Drew Simpson. Rutland, VT: Academy Books, 1984. 433 pp.

[Hamilton, James]. *Negro Plot. An Account of the Late Intended Insurrection among a Portion of the Blacks of the City of Charleston, South Carolina*. Published by the Authority of the Corporation of Charleston. Boston: Joseph W. Ingraham, 1822. 50 pp.

Harper, Frances Ellen Watkins. *A Brighter Coming Day: A Frances Ellen Watkins Harper Reader*. Ed. by Frances Smith Foster. New York: Feminist Press. 1990. 416 pp.

———. *Complete Poems of Frances Ellen Watkins Harper*. New York: Oxford University Press, 1988. 232 pp.

Henkle, M. M. *The Life of Henry Bidleman Bascom*. Louisville, KY: Morton & Griswold, 1854. 408 pp.

Henson, Josiah. *The Life of Josiah Henson, formerly a Slave, now an Inhabitant of Canada, as Narrated by Himself*. Boston: Arthur D. Phelphs, 1849. 76 pp. Posted at http://docsouth.unc.edu/neh/henson49/henson49.html.

———. *Truth Stranger Than Fiction. Father Henson's Story of His Own Life*. Boston: John J. Jewett and Company, 1858. 80 pp. Posted at http://docsouth.unc.edu/neh/henson49/menu.html.

———. *"Uncle Tom's Story of His Life": An Autobiography of the Rev. Josiah Henson (Mrs. Harriet Beecher Stowe's "Uncle Tom"). From 1789 to 1876* (London: "Christian Age" Office, 1876. 224 pp. Posted at http://docsouth.unc.edu/neh/henson/henson.html.

Higginson, Thomas Wentworth. "Denmark Vesey." *Atlantic Monthly* 7, 44 (June 1861): 728–44. Posted at www.theatlantic.com/issues/1861jun/higgin.htm.

Horton, George Moses. *The Hope of Liberty. Containing a Number of Poetical Pieces*. Raleigh, NC: J. Gales & Son, 1829. 22 pp. Posted at http://docsouth.unc.edu/southlit/horton/menu.html.

———. *Life of George M. Horton. The Colored Bard of North Carolina from "The Poetical Works of George M. Horton, the Colored Bard of North Carolina, to which is Prefixed the Life of the Author, written by himself."* Hillsborough, NC: Heartt, 1845. 20 pp. Posted at http://docsouth.unc.edu/hortonlife/menu.html.

———. *Poems by a Slave*. [Philadelphia]: [s.n.], [1837]. 23 pp. Posted at http://docsouth.unc.edu/southlit/horton1837/horton1837.html.

[Jacobs, Harriett]. *Incidents in the Life of a Slave Girl. Written by Herself*. Edited by L. Maria Child. Boston: For the Author, 1861. 306 pp. Posted at http://docsouth.unc.edu/jacobs/menu.html.

Jea, John. *The Life, History, and Unparalleled Suffering of John Jea, the African Preacher*. N.p.: The Author, n.d. 96 pp. Rpt. in *Black Itinerants of the Gospel: The Narratives of John Jea and George White*. Ed. by Graham Russell Hodges. Madison, WI: Madison House, 1993. Posted at http://docsouth.unc.edu/neh/henson49/menu.html.

[Jones, Thomas H.] *The Experiences of Thomas H. Jones, Who Was a Slave for Forty-Three Years. Written by a Friend, as Related to Him by Brother Jones*. Boston: Bazin & Chandler, 1861. 46 pp. Posted at http://docsouth.unc.edu/jones/menu.html. Note: also published in *Experience and Personal Narrative of Uncle Tom Jones; Who Was for Forty Years a Slave. Also the Surprising Adventures of Wild Tom, of the Island retreat, a Fugitive Negro from South Carolina.* Boston: H. B. Skinner, n.d. 48 pp. Posted at http://docsouth.unc.edu/jonestom/menu.html.

Kemble, Fanny. *Journal of a Residence on a Georgian Plantation in 1838–1839.* New York: Harper & Brothers, 1863. 298 pp. Posted at http://etext.lib.virginia.edu/toc/modeng/public/KemPlan.html.

Lee, Leroy M. *The Life and Times of Jesse Lee.* Richmond, VA: John Early, 1848. 517 pp.

Lockwood, John P. *The Western Pioneers; or, Memorials of the Lives and Labours of the Rev. Richard Boardman and the Rev. Joseph Pilmoor.* London: Wesleyan Conference Office, 1881. 211 pp.

Long, John Dixon. *Pictures of Slavery in Church and State; including Personal Reminiscences, biographical; Sketches, Anecdotes, Etc., Etc., with and Appendix containing the Views of John Wesley and Richard Watson on Slavery.* Philadelphia: The Author, 1857. 426 pp. Posted at http://docsouth.unc.edu/neh/long/menu.html.

Lyell, Charles. *A Second Visit to the United States of North America.* Vol. I. New York: Harper & Brothers, 1849. 273 pp. Posted at http://memory.loc.gov/cgi-bin/query/r?ammem/lhbtnbib:@field(NUMBER+@band(lhbtn+6866a)).

Mattison, H. *Louisa Picquet, the Octoroon: A Tale of Southern Slave Life.* New York: the author, 1861. Posted at http://digilib.nypl.org/dynaweb/digs/wwm97258/@Generic__BookView.

Mitchell, Joseph. *The Missionary Pioneer, or a Brief Memoir of the Life, Labours, and Death of John Stewart, (Man of Colour,) Founder, Under God of the Mission Among the Wyandotts at Upper Sandusky, Ohio.* New York: The Author, 1827. 96 pp. Posted at http://docsouth.unc.edu/mitchell/menu.html.

Mood, F. A. *Methodism in Charleston: A Narrative.* Edited by T. O. Summers. Nashville, TN: E. Stevenson & J. E. Evans, 1856. 207 pp.

Myers, Lewis. "Origin and Progress of Methodism in Savannah." *Methodist Magazine* 15 (1883): 252–58.

Offley, Greensburg Washington. *A Narrative of the Life and Labors of the Rev. G. W. Offley, a Colored Man, and Local Preacher and Missionary, Who Lived Twenty-seven Years at the South and Twenty-three at the North; Who Never Went to School a Day in his Life and Only Commenced to Learn his Letters When Nineteen Years and Eight Months Old; the Emancipation of His Mother and Her Three Children; How He Learned to Read While Living in a Slave State, and Supported Himself From the Time He Was Nine Years Old Until He was Twenty-one.* Hartford, CT: n.p., 1859. Rev. ed. as *A Narrative of the Life and Labors of the Rev. G. W. Offley, a Colored Man, and Local Preacher.* Hartford, CT: n.p., 1860.

Paine, Robert. *Life and Times of William McKendree.* Nashville, TN: Publishing House of the MEC,S, 1874. 549 pp.

Phoebus, George A. comp. *Beams of Light on Early Methodism in America. Chiefly Drawn from the Diary, Letters, Manuscripts, Documents, and Original Tracts of the Rev. Ezekiel Cooper.* New York: Phillips & Hunt/Cincinnati: Cranston & Stowe, 1887. 337 pp. Posted at http://docsouth.unc.edu/church/phoebus/menu.html.

[Pilmore, Joseph]. *The Journal of Joseph Pilmore: Methodist Itinerant.* ed. by Frederick E. Maser and Howard T. Maag. Philadelphia, PA: Historical Society of the Philadelphia Annual Conference of the United Methodist Church, 1969. 262 pp.

[Smith, James L.] *Autobiography of James L. Smith, Including Also Reminiscences of Slave Life, Recollections of the War, Education of Freedmen, Causes of the Exodus, Etc.* Norwich, CT: Bulletin Company, 1881. 150 pp. Posted at http://docsouth.unc.edu/neh/smithj/smithj.html.

Still, Mary. *An Appeal to the Females of the African Methodist Episcopal Church.* Philadelphia: n.p., 1857. Reprinted in Richard Newman and Patrick Rael, eds. *Pamphlets of Protest: An Anthology of Early African-American Protest Literature, 1790–1860.* New York: Routledge, 2001: 254–60.

Thomas, James. *From Tennessee Slave to St. Louis Entrepreneur: The Autobiography of James Thomas.* Colombia: University of Missouri Press, 1984. 225 pp.

[Thompson, Charles]. *Biography of a Slave; Being the Experiences of Rev. Charles Thompson, a Preacher of the United Brethren Church, while a Slave in the South. Together with Startling Occurrence Incidental to Slave Life.* Dayton, OH: United Brethren Publishing House, 1875. 102 pp. Posted at http://docsouth.unc.edu/neh/thompsch/menu.html.

[Travis, Joseph]. *Autobiography of Rev. Joseph Travis.* Ed. by T. O. Summers. Nashville, TN: Stevenson & Owens, for the MECS, 1856. 238 pp.

Truth, Sojourner. *Narrative of Sojourner Truth.* Ed. by Margaret Washington. New York: Vintage Books, 1993. 138 pp.

Turner, Nat. *The Confessions of Nat Turner, the Leader of the Late Insurrection in Southhampton, VA., as Fully and voluntarily Made to Thomas R. Gray . . .* Richmond, VA: Thomas R. Gray, 1832. 23 pp. Posted at http://docsouth.unc.edu/neh/thompsch/menu.html.

[Veney, Bethany]. *The Narrative of Bethany Veney: A Slave Woman.* With Introduction by Rev. Bishop Mallalieu, and Commendatory Notices from Rev. V. A. Cooper, Superintendent of Home for Little Wanderers, Boston, Mass., and Rev. Erastus Spaulding, Millbury, Mass. Worcester, MA: [The Author], 1889. 47 pp. Posted at http://docsouth.unc.edu/veney/menu.html.

Walker, David. *Walker's Appeal in Four Articles; Together with a Preamble, To the Coloured Citizens of the World, but in Particular, and Very Expressly, to Those of the United States of America.* Third and Last Edition, with Additional Notes, Corrections, &c. Boston: Revised and Published by David Walker, 1830. 88 pp. Posted at http://docsouth.unc.edu/nc/walker/walker.html.

Weld, Theodore Dwight, comp. *American Slavery As It Is: Testimony of a Thousand Witnesses.* New York: American Anti-Slavery Society, 1839. Posted at http://docsouth.unc.edu/neh/weld/menu.html.

[White, George]. *A Brief Account of the Life, Experience, Travels, and Gospel Labours of George White, an African; Written by Himself and Revised by a Friend.* New York: Printed by John C. Totten, 1810. 60 pp. Rpt. in *Black Itinerants of the Gospel: The Narratives of John Jea and George White.* Ed. by Graham Russell Hodges. Madison,

WI: Madison House, 1993. 60 pp. Posted at http://docsouth.unc.edu/neh/whitegeo/menu.html.

Whitefield, George. "A Letter to the Inhabitants of Maryland. Virginia, North and South-Carolina." In *The Works of Rev. George Whitefield.* London: Edward and Charles Dilly/Edinburgh: Kinkaid and Bell, 1771, pp. 35–39.

[Williams, James]. *Narrative of James Williams, a American Slave, Who Was for Several years a Driver on a Cotton Plantation in Alabama.* New York: American Anti-Slavery Society/ Boston: Isaac Knapp, 1838. 108 pp. Posted at http://docsouth.unc.edu/veney/menu.html.

York, Brantley. *The Autobiography of Brantley York.* Durham, NC: Seeman Printery, 1910. 139 pp. Posted at http://docsouth.unc.edu/nc/york/york.html.

Young, Jacob. *Autobiography of a Pioneer or, The Nativity, Experience, Travels, and Ministerial Labors of Rev. Jacob Young; with Incidents, Observations, and Reflections.* Cincinnati, OH: Cranston and Curtis, 1857. 528 pp.

Unpublished Sources

Colbert, William. *Journal.* Original is in the library of Garrett-Evangelical Theological Seminary.

Rankin, Thomas. *Journal.* Manuscript is located in the library at Garrett-Evangelical Theological Seminary.

African Methodist Episcopal Church

Allen, Richard. *A Collection of Spiritual Songs and Hymns from Various Authors.* Philadelphia: T. L. Plowman, 1801. Rev. ed. published as: *A Collection of Hymns and Spiritual Songs from Various Authors.* Philadelphia: Mother Bethel African Methodist Episcopal Church, 1987. 116 pp.

———. *Life, Experience, Etc., of the Rt. Rev. Richard Allen.* Philadelphia: Martin & Boden, Printers, 1833. 50 pp.

Arnett, Benjamin William. ed. *The Budget, Containing Annual Reports of the General Officers of the African Methodist Church of the United States of America: with Facts and Figures, Historical Data of the Colored Methodist Church in Particular, and Universal Methodism in General.* Xenia, OH: Torchlight Printing Co. 136 pp.

———, ed. *"The Budget of 1904:" Containing a Complete Organization of the Church.* Philadelphia: E. W. Lampton and J. H. Collett, 1903. 373 pp.

Butt, Israel L. *History of African Methodism in Virginia, or Four Decades in the Old Dominion.* Hampton, VA: Hampton Institute Press, 1908. 252 pp. Posted at http://docsouth.unc.edu/church/butt/butt.html.

Cannon, Noah Calwell W. *A History of the African Methodist Episcopal Church, the Only One in the United States of America, Styled Bethel Church.* Rochester, NY: Strong & Dawson, Printers, 1842. 42 pp. Posted at http://docsouth.unc.edu/church/cannon/cannon.html.

First Conference Minutes of the A.M.E. Connexion composed by Richard Allen in the City of Baltimore, 1818. Baltimore: Henry Shields, n.d. 14 pp.

Gaines, Wesley J. *African Methodism in the South: Twenty-five Years of Freedom.* Atlanta: Franklin Publishing House, 1890; Rpt.: Chicago: Afro-Am Press, 1969. 305 pp. Posted at http://docsouth.unc.edu/church/gaineswj/gaines.html.

George, Carol V. R. *Segregated Sabbaths: Richard Allen and the Rise of Independent Black Churches, 1760–1840.* New York: Oxford University Press, 1973. 205 pp.

Gregg, Howard D. *History of the African Methodist Episcopal Church.* Nashville, TN: A. M. E. Church Publishing House, 1980. 523 pp.

Handy, James A. *Scraps of African Methodist Episcopal History.* Philadelphia: A. M. E. Book Concern, 1902. 421 pp. Posted at http://docsouth.unc.edu/church/handy/menu.html.

Holmes, James A., Jr., and Richard Allen Leonard. "Early African Methodism in South Carolina." In *African Methodism in South Carolina: A Bicentennial Focus.* Tappan, NY: Seventh Episcopal District of the African Methodist Episcopal Church, 1987, pp. 25–29.

Jones, Absalom, and Richard Allen. *A Narrative of the Proceedings of the Colored People During the Awful Calamity in Philadelphia, in the year 1793; and a Refutation of Some Censures Thrown upon Them in some Publications.* Philadelphia: The Authors, 1794. Posted at www.geocities.com/bobarnebeck/allen.html.

Kealing, Hightower T. *History of African Methodism in Texas.* Waco: C. F. Blanks, Printer and Stationer, 1885. 238 pp.

Lee, Jarena. *Religious Experience and Journal of Mrs. Jarena Lee, Giving an Account of her Call to Preach the Gospel.* Revised and corrected from the Original Manuscript, Written by Herself. Philadelphia: The Author, 1849. 97 pp. Posted at http://digilib.nypl.org/dynaweb/digs/wwm9716/@Generic__BookView. Excerpt rpt. in William L. Andrews, ed. *Sisters of the Spirit.* Bloomington: Indiana University Press, 1986, pp. 25–52.

Morgan, Joseph H. *Morgan's History of the New Jersey Conference of the A. M. E. Church, from 1872 to 1887.* Camden, NJ: S. Chew, 1887. 265. Posted at www.njstatelib.org/NJ_Information/Searchable_Publications/.

Payne, Daniel Alexander. *A History of the African Methodist Episcopal Church.* Ed. by Charles Spencer Smith. Nashville, TN: Publishing House of the A. M. E. Sunday School Union, 1891. 502 pp. Posted at http://docsouth.unc.edu/church/payne/menu.html.

——. *Recollections of Seventy Years.* Nashville: A. M. E. Sunday School Union, 1888. 335 pp. Posted at http://docsouth.unc.edu/church/payne/menu.html.

Pinkett, Harold T. *A History of John Wesley A.M.E. Church, Washington, D.C.* Baltimore, MD: Gateway Press, 1989. 141 pp.

Smith, Charles Spencer. *A History of the African Methodist Episcopal Church: Being a Volume Supplemental to A History of the African Methodist Episcopal Church, by Daniel Alexander Payne, D.D., LL.D., Late One of Its Bishops: Chronicling the Principal Events in the Advance of the African Methodist Episcopal Church from 1856 to*

1922. Philadelphia: Book Concern of the A. M. E. Church, 1922. 570 pp. Posted at http://docsouth.unc.edu/church/cssmith/smith.html.

[Smith, David]. *Biography of the Rev. David Smith, of the A. M. E. Church Being a Complete History, Embracing Over Sixty Year's Labor in the Advancement of the Redeemer's Kingdom on Earth Including "The History of the Origin and Development of Wilberforce University."* Xenia, OH: Xenia Gazette Office, 1881. 135 pp. Posted at http://docsouth.unc.edu/neh/dsmith/menu.html.

Walker, Clarence E. *A Rock in a Weary Land: The African Methodist Episcopal Church During the Civil War and Reconstruction.* Baton Rouge: Louisiana State University Press, 1982. 157 pp.

Wesley, Charles H. *Richard Allen: Apostle of Freedom.* Washington, DC: Associated Publishers, 1935. 300 pp.

Wright, Richard R., Jr. *Encyclopedia of African Methodism.* Philadelphia: Book Concern of the A. M. E. Church, 1947. 688 pp.

African Methodist Episcopal Zion Church

Armstrong, James David. "A Review of *A History of John Wesley A.M.E.Z. Church, Washington, D.C.*" *The A.M.E. Zion Quarterly Review* 102, 1 (January 1990): 25–33.

Bradley, David Henry. *A History of the A. M. E. Zion Church.* 2 vols. Nashville, TN: Parthenon Press, 1956.

Hood, J. W. (James Walker). *One Hundred Years of the African Methodist Episcopal Zion Church; or, The Centennial of African Methodism.* New York: A. M. E. Zion Book Concern, 1895. 625 pp. Posted at http://docsouth.unc.edu/church/hood100/menu.html.

Moore, John Jamison. *History of the A. M. E. Zion Church in America. Founded in 1796, in the City of New York.* York, PA: Teachers' Journal Office, 1884. 392 pp. Posted at http://docsouth.unc.edu/church/moorej/menu.html.

The Rev. J. W. Loguen, as a Slave and as a Freeman, a Narrative of Real Life. Syracuse, NY: J. G. K. Truair & Co., 1859. 450 pp.

Rush, Christopher. *A Short Account of the Rise and Progress of the African Methodist Episcopal Church in America.* New York: The Author, 1843. 106 pp. Rpt.: New York: J. J. Zuille, 1866. Posted at http://docsouth.unc.edu/church/rush/menu.html.

Sketch of the Early History of the African Methodist Episcopal Zion Church with Jubilee Souvenir and Appendix. Charlotte, NC: A. M. E. Zion Publishing House, 1914. 93, 35 pp. Posted at http://docsouth.unc.edu/church/hood/menu.html.

Walls, William J. *The African Methodist Episcopal Zion Church: Reality of the Black Church.* Charlotte, NC: A.M.E. Zion Publishing House, 1974. 669 pp.

African Union Church/African Union Methodist Protestant Church

Baldwin, Lewis V. "The A.U.M.P. and U.A.M.E. Churches: An Unexplored Area of Black Methodism." *Methodist History* 19, 3 (April 1981): 175–78.

——. *Invisible Strands in African Methodism: A History of the African Union Methodist Protestant and Union American Methodist Episcopal Churches, 1805–1980*. Methuen, NJ: Scarecrow Press, 1983. 288 pp.

——. *The Mark of a Man: Peter Spencer and the African Union Methodist Tradition.* Lanham, MD: University Press of America, 1987. 86 pp.

Russell, David James. *History of the African Union Methodist Protestant Church.* Philadelphia: Union Star Book and Job Printing and Publishing House, 1920. 66 pp. Posted at http://docsouth.unc.edu/church/russell/menu.html.

Christian Methodist Episcopal Church

Gravely, William B. "The Social, Political and Religious Significance of the Formation of the Colored Methodist Episcopal Church." *Methodist History* 18, 1 (October 1979): 3–25.

Harris, Eula W., and Maxi M. Craig. *Christian Methodist Episcopal Church through the Years.* Jackson, TN: The Authors, 1949.

Lakey, Othal Hawthorne. *The History of the CME Church.* Memphis: CME Publishing House, 1985. Rev. ed.: Memphis: CME Publishing House, 1996. 756 pp.

Phillips, C. H. *The History of the Colored Methodist Episcopal Church in America, Comprising Its Organization, Subsequent Development and Present Status.* Third edition. Jackson, TN: Publishing House C. M. E. Church, 1925. 623 pp. Posted at http://docsouth.unc.edu/church/phillips/phillips.html.

Tatum, Charles Edward. *The Christian Methodist Episcopal Church, with an Emphasis on the Negroes of Texas, 1970–1970: A Study in Historical Cultural Geography.* Lansing, MI: Michigan State University, Ph.D. dissertation, 1971. 175 pp.

~

Index

~

About the Author

Religious historian J. Gordon Melton is the director of the Institute for the Study of American Religion, in Santa Barbara, California, and a research specialist with the Department of Religious Studies at the University of California, Santa Barbara. An ordained elder in the United Methodist Church, he is the author of numerous reference volumes and scholarly texts in American religious studies including the *Encyclopedia of American Religions* (seventh edition, 2003), *American Religion: An Illustrated History* (2000), and the *Encyclopedia of Protestantism* (2005). He is the coeditor of the *Encyclopedia of African American Religion* (1993) to which he contributed over one hundred entries. Early in his career he compiled the *Bibliography of Black Methodism* (1969), which marked the beginning of a life-long interest in African American Methodist studies. He has subsequently assembled a large collection of eighteenth- and nineteenth-century primary sources documenting the early history of African American Methodists.